Foxfire 9

Foxfire 9

**general stores, the Jud Nelson wagon,
a praying rock, a Catawba Indian potter—
and haint tales, quilting, home cures,
and log cabins revisited**

**edited by ELIOT WIGGINTON
and MARGIE BENNETT
with an Introduction by Eliot Wigginton**

ANCHOR BOOKS
A DIVISION OF RANDOM HOUSE, INC.
NEW YORK

ELIOT WIGGINTON, who started *Foxfire* magazine with his
ninth- and tenth-grade English classes in 1966, still teaches
in the Appalachian Mountains of north Georgia at the
consolidated Rabun County High School. Students in Wig's
English classes, as a part of their language arts curriculum,
continue to produce *Foxfire* magazine and the Foxfire book
series. Royalties from the sale of the books are directed back
into the educational program to pay salaries and expenses
involved in offering at the high school some sixteen additional
experimental community-based classes ranging from
television and record production to photography, folklore,
and environmental studies. Mr. Wigginton was voted
"Teacher of the Year" in Georgia in recognition of his
important contributions to education. In 1989, he was
awarded a MacArthur Fellowship.

FIRST ANCHOR BOOKS EDITION, 1977

Foxfire 9, like its predecessors, contains articles first
published in *Foxfire* magazine. This Anchor Book edition
is the first publication of *Foxfire 9* in a book form. It is
published simultaneously in hard and paper covers.

Library of Congress Cataloging-in-Publication Data
Foxfire 9.
    "Contains articles first published in Foxfire
    magazine"—T.p. verso.
    1. Country life—Appalachian Region, Southern—
Addresses, essays, lectures.   2. Appalachian Region,
Southern—Social life and customs—Addresses, essays,
lecture.   3. Handicraft—Appalachian Region,
Southern—Addresses, essays, lectures.   4. Folklore—
Appalachian Region, Southern—Addresses, essays,
lectures.   I. Wigginton, Eliot.   II. Foxfire.
III. Title: Foxfire nine.
F217.A65F694   1985   306'.0974   85-26803
ISBN-13: 978-0-385-17744-3
ISBN-10: 0-385-17744-5

www.anchorbooks.com

Printed in the United States of America
30 29 28 27 26 25 24

This book is dedicated to our readers. Your interest, your devotion, and your unflagging support of our work have propelled us through twenty years of continuing efforts to prove to high school students that they can not only achieve academically, but also make remarkable contributions to the quality of life in our global human community.

Stick with us. We've barely started. There's so much left to do.

CONTENTS

INTRODUCTION

This new volume, published at the conclusion of our twentieth year of work in the Rabun County schools, also concludes the numbered Doubleday series, and in so doing now allows us to explore a whole range of new publishing possibilities with our students.

The reasons for bringing this particular series to an end are numerous and have nothing to do with failure, exhaustion, or an end of subjects to research. In fact, exactly the opposite is true: seven million books in print to date is not failure, our energy level has only rarely been higher, and the number of new projects outlined and stacked in chaotic piles on my desk and on the floor around it is an unending source of frustration. I am being buried alive by great ideas.

The latter is the essence of the problem. Let me back up for a moment, though, and give you the full picture, for as a person who is presumably interested in our work, you deserve a fuller explanation. What's happening?

First, many of our early readers have lost track of us. Reviewers can find little new to say about the series and so they do not review the new volumes; bookstores, therefore, devote less shelf space to them since fewer people know they exist and request them (and when bookstores stock two or three copies of each of the titles, they have made a major investment in space that they could more profitably give to current bestsellers); and consequently I keep running into people who say, "The Foxfire series is wonderful. I have all three of your books." Despite that fact, thousands of you still manage to track down each new volume when it appears, and sales of each are still in figures that most authors would envy, but the handwriting is clearly on the wall. *Foxfire 26?*

Second, and even more to the point, is the fact that the format of the series has become confining. Physically, the size and shape of the books, the number of pages, the paper stock, and the black-and-white illustrations all serve to limit the style of presentation of many of the topics we present. In addition, the fact that traditionally there is a range of topics presented in each volume frequently causes each topic to be treated in less depth than it deserves; and it means that if a reader is interested only in folk pottery, for example, and thus buys *Foxfire 8,* he must also pay for chapters on chicken fighting and mule swapping, like it or not. It all comes with the package.

Finally, the narrow focus of the numbered volumes, with their emphasis on material culture and traditional customs of the immediate region, has precluded our being able to give quality time and energy to a number of other areas we would like to allow our students to explore. The pressures of collecting the information for the next volume in the numbered series have kept us from those endeavors; one of several unfortunate results is that we have run the risk of giving you a very one-sided portrait of the Appalachian region itself, a portrait that we know has led some readers to believe that our region is still—even in 1986—a geographical and cultural cul-de-sac peopled entirely by human artifacts of a different place and time. A living museum, if you will, or a quaint anachronism from which cable TV and satellite dishes and personal computers and Pizza Huts and even college educations have all been banned. (You may find it interesting in passing to note that a few hundred yards beyond Edwin Meaders's pottery kiln is the new home and studio of Xavier Roberts, the young mountain man who created the Cabbage Patch Kids and Furskins bears and was born and raised within shouting distance of his present house. Yes, we too are part of the twentieth century.)

So what *is* next? Four years ago, anticipating this moment, we began our own publishing house, Foxfire Press, through which we have presented a new series of books that are distributed nationally by E. P. Dutton. Like the numbered series, this one also documents our traditional culture, and our high school students are completely involved in its creation. Unlike the numbered series, however, each book features a single topic, and each has a distinctive size, shape, design, and "feel." The results of a questionnaire distributed to every subscriber to our magazine, *Foxfire,* helped us determine our master list of topics—initiated in the magazine and the Doubleday volumes —which readers wanted to see treated in greater depth. Published every fall at the rate of one book per year, each book in the new series also contains a response card, which readers can use not only to comment on the new book but also to make suggestions for future volumes.

The inaugural volume, published in 1983, was completely devoted to Aunt Arie Carpenter. Containing material gleaned from years of tape-recorded conversations and scores of photographs, it stands today, I think, as the warmest, most human book we have ever published. Others shared that view, for shortly after its publication it won a Christopher Award.

Aunt Arie: A Foxfire Portrait was followed by a fat cookbook of traditional recipes and foodways that included interviews with some of the men and women who contributed the information. It was runner-up in the French Company's Tastemaker competition for the best cookbook published in 1984. The next fall the *Foxfire Book of Toys and Games* appeared, and it was immediately chosen as one of the offerings of the Better Homes and Gardens book club, and six weeks after publication it went into a second printing.

The Dutton series, therefore, is off to an auspicious start with strong acceptance of the first three volumes, and three more volumes, all requested by readers, are being researched and created by teams of students at this moment.

At the same time we are experimenting with some five other types of books, most of which would be published and distributed through Foxfire Press itself rather than through a national publishing house. They include:

First, a series of children's books, both fiction and nonfiction, written and illustrated by elementary school youngsters for their peers. Local elementary students have already written and illustrated nonfiction narratives that we have printed and distributed as self-contained, removable inserts in issues of *Foxfire,* and soon we will begin to build on that embryonic effort. From an educational point of view, this effort has been of particular interest to me for years because of the possibilities it creates for having talented, sensitive high school students working with groups of younger students in the same kinds of ways that we have been working with the high-schoolers, to say nothing of the additional interest in reading that we may be able to generate by being able to give children books written by other children with whom they can readily identify, and whose common experiences they share.

Second, a group of titles that explore, in plays as well as prose, the broader and more current experiences of Appalachian people. Recently, for example, we published an oral history play called *Cabbagetown, Three Women* in which three elderly residents of the Appalachian Cabbagetown district of downtown Atlanta reveal what happened to their lives after they moved out of the mountains in the early 1900s to the company town created by the Fulton Bag and Cotton Mill which offered steady year-round employment. They and their neighbors—all mountain families who suddenly had to adapt to a completely different environment—worked for the mill for years until it finally closed, leaving behind the empty silent factory buildings and a now poverty-racked, deeply troubled mountain neighborhood that stands today in the middle of one of the most prosperous cities in Sun Belt America. A grant from Foxfire sponsored the collection of the initial interviews by young people from Cabbagetown and the publication of a subsequent book and photographs, and Brenda and Cary Bynum, two Atlanta playwrights, used the material in that book to create the play itself. We now hope to explore the possibility of similar kinds of relationships and endeavors.

Third, the discovery and acquisition of the complete collection of prints and negatives of the talented amateur photographer R. A. Romanes has opened a whole new area of activity. Romanes, who photographed our section of the mountains extensively during and following the Depression, and who was a native and resident of the area, left behind a stunning collection that documents rural life here in a way that we have been unable to do. Small groups of our students have been working for over a year to catalogue and index the negatives, and to locate still living subjects for a series of publications of primarily regional interest that we will begin to release shortly.

Fourth, under consideration is an effort that would put back into circulation long out of print works of high merit by Appalachian authors who deserve an audience today. Lists of possible titles are being compiled, and financial support is now being sought to help in what could be an important project.

Fifth, we are also working toward the creation of materials that we hope will be of use to elementary and secondary public school teachers both in the mountains and beyond. A bit of background is helpful here: by the early 1970s we had already begun to work with teachers from Maine to California who wanted to transplant certain aspects of our work to their classrooms and their communities. Hundreds of publication projects resulted, and a network of teachers began to grow, serviced by a small newsletter, *Hands On,* which we still print and distribute as a way of providing a forum through which those teachers can exchange news and ideas. Partly because of this work, the issue of effective education itself became increasingly fascinating. What other activities could students become involved in that would stretch their talents and capabilities? How else could the overall philosophy of community-based experiential education be applied within and beyond the language arts curriculum to serve not only the more narrow, state-mandated academic agenda but also, simultaneously, certain other needs of the students themselves and the communities from which they came?

Those of you who have followed our work and read the introductions to the previous volumes in this series know how we then expanded our efforts into video and television, radio production, music and record production, community economic development, and so forth. Some experiments have prospered in terms of their educational benefits, and some failed, but all were in the service of the original goal of the original *Foxfire* magazine: to bring learning to life for the teenagers in our school, at the same time testing options that other teachers might want to try.

By 1979, as word of the experiments spread and as requests for more information arrived from teachers and school districts alike, I was well into a book for my peers that Doubleday released in the fall of 1985. By the time that book, *Sometimes a Shining Moment: The Foxfire Experience,* appeared, the current educational reform movement was also in full cry, with most commission reports pointing to the need not specifically for projects like Foxfire, but for precisely the *kinds* of activities in schools with which we have been experimenting for years. The educators who composed the National Commission on Reading, for example, and wrote *Becoming a Nation of Readers,* concluded in part:

> It is a mistake to suppose that instruction in grammar transfers readily to the actual uses of language. This may be the explanation for the fact that experiments over the last fifty years have shown negligible improvement in the quality of student writing as a result of grammar instruction. Research suggests that the finer points of writing, such as punctuation and subject-verb agreement, may be learned best while students are engaged in extended writing that has the purpose of communicating to an audience. Notice that no communicative purpose is served when children are asked to identify on a worksheet the parts of speech or the proper use of "shall" and "will."

John Dewey was right. Before any of us was born, he warned that a student internalizes and masters the basic academic skills not by studying those skills directly and exclusively, but by doing projects in a real world context where those skills must be utilized. To say it another way, a student may memorize the component parts of a bicycle (read: parts of speech, dates, formulas), and make a perfect score on that section of a state competency test, but that fact has absolutely nothing to do with the student's ability or desire to ride.

One very real problem is that many teachers today simply were not themselves taught within a school system that followed that philosophy, and consequently they have no real patterns to go by. Those who come to us for help usually want concrete examples of the philosophy at work in responsible, compelling ways *within* the typical school system. It may well be presumptuous of us to try to help them, but we have examples in spades, and a series of materials for teachers published by Foxfire Press may turn out to be the most efficient and logical way to share those examples with our colleagues.

Numerous questions remain.

Will we publish anything else with Doubleday? I certainly hope so. In the future, however, it will be a different kind of title from this one. *Sometimes a Shining Moment* inaugurated our new relationship, and my editor at Doubleday and I are watching somewhat anxiously to see how that book does.

Will Foxfire Press ever generate enough income not only to survive financially on its own, but also to achieve our collateral dream that it become a successful, viable business in our county that can employ a number of local people? I just don't know. It hasn't come close in four years, and many of the projected titles, being of purely regional interest, will probably have difficulty earning out their costs of production. The play, for example, has yet to sell five hundred copies.

Does it really matter? Well, yes and no. The realist within me says, "Of course it matters. You can't play if you can't pay." The less pragmatic individual within me says, "Look, the experiments are worth trying if only for what new lessons can be learned from them, and for the fun we'll have in the doing."

We'll see. I can't resist the notion, though, that a fitting initiation of our twenty-first year is not the continual repetitious application of a so far successful formula, but putting what we've learned so far to work on a clean slate.

BEW

Foxfire 9

FOXFIRE—WHAT IS IT?

For years, readers have written us asking for information as to just what the organic substance foxfire *is* and how to find it. Now, finally, we think we have some information that is solid enough to pass on.

This chapter has two parts. The first is an explanation of its botanical characteristics—the what is it and why does it glow? It was written by Curt Haban, a high school senior at our school, as a research paper for a college English class.

The second is an interview with Clyde Hollifield who lives with his wife, Adrianne, in the mountains of North Carolina near Old Fort. Together, they have acquired a reputation in the region not only as puppeteers who provide quality entertainment for public elementary school audiences, but also as people who occasionally, in special circumstances, put on "light shows" at night with foxfire, and who appreciate more fully than most its almost supernatural qualities.

MUSHROOMS THAT GLOW

Down through the ages, glowing plants have been wrapped in superstition, associated with witches' brews, sorcerers, and little elfin people, and linked to magic and religion. It is quite natural that these plants that reveal no roots or leaves and seemingly pop up out of the ground overnight and exhibit so many other strange qualities be treated with awe and wonder.

Foxfire is one of these fascinations. The book *Ingenious Kingdom* uses a description which states, "Imagine entering a secluded forest glen on a moonless night and finding mushrooms glowing in their own eerie light."[1] An author of Compton's Pictured Encyclopedia

[1] Harry T. and Rebecca T. Northen, *Ingenious Kingdom* (Englewood Cliffs: Prentice-Hall, Inc., 1970), p. 48.

PLATE 1   Time exposure taken of some foxfire glowing on decayed wood that Clyde Hollifield gave us.

PLATE 2   Student Al Edwards taking the time exposure for the foxfire picture.

ponders the same qualities, writing, "On rainy nights, they glow through the dark forest in a most eerie manner. One could easily picture elfin creatures dancing in the glim, their king and queen, perched on the largest and brightest mushrooms, ordering tricks to be played on human beings. The sudden appearance of a perfect ring of mushrooms in a open field would not be difficult to interpret as the scene of a fairy carnival the night before."[2]

These are the same qualities that have inspired authors to include this phenomenon in their literature to establish a mysterious, secretive, even a magical atmosphere. Mark Twain and Sterling North both used foxfire, in *Huckleberry Finn* and *Rascal*. In both cases foxfire was used because of its soft, yet exciting, luminous quality. In the book *Rascal*, for example, Sterling North described foxfire as "a real curiosity—a phosphorescent stump which gleamed at night, as luminescent as all the lightning bugs in the world—ghostly and terrifying to boys who saw it for the first time."[3] Mark Twain gives foxfire more practical qualities. In *Huckleberry Finn*, Tom and Huck plan to dig an escape tunnel into the cabin where the slave Jim is being held. They realize that a lantern would make too much light and might call attention to their activities: "What we must have is a lot of them rotten chunks that's called foxfire, and just makes a soft kind of glow when you lay them in a dark place."[4]

After reading about foxfire in those books, I was still uncertain about it. I still did not know what foxfire really was. Many things in nature are luminescent. Certain kinds of saltwater fish, as well as the more obvious lightning bugs, glow in the dark. But what, exactly, is the thing called foxfire?

A dictionary defines it as "an eerie phosphorescent light, the luminescence of decaying wood, any of various luminous fungi as *Armillaria mellea* that cause decaying wood to glow."[5] The book *Ingenious Kingdom* explains foxfire as "a faint luminescence that can be seen only on dark nights which is given off by several kinds of mushrooms, in some by mycelium, in others by the cap or gills, and only when these parts are young and fresh."[6]

The most common fungi responsible for foxfire are the *Clitocybe illudens*, *Panus stypticus* and *Armillaria mellea*. "These fungi are members of the Basidiomycete class which includes many types of gill fungi or

---

[2] "mushroom," Compton's Pictured Encyclopedia (Chicago: F. E. Compton & Co., 1960).
[3] Sterling North, *Rascal* (New York: E. P. Dutton & Co., 1963), pp. 15–16.
[4] Mark Twain, *Adventures of Huckleberry Finn* (Cleveland and New York: World Publishing Co., 1947), p. 310.
[5] "fox fire," Merriam-Webster's Third New International Dictionary, 1966, p. 900.
[6] Northen, p. 48.

mushrooms. These fungi are usually found in rich soil or on decaying logs. Many of the species are parasitic and grow within the tissues of their host."[7] However, one cannot see mushrooms actually growing on the wood that glows. Foxfire does not appear as a mushroom. It resembles instead a stain that has been applied to the wood.

I discussed this with the biology teacher at Rabun Gap-Nacoochee School, Billy Joe Stiles, and we arrived at an explanation. When wood or a stump is decomposing, certain fungi or mushrooms grow within the wood to aid the decomposition process. All mushrooms start their lives in the form of spores, which later grow to what are called buttons, the young mushrooms. The dictionary defines a button as "an immature whole mushroom, one just before expansion of the [umbrella-shaped upper cap]."[8] According to Mr. Stiles, these spores (numbering in hundreds of millions) can grow on a decomposing stump. These spores later grow into buttons, then eventually to full-grown mushrooms. Throughout this mushroom's life, it lives off the wood or stump itself like a saprophyte. It is the mycelium (one mass of branching, threadlike filaments that form its main growing structure) of the young mushroom, or button, that glows—not the full-grown mushroom.

Now that foxfire's physical appearance was better understood, I was still confused about how decomposing wood and the fungi associated with it actually glow. I referred to botany and plant physiology books for an answer. According to those books, the light is the result of a complicated chemical reaction within the fungi pigment molecules. Phosphorescence is a product of photosynthesis. Photosynthesis is the process by which a plant manufactures its own food. One book explained phosphorescence as the return of a luminous mushroom's pigment molecules from a higher energy level, which is caused by light energy absorption, to its normal level.[9] After studying this, I was still confused about what actually happens. I consulted with Clayton Croom, my physics teacher at Rabun County High School, and arrived at an answer. The process is started when light energy is absorbed by the fungi, either directly by sunlight or through ultraviolet rays, which, according to Mr. Croom, can penetrate wood, stumps, or soil to reach them. It is also possible for the excess energy

[7] Harry J. Fuller and Donald D. Richie, *General Botany* (New York: Barnes & Noble, 1967), pp. 168–69.

[8] "button," Merriam-Webster's Third New International Dictionary, 1966, p. 305.

[9] Robert M. Devlin, *Plant Physiology* (New York: Van Nostrand Reinhold Co., 1969), pp. 181–86. Phosphorescence and luminescence are described and explained in Chapter 11, "Light and Dark Reactions of Photosynthesis." Within the chapter, reasons are given explaining how light is absorbed by plants, how it is transported, and what intermediates are involved, along with the reactions that accompany these processes.

left in a stump or piece of wood from a lifetime of absorbing light energy to be released in the form of phosphorescence as the stump decomposes if the correct fungi are present. When the proper fungi are present and conditions are right, decomposing wood glows. Therefore not every plant and not every piece of decomposing wood glows.

According to the laws of physics, energy, whatever its origin, cannot be created or destroyed. This process is known as the conservation of energy.[10] Consequently, the energy absorbed by the luminous fungus molecules must reappear again sometime in some form, such as light. When this energy is given off the luminous fungus as light, it is known as foxfire.

CURT HABAN

CLYDE HOLLIFIELD

I've been pretty curious about foxfire the last four or five years. In Scotland and Ireland, foxfire was called fairy fire for obvious reasons. I don't know where the term "foxfire" comes from, but I have a feeling that it's an anglicized word. In Irish fairy tales and folklore, it's usually called fairy fire or will-o'-the-wisp. Maybe they're talking about swamp gas, foxfire or who knows what, but they call both by the same common name—will-o'-the-wisp or Jack of the little fire or Jack-with-a-lantern. Like a lot of Irish folklore, most of the stories I've seen didn't deal with foxfire directly, but it was just part of the story. Irish fairy tales are kind of gruesome, a little bit bizarre, and the fairies aren't to be trusted. The general story goes that somebody is going across the moors at night [and sees foxfire] and thinks it's a cabin. They go toward it and end up falling in the lake and drowning or getting led off into the moors by this foxfire, fairy fire, will-o'-the-wisp, or whatever. So they didn't think of it as a particularly good thing.

The stories I've heard locally around here are mostly about somebody that had seen foxfire on a hunting trip. "We got up there in the woods and it was just a-glowing all the way to the top of the mountain." That kind of thing.

I'll give you my own personal ideas about the little people that lived on top of the Smokies. I don't know anyone else particularly that has the same feelings I have, but I know some Indian people that

[10] Arthur W. Greenstone, Leland G. Hollingworth, Frank X. Stutman, *Concepts in Chemistry* (New York: Harcourt, Brace & World, Inc., 1966), p. 156.

PLATE 3   Clyde shows Wig how to dig at
the roots of a rotten stump to find foxfire.

talk about the little people. This one Indian fellow I know talks about
four different kinds [of little people]. [All of them] were white. Some
little people lived on top of the mountains, some little people lived in
broom sage, some in laurel thickets and some lived in deep woods.
Fairy fire or foxfire may be [the little people's] fire. It's sort of underground, the opposite of our fire. Their fire is cold and blue; ours is
hot and red. Theirs is wet, yet at the same time it's burning, oxidizing
wood and giving off light. Their fire is at the other end of the spectrum, sort of opposite our world. I think the literal translation of the
Cherokees' term was something like cold fire or fire that's cold. All
the phosphorescent lights, the Brown Mountain lights and all the
others, have some Indian legends about their association with spirits
and stuff. I think that's one of the real magical qualities of these
mountains. It's just the fact that on summer nights they are glowing
out there all over the mountainside. Lightning bugs, glowworms,
mushrooms, foxfire, and a few Brown Mountain lights drifting
through. So, who's to say what's an elf or a fairy if you see a light in
the woods at night?

   To me, it has that elfin quality, that cool, blue-green lunar sort of
elfin color. Most people, especially kids, seem really fascinated by it.
When they see a chunk of foxfire, they take to it instantly and want to

handle it or break it up. Foxfire is a real curious thing, which to me hints to the elfin world, but if foxfire is an elfin thing and if you mess with it, you're very apt to come to the attention of the little people. You'll be noticed if you play with something that's in their element. Foxfire is just barely in our physical world. It's more in their element. Not only is foxfire one of the real mysteries and magic of these mountains, but also things like the Brown Mountain lights, things that nobody quite understands. I just wonder sometimes if these natural lights aren't somehow connected to part of a larger phenomenon.

At night when you dig around a stump, it will look like a castle, like deep openings and a light coming from deep down in the ground. All around the stump will look like a castle with a party going on inside. Once we pulled up an old stump and where the tree came out of the ground, it left a cavity and that cavity was just a city down there all lined with lights.

At night, foxfire looks like a jewel and the next day it's just rotten wood. That's another reason I think of this stuff as sort of having a magical quality. It's like those fairy tales of getting a pot of gold and the next day it turns out to be oak leaves or rotten logs.

I remember the first time I saw foxfire. I was just a kid on a camping trip. Me and my cousin camped on Mackey's Creek and we just happened to disturb a bunch of foxfire when we were getting firewood. It was just there. I looked at it more closely and sort of saw what wood it was in and what it looked like and where we dug it up. We just loaded up jars full of it and thought we'd have [the glow] from then on. The next night it didn't glow at all and we were so disappointed. We thought as long as we kept it in that jar, it would glow.

After we found that foxfire, we started trying to find out its life cycle and what it was. We realized pretty quickly the foxfire didn't glow until you busted it up and let it have a chance to get to the air. There's something about it having to oxidize. It takes four or five hours to start glowing.

One time [near a creek bank], I saw all the oak leaves on the ground were glowing. If you turned 'em over, the whole ground was glowing. It was glowing all through the earth!

Foxfire lasts a long time. We've gone camping and found it in big logs and it would still be there the next year. We even piled a bunch of foxfire up near a creek [we go to] and threw some logs on top. The next time we went back, it was all in the pile and still spreading.

Two years ago, I cut some trees for the house [I was building here]. The [scraps] and small pieces of log have been laying around up on the hill and foxfire is beginning in them. Then the next year there'll be more and more. In five or ten years those small poplar logs will just about have rotted away and maybe it will be just about solid foxfire.

Recently we dug some on a creek over near Murphy [North Carolina] in Hayesville. The place was an old sawmill site. The sawmill was closed in 1928 and the logs have been laying there ever since. They've been rotting fifty years and will probably continue to rot another fifty.

Foxfire is just barely visible, sort of faint. On moonlight nights, you can hardly see it. There's too much light on a moonlit night to see it. If it's lying on the ground, it looks like moonlight on dry leaves. Foxfire could be everywhere and you'd think it was moonlight scattered about. It takes a real pitch-black night to see it well.

I think foxfire is barely within our range of vision on the blue-green end of the spectrum. When you can't see it, it may still be glowing beyond our vision. That's a thought. You can take a flashlight or a cigarette lighter or a red light and flash it on foxfire momentarily and it makes a sort of strobe light. It sorta jumps at you because of your eyes trying to compensate suddenly for a red light, then a moment of blindness before you can see the green light again. Your eyes are trying to go back between two drastically different wavelengths. It's like looking at some signs that are painted in bold red and bold blue and they kinda vibrate a little. Foxfire kinda jumps a little bit in an unnatural way, like you wouldn't expect. It does that sort of thing.

I have no idea why foxfire glows. You could make a case for a lightning bug glowing for mating purposes, but why would that mushroom glow? Doesn't make any sense. There's at least three or four different mushrooms that are like foxfire. I used to think it was one mushroom that grew on poplar trees, but it's at least three or four other ones that glow, too. The glow all looks the same. You can't tell the difference in appearance. My interest is not only foxfire but all these bioluminescent things. I know at least a good half dozen or more things that glow like foxfire, glow all the same color. There's big pink caterpillars and these little glowworms you see in the grass. There's several different mushrooms themselves that glow, and of course lightning bugs. There's some sort of light that drifts along through the woods, sort of like lightning bugs.

In the middle of the summer, go along any little ol' stream or creek where it's good and damp and where there's roots hanging over the creek and there's an undercut. Stick your head down and look up under there. There's almost always a little city of lights all up along the banks. It's very tiny, whatever it is, and it has the ability to move like a little insect moves. You can jab around there with a stick and the little lights will move around, but you can only disturb them so much and they'll move once or twice and then they'll settle back down and they won't move again. I've got down with a flashlight and tried to determine what they are, but they're just so tiny [I couldn't see them very well].

Foxfire is a fungus and it's very, very wet. It has skin around it like a membrane around wood that holds the water in. When you break it open to look at it, it starts to form another membrane down a little further.

PLATE 4   Clyde points out the mushy tex-
ture and streaked surface of the wood in
which the foxfire is found.

You've got to break it up fairly small where air can get to it and dry the wood completely out. It's so rotten and soppy you can squeeze water out of it. It has to be that wet or [foxfire] won't grow there. Find where an old poplar tree or a white oak has died, is totally dead and the tree has fell over and the bark has fallen off and it has a real rotten stump. You'll be able to tell by the bark and the color of the stump. The stump will be real super wet and mushy. Then you dig a couple of inches down in the ground and foxfire will be in the roots and up in the stump. You bust the whole thing up and the whole stump will be glowing. Even though foxfire's not in contact with the ground, streaks of it will be going all up through the stump there. If there's a big log laying on the ground, foxfire will be all over the bottom side. You can see foxfire anywhere that stays wet.

Poplar seems to be the brightest and glows the quickest. Oak is a little less reliable. One time I found it in birch and it was really bright. I've never found it in walnut, pine, or any kind of fir tree—no kind of tarry or resin-producing tree. I've never found it in an evergreen. I've never found it in any super hard wood either except for oak. Most every time I've found it, it's been in a light-colored wood like the poplar, beech and birch. I guess you might even find it in maple or ash or some of the other white woods, but I've never found it in any dark wood like red oak or black walnut. Oak seems to take a little longer to come on in the summertime. A good four hours for all of it to get glowing really bright, although sometimes you'll find pieces that begin glowing sooner. Foxfire glows where the air hits it. If you take a big chunk and it's glowing a little one night, you bust it up a little more the next night and bust it up some more the next night, and it will keep glowing on and on. If you dug some today, it would glow tonight and that'd be it [if you didn't bust it up]. Basically it just glows one night, and foxfire doesn't always perform for you one hundred percent. You have to gather about twice as much as you actually need.

Practically every old rotten poplar log laying on the ground or just the stump has got [foxfire] in it. You can see a physical difference in the wood with just your eye. It has a certain look about it and it's streaked-looking. It has black lines in it, looks a little bit like water-marks. When the wood has a streaked look of black lines and circles, it's called spalling. If you look at [that wood] at night, the whole piece of wood won't be glowing, only some of the inside circles. The more you break it up and mess with it, the more active [the foxfire] gets.

In the wintertime, you can find [foxfire] underground, below where it might freeze. It doesn't glow hot like it does in the summer. Foxfire seems to glow better in the summer. [In the winter] it takes three or four times as long to start glowing after you break it up. May take a day or two, but it's just not as bright. It's just a faint glow. Maybe the fungus is not growing as hard or something.

I've seen [foxfire] of every consistency from hardwood all the way to something that is like jelly. Some oak will be very hard and then some poplar will be mushy. As the wood gets more and more rotten, it gets softer and softer, but it's the same color of glow. The color doesn't vary with the kind of wood. It seems to be the same.

A neat thing to do with [foxfire] is to get a bucket of it and throw it in the creek above a waterfall, because water won't make it go out. It'll go over the waterfall and down in the side currents. Little bits and pieces will go for half mile down the creek. The whole creek will be lit up with little fragments of it running around and doing stuff; or you can hang it on leaves and branches, hang bits and pieces on a string in the woods, and it will be kind of dipping and moving all down through the woods but it goes out quicker because it gets more air.

You can break up a piece in the woods, put it in water and keep it for a few days. When you take it out of the water, it will start glowing a few hours later. You can kind of delay [the glowing] if you want to use it for some purpose, like showing some kids or something. You can bring chunks of it and bury it in the ground beside your house and it will just stay there indefinitely. Every time you dig it up, it will glow a little more because you keep breaking it. You can get a log and bury it by your house and six months later, it's still [glowing].

These old mountains have lots of magic and the glowing things are just some of it.

Article and photographs by Allison Adams, Kyle Conway, Greg Darnell, Hedy Davalos, Al Edwards, and Chet Welch.

REMEDIES, HERB DOCTORS AND HEALERS

Since the publication of *The Foxfire Book* with its list of home remedies we had collected to that date (pages 230–48), we have continued to add to the list. The additions, all from within a thirty-mile radius of our school, appear here accompanied by the names of those who contributed them. The list is sandwiched between two other relevant contributions to the topic.

Preceding the list is a major article about Flora Youngblood whose father was an herb doctor and faith healer who lived in the Sautee-Nacoochee Valley only a few miles from here. Flora learned many of his cures, used most of them herself, and contributed extensively to the new list. This section, which features Flora as a person, is unique for showing the remedies themselves in the overall context of one healer's life, and being used on a daily basis by a living human being. At the same time, Flora also shares with us a craft from which she derives additional pleasure—that of making honeysuckle baskets.

Following the article about Flora and the list of remedies is an article about Doc Brabson, Aunt Arie's doctor, and a legendary figure in the Macon County, North Carolina area. Doc Brabson, the grandfather of John Bulgin, a blacksmith we featured in *Foxfire 5*, represents the transition between home herbal healing and modern medicine—a doctor who rode horseback into the mountains to ease pain, whose feet sometimes froze to the stirrups of his saddle while he rode on winter nights from patient to patient, and who received produce and labor in return for his services far more often than he received cash—a fact eloquently attested to by his ledger, still owned by John Bulgin. Material from that ledger is reproduced in this third section, and it gives unshakable credence to the stories we have heard of doctors accepting goods for services.

Concerning the remedies we have printed, a note of caution is appropriate: we have tested none of these remedies ourselves, and though we do not dispute their efficacy, we must warn that—due to the pressures of the interview situations, or tape noise and interference, or the failure of the human memory—essential ingredients or quantities may have been misunderstood or left out; and the names of ingredients such as plants, because they are frequently called by their common colloquial names around here, may be misleading.

In addition, several of the plants advocated (yellow ladyslipper, for example) may be on endangered species lists.

For the above reasons, we cannot advocate or stand behind the actual use of these remedies, and we do not encourage you to employ them. We present them here purely for their historical and cultural interest, not as viable alternatives to modern medicinal products.

FLORA YOUNGBLOOD

Our first visit with Flora Youngblood was in July of 1984. At the beginning of the summer, one of her daughters, Mamie Waycaster, wrote us about her mother's knowledge of herb remedies. Mrs. Youngblood had acquired this information from her father, Henry Cantrell, who had been an herb doctor in Sautee, near Cleveland, Georgia, from the time he was a young man until his death long after Mrs. Youngblood was a grown woman. Some of the students working for Foxfire during the summer went to interview her at her home in Buford, Georgia, a small town about twenty-five miles north of Atlanta.

That first trip was made with the intention of doing a story on the herb remedies, but we came back with a great deal more. As it turned out, Mrs. Youngblood not only knew of some remedies of which we had never heard, but she has talents in the honeysuckle basket-making field and also told us many amusing tales of her childhood. Unfortunately, she had no honeysuckle vines with which to make baskets that day. Therefore this fall several of us—Richard Edwards, Lori Gillespie, Allison Adams, and Cheryl Wall—traveled back to Buford for a second interview and brought along a big box of vines gathered by Cheryl and Steve West on the Foxfire property the day before.

After almost two hours of driving and another round of "How much farther?" our destination came into view. We were in a rural area and the houses were set back from the road, each with a spacious yard. Mrs. Youngblood's house was located on a one-lane dirt road used primarily by the members of her large family, many of whom live nearby. She has twelve children (eight daughters and four sons) and although none of them still lives with her, most have homes close by. She has about thirty-nine grandchildren and several great-grandchildren.

She lives in a well-kept one-story red brick house sitting on a little hill. There is a small wooden shed in the backyard and the house is surrounded by tall trees and a lush green lawn. It was a warm, sunny day in early September and we arrived about midmorning while the grass was wet with dew.

As we walked across the carport to the door, we were taken aback by seeing two large street bikes parked in there. They were quite a contrast to the smiling, small, grandmotherly woman standing behind them at the door. She explained to us that they belong to her sons who don't have room to park them at the place where they live.

Although she is small, Mrs. Youngblood is sturdily built. Her silver-gray hair was pulled into a bun at the base of her neck and held in place with two metal combs. She is fair-complexioned and was tanned from the summer's outdoor work, needing no makeup to enhance her coloring. Her bright blue eyes sparkled behind the black horn-rimmed glasses she was wearing. Her cool summer dress with a pastel floral print added to the grandmotherly aura that surrounded her.

PLATE 5   One of Mrs. Youngblood's daughters, Reba Hunt, helps prepare the honeysuckle for a basket.

She greeted us warmly and made us all feel very special, as if we were her own grandchildren coming to spend the day. She invited us in and we began setting up the tape recorder and positioning our cameras as we explained what was most needed in this second interview. She began preparing the honeysuckle vines in her living room, a small, comfortable room adjacent to the kitchen. There were a couch, several chairs and a coffee table there. The walls were covered with pictures of the Youngblood family. With all of us there, the small room was crowded, so we moved into the kitchen where she was ready to begin boiling the vines in a large pot on the stove. This was the first step in making the basket, which will be shown in detail in the article following.

There was a table at either end of the kitchen: a linoleum-covered table near the sink and a larger dining table where we sat as she showed us how to make the basket. Knickknacks knitted by Mrs. Youngblood decorated the cabinets above the stove and kitchen counter opposite the kitchen table. Shelves laden with a variety of colorful home-canned foods and several kitchen appliances stood against the wall behind the dining table. The kitchen, lighted by two ceiling fixtures, had the warm atmosphere of a favorite gathering place for family and friends.

Mrs. Youngblood seemed slightly nervous at first (and so were we), but all of us soon relaxed and became engrossed in the conversation and basket weaving. The atmosphere was light and fun, and time went by quickly. We were all involved in drawing diagrams, making photographs and getting all our fingers into the weaving of the basket. Two of her daughters were there most of the time and they contributed much of the information we came after.

As the morning stretched into lunchtime, we began to think about letting Mrs. Youngblood take a breather while we went to a nearby McDonald's for french fries, hamburgers and Cokes. Mrs. Youngblood had other plans for our lunch. After helping to get the dishes and food onto the kitchen table which sits beneath a window overlooking the backyard populated by birds and squirrels, we filled ourselves with ham, gravy and biscuits, cheese biscuits, iced tea, and cake until we could barely get up out of our chairs!

Even during lunch, we asked questions about Mrs. Youngblood's early childhood and later life with her husband and children. Mrs. Youngblood is a robust and energetic woman, typical of what we think of as a mountain woman, one who carries about her an air of gentle pride for having grown up in the severity of harsh mountain winters with a lack of what we consider modern conveniences. Her smiles were quick and warming as she told us some tales that had us laughing and others that amazed us.

She drew for us a diagram of the Cantrell family home located near Cleveland in Georgia's northeast mountains. Since she had talked about the rag dolls she played with as a young girl, she drew us a pattern for those and told us how they were made. She had made "butterfly" dresses for her daughters when flour sacks came in pretty printed cloth, and she gave us that pattern to include in this story about her. Primarily, though, she showed us how to make lovely baskets of honeysuckle vines and we have included all those steps so that anyone interested can follow her directions. And her knowledge of herb remedies is impressive. We feel an obligation to preserve this material before it is lost forever because so few have been careful to remember and pass this information on.

ALLISON ADAMS AND LORI GILLESPIE

Interviews, photography, transcribing, editing and layout by Allison Adams, Richard Edwards, Al Edwards, Teresa Thurmond, Lori Gillespie, Chet Welch, Cheryl Wall, Kelly Shropshire, and Joseph Fowler. Special thanks to Oh Soon Shropshire for drawing the basket diagrams.

I was born the thirty-first of January, nineteen and six. I was raised up in [White County, Georgia] and was the seventh child out of nine. My father was Henry Cantrell. He was pretty big, kinda stocky-built, medium height. He was just quiet and calm, never got mad or angry about anything. He was just as calm as he could be. I never saw him get 'ary a bit fluster-rated. He was fond of his kids. I mean he was! Any children! I never heard him ever raise his voice to us kids, even after he'd taken down with arthritis and wasn't able to do anything.

He was the baby of his family. There were sixteen children in all and he was youngest. His family farmed for a living and raised everything they ate, but he always was interested in remedies. There was an Indian chief who lived in the same neighborhood that [my daddy's family] did, near Cleveland, Georgia, in White County. He would come out and talk with my daddy a lot in their young days. That got him interested and wanting to know about [the Indians' remedies].

Back then, you know, there wasn't many doctors. People just sort of doctored themselves, so his parents were really interested in my daddy learning this stuff. His family wanted him to go [stay with the Cherokees] to learn about their remedies. He was the only [member of his family] that wanted to learn, so they let him. The rest of 'em didn't want to, so he just went and joined their tribe near Robbinsville, North Carolina, when he was twenty-one years old. He learned all their remedies from them. That's the reason he went over there, but [while he lived with them] he would do whatever the Indians were doing [to earn his keep]. He stayed with them for ten years and then he came back home.

He started gold mining and started his family then [when he was thirty-one]. A lot of people digged [for gold] back in them days and he was just raised up with it. He gold-mined near Hiawassee and in Gilmer County, all back in there. Lawd! He was a real gold miner! [laughter] He could tell [where there was gold] by the color of the sand and the little rocks. He'd say, "Now at the end of this, there's gold," and they'd start following the little trail [or vein]. They'd dig tunnels or channels where they saw the vein, start turning under, following that little vein with picks and shovels. If they ever found a ledge or rock, they'd take that pick and go through that rock because that was where the most gold was. Then they'd trench their water into little troughs. They had pans and they'd dip those pans in [that water] and turn them every which way and let the water run through them. That way, the gold would stay in the bottom [of the pan] while all the other stuff would run out. [My mama still had the pans but I don't know what she did with 'em.]

They'd heat [the gold] to get all the black dirt off of it. Then they'd sell it by the ounce. Just an ounce of gold would bring a lot of money. Them gold nuggets *really* brought in a lot of money!

He would [plant his crops and tend them] get that done. Then [while they were growing] him and his brothers and some of their neighbors would gold-mine together. When it come time to gather [the crops], why then he'd come back to the fields and get them all in and go back to gold mining.

In the winter months, he'd gold-mine a lot. He was a real gold miner back in his young days! That's what gave him the arthritis— exposure in the creeks and everything. He panned gold and he would come in in the wintertime so wet and freezing to death!

He took down sick when I was small, so I never got to go [to the gold mines] with him. I've been to the gold mines after he got to where he wasn't able to go. I saw where they had worked, but when I was there, there wasn't anybody working. I don't know why they all quit gold mining back up in there. My sister can remember him having some gold nuggets when he first got down sick. She can remember playing with them *[laughter]*, but he finally sold them all.

[When he could no longer gold-mine because he was so crippled up with arthritis, he still did herb doctoring. He would ride around in an oxcart that my brothers built for him.] It was made by taking the two front wheels and the axle from a regular one-horse farm wagon, and adding a little bed [about three feet long and just wide enough for two people to sit side by side]. Instead of the wagon tongue, they put shafts on each side of the wagon and put a steer between these to pull the cart.

They fixed the cart where it would lean down and Daddy would sit down on it [facing backwards] and then they'd take a stick and raise [the cart] back up and lock it [in place]. That would fasten [the cart level] to where he could sit right.

[One of my brothers] would just get up in the front and drive it like a horse-drawn wagon. One of us little ones would sit down by my daddy in the back. They'd [usually] send me with him because I was the size that he needed to go with him and I'd take care of his crutches for him. When he'd get [ready to get out], the big boys would let the cart down with the lever and he'd stand up. He couldn't use his arms much, so I'd stick his crutches under his arms and walk along with him.

He'd go squirrel-hunting like that. He'd tell me to [get down from the cart] and go around the tree and chase the squirrel to where he could shoot it. I'd go 'round behind the tree and make a fuss and the squirrel would run around [toward him] and he'd shoot it. The older ones would dress [the squirrels he shot] and put the hides on a board and sell them things. My mama would make squirrel dumplings. My daddy *loved* squirrel dumplings!

He possum-hunted a lot, too. I wouldn't eat the possum but the rest [of the family] liked 'em. They'd dry out the possum skins and sell them too.

We'd go back up in the mountains in that oxcart. He'd say, "All right, get that mayapple. There's some mayapple." I'd hop off the oxcart and dig it up for him with a little shovel or a little ol' mallet, whichever one he'd have in his hand. I'd have to gather the whole plant, usually, but for some he'd just use roots—blackberry, for instance.

We'd trim off the dead leaves and any that wasn't good and alive. We'd wash 'em real clean to where there wouldn't be a bit of grit on 'em nowhere. Then we'd trim 'em and fix 'em. He'd take the leaves and make different things out of them and he'd make other stuff out of the roots.

He'd take the roots while they were fresh and beat them up and make little poultices for sores. It'd draw that infection out and the sore'd heal right up. [Usually, he prescribed medicines to be applied] externally as poultices.

He also dried a lot of his stuff. [To powder up the roots and leaves,] we'd stick 'em in a pan and put 'em in the stove to dry. Then we'd put 'em in a cloth and beat 'em with a hammer, just like you were beating up pickling spices to put up pickles. I've powdered for a half day at a time. *[laughter]* After we had it powdered up, he'd put it in little bottles and he'd keep all his stuff in a certain cabinet. He had a chart on his cabinet and all the bottles were numbered. Now if he [knew his patient] had this certain kind of disease or illness, he had a number [he'd go to]. When people came, they mightn't know what was the matter with them. He'd diagnose what they had and then he'd get the herbs that went with that disease and dose 'em up. He'd know how much to give and he'd take a little spoon and [dip that much out of one of his bottles]. He'd give them the powder and tell them how much to put in a glass and how much water to pour over it to make the tea. They were supposed to let the tea sit so long, then strain it and drink it.

We lived close to a spring so we had a springhouse built. My daddy hired a man to make the bricks for it and it had a little oak shingle roof on it. [At that time] he'd make fresh herb teas and medicines every week. He'd put the medicine in little jars and we'd set the bottles down in the water [in that springhouse] to keep them cool because there wasn't such things as Frigidaires then. It would keep [the medicines] fresh for more than a week. He would [prescribe] all [his herb medicines] in the tea form if it was [to be taken internally]. Tea was the easiest way to take [the medicine]. Some of [his patients] wouldn't drink [the teas] without sugar to sweeten it a little bit, but if they would, he preferred to have them take it without sugar.

There wouldn't be many days unless it was real bad weather that somebody [didn't come to be treated]. [He had patients] that'd come from a long ways, some from Alabama and some from Tennessee. They heard about him through their kin people. "Why don't you go see Henry Cantrell? He can cure that."

[So they'd come see him and say,] "My cousin [or my aunt or my uncle] told me about you. Here I am."

Someone that had ulcerated stomach and hemorrhoids came from Five Points in Atlanta. He mixed a teaspoonful of alum and about a Vaseline jar-sized amount of pure hogs' lard together, worked up into a salve, and give them a little jar of that. He'd just cure 'em up in a little while. We kept that salve mixed ahead of time, 'cause it didn't spoil.

[People used to come to him with pellagra.] They'd turn red from the elbows down and knees down and their skin would peel off. It'd look like a bad case of sunburn but it don't ever turn no color but red till [the skin] starts peeling. I ain't saw none of that in years but people'd come to him with that and he'd fix this tea out of the stalks of the barbell plant and some whiskey. Barbell's a long, slim plant that rises up in a pile about as high as my head. It has yellow-gold-colored blooms that look like little bitty bells hanging on the underside of little clusters. It [grew] back in the mountains around Cleveland. [He'd prescribe] a good teaspoonful *before* each meal, three teaspoons a day. He'd put a little whiskey in [with the stalks] to preserve [the barbell] if there wasn't a cool place to keep it. The whiskey had to be pure corn liquor, not any that was made with sugar and stuff. [The sugar] made the pellagra act up worse.

Barbell was the only mixture he'd use with whiskey. [My brothers] went and got his liquor for him. [They'd go] way back there in the mountains towards Hiawassee. There was one place up there that they knew [our family] so they'd let the boys have it for medicine. It cost them ten dollars a gallon. [When they] went for it the first time, [the moonshiners] give the boys a hard time. "Who's sick? What do you want with it?"

The revenue officers would stop them and they'd tell 'em, "Why, I was getting this for such and such a one that was sick. Gettin' it for my daddy to make medicine out of," and then they'd leave 'em alone. They knew my daddy was a herb doctor [so they] knew what it was all about.

There was what they called snake button plant. It had little ol' buttons on top of that plant and he used that on warts and corns and bunions on your toes and feet. It'd draw the soreness out and the corns or whatever would peel off. I ain't seen none [of the snake buttons] down here. All that stuff was mostly found back in the mountains.

[My daddy treated all the family when we were sick or hurt.] When I was about seven or eight, just old enough to walk the three miles to school, my mother got *shot*. My brother-in-law had brought a Mr. Loudermilk up to our house to sell him my daddy's gun. [The gun was] one of these kinds that loaded a whole lot of shells, an automatic. My brother-in-law took it and started to put a shell in. [When he] pulled the bolt back, it was supposed to throw its shell out. He pulled the bolt back but the gun didn't throw its shell. It always had before, but it didn't that time. Well, he pushed the bolt back up and the gun went off and shot my mama. The bullet went through her lung and lodged in her shoulder blade.

Back then we didn't have phones, [so we] couldn't call a doctor. My brother-in-law had to go get him. We thought the doctor might get the bullet out, but he couldn't because it [had] lodged against her shoulder blade. They never did get that bullet out and she didn't have no surgery. Daddy doctored her. He fixed a walnut poultice [to put on the wound]. To make the walnut poultice, crack the walnut hull and get the walnut out. Beat the hull up and put table salt and a little bit of flour in with it and smear it on a little piece of soft, clean cloth, like a piece of old sheet or pillowcase. He put that on the wound and changed it every twenty-four hours.

He also gave her a blood purifier made of a teaspoonful of sulfur mixed in a pint can of honey all stirred up good. She had to take one teaspoonful of that mixture every day. She got all right [after] staying in bed ten days, and could use her arm like always. She lived to be ninety-one.

He never did just set a price for his doctoring because he didn't think that was right. People would just pay him by working for him or they'd trade him stuff from out of their garden or produce or something like that.

The patients would just come in the living room because he had to stay in one place due to his arthritis. He didn't get about much, maybe a little bit on crutches, but not much. Sometimes he'd get himself able to get up and out and around, and then he'd go right back down. He'd usually just sit in the living room in a chair [that was high off the floor]. He couldn't sit down in a regular chair [and get back up] like we do. He had to be up real high.

[After he got so disabled that he couldn't get around much at all,] he'd sit and read his Bible. If nobody wasn't there to talk with him, he'd sit there and read that Bible. He wouldn't read the newspaper; he'd read the Bible.

He died in '36 when he was seventy-nine.

My mama's name was Rachel Chadwick. She was from Ellijay, Gilmer County [Georgia]. She was about five feet tall and had gray eyes, the color of mine. Her hair [was] kind of a reddish color and she wore it in a bun.

She met Daddy when he came back home from living with [the Cherokee Indians]. She was sixteen [and he was thirty-one] when they got married. They moved to Cleveland [Georgia, White County].

Mama sewed with her fingers and made all our clothes. Her mama had taught her to sew. It was just something passed on down from mother to daughter. She also sewed for other people. She'd make dresses and men's clothes and suits. [She processed the cotton that she wove with.] We didn't grow any cotton; we bought it from other people around us. Before [we] could go to bed at night, every child had to pick seed out of so much cotton. I learned how to card and make bats and rows with her. She had a spinning wheel set up and I'd turn the wheel while she'd spin and make big balls of thread on corncobs. She didn't have no bobbins.

She'd weave with that cotton thread. She'd run it in that loom and weave her cloth to make clothes and curtains. A lot of times she'd weave a little wool in with the cotton. She'd trade for wool fleece and card that wool, too. She would knit boys' wool socks and babies' booties out of that wool.

She quilted all the time. [She had a quilting frame] just like I've got. It hung from the ceiling. She'd roll it up to the top of the house at night, plumb up out of the way. Roll it down in the day. She'd make her own quilting bats, cotton padding, to put in the quilts. She'd place the bats on the flat lining, then she fixed the rows with thread. They was little rows, with the thread doubled on the spinnin' wheel by twisting two [strands] of thread together.

When she didn't have a quilt, she'd sit and crochet. She'd crochet lace on the pillowcases and wide lace on our hand towels and bedspreads. When she'd lay her crocheting down to go in and fix a meal, I'd get it up and see how she'd done it. I'd just work while she was gone. I'd hear her coming and I'd ravel it back out. I wouldn't realize I was getting the thread dirty. She knew, but I thought she didn't know it. I can't remember learning [to crochet]. I just copied her. Mama learned us all how to quilt and crochet and make dolls. So that's the way I learned.

[My mama usually] fixed biscuits and ham gravy for breakfast. She'd fry the ham and take that grease and make gravy. She would thicken it with flour and make thick gravy. She's the one that learnt me to make biscuits.

She'd always cook whatever kind of vegetables she had for dinner and supper, and cornbread and we always had milk and butter. She had a big wood stove she cooked on, and we children had to gather all the wood [for it].

Mama was pretty bad in real cold weather to make cornmeal mush, they called it. She was pretty fond of that for supper. To make it, just sift the meal and instead of making cornbread with milk and cold water, just stir in boiling water to thicken it. Then take that up and eat it with butter and milk. It was kind of like oatmeal and I didn't like it too good.

My favorite meal was ham and gravy. Any time she cooked it, I'd eat it. The ham was country cured, salted down in a big ol' meat box. The meat box was like a big cedar chest made out of oak. It was kept close to a window inside the kitchen part of the house. The bottom would have wide cracks in it to let the salt drip through, but the rest of it was pretty tight. They'd layer that meat in there—ham, shoulders and middlin's. (Middlin's is the side, between the shoulder and back—down the spine. They'd go right down the hog's backbone and cut that out and that's a square middlin' of meat.) They'd put a layer of salt, layer of meat, layer of salt, and at the top they'd cover the meat completely up with salt so nothing could get to it and where you couldn't even see none of it. Then they'd let it set for about a week. When the salt started melting on the meat, we'd put a big pan under there to catch the salt. We had to empty the pan out every now and then.

Mama would take the trimmings of the meat and grind them up to sausage. Then she'd put the flavoring and the salt in. She'd use sage most of the time and a little bit of hot pepper sometimes. Different stuff you know, whatever way everybody liked it. My mama was bad to put it up two ways, some with sage and some with just pepper.

Sometimes she would shuck corn, break the corn out and put [sausage] up in the dry corn shucks. She'd wash that shuck and pack that sausage and salt in it. She'd close it back up and tie the shucks closed with little wires. Then she'd hang them in the smokehouse and let them dry out. It'd keep for as long as we needed it, all winter. Nothing would get in [the sausage] with it wrapped up in that shuck. Sealed it up.

Mama kept such a yard of chickens, we'd pick up eggs hours at a time. They was just laying everywhere, some under the house, some nesting in the barn, some in the little out sheds and all around. We [built] a chicken house and lot and built nests for the hens in little boxes. We put straw in those nests and got the hens to lay their eggs there. We had guineas and turkeys, too.

When it got to where Daddy couldn't get around, us kids took the farming over and we did it! We growed cabbage, collards, corn and two kinds of potatoes, sweet potatoes and Irish. We didn't grow cotton but we grew just about everything else. We would grow acres of syrup cane. We were close to a syrup mill and we would cut our cane down and take it there to be ground. The mill was pulled by a mule. The juice was cooked till it got thick. Then [the foam on top] was skimmed off and the syrup poured into tin buckets that held about four pounds of syrup. Sometimes we'd put our syrup into a ten-gallon barrel, just a plain barrel with a hole and stopper in it, so we could tilt it over and pour out what we needed. We would sell syrup by the gallons.

Mama was bad to cook syrup gingerbread. It was delicious. She'd make tea cakes, too. We'd eat syrup and butter and biscuits, also. We used a lot of syrup.

My mother never would can too much, just berries and peaches and apples, stuff that wasn't hard to can. She preserved some vegetables in barrels. She'd fill one barrel full of beans. We would pick 'em, string 'em and break 'em all up. Then cook 'em half done and pack 'em down in a barrel with layer of salt, layer of beans, layer of salt, layer of beans till we got that barrel full. Then she would take cabbage leaves and cover the top. Then take a white cloth and pack it down in there and cover it with salt. Then she'd put a lid on that barrel and let those beans sit there to sour. It'd take about a week to sour and then they'd be ready to eat. They'd just last and last; they wouldn't ruin 'cause they was soured.

She had one barrel she'd put up with kraut, put it up same way as the beans. We didn't cook the cabbage. Just chopped it up in another container using a straightened-out hoe, sharpened just as sharp as they could get it. In the barrel she'd put a layer of cabbage, layer of salt, layer of cabbage, layer of salt. Then put the cloth over it and let it sour. That was sauerkraut. That made the best sauerkraut. It was delicious and there wasn't no spoilin' to it. You'd have that till you used it up.

When I was real little, we lived down in a low place, kinda in a valley like. Well, it came a lot of rain one time. Just rainin', rainin', rainin', rainin', and I heard [the grown-ups] talk about the floods, you know. My daddy [had been] reading to me [about Noah's ark] in the Bible, back when the flood came. Well, I was too small to understand what it was all about, but I knowed just a flood came and washed everybody away. That's all I had in my mind. Well, it rained and rained and we couldn't go to school because it was so rainy. I got out in the yard one day and came running back in the house, "Mama, Mama, it's comin' a flood!"

Mama said, "How do you know it's comin' a flood?"

I said, "There's just water everywhere." I was scared, just as scared as I could be.

Then my daddy called to me. He said, "Come here. Let's get this straight now. Back in them olden days, back when people was wicked, God seen people destroying the first world. A flood came and washed everybody away but the ones that was ready to go. Noah had built an ark for [them]. The ones that wasn't ready to go in the ark—well, they was washed away."

So that kinda satisfied me a little and I calmed down. *[laughter]* I just knew we was all gonna be washed away, you know, 'cause there was water everywhere! [My daddy] told me the big flood's already been and it took away all the mean people. Well, that satisfied my mind right there.

PLATE 6 An old photograph of the house described below, located in White County, Georgia. Flora's mother, Rachel Cantrell, is holding Coleman, and Myrtie, Flora, and Florrie are standing with them.

"When I first started school we lived in an old, old log house with wood shingles. It just had two rooms and it was built so you could go between them. You could drive a car between them two rooms. There was one big room and then the [people who built the house] skipped the width of a wagon and built another big room. You had to go out of the living room and cross through [that open space] to get to the kitchen. It wasn't covered between the two rooms; you just walked out in the weather. [They called it] a dog trot, except dog trots are usually joined and ours wasn't. When we moved there, the wagon was driven up between the two rooms to unload the furniture. We lived in that house for ages. Now *that* was a mountain house."

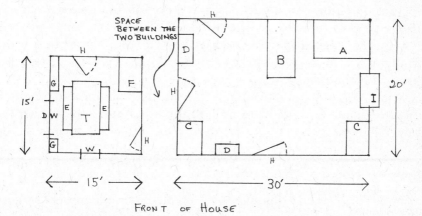

PLATE 7 A diagram showing where the furniture was located in this two-cabin house. A. Father's bed, B. Mother's bed, C. Child's bed, D. Chest of drawers, E. Benches, F. Stove, G. Shelves, H. Door, I. Chimney, DW. Double window, W. Single window, T. Table.

* * *

We'd start school in September, go to school for oh, six months in
the winter. Then we were out for about four to six weeks or so. We
missed a good many days on account of the weather because we had
no transportation. [We had to walk.] We'd put on a raincoat if it was
rainin' and go to school, just so's it wasn't real freezing cold.

The first school I went to was in a building near the asbestos mines.
I didn't get to go when I was six years old. I had to wait awhile till I got
old enough to where I could walk that far. It was a pretty good little
piece, about a couple or three miles.

It was a one-room schoolhouse and we had little benches, not
desks. They had a primer, first grade. And then they had [second and]
third grade and fourth grade and on up through the seventh. But
there wasn't very many in neither grade, just maybe two or three.
Now when I got in the fourth grade, it was me and one other girl. We
was in the fourth and fifth grades for two years by ourself. I don't
know how old our teacher was but she was young. [She didn't have
any formal teacher education] that I knew of.

Later, I went to high school in Nacoochee Valley. One day we had a
fire drill at school. They told us we was gonna have one and then we
heard the bell. The little bitty ones was on the first floor and I was on
the second. The school was three stories high. When the bell was
tapped, we had to see how quickly we could get out. There was
banisters and steps that went down; they weren't very wide. Well,
ev'rybody broke into runnin'. I didn't get out fast enough and the
third-graders come down and pushed me over the banister. I fell off
and broke my arm.

There was a man who just helped around the school but he wasn't a
doctor. He knowed about as much as a doctor, but he didn't have a
license to doctor. If one of [the students] got hurt, he could give 'em
first aid. He placed my arm back as best he could and put a towel
around it. He let my sister take me home. We had to walk three miles
—me with that broke arm.

[When we got home,] my daddy fixed it. He held one end real tight
and pulled and had Mama to pull on the other end and they set the
bone. They bandaged it up real good with a cloth. He wrapped it up
with the cloth fixed where it'd stretch. Then he put it in a sling. I went
back to school the next day and I haven't had any trouble with it since.

[All of us children would play back up on the mountains near where
we lived. There were rocks we'd crawl up on and through.] We [also]
had a jumpin'-off place where we'd [go]. You see, back in the Indian

war one of the Indians got to dating one of the white girls and her
daddy tried to stop her [from courting him] but she wouldn't give
him up. So her daddy tried to get rid of him. He took him up to the
jumpin'-off place and pushed him off. Well, she jumped off after him.
We used to boil eggs and eat what we wanted, then throw the rest of
them off down there, just for the fun of it, to see how far they would
fall.

We had a milk cow and Mama went to milk it [one day]. I went along
with her and there wasn't a thing in the world wrong with the cow that
day. She was just as fine as you ever seen. The next mornin' Mama
went down and milked her and the cow didn't much want to let her
milk it that time. She went ahead and milked anyway and then turned
the cow out in the pasture. It went right around that pasture fence a-
goin' towards the branch, kinda leanin' on the fence. When the fence
give way [under the cow's weight], the cow fell over in a little low, flat
place. It died. A heart attack, they said. Well, the boys went out there
then and dug a hole and buried her where she died.

I worried and worried about where we were going to get our milk.
The only milk cow we had died. They bought another one but us
young 'uns didn't know no better. We bawled our eyes out 'cause our
cow died of a heart attack.

I was still crying about the cow when me and my sister, a little older
than me, started across the creek. There was a big ol' turtle setting up
on a rock. I wanted to take it to the house and make me a pet. I didn't
know then how dangerous they was. My sister run to the house and
got my mama and she come and got the turtle and took it up to the
house. Then she just took and chopped its head off and she cooked it!
I did cry then. She'd killed my pet! We bawled our eyes out. That was
the prettiest thing we'd ever seen and she just took and chopped its
head off and cooked it. They say they are real good [to eat], but I
wouldn't eat a bite. That was my pet. I found it and I thought it ought
to have been mine. We kept its pretty speckledy shell for years.

Right about where the turtle had been in the branch was a big ol'
plum bush. We'd go down there and get them big ol' plums. They
called 'em hog plums back then. Mama would tell us, "Don't you go
down there and get them plums!" We'd go down there anyway. She
didn't like for us to eat 'em atall 'cause she said they wasn't good for
us, they would just kind of make your stomach hurt. Us kids didn't
care. We'd eat 'em anyhow—like a crab apple, you know.

We'd eat persimmons, too. We'd bite 'em when they was green and

see who could eat 'em and not make a face. It draws your mouth
inside out! After the frost was on 'em, when they was ripe, they was
good and we'd eat 'em.

Now we didn't have no rural mail [delivery]. We'd have to walk
three or four miles [to the old Sautee store] to get our mail. We did
our trading there and everything. They might have [rural delivery]
down in the lower country but not back in the mountains. When they
finally did get to deliverin' mail [to us], it was ridin' horseback. Had
these mailbags they'd put on each side of the horse's back and then
put the saddle on and take off with the mail.

We did our trading there [at the Sautee store], too. We'd trade eggs
and chickens and swap 'em for whatever we couldn't raise. We'd tie
three or four fryers up by the feet and lay 'em on our arm and go swap
'em for something we couldn't raise. We'd take buckets of eggs and
trade 'em for coffee, sugar, salt, soda and something like that, 'cause
we growed nearly everything else. That store had about everything in
there.

We children would cut broomstraw. It would be as high as your
head. We'd take what we always called 'tater forks because we used to
dig 'taters with 'em, and get the husks off the straw with them forks.
We'd clean it real good. We'd carry big bundles of that broomstraw to
the Sautee store and trade it for goods. We'd have to carry it [walking]
because we didn't have any other way of going much except footin' it.
They'd buy every bit of it. They'd just take the bundle of straw from
us children and they'd make it into brooms. They'd [sell them for]
about seventy-five cents for the broom and [give us] about ten cents
to the bundle. We could've made it into brooms but they said, "Just
bring it on."

We made our own brooms [for use at home]. We'd cut out about
that much straw [about four inches in diameter] and wash it real
good. [Then, we'd] take a potato fork and strip all that husk off. Then
take a good, stout cord (not too big around, something like a fishin'
cord) and make a loop. We'd run that cord down a little more than
halfway of the straw and then just wind it up to the top. You wouldn't
tie the cord, but just stick it back down in the straw as far as you could.
Then, we'd cut the ends off the straw at the bottom and just sweep the
floor. I love a homemade broom 'cause you can get down under
anything with one hand and sweep it out.

I [lived in White County] until [I married Johnny]. We moved first
to Banks County and then here to Buford. I was seventeen and he was

eighteen when we married, and that was on October the fourteenth, nineteen and twenty-three. I had met him in White County at Blue Creek Church when he boarded with his uncle.

Just after Johnny and I had got married, we had his daddy's car one

PLATE 8   Flora and Johnny Youngblood, taken shortly before his death in 1980.

day. We started to his daddy's house and had my brother and his girlfriend with us. We had started up a pretty good little hill when the kingpin split open and we started going back down that hill. The brakes wouldn't hold and we couldn't stop. [Johnny] swerved the car around and cut it into a dirt bank. One wheel went up faster than the others and the car just landed sideways. My brother's girlfriend weighed about two hundred pounds and she got to the other side of the car and it just set back up. We just liked to have wrecked, but we didn't after all.

[Later on, when we lived in Banks County, I tried driving a car.] Johnny said, "I'm tired. You wanta drive?"

I said, "Might as well." So I got under the wheel and let him hold the baby. Well, I was going along pretty well and I passed a road where there was some dump trucks hauling dirt. One dump truck had a back tire to blow out as it passed us. I turned loose the wheel, took my feet off of everything and said, "Get it." Johnny grabbed the wheel. I thought that dump truck had hit us [when I heard its tire blow], but we didn't wreck. I don't know why, but I never did drive anymore.

We hadn't been living in Banks County long when Johnny decided to farm a crop. [He borrowed a mule] and plowed all day. When he took the mule home, it got sick. Well, he went on over that evening [to the man's house that he had borrowed the mule from] to help him with it.

[I was there at our house alone except for the two babies.] Ruth, the oldest child was little, and Ruby, my second child, was a baby. There wasn't but a year and three months between 'em. I had Ruth setting looking at the Sears and Roebuck catalog while I got the little one to sleep. I heard something coming out the driveway. It sounded like a whole lot of people walking. I never heard so much racket. The old house had wooden shutters so there was no way to see out without opening up a window. Well, it was after dark and I wasn't about to open that window. There was a family of colored people lived out from me. I wasn't used to no colored people, because they weren't allowed back in Cleveland [Georgia]. Everybody knew I was scared of 'em. The trail [of noise] was coming from the way [the colored family lived]. So I just knew that those folks knew that Johnny was gone and they was gonna come out there to my house. There was a well in the front yard that we drawed water from, and when they came to the house that well bucket went off [the shelf]. I thought it was them and they was drawin' a bucket of water. I got scared and I could just see 'em in my imagination drawing a drink of water.

Well, [the noise] went on around the house. We had filled up the straw bed with new straw and there was some [leftover straw] out on the grass. They was making a racket there. I pictured in my mind that I could hear 'em and I thought, "They's a bunch out there and they're talking real low." Well, I got scareder and scareder, and I went and got down a sixteen-gauge shotgun. I wore an apron then and I filled my apron full of [shotgun] shells. I set down there with that gun and watched the door. If they had touched [the door] like they was gonna come in, I was just gonna shoot through the door. There was just a little ol' bitty porch there and it's a wonder [whoever or whatever was there] hadn't touched the door.

Then I heard Johnny coming up. I learned the way he would walk and could tell his walking ahead of anything else. So when he got to the door, I jumped up and undone it right quick. I said, "Come on in." He saw I was scared and cold. [I always get cold when I get scared.]

He said, "What's the matter?"

I said, "There's a bunch of them colored people at the back of the house."

He said, "Aw, there's not."

I said, "They are, too, because I heard 'em coming from the house and they're right around there."

He said, "Set down. That's a mare and colt. They're out there eating that straw." *[laughter]*

I'd done got scared to death and it wasn't nothing. Boy! Was I ever scared, though!

In 1938 I was pregnant, seven months to the day, when I got hurt by a mule. It was an early Sunday morning before church and I went to turn her out into the pasture. When I opened the stable door, she didn't come out. I said, "Come out of there, Kate! What you doing? Come on out!"

Then I just stepped back for her to come out. Well, she just leaped up in my face. She took her foot and laid my leg plumb out. It didn't break the bone, just chopped the flesh up. She also bit me in the back and stomped me.

After a while, Johnny woke up and looked out the window. He said a low voice woke him up saying, "Johnny" real low. He saw me trying to crawl through a little place [in the barn]. The mule was still pawin' at me. He jumped up and ran out and run the mule off and got me to the house. They got the doctor there and got me all done up. I came to enough to know something had happened. I had false teeth, hadn't had 'em but a little while. Well, I missed them and I was a-beggin' them to get me my teeth. They hunted and hunted and finally found them up under the cow box, where we fed the cows. [The box was nailed off the ground.] They weren't even broke. They was still clean. I stayed in the bed two months. I didn't lose the baby. It was a twelve-pound boy.

I had eight girls and four boys. There was three girls—Ruth, Ruby, and Rosalee, and then three boys—Grady, Hoyt, and Herman. Then there was Mamie, Gene, Johnny May, Grace, Mildred and Rosie. [I had a midwife] come to the house [for the first six]; then the doctor [delivered the last six]. All of 'em were born at home but the last one. I went to the hospital with her. That's my baby. She was the tiniest and she weighed six pounds!

When the doctor delivered the babies at home, he brought scales with him. They were those kind that had a scoop in 'em. They'd weigh [the babies] first and then dress 'em. I had two that weighed twelve pounds. Most of them weighed eight and a half to ten pounds.

We farmed the first few years [we were married]. We done everything! Johnny would kill hogs and dress 'em, salt 'em down and everything. We raised our own milk cows and one time I got one to a pretty good size. Some people came over to buy it and I said, "No, I don't want to sell this one." She was so pretty. She was my pride and joy and I wasn't gonna sell her. I wanted to save her and raise her into a milk cow.

Well, they went on back and didn't try to buy her no more. Two days from that, that calf didn't come up to the barn. I got out and hunted, but I couldn't find her. Johnny said, "I'll go see if I can find her. Maybe she's hung up somewhere down in the pasture." He went down through the pasture then and found where she'd fell over in a ditch and broke her neck. I said, "Well, I should have sold her, but I didn't want to."

When the Depression hit, we had four kids and by the time the Depression was over, we had two more. [Johnny] had to leave home to find work. I just kept house and kept the kids here in school. That was a full-time job. I ain't ever worked away from home. Never have. Johnny'd work and send us money home. [I ran the farm] when Johnny was working away. We just raised produce stuff. We didn't raise no cotton. [We grew stuff] just for our own use.

PLATE 9   "I've quilted a lot of quilts! It's a sight at the quilts I've quilted for outside people. And I would crochet cushions to sell, but I did not make any clothes to sell." Mrs. Youngblood.

[Johnny worked] in Atlanta during the Depression. He'd ride the bus down there and back. He didn't have to work too long until he got to where he could buy a T-Model [car]. [He'd stay in Atlanta through the week, boarded there] and come home on the weekends.

After he got the car, he still boarded because he couldn't afford the gas to drive back and forth. [And then, during the Second World War, there were many shortages and we had to be issued rationing stamps for food and for clothes.] There wouldn't be much cloth in the stores and when they got some, they rationed it—so many yards to this one and so many to that one. [Flour and feeds for animals and chickens came in cloth sacks back then that had pretty prints on them or were plain colors and were suitable for reusing.] I made all my kids' clothes. I've made my boys many a flour-sack shirt. It took about two hours to make one. I had a pattern to go by. I'd put [the buttons] on just like a regular shirt and it had a collar. [The cloth] looked like broadcloth and came in white, so I left it white. It was easier to take care of.

A lot of times I'd hold my baby on my lap and cut a dress out from [what I called the] butterfly pattern. Grab it up, sew it on the sewing machine, and put it on who was going to school in time to catch the bus. [For that dress], you only had to hem around the sleeves which were like cap sleeves, around the neck which was round, and at the bottom for the hem. You didn't have much change in clothes then. You done well if you had three good dresses.

They had shoes rationed. You got one pair a year and they had to do you. They put a shoe repair shop up at Buford where they could keep 'em patched and sewed and cleaned. I made all of my little ones' shoes out of Johnny's felt hats. He'd wear a hat till it was unfit to wear and I'd take it and make my babies shoes. They weren't out-on-the-ground shoes. I'd double the felt when I cut them out. I'd just cut them out in the shape of a boot and sew the two pieces together and then put a sole in. I didn't have a pattern for those.

Meanwhile Johnny helped frame houses, carpentering. He read blueprints. A lot of other people couldn't read them, but he could. They'd always holler for him. He made good money but he had to stay gone nearly all the time. He joined a carpenters' local [union] and they would hunt him a job if he got out of work. He built houses everywhere. He left Atlanta to help build an H-plant in Jackson, South Carolina. Then he went to Indiana and helped build a hydrogen plant there and then one in Tennessee. [You couldn't come out and say a word to nobody 'cause everything was secret.] That was back in the war times. He helped build a bomber plant in New York State. He went from there to Niagara Falls to work on the dam.

I went to Niagara Falls [to visit him] on an airplane. I hadn't flew [before], hadn't been nowhere by myself. I took off up there and stayed a week. I enjoyed it!

As for the ride—it was good and smooth riding until we hit a air pocket. The stewardess was always giving you something. They give me a cup of coffee and if I started to take a drink, I poured it on me. They give me mints to chew so I wouldn't get airsick. I'd felt better if I'd had somebody to go with me, but I went by myself.

[The pilot] got to telling how high we was and I thought to myself, "Now that's high enough." We went so high you couldn't see a thing in the world but the little thunderheads in the sky. Now they are pretty up there, the prettiest things you ever seen.

It took us two hours going up to get to Pittsburgh and then I changed planes. I said to the man there at the door when I went to get out, "I'm supposed to change planes," and I showed him the number on my ticket.

He said, "Go to that plane right out there." There was a soldier boy walking along there and he had the same number plane to go to. [The man at the door] told him, "You see that she gets on that plane," and he said to me, "You follow him." Well, I just followed him on out there then and he stepped back and said, "You go up first," and I went on up the steps.

I got up [to Niagara Falls] and we went around and saw a lot. We went to the whirlpool at the end of the Great Lakes. There ain't no bottom to it. It's where [the water] goes around and around. They had a place built on each side and a thing you could ride across on cables. I wouldn't ride *[laughter]*; I was off the ground enough. They done said there wasn't no bottom to it. I wasn't about to get up there.

The airplane that I took up there didn't get back. They said it was about tore up and they kept it to be repaired. So when the time came for me to come back home, I had to come back first class in a big sightseeing plane. We came back low and I could look out the window. It was just beautiful. Going over housing projects that looked like little rabbit boxes. They would tell us where we were, but I can't remember all the towns we flew over. We flew four hours before we even lit at all.

You know, it just cost me eighty-eight dollars and fifty-five cents for a round-trip ticket. Now it would cost you that from here to Atlanta. Everything's went up so.

Johnny was a member of the carpenters' local [union] for twenty-five years. He had to pay dues so I told him that was buying a job. They'd find jobs [for him] and that's how come he was going to so many different places. [After he retired] he got a pension and drawed that until he died. That was the twenty-eighth of June in '80. He was seventy-eight. He had emphysema of the lungs and then he took pneumonia. He also had bleeding ulcers and they couldn't doctor the emphysema without settin' the ulcers off to bleeding. Just one thing brought on another until he just couldn't make it. We just lacked from the twenty-eighth of June until the fourteenth of October being married sixty years when he died.

As Mrs. Youngblood demonstrated to us her method for making honeysuckle baskets, she told us:

PLATE 10   A completed basket.

Back in the mountains [when we were children], we didn't have nothing much to do. We didn't have nowhere to go, so such things as this [basketmaking] was pastimes. When we would see anything made, why we would want to fix [us one] too, so we'd copy it. My mother would make our Easter baskets, and she'd also make big baskets, big enough to put beans in [when we picked them. That's where I first learned how to make a basket.]

[Then I married and] moved to Buford and still made baskets as a pastime. [Making baskets out of honeysuckle vines] was interesting to me because it's something from nature. I just enjoy things like this—you can start from nothing and make something out of it.

The best time [to gather honeysuckle vines] is in the spring of the year. They're tender then and they won't break as bad as when the sap goes down later in the year. You can find some patches where the vines do not have many knots [or joints] in them. Little knots will be all right. They won't [interfere with the weaving]. Take [off those] that'll come off easy and leave the rest. You can work a few in, but not too many.

It takes a good-sized boxful of vines to make a medium-sized basket, a lunch basket about eight inches around and about seven inches high. It doesn't matter what size vines you collect. Larger ones [a little smaller than the diameter of a pencil] make the ribs of the basket, and smaller ones [are used] for the webbing or filling.

We can just wind some [of these vines] up and put them in this eight-quart pan. Let me put in about a cup of washing powder and cover the vines with water, put a lid on 'em and boil them till that skin'll start slipping off of 'em. The longer you boil [the vines], the better they'll skin. To see if they've cooked enough, just pick up one once in a while and see if all that bark'll slip off. Some don't have to cook long and some have to cook [from thirty minutes to an hour]. The soapsuds make the [bark] come off quick. Just run your thumbnail down the vine and take the bark completely off. The vines need to be soapy when you're stripping them. After they're stripped, put them in a pan of clear, cold water and they'll stay good for as long as a week [if you don't have time to weave your basket right away. If they do dry out, you may soak them again later when you are ready to weave your basket].

When my kids were little, I'd boil [my vines] outside in one of them old-timey black washpots. I'd keep 'em in the water till I worked 'em up, peeling them and all that. Then maybe the next day, I'd make my basket.

It doesn't take but about a couple of hours [to make a lunch basket like this] once you get started. Main thing is gettin' your stuff all ready. [Then after the basket's made,] it'll dry out in a little while, about two hours. I haven't, but I guess you could [dye some of the baskets]. I don't [even] shellac them. I just let them stay natural.

There was a collar shop up here in Buford and I'd get out and make these baskets and sell 'em to the ones that worked there. My husband also sold them. Later, I sold 'em out of my house.

I made what they call a tumbler. [Those are baskets that are] as big as a glass or a pint fruit jar. You put flower pots in 'em. They sell like

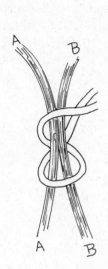

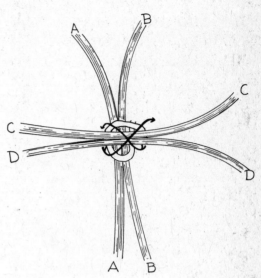

PLATE 11 Lay two of the longer ribs (A and B) side by side. Using a piece of thin vine, make a figure 8 around the two ribs.

PLATE 12 Lay two more long ribs (C and D) side by side across the first two.

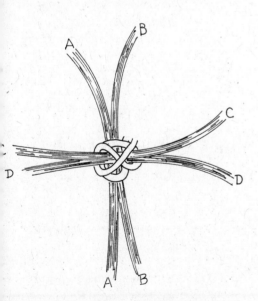

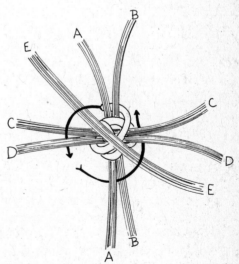

PLATE 13 Continue with the thin vine, making another figure 8 around the two new ribs. Keep pulling, as tightly as possible, the vine with which you are weaving.

PLATE 14 Lay one long rib (E) across the other four.

PLATE 15 The ribs being placed as described in the diagrams.

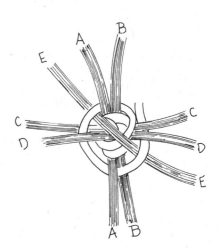

PLATE 16 Proceed weaving with the thin vine going through the ribs, over two, under two, making one complete circle.

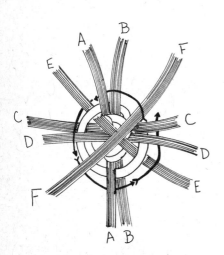

PLATE 17 Add another long rib.

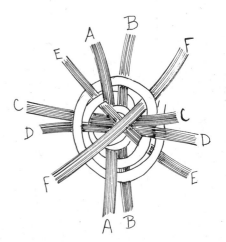

PLATE 18 Continue weaving over two, under two, for another complete circle.

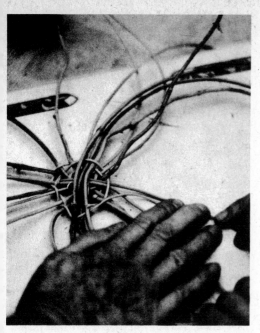

PLATE 19 Add ribs until all thirteen have been used.

PLATE 20 Mrs. Youngblood weaving the basket.

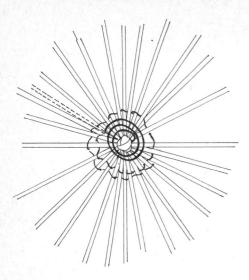

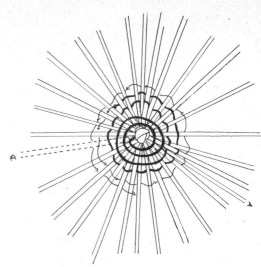

PLATE 21   After all long ribs are in place and the last circle woven, begin weaving over one, under one. After making one complete circle like this, begin adding the short ribs. Place them at random, wherever there is a wide gap between two ribs. Insert them toward the center as far as they can be pushed.

PLATE 22   Continue weaving over one, under one, until all fifteen have been used. Weaving note: When one piece of thin vine is almost completely used up, push the last inch or two into the weave and begin with another vine by pushing the first inch or two of that one into the weave and start with the over, under process again.

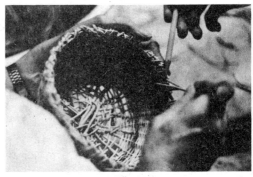

PLATE 23   After the diameter of the basket is the size desired, start lifting ribs slightly upward to form the sides. Create the shape you wish the basket to be, curved or straight up, by controlling how tightly you weave.

Continue weaving until basket reaches height desired. Mrs. Youngblood told us, "You could keep adding to this. Keep going 'round and have it as big as you want it." Weave a long vine vertically into the basket (about one inch) to end this phase. Ribs will still be sticking above the weaving. Cut ribs off two inches above weaving.

Insert a new piece of thin vine into basket's weaving and begin bending ribs along the edge, sewing them as you go.

PLATE 24   Go completely around the basket. With another vine, sew in opposite direction along rim to secure top edge. When finished, clip the vine, leaving about two inches. Run this vertically into the basket's edge to give a smooth finish.

To form the handle, braid three honeysuckle vines together. Leave about two inches unbraided on each end. Weave these ends vertically into the sides of the basket, starting on the inside.

everything! I sold I don't know how many till I got rid of every one. I gave the last one I made to somebody for their birthday. I don't even [have one left] for a pattern and I do try to keep one of everything for a pattern. I kept saying, "Well, I'll make me some more," but I never got 'round to it.

REMEDIES

Aching Feet

PLATE 25 Maude Houk gathering herbs for a remedy.

Bathe feet before bedtime in a strong solution made from white oak bark.

DIANE FORBES

Make a real hot tea out of burdock. Soak feet in the tea just before going to bed. To make the tea, use the whole plant, including roots.

Pull it up, wash it, chop it up and put in a pot of water, and boil and steam. Burdock may also be dried and the tea made during the winter.

FLORA YOUNGBLOOD

Arthritis

Make a tea by boiling the roots of ginseng. That gets the strength out of them. Drink the tea or rub it on the joints, and either will have the same effect.

NUMEROUS MARCUS

You can mix the roots of ginseng and goldenseal together in liquor.

NUMEROUS MARCUS

Eat lots of raw vegetables and fruits.

DOROTHY BECK

Take a buckeye and put it in your pocket and carry it around with you.

ELIZABETH ENDLER

My daddy used barbell. It has a yellow bloom. The little flowers are shaped like little bells and hang on the underside of the leaves. Cut the barbell plant down to the ground. Use the stems. Chop them up and put in a pot and boil them about twenty-five minutes. Strain the tea and drink it. It'll limber you up just right now.

FLORA YOUNGBLOOD

Asthma

Use the inner bark of wild yellow plum trees. Knock the old bark off and scrape down next to the wood and use these scrapings along with mullein leaves. Boil these together with sage leaves for about twenty minutes. Add alum to the tea after it is strained—one level teaspoon of alum to a quart of tea. Drink about two big tablespoonfuls of the tea every morning and every night, about twelve hours apart on the doses. It'll cure asthma.

FLORA YOUNGBLOOD

Bedbugs

We'd tote our bed frames and the slats outside and scald them every month or two in boiling water and lye soap. The bedbugs laid their eggs in that wood. Then we would change the straw in the ticks every fall. Whenever they would start threshing the wheat, we'd take them empty bed ticks and boil them real good. Then when they got dry, we'd stuff them with that fresh wheat straw.

FLORA YOUNGBLOOD

Apply kerosene liberally to all parts of the beds.

DIANE FORBES

Bleeding

Bandage the cut real tight. Tie a cord below and above the cut and repeat Ezekiel 16:6. The blood will stop immediately. Take the cords off and cleanse the wound with warm salty water. Use just enough salt to purify the water. Then bandage.

FLORA YOUNGBLOOD

Put kerosene oil on the cut.

ANNIE MAE HENRY

To stop bleeding, take soot from the back of a fireplace in an old chimney and press against cut. Wash the soot out when blood clots or it will leave a scar.

AMY TRAMMELL

Blood Pressure

Sarsaparilla, or "sasparilla tea," is good to correct blood pressure.

AMY TRAMMELL

Blood Purifier

When you hit your hand or cut your arm or anything, and it gets infected instead of healing up, you need a blood purifier. Mix just a tiny bit of alum and saltpeter together in water and drink it. That purifies the blood.

FLORA YOUNGBLOOD

Make a tea of either burdock roots, or spice wood in the spring.

AMY TRAMMELL

Blood Tonic

Buy a box of sulfur at the store and mix a small amount (about the size of a pinto bean) in a teaspoonful of honey. Take that teaspoonful and then drink a glass of water. We would do that every spring. Mama would fix it up and we'd all get purified up for summertime. That's a tonic to purify your blood.

FLORA YOUNGBLOOD

Buy a box of sulfur at the store and mix a small amount (about the size of a pinto bean) in a teaspoonful of molasses. Take that teaspoonful and then drink a glass of water.

AMANDA TURPIN

Make a tea of bloodroot.

AMY TRAMMELL

Soak rusty nails in water and drink the water.

AMANDA TURPIN

Boils/Risings/Sores

For boils, grind up green walnut leaves or the hull of walnuts (the big green outside hull) with table salt, using one teaspoon of salt to a half cup of ground-up leaves or walnut hulls. Make a poultice. It will draw the boils out.

FLORA YOUNGBLOOD

Make a poultice of the houseleek plant and apply to boil.

MRS. C. E. PINSON

Mash up a rotten apple, place on the rising and tie a cloth around it.

FLORENCE CARPENTER

This recipe for "Green Salve" is good for boils or any kind of sore.

    One ounce beeswax
    Two ounces mutton tallow
    One ounce olive or sweet oil

One ounce oil of amber
One ounce verdegrease [verdigris]
One ounce resin
One ounce oil of spike

Simmer first four ingredients together; add verdegrease and resin, well powdered; then add oil of spike.

MRS. ALBERT ECKSTEIN

Make a mixture of kerosene, turpentine, Vaseline and old-time soap.

CONNIE MITCHELL

Make a salve made of heart leaves gotten out of the ground in the woods. Boil the leaves. Add lard and turpentine. Continue to boil until the mixture gets thick. Put the salve on sores as needed.

FLORENCE CARPENTER

Peel down outer bark of slippery elm sapling. Scrape off the inner bark and put those scrapings on a cloth and bind that on the risin'; or put piece of fat pork on it; or put a poultice on it made from bread and milk.

HAZEL LUZIER

To pull the core out of a risin', fill a bottle with very hot water. Let it sit a minute, then empty. Put the mouth of the hot bottle over risin' and hold it there.

ELIZABETH ENDLER

Buy some flaxseed meal. Make a poultice and put on risin'.

ELIZABETH ENDLER

This salve is good for anything that you want to draw, or any kind of sore. If you stick a nail in your foot or cut yourself or stump your toe, it's to draw out the infection.

The main ingredient in the salve is beef tallow. Make this by taking the fat off the beef just as you would a hog. Then put a little water in a pan or pot to keep the fat from sticking as it cooks, add the fat and cook it, stirring it so it doesn't burn. After all the fat has melted out, strain out all the cracklings and set the tallow aside to harden. The tallow will keep for years in a jar.

When ready to make salve, take out a palmful of the tallow and add

PLATE 26   After Amanda Turpin had gathered the ingredients she needed to make her salve for us . . .

PLATE 27   . . . she mixed them in the palm of her hand.

a level teaspoon of brown sugar, a level teaspoon of salt, and a few drops of turpentine. Mix all ingredients thoroughly together and then add a few drops of camphor oil.

Make the camphor oil by getting two blocks of camphor gum at the drugstore and chipping it up in a pint of moonshine whiskey. I think that the camphor is the medicine. Whiskey just keeps the camphor gum. You know, camphor gum will evaporate just by itself.

After the salve is mixed up, apply it directly to the wound and cover it with a bandage. If you put it on at night, let it stay all night. If it's not done enough work by morning, put on another application and let it stay all day.

Amanda Turpin

Burns

Mix two tablespoons soda with one and one-half tablespoons water, put that on a rag and wrap the rag around the burn.

Samantha Speed

Use castor oil on burns.

Annie Mae Henry

Put baking soda on the burn.

Florence Carpenter

The white of an egg and castor oil stirred up together is just as good a thing as you can put on a burn. Stops the pain and makes it heal up right quick.

Annie Mae Henry

I can cure a burn in just a few minutes. Cut an Irish potato in two at the middle and lay the cut part of the potato against the burn. Bind that potato to the burned place with a handkerchief. In ten minutes, you can't even tell you've been burned. That's the truth. I've doctored myself. I know. The heat is gone. Let that potato stay there until it turns black. Then the place where the burn was will be as white as cotton. If you get that potato on there fast enough, it won't even blister.

Kenny Runion

Apple vinegar on minor burns will take out the fire. Or blow your nose and wipe the mucus on the burn.

ANONYMOUS

Sulfur will heal a burn after the fire is drawn out.

GLADYS NICHOLS

I blow out fire using a Bible verse. You blow right direct on the burn and just talk the fire out of the burn. If you get it when it first happens it won't blister, but if you have to wait it will make a water blister. Then I would put sewing machine oil on it. Just bind it up in sewing machine oil and that would take care of it.

It is the seventh child that can blow fire out, my daddy learned me. I haven't told my seventh child. I'd better do that. I should write those verses off and leave 'em with somebody. [See *The Foxfire Book*, page 367.]

FLORA YOUNGBLOOD

Chapped Hands

Rub hands in a mixture of homemade soap and cornmeal. Bring the soap and meal to a good lather.

BEULAH FORESTER

My father made an ointment for that out of persimmon bark. Scrape persimmon bark down and cook it down to where it would be good and strong. Then put sweet milk or cream in it. Keep it rubbed on your hands and lips. I don't make it like I used to. When my children were all at home and the Depression was on I made lots of it.

FLORA YOUNGBLOOD

Use warm mutton tallow. When the sheep are killed, the fat is taken out and fried. The tallow is made from the grease.

ANONYMOUS

Chewing Gum Out of Hair

Take a half a teaspoon of peanut butter and smear it together with the chewing gum until the gum dissolves. Then wash out.

HELEN WALL

Just wet a cloth with kerosene and strip it down the hair (from the roots to the ends) and it'll take every bit of that out. Kerosene won't hurt the hair and it won't hurt the scalp if it gets on it.

FLORA YOUNGBLOOD

Chills

Drink a strong tea made from the leaves of pennyroyal.

AMY TRAMMELL

You would buy quinine from the drugstore. You would put just what would lay on the point of a knife blade in a teaspoon of water and stir it up. Take that and it would break the chills just like that.

FLORA YOUNGBLOOD

Colds

Make an onion poultice and put on your chest to break up a cold. To make the poultice, fry chopped onions in grease until well done. Put on a cloth and lay on the chest while still warm.

MRS. C. E. PINSON

When making tar, the flow of pine tar itself is preceded by some white smoke, then water. (See *Foxfire 4*, page 252.) A swallow of this water is good for a cold. The pine tar itself, rubbed on the chest, will loosen up a cold.

DAN HAWKES

Chew the leaves and stems of peppermint.

LAURA PATTON

Mix mutton tallow and alum together. That's good for colds. When you kill your sheep, cut the fat off and render it out. Put some alum in with it and mix it up. Then you put it in a jar and let it harden and make a grease cakelike patty out of it. Then when you get a cold or something you just rub it on your chest and neck. It will break a cold up.

NUMEROUS MARCUS

Put ginger and sugar in hot water. Drink this and go to bed.

GLADYS QUEEN

PLATE 28   Maude Houk.

For bad colds, make a tea of the leaves and stems of boneset, goldenrod, and wild rosemary. Boil these together until the water turns to a brownish tea color. If large bunches of the herbs are used in a small amount of water, the tea will turn very dark, like strong coffee. Strain and serve warm at bedtime. This should sweat the cold out of the patient. The goldenrod should be picked when it is in bloom, but do not use the blossoms.

In the fall before first frost, I would gather bunches of all three of these herbs. I'd tie each bunch up and hang it on the porch to dry. Then I had the herbs as I needed them.

MAUDE HOUK

We would make a tea out of the roots of butterfly weed. If it's just a runny nose and coughing we would make it weak. We would make it strong if we came down with a heavy cold.

FLORA YOUNGBLOOD

Colic

Stew down some calamus root and mix a few drops with catnip tea. It's good for colic in babies or in a grown person, either one.

SUP NUMEROUS MARCUS

[Editor's note: calamus is now a suspected carcinogen.]

Beat up a bulb of garlic. Make a poultice of bulb and juice and lay on the stomach.

SAMANTHA SPEED

Chest Congestion

Mutton tallow salve is good for relieving chest cold congestion. Spread it on chest and back between the shoulder blades and cover with flannel.

MRS. ED NORTON

Mix some lard and turpentine together, put it on a cloth, and put that on your chest.

AMY TRAMMELL

Make a tea from just the leaves of catnip. Pour boiling water over the leaves and sweeten it. To keep catnip through the winter, gather the leaves, dry them out, and keep them in a container where they can get a lot of air. They'll keep a long time.

NUMEROUS MARCUS

Take mustard seeds and beat 'em up and mix a little flour with enough warm water to make a kind of paste. Smear it on a cloth and make a little poultice and place it right across the chest. It'd be warm and it would just turn the skin red.

FLORA YOUNGBLOOD

Constipation

Make a tea from senna leaves.

AMY TRAMMELL

Take about two teaspoonfuls of turpentine.

GLADYS QUEEN

Buy croton oil at the drugstore. Put one drop of the croton oil in a glass of water and drink that.

FLORA YOUNGBLOOD

Give kids two teaspoons of castor oil and give adults two teaspoons of Epsom salts.

SAMANTHA SPEED

Cooties/Lice

Shave head and wash with apple vinegar.

BILLY JOE STILES

Make a tea from the stems and leaves of the larkspur. Wash your hair twice in that tea and you won't have any more lice.

FLORA YOUNGBLOOD

Corns

Tie five little flint rocks up in a rag. Throw them away at the forks of a road. When someone picks up the rag to see what's in it, your corns will go away and they'll get them.

ANNIE MAE HENRY

Take aspirin tablets worked in with a little bit of lard or Vaseline or anything to make a kind of salve. Bind the corn up with the salve and it'll just come right out in a day or two.

FLORA YOUNGBLOOD

Cough

We would go up and down Sautee Creek and get the bark from red alder. We'd boil that and make tea. Add a lot of honey to it. That was our cough syrup.

FLORA YOUNGBLOOD

Drink ginger tea. Make it by mixing one tablespoon whiskey and one teaspoon honey and a dash of ginger mixed in one fourth cup hot water.

SAMANTHA SPEED

Mix honey and soda together. Take a teaspoonful before you go to bed and a teaspoonful when you get up.

FLORENCE CARPENTER

Boil five lemons in a small amount of water. Slice them while hot into a clean enamel pan. Add one pound sugar. Return to fire. Add one tablespoon of oil of sweet almond, stirring constantly. Take one teaspoonful at the first onset of coughing.

DIANE FORBES

Gather holly bush limbs and boil them to make tea. Drink one cup.

BEULAH FORESTER

Wrap an onion in wet paper and bury it in hot ashes. Let it roast about thirty minutes and then squeeze out the juice. Add an equal amount of honey to the juice, mix well and take by the teaspoon as you would any cough syrup.

Or take the fat from a skinned 'possum, cook the grease out of it and keep it in a jar. As needed, take the grease and rub it on your chest to loosen cough.

BOB MASHBURN

Heat together two tablespoons kerosene oil, one tablespoon turpentine, one tablespoon camphor (if available) and one cup of pure lard. Rub the salve on temples and the upper lip for head colds and on the Adam's apple and chest for coughs and chest colds. Cover salve on the chest with a flannel cloth.

STELLA WALL

Use one part olive oil to one part whiskey and take two tablespoons every four hours until the cough is gone.

MRS. VERLAN WHITLEY

Mix one cup liquor to one half cup of honey and the juice of one lemon.

DOROTHY BECK

Add a pinch of soda to a spoonful of sorghum syrup (just enough to make it turn white) and stir and take.

ETHEL OWENS

Make tea by putting pine needles and boneset in boiling water.
Sweeten with honey.

Or put some ground ginger from the store in a saucer and add a
little sugar. Put a little of this mixture on the tongue just before
bedtime. It burns the throat and will stop a cough most of the time.

ANONYMOUS

Croup

To prevent croup in children, make a bib from a piece of chamois
skin. Melt together some pine pitch and tallow and rub it into bib.
Have the child wear it all the time.

DIANE FORBES

Make a little ball up of a half teaspoon of sugar, a drop of kerosene
oil, and about a half teaspoon of Vicks salve. Swallow this.

ANNIE MAE HENRY

Mix groundhog grease, turpentine, and a little lamp oil together.
Dip a rag into the mixture and saturate it. Then lay that on your chest.

WILMA BEASLEY

Dip the hot ashes right up from a fireplace. Put enough ashes in a
half glass of cold water to raise the level of water to the top of the
glass. Let it settle until every bit of the ashes settles to the bottom.
It'll be just as clear on top and you take a spoon and spoon off some
of the water. That cold water will cool the ashes down by the time it's
ready, so it will be cool enough to drink. I still use that for the
grandchildren when I can find the ashes. It'll knock the croup out just
like that.

FLORA YOUNGBLOOD

Cuts and Sores

Pound a dock root until it's soft and juice comes out of it. Put
enough sweet cream on it to cover it. Rub the mixture on a cut or
sore.

LOTTIE SHILLINGBURG

Bathe the sores off real good in warm salty water. Then you get
Vaseline or something where the cloth wouldn't stick and wrap it.

But if a sore got infected then they'd use the walnut poultice (ground walnut leaves and table salt).

FLORA YOUNGBLOOD

Diarrhea

Boil a lady-slipper plant in water. Strain the water and drink.

GLADYS QUEEN

Get some soot off the back of the chimney. Put a teaspoon of that soot in a glass of water. Let the soot settle out and drink the clear water.

FLORA YOUNGBLOOD

Pull up some blackberry roots and clean them and boil them. Strain and drink the water.

FLORENCE CARPENTER

Diphtheria

Make a little mop to mop the throat by getting three long chicken feathers and stripping most of the little feathers off the quills. Leave a few up on the end. Tie the quills together with thread with those three little bunches of feathers up on one end.

Then take some copperas and put it in a little metal lid (like a snuff can top) and set it on the hot stove. Let that copperas burn till it makes ashes. Pour honey into the copperas and work that up together. Dip that feather mop into that mixture and mop out the throat; three moppings and the diphtheria was gone. I had diphtheria and they used it on me. I have used it on my kids for real bad tonsillitis or any kind of tonsil trouble.

FLORA YOUNGBLOOD

Diphtheria, Prevention of

Put a lump of asafetida in a small muslin bag. Put a string on the bag and tie it around your neck so that the bag rests against chest.

ELIZABETH ENDLER

Dysentery

Boil plantain leaves *(not* the roots) and drink the tea often. This will cure dysentery.

Also, a tea made from dried strawberry or blackberry leaves will stop dysentery.

AMY TRAMMELL

Drink strong, sweetened tea; then eat five ounces of any good solid cheese with bread. Everyone knows that cheese is binding.

DIANE FORBES

Daddy used soot off the back of the chimney for dysentery (just as for diarrhea). Put it in a glass of water and stir it up good. Then let it set until the soot settles, and then just drink the water.

FLORA YOUNGBLOOD

Earache

Blow smoke from rabbit tobacco in the ear.

AMY TRAMMELL

Take the good meat out of a walnut. Put it into a rag and beat it up. Then dip this into warm water. Afterwards, squeeze the excess water and walnut oil into the ear.

WILMA BEASLEY

Boil pennyroyal. Pour the tea into a pitcher and put a cloth over the pitcher. Put your ear on the cloth.

VON WATTS

Put one block of camphor gum into a half pint to a pint of whiskey. Let it dissolve and add more camphor gum and let the mixture set idle. Rub it into the ear thoroughly. Use a lot. It will draw the poison out.

CLELAND OWENS

Use warm Vicks salve. Put it on a cotton ball and place that in the ear.

GENELIA SINGLETON

Put a drop or two of warm castor oil in the ear.

ANONYMOUS

Eye Trouble

Take a medicine dropper and drop warm salty water right in the corner of the eye. Hold your eye wide open and just let that salty water drain down through it. It burned a little bit. That's good for something in your eye, or the sore eye or a scratched place on the eye.

FLORA YOUNGBLOOD

Fever

Teas made from boneset, or from the roots of butterfly weed, or from wild horsemint, or from feverweed are all good for colds, flu, and fevers.

AMY TRAMMELL

Boil half a cup of wall ink vine leaves to a quart of water. Give two teaspoons three times a day.

LAURA PATTON

A tea made of rabbit tobacco will break a fever.

AMANDA TURPIN

Pull up poor john (feverweed), making sure to get roots. Put roots, leaves and all in pan with water and boil. Strain. Add sugar to taste and drink.

DOROTHY BECK

Take several bulbs of garlic and wrap them in a cloth. Take a hammer and just beat them up. Tie the cloth around both wrists right where the pulse is. The fever will come down in maybe thirty-five or forty minutes. Back when the kids was all little I did things like that.

FLORA YOUNGBLOOD

Fingernail—Puncture

Dampen a wool rag with turpentine. Heat the rag and tie around the puncture.

ANONYMOUS

Fingernail—Smashed

If we got our fingernail smashed or cracked, or you know, torn in any way, we would take a little elm tree bark. We'd peel off the inside of the bark and bind it to the fingernail.

FLORA YOUNGBLOOD

Put wet chewing tobacco on it.

ANONYMOUS

Fretful Child

For a baby that's squalling, take some 'sang root [ginseng] and put it in a saucer. Pour a little hot water on it and give the baby two teaspoons of that. In a few minutes it is all over.

HARV REID

Take a level teaspoonful of sugar and a drop of turpentine according to the age. If it is a little bitty baby, use about one drop of turpentine. Make that up in a little bit of water and give to him. It'll just quieten down. I've done that many, many, many of a time.

FLORA YOUNGBLOOD

Frostbite

Just go to the spring and get that water—it takes spring water, not well water. Just warm it and soak the affected area in it and it'll draw every bit of that frostbite out.

FLORA YOUNGBLOOD

Men would pour whiskey in their boots as a protection against frostbite. It was said to keep their feet warm for a long long time and didn't even wet their boots or shoes.

AMY TRAMMELL

Headache

Find some lady-slipper with a yellow bloom on it. Dig the roots and make some tea and drink that about once a week and it'll cure a sick headache.

MRS. E. H. BROWN

Soak strips of brown paper in warm vinegar. Bind them onto the forehead with a white cloth, or bind warm fried potatoes to the forehead with a rag.

ELIZABETH ENDLER

A headache is an inner fever in the stomach. You've got a fever in your stomach and it don't show up anywhere else but up here in your head. You take something for the stomach, like a wee dose of Epsom salt. You take a teaspoonful to a half a glass of water. Stir it up real good and drink it down. That cures the headache.

FLORA YOUNGBLOOD

Heart

Dandelion tea is a heart stimulant.

AMY TRAMMELL

Hiccups

Putting vinegar on sugar in a spoon and taking that is said to stop them.

AMY TRAMMELL

Wet a leaf of tobacco and put it on your stomach.

VON WATTS

Take nine sups of water and you will quit hiccupping.

ANNIE MAE HENRY

If you could remember the last place you seen a frog that had been run over by a car on the road, it would cure the hiccups.

KENNY RUNION

Swallow three swallows of cold water without getting your breath, no more or no less. They'll just go away. It still works. I've done it.

FLORA YOUNGBLOOD

Hives

Boil a bunch of catnip in water. Strain and drink.

GLADYS QUEEN

Hivey Babies

Get ground ivy and make a tea of the leaves and stems. Give some of this to a baby and it'll just break them hives out. When they laugh in their sleep and wall their eyes, it's because they're not broke out. After they break out in a kind of a rash, they'll rest from there on out.

FLORA YOUNGBLOOD

Inflammation

Boil a beet leaf and put it on the inflamed spot and tie a cloth around it.

FLORENCE CARPENTER

Itch

Make ointment out of one teaspoon of sulfur and four teaspoons of lard.

ELIZABETH ENDLER

Kidney Trouble

Make a tea from boiling mullein roots.

AMY TRAMMELL

Gather a large amount of peach tree leaves, boil in water to make tea, and drink.

BEULAH FORESTER

Get the dead silks off an ear of corn. Boil in water, strain and drink.

GLADYS QUEEN

Make tea either from the whole spearmint plant, or put three or four leaves into a cup and pour boiling water over them and cover until cool. Then drink.

LAURA PATTON

Measles

Drink diluted sheep manure to ensure that the measles will "pop out." Sheep manure has a high temperature quotient.

DIANE FORBES

Drink a cup of hot lemonade, then a cup of cold lemonade.

ANONYMOUS

Mumps

To keep mumps from going down into breasts and privates, tie a silk ribbon around a girl's neck (snug, but not too tight), or a silk tie around a boy's neck.

LOTTIE SHILLINGBURG

Nerves

Use the root of a yellow lady-slipper. Boil the root a long time, until the water turns a brownish tea color. Strain and drink.

MAUDE HOUK

Make a tea of elder flowers by steeping them in boiling water only a few minutes, then strain off. Tea may be sweetened or taken plain.

DIANE FORBES

Nosebleed

Take a small piece of a brown paper sack and fold it into a square and put it under lip and press.

LESTER J. WALL

Pull the hair on top of your head straight up until bleeding stops.

BEULAH FORESTER

Let your nose bleed on a knife blade and stick the knife in the ground. Your nose will stop bleeding.
Or take a pair of scissors and run them down the back of your neck.

ANNIE MAE HENRY

Stopped-up Nose

Use two teaspoons of salt to one pint of water. Pour three or four drops in each nostril every three to four hours.

HELEN WALL

Inhale the steam from boiling salt water.

AGNES BRADLEY

Pain

Apply a poultice of comfrey roots to ease pain. To make the poultice, boil the comfrey roots in a small amount of water. Take roots out and add about a cupful of cornmeal to about a pint of the water. Cook the meal until it thickens and then put it on a cloth. Cover with another cloth and place on painful area. This is also good for a sore throat, for which you apply the poultice to the neck.

AMY TRAMMELL

Pimples

Put about a half teaspoon of alum in about a tablespoon of water and make it real strong. Keep the pimple rubbed and it'll go away.

FLORA YOUNGBLOOD

Try rubbing your face with a wet baby diaper. Works every time if you can stand the smell.

DIANE FORBES

Poison Ivy

Take a bath in table salt water, then grease in Vaseline. That salt will kill out every bit of that poison and the Vaseline will keep it from itching and you won't scratch it.

FLORA YOUNGBLOOD

Boil milkweed leaves in water. Rub this water on the poisoned skin.

FLORENCE CARPENTER

Use gunpowder and buttermilk mixed together to put on poison ivy.

NELLIE TURPIN

Rub some leaves from a touch-me-not plant on the place where you've got it. It'll cure it.

KENNY RUNION

Make a mixture of vinegar and salt and put that on it. Or wet skin with water and then put baking soda on it. Diluted bleach will work, too.

DEBORAH WILBURN

Rheumatic Fever

Heat apple vinegar and wet a cloth in it. Apply the cloth, as hot as you can stand it, to ease the pain.

Or apply a poultice of mullein roots to ease the pain in the legs caused by rheumatic fever. Follow my recipe for comfrey poultice [under **Pain**] but use mullein roots instead.

AMY TRAMMELL

Rheumatism

Chew ginseng root or make a tea from the roots or drink a celery tea made by boiling a handful of celery stalks in a pint of water until the celery is limp.

AMY TRAMMELL

He did the same thing for that that he did for arthritis. Just make the barbell tea a little bit stronger.

FLORA YOUNGBLOOD

Gather a pokeroot about an inch long. Put this along with some yellow ivy in a quart of whiskey. Drink a teaspoonful a day.

BEULAH FORESTER

Make a tea out of the bark of the witch-hazel tree, and drink it.

ANNIE MAE HENRY

Let snakeroot sit in white liquor for one month. Then take one tablespoonful every twelve hours for up to three months.

LESTER J. WALL

Ringworm

You take turpentine and work it in pure hog's lard. Put that on the ringworm and pop it right out.

FLORA YOUNGBLOOD

Put the juice from a green walnut hull on the spot to stop the ringworm.

AMY TRAMMELL

To Make a Baby Sleep

Bore a small hole in a raw onion, put sulfur in the hole, wrap the onion in wet rags and put it on the hot coals of a fire and roast it. When roasted, take it out and squeeze the juice out of it and give about a teaspoon to the baby.

MELBA DOTSON

Snakebite

I heard Daddy say a lot of times if you got snakebit take a knife and cut a cross place on the bit place. Then cut the hollow neck of a gourd where you could suck through that gourd. Cap it over the snakebite and draw that poison out that way.

FLORA YOUNGBLOOD

As soon as bitten, spread some ammonia over the bite and then swallow a few drops of the ammonia mixed with water.

DIANE FORBES

Salt has been used to draw the poison out of a rattlesnake bite. People used to use gunpowder, too.

PRUDENCE SWANSON

Never take whiskey when snakebit. Pour a little turpentine on the bite. Or put the bark of the lino tree (some call it basswood) on it. It draws the poison.

Or cut the fang mark and put turpentine and sugar on it. Some use kerosene.

ANONYMOUS

Mix together two thirds pint of vinegar and one third pint of camphor and apply. This will draw the swelling out.

GLADYS NICHOLS

Put the entrails of a freshly killed chicken on the affected area.

ANONYMOUS

Take a meat tenderizer and make a paste with water. Put it on the bite. Occasionally replace it with new paste.

ELIZABETH ENDLER

Salt and onions was good for snakebites. You'd beat the onions up and put in a lot of salt and apply that to the place and that would draw out the poison.

AMANDA TURPIN

Sore Throat

Boil the inner part of some red oak bark. Strain and gargle with it.

FLORENCE CARPENTER

We'd use the honey and copperas for any kind of sore throat. For a plain sore throat you would make it real weak and thin enough where you could gargle it and spit it out.

FLORA YOUNGBLOOD

Boil onions in molasses and eat it to relieve pain of sore throat. Or make a comfrey root poultice (see directions in "PAIN" remedy).
Take a silk stocking and saturate it with lard or cream. Place spirit of turpentine and Vicks salve in the stocking and tie around neck.

DOROTHY BECK

Boil cottonseeds until soft. Beat them up and make a poultice. Apply it to sore throat.

MRS. C. E. PINSON

To swab throat, use a peach tree stick with a rag wrapped around it.

GLADYS QUEEN

Sprains

Take three or four mullein leaves. Dip them in vinegar. Put them on the sprain and bind.

LOTTIE SHILLINGBURG

Take mullein leaves. Pound them just a little. Put on sprain.

ELIZABETH ENDLER

Take cornmeal and table salt and work it together. Mix it with warm water and make a poultice. It just draws out all the soreness. My kids, jumping rope, would sprain their ankles, legs and knees. I'd just make that salt poultice and wrap it around and it would be all right.

FLORA YOUNGBLOOD

Spring Tonic

Make a good tea from sassafras roots or the limbs of a spicewood bush for a fine spring tonic.

MRS. C. E. PINSON

Stings

Lay a cloth down and put about four tablespoons of wet salt on there. Then pull it tight around the sting and in ten minutes you can't even tell you've been stung.

KENNY RUNION

Make a paste of one half teaspoon of baking soda and one half teaspoon of honey and apply to sting.

DOROTHY BECK

Put tobacco or snuff on a sting. Homemade tobacco is the best of all. Take a leaf of homemade tobacco and wrap it around anything to take the swelling out.

ANNIE MAE HENRY

Stomachache

Boil some yellowroot and strain it. Add honey to it and take two tablespoons before meals.

FLORENCE CARPENTER

Sick stomach: Cut a peach tree limb and scrape the bark off into a glass of water. Let this sit a little while. Then strain and drink this water often.

A tea made from black snakeroot is also good for the stomach.

AMY TRAMMELL

Castor oil is good for stomachache. Just drink a dose. It heals as it goes down.

ANNIE MAE HENRY

Drink a tea from ginseng roots.

Or drink a tea made from the lining of a chicken gizzard.

Or eat some garlic.

ANONYMOUS

Put a few drops of British oil in a tablespoon of milk. For a baby, use one drop of oil.

Make tea of four teaspoons of anise seed to one pint water. Add sugar to taste. Take three times daily.

ANONYMOUS

Sunburn

Make a strong tea with sage leaves and rub on sunburn.

MRS. C. E. PINSON

Swellings and Inflammations

Prepare a poultice of stewed pumpkin. Renew every fifteen minutes.

DIANE FORBES

For a swollen breast, make a poultice of the roots of boneset grass by drying them, powdering them and adding a little water. Rub on breast.

ANONYMOUS

Bind that swelling with a salt poultice.

FLORA YOUNGBLOOD

Teething Babies

Steep one teaspoon of chamomile flowers in a cup of boiling water for three or four minutes. Then strain. Sweeten slightly and give the baby two or three teaspoons of the warm liquid.

DIANE FORBES

Take a mole's foot (his left front paw) and tie that around the baby's neck and you won't hear a sound out of it.

Or take a dime with a hole in it and hang it by a chain around his neck.

ANNIE MAE HENRY

Thrash (Thrush)

Can be cured in the spring by drinking water from a creek bed just after it has rained.

ANONYMOUS

Drink sage tea made from the leaves of a sage plant.

ANONYMOUS

Thrash [thrush] is caused by a regurgitating stomach. The formula, if they are put on a bottle, and sometimes the mother's milk don't suit 'em [the babies], they'll regurge it back. When they spit it up it irritates their mouth. The acid in it blisters their mouth. There's a yellow and a white blister, but you doctor them just alike. It takes a little longer to cure the yellow than it does the white if they let it run on a long time.

Well now there is a verse you repeat and you repeat this verse in your mind three times as you blow your breath into their mouth. You have to see 'em every morning for three days in a row that first time. Then I would make a mouthwash and let them start washing their mouth. I'd take persimmon tree bark, scrape it and make a strong tea.

Then we'd put a small, little pinch of alum down in that and stir that up. Strap a white cloth around your finger and scrub all around in their mouth with it. Why we make that tea is to get that white out and not let 'em swallow it. The mouth will be just as white and it'll start shedding off. Looks like they got a mouth full of cornmeal. Then the second morning, you give them something to work their stomach out, a laxative like castor oil or Castoria. They'll swallow some of that down in their stomach and [what you give them for their stomach] keeps it [the thrush] from setting in their stomach. Then by the time they come back the third time it's all gone, but you do it [say the verses] the third time.

I've cured so many—oh, you wouldn't believe. The doctors send 'em to me, they don't know what to do with 'em. I was in the hospital and they brought the babies in to me in there in my room. I've had three in one day, especially in the spring of the year. I don't know how many little young babies [I've cured] just right here lately.

One brought their baby here and it [the thrush] had run on so long that I didn't know if I could even bring it through or not. I did, but they had to bring it more times because it was so bad. Of course I didn't blow in its mouth but the three times, but I had to help 'em wash its mouth out. I finally got on ahead and got it over it.

Some will bring 'em and after the second time they're so much better they don't even bring it back. But I tell 'em, "Now, if you ain't gonna bring it three times they ain't no need in trying." 'Cause in maybe two or three days it'll come right back up and get worse. It's embedded in the locks of the jaws, where your jaws come together, and it'll start spreading back out. I had to doctor some of 'em twice like that.

You boil everything that the baby has anything to do with in sody water [use one teaspoon of baking soda], its nipples, bottles, bibs, anything it has about its mouth. Be sure you don't kiss 'em around the mouth or you can get it, it's catching. Now one [time] a grown man come. He said, "I've caught that thrash sure as a world." I'd doctored his grandbaby with it, I got it well. He said he'd been a-kissing his little grandbaby. I said, "Don't be kissing on 'em around the mouth." I said, "Kiss 'em on the back of the neck or somewhere." I doctored him like I doctored babies.

FLORA YOUNGBLOOD

Toothache

Make a peach tree poultice from peach tree leaves boiled until soft, mixed with cornmeal and salt. Place on the outside of the jaw for abscessed tooth.

FLORA YOUNGBLOOD

Put some burnt soda on the tooth.

FLORENCE CARPENTER

Smoke rabbit tobacco.

AMY TRAMMELL

Pick around the ailing tooth with a pine toothpick until it bleeds.

LOLA CANNON

Pound some horseradish leaves fine. Put them in a cloth and hold it against your tooth.

ANONYMOUS

Ulcerated Stomach

Make a weak tea from yellowroot and drink it.

FLORA YOUNGBLOOD

To Induce Vomiting

Beat the white of an egg and add a pinch of alum. Give it to a child to make him vomit.

MRS. C. E. PINSON

Warts

Well, Daddy conjured the warts with a piece of fat hog meat. You cut off three little chips of fat meat. Take a little chip and rub the wart. Then you accidentally lose the little piece of fat meat. You don't go put it in no certain place, you just kind of walk around with it and after while you look down and that little piece of fat meat is gone. Then you do it the next day and the next day, for three days, and the warts will go away.

FLORA YOUNGBLOOD

Get nine unbroken green beans. Rub them on each wart nine times (with each bean). Bury the beans and the warts will go away.

MRS. BUCK CARVER

Sell the wart for a penny. Then throw the penny away.

LOTTIE SHILLINGBURG

Put some cow manure on them.

ANONYMOUS

When the sap is rising in trees, make a cross on the wart with a knife.

OAKLEY JUSTICE

You count the number of warts you want removed and write that number on a piece of paper. Give that to the person who is going to take them off. They'll go away.

ANNIE MAE HENRY

Take a small Irish potato and rub it over all the warts. Don't let nobody know much about your business. Go out of the house and buy that potato where the water runs off from the eave of the house. When the potato rots, the warts will be gone.

Take a stick about a foot long and rub it over all your warts. Cut a notch for every wart and go to where there is a swamp branch. Walk backwards and stick it in the ground and don't look where you put it.

KENNY RUNION

Whooping Cough

Mix alum powder and honey together in a bowl. Take a teaspoonful when you start coughing.

FLORENCE CARPENTER

Make a chestnut leaf tea. Add enough brown sugar to make into a syrup. Take four times weekly.

ELIZABETH ENDLER

Mix honey with lemon juice or alum.
Or mix olive oil with laudanum.
Or make a tea from holly tree berries, adding honey and sweet oil.

Or boil a hornet's nest to make a tea, adding lemon juice and honey.

Or mix lemon juice, salt, brown sugar and olive oil; give one teaspoon several times a day.

Or boil together one pound brown sugar, one ounce paregoric, and one cup water. Let cool and add one pint whiskey [Mrs. Pinson recommended the "good old kind"]. This is good for any kind of cough.

MRS. C. E. PINSON

Gargle with warm salty water. If the baby is too little to gargle, just give it a little bit and just let it slide down.

FLORA YOUNGBLOOD

Worms

Drop turpentine on a teaspoonful of sugar. Mix together. Give it according to age. If they're one year, give 'em one drop and it's a drop for every year till he gets on up pretty good size. Give that for three mornings. Also run turpentine on the child's navel. That's where the worms come up to and they'll hang there. They'll bite down on the child and that makes the child grumble with a stomach-ache. That turpentine will make them turn loose and the child will pass 'em. This remedy is used mostly for pinworms.

ANONYMOUS

Use the root of samson snakeroot. The roots are pink and measure six to eight inches long. Use three to four roots for each dose. Boil the roots in a small amount of water until the water turns a yellowish brown color. The tea can then be sweetened with syrup.

SAMANTHA SPEED

Get the seeds out of a Jerusalem oak and boil them in syrup until it makes a candy. Give the person with worms a piece of the candy every other day.

FLORENCE CARPENTER

Gather red sassafras bush roots. Boil about a half a cup to a quart of water and drink the tea.

LAURA PATTON

Yellowroot tea will get rid of worms in children. Boil about one half cup of small roots to one and a half quarts of water. Let boil until about one quart of water is left. Strain and drink about a half a cup every day.

LAURA PATTON

Eat gourd seeds for worms.

BARNARD DILLARD

Dampen a wool rag with turpentine. Heat the rag and lay it on the navel and rub it on the neck.

SAMANTHA SPEED

Yellow Jaundice

Drink apple cider often.

VON WATTS

Make a tea from yellowroot or soak the roots in whiskey. (Whiskey is good because it draws the strength from root and it won't go bad if you set back for a while.) Then drink some.

ANONYMOUS

You make a little cross with a razor blade right between the shoulders. You put a little funnel or any little suction cup over that and draw out the blood. Then you get the blood up in a spoon and weaken it down with a bit of water. Some babies you can give a teaspoonful and some babies it'll be a half. That'll cure the jaundice. I've seen it done, but I never did do it. Mine never did have it.

FLORA YOUNGBLOOD

DOC BRABSON

So far in this section, we have shown you different types of herb remedies that were used, and are still being used, in the southern Appalachians. However, these people did not always depend solely on home remedies. By the mid 1800s there were also a few qualified physicians in their area.

On an earlier visit with two of our frequent contacts, Mr. and Mrs. John Bulgin, they mentioned to us that Mr. Bulgin's grandfather, Alexander Crutchfield Brabson, had been a doctor. The Bulgins have a collection of operating tools that Dr. Brabson actually used and a ledger of accounts from his practice. One interesting point about the ledger is the manner in which many patients paid Dr. Brabson for his services. The payments to him were often made not in money, but in things such as animals and produce from his patients' farms and gardens, homemade quilts, or services. To get a more detailed account of Dr. Brabson and his practice, during July of 1984 Cheryl Wall and I went to the Bulgins' home in Franklin, North Carolina, about thirty minutes from Rabun Gap.

The Bulgins' home is a large, modern two-story house built on top of a hill. It is surrounded by several barns, workshops, and a small greenhouse. Mrs. Bulgin has filled the house with antiques—especially clocks. On the hour, the house almost seems to quake with the chiming of the many clocks in the living room.

We sat in the Bulgins' large, sunny kitchen during the interview. As we talked at the oak breakfast table, Mrs. Bulgin would occasionally wipe the counters of the clean, bright-colored cooking area. The windows from the kitchen look out upon the backyard where several birds pecked at the seed thrown out for them.

When we settled down to the interview, Mr. Bulgin surprised us with some new information: not only was his grandfather a doctor, but so was Dr. Brabson's father-in-law, Dr. G. N. Rush. Dr. Brabson studied medicine under Dr. Rush and later attended Emory University, and they both served in the Civil War. Together, they perfected a cure for a usually fatal disease called milk sickness.

Mr. Bulgin said that Dr. Brabson was devoted to his work. No matter how bad the weather or what other obstacle stood in his way, it seemed that he was always able to get to his patients to treat them.

Mr. Bulgin is a tall, lean man in his early eighties. On the day we visited with him, he had been working in his metal shop, so he was wearing a baggy pair of army-green workpants and a matching workshirt. His large, knobby hands are strong and skillful-looking. His ruddy face is oblong and wrinkled from a combination of sun and age. Behind thick, black-rimmed glasses is a pair of eyes that are full of life and laughter and he grins impishly.

Mr. and Mrs. Bulgin, as always, were enthusiastic and eager to talk to us, and the following is the result of our most recent visit.

ALLISON ADAMS

John Bulgin: My great-granddad's name was G. N. Rush. [He became a doctor when he graduated from] the University of Nashville in the Republic of Tennessee before it became a state. The date was 1854 the best I can make it out on his diploma. That diploma is actually on the skin of a sheep, and it's all in Latin. He was an ordained elder in the Ebenezer Presbyterian Church and later at

PLATE 29   John Bulgin showed Cheryl Wall
Dr. Rush's medical kit:
"[These medical tools] were Dr. Rush's
graduation present. He graduated in 1854,
so they're at least that old. I've found one set
[of medical tools] like this in a museum in
Raleigh [North Carolina], but it's not as complete as this one. There's even a tourniquet
and one of the needles in here. I don't know
how they kept [the tools] clean. Doctors have
told me they used carbonic acid.
"Dr. Rush gave this [medical equipment]
to my uncle in Cornelia. Then my mother
said, seeing that I was the oldest grandson,
she wanted me to have [the kit]. So some of
'em gave it to me."

Morrison Presbyterian Church (which still exists) from which he retired.

Dr. Rush was in the Civil War. He had his degree then. I still have
his watch. It has a hunting case and a key, and it still runs and is in
good shape. He would carry it in his vest pocket with the key on it.

My grandfather's name was Alexander Crutchfield Brabson—Dr.
A. C. Brabson. I wish I had been old enough to remember him, but I
was about four years old when he died in 1916. He was in the Civil
War, too. Of course he was quite a bit younger than Dr. Rush. They

PLATE 30

were both medical aides for the South. After the war, when they came to this area from Washtown, Tennessee, they settled about eight miles from Franklin in what they used to call Riverside.

Grandpa Brabson read medicine and studied it under Dr. Rush. He then went to Emory University [before it was named Emory]. He lived where Bryant McClure's restaurant is in Otto, North Carolina. He lived right across the ridge from [where the restaurant is now] within hollering distance, nearly. That old house is still standing.

Mrs. Bulgin: John's grandfather and grandmother were considered to be the affluent society. They had a nice home, they had plenty of food, and they had house servants, but how they got the money to pay for them, I don't know. He didn't get any fee, hardly, for what he did. He didn't question whether [patients] had money or didn't. I'm sure he knew that if they had money, they would pay him, and if they didn't have money [it didn't matter]. They still needed something done for them.

John's grandmother used to have one woman that came and moved in during the wintertime. She'd come right after Christmas or around the first of January and stay with them through the winter months. I'm not sure whether she was an old maid or whether she was a widow, but she didn't have a family. She'd sew, quilt, card wool, spin, and weave. John's grandparents had seven children—a big family—so his grandmother didn't have time to do all the mending and all the darning of socks and all of that. John's mother, Blanche Brabson, was second to the oldest of the children.

I've heard her talk about some of the remedies [Dr. Brabson used], but I never used them except one for yellowjacket stings. When my kids would get stung in the yard, I'd make a poultice with three or four plantain leaves—wet them and tie them on the sting with a cloth. It'd take the sting and the swelling out.

We cannot conceive of the hardships [they faced back then]. Diphtheria was a big killer in those days. If that hit, there wasn't a thing anybody could do about it. They usually didn't live long after they contracted diphtheria. [Dr. Brabson had a lot of cases of] that as well as scarlet fever and typhoid fever. They also used to have a disease called milk sickness. People got it from using the milk of [infected cows]. Cures were rare, but Dr. Rush and Dr. Brabson perfected a treatment for it, and Dr. Brabson taught the cure to Dr. Neville from Dillard, Georgia, and he taught it to two or three other doctors around here. But the actual remedy they used has been lost now. [It died with those doctors.]*

John Bulgin: Grandpa Brabson worked mostly out of his house. He had a horse and buggy that he went to Hayesville in. He probably had to stay the night somewhere before he got to Hayesville because it's about forty miles from here. During a childbirth, he'd have to maybe spend the night or a couple of days at the home according to how the patient got along.

His favorite words were, "Ye old son of a bitch." He would tell

---

* Milk sickness was a common and greatly feared disease not only in the Appalachians, but also in the Midwest. Doctors that were able to treat it were widely respected and greatly valued members of any community. Dr. Neville, for example, in our community, was often described to us on interviews as "the only doctor around here that could cure the milk sick."

Gerald W. Sanders, the lead technician at the Lincoln Boyhood National Memorial in Lincoln City, Indiana, was kind enough to send us several materials regarding the disease. One was a booklet entitled "Milk Sickness Caused by White Snakeroot" written by Edwin Lincoln Moseley (professor emeritus of biology for the State University at Bowling Green, Ohio) and published in 1941 jointly by the Ohio Academy of Science in Bowling Green and the author. Another was a handout for visitors to the Memorial entitled, "The Plant That Killed Abraham Lincoln's Mother: White Snakeroot." (No author given.) The latter reads, in part, "By definition, milk sickness is poisoning by milk from cows that have eaten white snakeroot. Many early settlers in the Midwest came into contact with the sickness.

"In the Fall of 1818, Nancy Lincoln died as milk sickness struck the Little Pigeon Creek settlement. The sickness has been called pucking [sic] fever, sick stomach, the slows and the trembles. The illness was most common in dry years when cows wandered from poor pasture to the woods in search of food. In man, the symptoms are loss of appetite, listlessness, weakness, vague pains, muscle stiffness, vomiting, abdominal discomfort, severe constipation, bad breath, and finally coma. Recovery is slow and may never be complete. But more often an attack is fatal. And so it was for Nancy Hanks Lincoln. She died on October 5, 1818."

PLATE 31   An old photo of Dr. and Mrs. Brabson which was hanging in Mr. and Mrs. Bulgin's home.

them, "Ye old son of a bitch, you ain't gonna die! They ain't no use of you coming to see me."

But I don't reckon he ever turned anybody down. He didn't think of it. I remember a story about a guy somebody shot. He was stealing stuff out of a man's garden. I don't know the particulars, but it was dark and he ran and got caught in a cockleburr patch. The [owner] shot him with a shotgun. It was pouring down rain and a guy come in the middle of the night after Grandpa. He told the guy he wasn't gonna go see that old son of a bitch [because] he wasn't worth saving. But Mama said that all the time [he was saying that], he was getting up and putting on his clothes. He told the man to go over to the barn and "catch Alec and put the saddle on," and he rode over there and scooped out the cockleburrs and sewed that man up, and he lived.

And I remember Mama telling about him coming home from Hayesville late at night or in the early morning hours when it was real cold and raining. His feet would be frozen to the stirrups and he couldn't get off. He'd ride up right in front of the house and she would take a kettle of water out and pour on his shoes to loosen them so he could get them out of the stirrups. If he was lucky, he got two dollars for that call, wherever it was.

I imagine there were lots of [debts] in that ledger that was never collected. Most of the patients would pay something, though. Maybe they'd just have fifty cents to pay him, and he'd mark it down and give them credit. When he delivered a child, it was two dollars and a half or three dollars. He always carried medicine with him, and the medicine charge would be fifty cents.

The ones that couldn't pay cash bartered. One old guy made a bunch of those split rails—I believe it was a hundred—for [credit of] seven dollars and a half. In [the ledger] you'll see where people cradled wheat for fifty cents a day. They'd give him dried apples, a bushel of peaches, syrup, maybe a quarter of beef. Sometimes just a day's work [would pay the bill], maybe hoeing his corn or working in his garden. He was quite a watermelon raiser. Mama said he would always plant his watermelon seed down on the creek bottoms on the seventh of May whether it was Sunday or not.

Actually, I still barter some myself, but the Internal Revenue frowns on it. But I do some work for the dentist and I do some work for the eye man and we swap out a lot.

Following is a list recorded in Dr. Brabson's ledger of items that he accepted from patients as payment for his services:

Payment to Dr. Brabson for services	amount
2 pigs	[$]5.50
1 day rock hauling	2.00
gallon kerosene	.25
36 lbs. beef	2.22
mowing	7.50
10 bushel turnips	2.25
1 stack fodder	2.00
buffalo horns	3.00
1/2 bushel dried grapes	.75
pasturing	8.00
plowing 5 acres	4.00
pulling corn	.50
work in meadow	4.50
patching roof	.50
churning	1.00
photographs	2.50
dehorning cattle	.50
ranging cattle	4.50
1 lb. tobacco	.20
beef skin	2.00

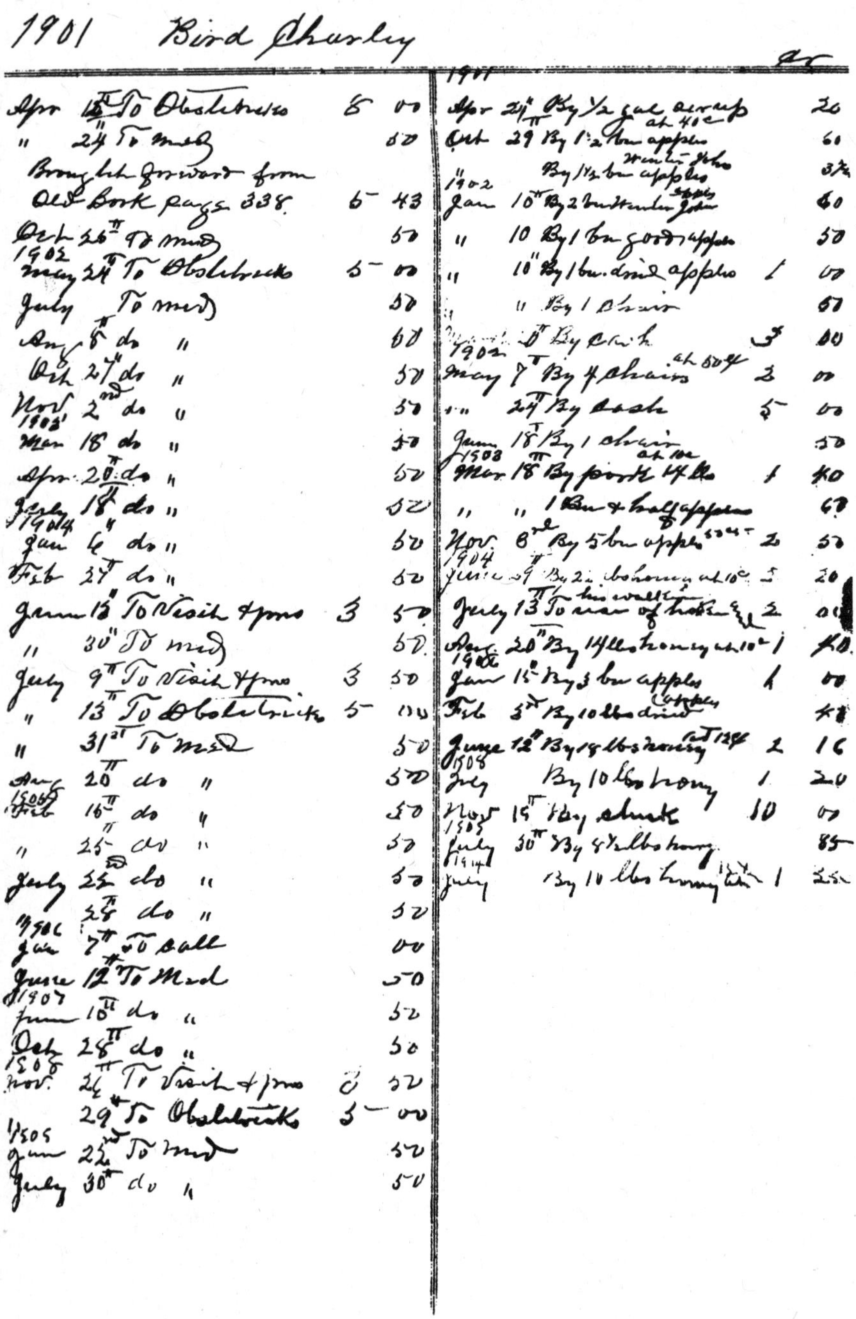

1901 Bird Charley — Cr

1901 Apr	15th	To Obstetrics	5 00
"	24th	To med	50
		Brought forward from Old Book page 338.	5 43
Oct	26th	To med	50
1902 May	24th	To Obstetricks	5 00
July		To med	50
Aug	8th	do "	50
Oct	27th	do "	50
Nov	2nd	do "	50
1903 Mar	18th	do "	50
Apr	20th	do "	50
July	18th	do "	50
1904 Jan	6th	do "	50
Feb	27th	do "	50
Jan	13th	To Visit & pres	3 50
"	30th	To med	50
July	9th	To Visit & pres	3 50
"	13th	To Obstetricks	5 00
"	31st	To med	50
Aug	20th	do "	50
1905 Feb	16th	do "	50
"	25th	do "	50
July	22nd	do "	50
	23rd	do "	50
1906 Jan	7th	To call	00
June	12th	To Med	50
1907 Jan	10th	do "	50
Oct	28th	do "	50
1908 Nov.	24th	To Visit & pres	3 50
	29th	To Obstetricks	5 00
1909 Jan	22nd	To med	50
July	30th	do "	50

1901 Apr	24th	By 1/2 gal syrup at 40c	20
Oct	29	By 1 1/2 bu apples	60
		By 1 1/2 bu apples Winter John	37 1/2
1902 Jan	10th	By 2 bu Winter John apples	60
"	10	By 1 bu good apples	50
"	10th	By 1 bu dried apples	1 00
"	"	By 1 chair	50
1902		By cash	3 00
May	7th	By 4 chairs at 50¢	2 00
"	24th	By cash	5 00
Jan	18th	By 1 chair	50
1903 Mar	18th	By pork 14 lbs at 10c	1 40
"	"	1 bu & half apples	60
Nov.	8th	By 5 bu apples 50¢	2 50
1904 June	9th	By 2 ... hominy at 10c	2 20
July	13th	To use of his wall ...	2 00
Aug	20th	By 14 lbs honey at 10c	1 40
1906 Jan	15th	By 3 bu apples	1 00
Feb	5th	By 10 lbs dried apples	40
June	12th	By 18 lbs honey at 12¢	2 16
1908 July		By 10 lbs honey	1 20
Nov	15th	By shuck	10 00
1909 July	30th	By 8 1/2 lbs honey	85
1914 July		By 10 lbs honey 12 1/2	1 25

PLATE 32 A sheet from Dr. Brabson's ledger.

Payment to Dr. Brabson for services	*amount*
chimney work	[$]2.50
1 blanket	2.50
fly brush	.75
saw	1.85
3 pecks onions	.37½
3 days foddering	1.50
160 feet lumber	1.60
1 gallon syrup	.40
cutting wood	.50
cotton	.25
fruit jars	.90
4 days harvesting	6.00
sack of salt	1.00
hauling 274 lb. wire	1.37
25 lb. flour	.75
2 days planting	2.00
quilting	2.00
1 sheep	1.65
½ lb. yarn	.30
soup recipe	1.50
12 socks	.30
soap	.25
1 bushel dried apples	.50
¾ days cradling	.75
1½ bushel peaches	.75
350 rails	7.00
2 days hauling	3.00
haying	2.25
2 bushel potatoes	1.25
2 days sawing wood	1.50
eggs	.60
coffee	1.00
splitting wood	.30
25 lb. sugar	1.25
7½ bushels wheat	7.50
blackberries	.50
chair	.50
12½ lbs. pork	1.00
lumber	1.75
180 ft. culls	1.25
shotgun	7.00
spinning	.50
12 lbs. honey	1.50
1 day wagon and team	1.25

Payment to Dr. Brabson for services	*amount*
8 gal. ware	[$] .75
knives and forks	1.25
pair of cards	.37
1300 shingles	2.60
1 bushel oats	.40
7 brooms	.70
shoeing 2 horses	.80
24 lbs. bacon	2.40
1 barrel	.50
lard	1.20
1 pair shoes	1.25
drill 1 days work	.50
making gate	1.00
32 stakes	2.06
1 peck chestnuts	.25

THE GENERAL STORE

Most communities in the mountains, as else-where, failed as viable communities without several essential institutional and social anchors: a post office, several churches (which usually doubled as schoolhouses on weekdays), a grist mill, a blacksmith shop—and a general store. Up until now, we have not looked at the last in any concentrated way in this series of books, but in the past few years we have been lucky enough to learn about several ledgers from general stores that existed in our area, and this information simply whetted the appetites of the students, who began to search for them. Some searches have not been successful, like our attempts to find the one Christine Wigington told us about:

"One of my daddy's first cousins, old Mr. Bob McCall, used to live at Cashiers [North Carolina]. He was quite a character. He had a big store there, one of the biggest—which wasn't real big, but it was big for Cashiers back then; and he sold everything, too. He couldn't read or write, but he had his ledgers that he kept his records in. When a person bought something on credit, he'd draw pictures of what they bought and they'd write their names down. Nobody beat him out of anything. Used to own practically all of Cashiers.

"I remember one time they laughed at him. He had a round picture with a hole in the center of it, and the man that signed come in to pay and he charged him for a hoop of cheese. Well, that man hadn't bought any cheese, and they couldn't figure it out, and they thought and thought. Finally he remembered he'd bought a grindstone. But he'd put that down and he thought it was cheese!" [laughter]

Other searches were more fruitful, however, and these discoveries captured the interest of the students who combed through them to the point that a series of articles became inevitable.

In hundreds of previous interviews concerning how mountain people survived during the period of extreme self-sufficiency (which lasted, around here at least, from the 1820s, with the arrival of the first permanent white settlers, for at least a hundred years), the people interviewed explained to the students again and again how little they and their families had bought in the few stores that existed: a bit of coffee, some salt, some sugar. Otherwise, they said, they were virtually on their own, and they even had acceptable substitutes for coffee (parched wheat, for example), and sugar (sorghum molasses) when times were truly tough. That information—which we are not contradicting, by the way—led all of us to assume that the bare staples like coffee and salt were the only items these stores stocked at all.

That assumption came completely unraveled with the discovery of the ledger from the Fort Hembree store (located in what is now Hayesville, North Carolina) dated 1845–1847—a ledger owned and fiercely protected by student John Singleton's grandfather, Frank Moore, while he was living. The assumption was shattered, in fact, by the array of available goods that appeared on the master list of products John and his classmate, Vaughn Rogers, amassed from reading the accounts from this modest pre-Civil War business—a business that, rather than serving a city, served instead the tiniest of rural communities in a mountain valley that was almost inaccessible to the outside world except by horseback. Think of a K-Mart with groceries, its contents jammed into a tiny frame building, and you begin to get the idea.

This five-part chapter, then, is about the general store—but more than the stores themselves, it also features the families that owned them, our attempt being to set the stores into the context of the owners' larger lives rather than looking at the stores simply as artifacts; to set them into a background of lifestyle and activity.

The first section is about the Moore family and the Fort Hembree store. Moving chronologically through time, the second is about the P. D. Queen store in Passover (now Mountain City), Georgia, the ledgers from which were dated 1898–1907. The last three sections are about Depression-era establishments, all of which, like the former two, are now closed. In the latter instances, however, their owners are still alive and were interviewed for their firsthand experiences. Of these last three, the final one lasted until most recently. Rance Gillespie conducted the interviews with his grandfather, Earl Gillespie, whose produce business was located in Clayton, our county seat, and lasted until the mid-1970s. Earl's store was unusual in our county, not only because of the people involved and the various services it

PLATE 33   The typical general store was crammed from floor to ceiling with goods. The T. M. Rickman store, which still exists near Franklin, North Carolina, is one good example. This view shows the interior of his store as seen from the front door.

PLATE 34   Mr. Rickman and his nephew behind the counter.

provided, but also because up until the very end, a portrait of Franklin Roosevelt hung proudly above one of the most spectacular cash registers in the mountains.

In rural areas like ours, older people still say, "I trade at _____," rather than, "I shop at _____." That expression has honorable roots, abundantly illustrated by this remarkable chapter about a social institution called the general store.

THE FORT HEMBREE STORE AND TANNERY

Eight Generations of Moores

I care a lot for my grandfolks. I've visited them since I was a child, and I remember those visits fondly. Their sensitivity is one thing that makes them so unique. Their concern goes out in all directions, and their generosity is never far behind. They've left me with memories I will tell my grandkids, and if those grandchildren ever feel the same way about me, I will know I'll have been a success.

I never dreamed I'd be able to give my grandparents anything back that would mean something special to them. But after working with Grandpa on our family's history, I've become sensitive in a way I never was before to my background and to why he has saved all the letters and photographs and documents and scrapbooks he has over all these years. Now I care about our family in the same way my grandparents do.

For older people out there who have given up on the younger generation, I can say that there are a lot of us who are learning to listen to you. There are still some of us whose opinions aren't so hardened that they can't be molded to your wisdom. Many who realize how much you have to contribute.

I guess it can be a scary feeling if you convince yourself society has no room for you—that the hotel of life is filling up and soon there'll be no vacancies. I guess society sometimes seems like a pack of wolves that follows the caribou herd, feeding on the young and the old, the sick and the lame.

Yet in the coming generation there is a growing number of people who care. Only an optimist could speak of it as a plethora, but the number is far greater than it was a few years back. Maybe with a little time, these seeds of concern will grow and bear fruit; and maybe, before long, many will see and appreciate what only a lucky few of us have seen so far.

JOHN SINGLETON

John began this article about his family during this last winter quarter of school while I was working on another article. I saw all the documents and

PLATE 35   John Singleton with his grandfather, Frank Moore.

ledgers he had borrowed from his grandfather and I said to myself, "That stuff looks real interesting." So after I finished my article, I decided to spend the spring quarter helping John finish his.

The first thing I worked on was the 1846 ledger from the general store at Fort Hembree run by John C. Moore. I went through a number of the accounts, some of which are reprinted in this article, to see if I could tell anything about the people by what they bought.

John and I both had problems with the meanings of some of the words and with the handwriting on some of the older letters, and so Wig, John, and I spent part of a day at the State Archives in Atlanta where Pete Schinkel and Linda Leslie were able to straighten us out and come up with some ideas for ways we could use some of the material we had. One thing they had that helped a lot was a Webster's dictionary that was published in the 1880s.

Later, we went back to John's grandparents, Frank and Nannie Moore, over near Hayesville, North Carolina, to clear up some questions about the store and some of the family members. It was John's third trip in connection with this article, but it was my first, and I was really glad to meet them. We went in the living room and Mr. Moore got out his records and scrapbooks and photographs, and we started going through them looking for the answers to our questions while Mrs. Moore put out a huge dinner for us in the dining room. I was completely amazed at the things they had saved and how well they had been preserved. We have reproduced many of the documents in this article so that you can share our excitement, too.

The Moores really have a sense of value for their heritage and for the people

*who settled this part of the country. They are also very generous people. Mr.
Moore has given away at least as much as he has saved. They're all-around great
people with much to share, and they have their past to keep them strong in a part
of the country where their roots go deep—a community that has now changed so
much that they sometimes feel like strangers. I'm glad John was willing to share
them with me, and I hope we're going to be friends for a long time.*

VAUGHN W. ROGERS, JR.

The chart below shows John's family line at a glance—from Aaron
(the Moore who immigrated to America from Ireland) to John himself. The family does not know who Aaron's ancestors were.

Aaron Moore	Aaron married and had six daughters and three sons, one of whom was John, born November 19, 1777.
John Moore	John married Martha Covington, and they had four daughters and four sons, one of whom was Joab, born on December 15, 1800. [John Covington Moore, who ran the general store at Fort Hembree, was another of John's sons.]
Joab Lawrence Moore	Joab married Martha Patton, and they had six daughters and five sons, one of whom was William, born February 5, 1831.
William Patton Moore ("Irish Bill")	Irish Bill married Harriet Naomi Gash, and they had five daughters and five sons, one of whom was Lawrence, born November 15, 1870.
Lawrence Richardson Moore	Lawrence married Caledonia Ledford, and they had three daughters and two sons, one of whom was Franklin, born August 17, 1902.
Franklin Charles Moore	Frank married Nannie Lou Chambers, and they had two sons and two daughters, one of whom was Sarah, born November 25, 1932.
Sarah Lou Moore	Sarah married Edward Singleton, and they had two sons, one of whom was John, born February 25, 1962.

John Lawrence Singleton

John is the high school senior who authored this article. [After he graduated from Rabun County High, he majored in journalism at the University of Georgia.]

Aaron and John Moore

Aaron Moore is my great-great-great-great-great-grandpa. He was born in Ireland. It's not totally known why he left his home but it's probable he left because of trouble. The Catholics at that time were under persecution and although it isn't known what religion he was practicing, it is doubtful that he or anyone else in Ireland could remain neutral. Add to this the fact that Ireland had still not accepted the then imperialistic British rule, and it is easy to see why he might have decided to become part of the growing exodus from Ireland to this country.

He arrived at Pennsylvania sometime during the 1740s as just another immigrant, but he soon found himself a captain in the Army. He even survived General Braddock's defeat and eventually came south. None of the records during this nomadic stage have been preserved to our knowledge and they are probably gone forever. It is known that he settled in what is now Rutherford County. It was here that his children were raised.

One of these children was John Moore. In all truth, he was the first true-blooded American ancestor of my family. Born December 15 in 1800, he grew up in Rutherford County on the banks of the Broad River. Not much else is known of him except that he gave birth to four sons, two of whom were Joab Lawrence Moore, and John Covington Moore. The latter first came and settled in Clay County, North Carolina, [then Haywood] and Joab Lawrence, evidently after hearing of his move, also came. It was Joab who bought the farm that is still in the hands of what's left of our family.

John C. Moore

John C. Moore was the son of John Moore. He was born in 1811 in Rutherford County. Being the expansionist and adventuring person he was led to his being the first white man to move into the Tusquittee Valley area. After his runaround with Indians, he showed them where he stood and they got along fine after that. He settled a large area of land by which he made his living. He started a whole new community, which is a remarkable feat. Here Frank Moore talks about him:

This newspaper article [reprinted after Frank Moore's comments] gives some of the facts about John C. Moore. There are some other things that I remember hearing about him. The first trip he made in here—it wadn't when him and his wife come, but he'd been over here before then. He come down on the head of Perry Creek. Indians lived on the head of the creek there, and he stayed all night with the Indians there. He said during the night they was a-talkin', you know, and said the Indians would come in at the door and just come right by you and look you in the face and just walk right on and wouldn't speak. They'd just walk right on through into the kitchen and they'd grab down into a big barrel of hominy. They'd stay in there and they'd eat hominy awhile and then said they'd come in, sit down, and go to talkin'. But said they wouldn't speak or nothing till they went on through yonder and got 'em a run of hominy. Then they'd come back, sit down, and go to talkin'.

Later he built him a little log cabin in Tusquittee Valley, brought his wife over and stayed friendly with the Indians. He needed a wagon and some stuff to farm with, so he left his wife with the Indians, and he went away into Tennessee or Alabama—somewhere down in there —to buy him a wagon. He bought the wagon and got as far as what was then Cherokee County. They wadn't no road in here to bring the wagon on to get in, but there was an Indian trail up the Hiawassee River. He had to take his wagon apart and carry it wheel by wheel, piece by piece, up the river. That's how he got it up here. After he brung it up here, piece by piece, then he put it back [together]. That was the first wagon that ever came in.

Then right after that, he went down to Hayesville there and put up the first big store in western North Carolina. He got a fella by the name of McCrae to run the store, but it belonged to both of them. Then John C. put up a big tannery by the side of the store down there just beyond Hayesville. They called it Fort Hembree, and they run that tannery and store. I've got the books, where it was run for years there [see records following the reprinted newspaper article]. They come from Georgia, North Carolina, and everywhere to trade there.

The following is a newspaper article about John C. Moore, probably printed in the Franklin, [North Carolina] *Press.* Frank Moore had it in his scrapbook.

"John C. Moore was born in Rutherford County, North Carolina,

PLATE 36   This historical marker stands on the courthouse lawn in Hayesville, North Carolina.

in the year 1811. When grown, he moved to Macon County where he won the heart and hand of Miss Mary Bryson as his help mate. After many fond dreams and thoughts of a fortune in the future, they each agreed to cast their lot among the Indians in the fertile Tusquittee Valley. They packed two horses with household effects and their first born, little Bill, and started across the Chunkie Gal Mountain, the road being a precipitous Indian trail at that day. They soon safely landed at a small Indian cabin in the bottoms at the side of the road just below W. H. Johnson's residence.

"Mr. Moore, being an expansionest and endowed with pluck and brains and capital enough for any young man to earn a living, he set out to felling the monster trees and clearing land to grow Indian corn, the staff of life.

"One day, when erecting his fence, an Indian came along and protested against the fencing enterprise on their possessions. Each of them grew into a combative spirit and tried their luck at fist and skull fight, Mr. Moore biting the Indian's thumb nearly off and the Indian retreating hollowing 'Wa Wa.' Later other Red Men came and Mr. Moore got his old Flint Lock Gun, set up a board shooting hole demonstrating to the Indians his coat of arms to protect himself in case of wars. The Indians seeing this, all retreated never to molest him again.

"Garden work well along and crops about ready to store in his new garner, he secured an Indian woman, Sallie Peckerwood, Jim's wife, to stay with Mary and little Bill while he returned with his two horses to Macon County to get more household equipment for icy winter's cold winds. Loading and leading one horse packed to wonderous capacity, he then started for old Tusquittee via Chunkie Gal Mountain. The first day's travel landed him at the head of Tusquittee at an Indian's by the name of Yone Connahut, the good family giving their guest plenty of Connie Honie [Hominy] for supper. After supper several Indians came in to display to their white man their mode of dancing, one of them getting drunk and vomiting part of his Connie Honie. The next morning, after loading his horses, Mr. Moore wended his way by an Indian trail a few hours later reaching his new home to find Mary and little Bill. While he had been gone, Sallie Peckerwood had day by day tied little Bill Moore in the blanket, Indian style, for her papoose taking him up Johnson's Creek to pick up chestnuts under the rich October skies.

"This being several years prior to the land sale, when the land sale came, he bought what is now the Shearer and Evans property on Tusquittee.

"As the years sped by more bright children were added to this new home, Sarah Elizabeth, Joab, and Lizzie. Seeing the needs of these buds of promise and the needs of his farm, he got two other stalwart men, rigged his horses with harness, the collars being made of shucks, and started for Tennessee to purchase the first wagon to ever track the soil of Clay County. These three men with axes trimmed their road as they went. As they came up the Hiawassee River and reaching the shut in at the Leatherwood Bluff below Hon. J. C. Herbert's, they had to take the wheels off the wagon and carry it piece by piece around the mountain. Resuming the former way of clearing the road, they reached his Tusquittee home where Bob Evans now lives.

"Just imagine the radiant smile of his wife and children and Indian neighbors as they stood gazing at the new wagon—the new Ford car at that time. These gleeful children thought they were riding some in this new wagon.

"Later Mr. Moore sold these possessions to James Allen Shearer and purchased a lot of the Ford property and the Warne property at Brasstown, starting his vocation of farming and fencing again. One day while fencing, he went to fell a sapling for a ground pole, hit something with his axe causing it to glance off. This broke his axe and on examining the rock he discovered he had with his monstrous blow struck the lick of fortune. Looking at this rock and others his keen eyes beheld plenty of shining gold. With bold steps and smiles of fortune on his face, he carried some of these rich treasures to his wife. Fortune, they say, knocks at every man's door and Moore's fencing proposition was the key to turn him in. Later Moore sold these lands and his gold mine to Warne and Bill Boe, thus the Warne Gold Mines were started. He received quite a handsome sum of money for the mines for that day. Then Mr. Moore started for Tusquittee again buying a large farm from Lovelady. Here he died at the age of ninety-two years; his wife being about ninety.

"Their son Bill located in Asheville and reared sixteen children. Lizzie married John Robbins who taught the first school at Robbins-ville, this town being named in his honor. Sarah married the Hon. William Herbert; the Hon. J. C. Herbert being then our Senator, two of their sons became physicians. Miriam Moore married Abner Moore; T. C. Moore was born to this union. T. C. Moore married a Caldwell; to their union fifteen children were born to do honor as teachers and various honorable vocations to J. C. Moore's name.

"Mr. John C. Moore came to Tusquittee and lived among the Indians five to seven years before they were removed from this section. Douglas Davis was the second white man to locate here. The writer of this sketch has often sat and listened to Mr. John C. Moore as he would rehearse his life among the Red Men and tell of their habits, ways of living, dances and ball games. One of the most out-standing incidents was that the Indians would go to a mountain between Jay and Paul Moore's and get silver ore on the sly and take to their furnaces and run bars of bullion. This they took to Tennessee and traded for coin.

"He was a man of fundamental principles of the Bible. Psalms XLI, 'Blessed is he that considereth the poor: the Lord will deliver him in time of trouble. The Lord will preserve him and keep him alive and he shall be blessed upon the earth; and thou wilt not deliver him unto the will of his enemies.'

"Mr. Moore's lineal descent was German, Dutch, Scotch, Irish and English. He affiliated with the Presbyterian Church where he imbibed a lot of his lofty ideals and noble principles.

"Joab Moore, son of John C. Moore, was one of the most eminent physicians of the State of Texas."

The ledger from the Fort Hembree tannery for 1846–47, which Frank Moore still has, makes fascinating reading for those interested today in the kinds of sales and purchases such a tannery made in a

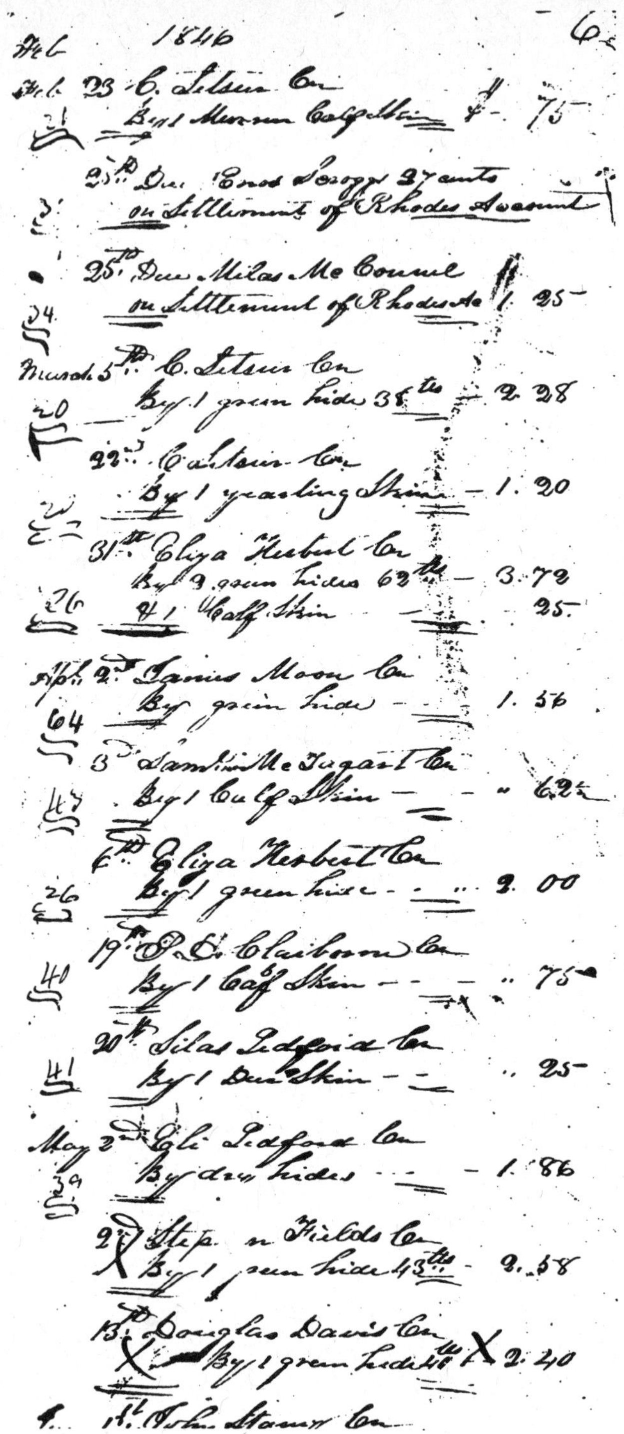

Feb 1846 6

Feb 23 C. Tilson Cr
By 1 Morocco Calf Skin 4 – 75

25th Due Enos Scroggs 37 cents
on Settlement of Rhodes Account

25th Due Milas McConnel
on Settlement of Rhodes Ac 1.25

March 5th C. Tilson Cr
By 1 green hide 38 lbs – 2.28

22nd C. Tilson Cr
By 1 yearling Skin – 1.20

31st Eliza Herbert Cr
By 2 green hides 62 lbs – 3.72
By 1 Calf Skin – 25

Apr 2nd James Moon Cr
By green hide – 1.56

3rd Saml McTagart Cr
By 1 Calf Skin – .62½

6th Eliza Herbert Cr
By 1 green hide – 2.00

19th P. D. Claiborne Cr
By 1 Calf Skin – .75

20th Silas Ledford Cr
By 1 Deer Skin – .25

May 2nd Eli Ledford Cr
By dry hides – 1.86

2nd Stephen Fields Cr
By 1 green hide 43 lbs – 2.58

13th Douglas Davis Cr
By 1 green hide 40 lbs – 2.40

14th John Stamey Cr

PLATE 37 One page from the Fort Hembree tannery ledger. It shows purchases and payments made between February 23, 1846, and May 2, 1846.

mountain community. We went through its pages and listed the following sales to give you an idea of the variety:

5¼ pounds [of] harness	[$] 1.75
1 side [shoe] sole [leather]—7 pounds	·2.10
1 side [shoe] upper [leather]	3.00
1 piece shoe leather	1.00
Tanning 1 kip skin	1.00
Bridle leather	.50
Leather remnants	1.00
2 sides bridle leather	5.00
2 bell collars	.87½
1 bell collar four feet by three inches	.30
Tanning and dressing 1 sheep skin	.75
1 sheep skin for saddle	1.50
1 pair bridle reins	.37½
1 plow line	.50
Strap and leather for coat pad	.25
1 side harness leather	3.00
Tanning 1 calf skin	.75
Deer skins to a saddle at Blairsville	1.00
2 dog skins	1.00
1 hog skin and back band	1.25
1 deer skin for whangs	.25
Whang leather	.37½
4 sides harness leather—40.33½ pounds	13.33½
Tanning 1 colt skin	.50
1 set bridle leathers	.75
4 sides [shoe] upper [leather]	9.00

Though we cannot explain several items on the list—why someone would want two dog skins tanned, for example—we have learned from our contacts something of how such tanneries worked. We know, for example, that with cow hides, they usually worked in terms of sides—each hide being split down the backbone into two equal pieces. Sometimes a farmer would bring a cow hide in to be tanned and when the job was done, he would get one side for his own use on the farm, and the tannery would keep the other side as payment. They could then sell that side to shoemakers, for example, who might not have the time or capacity to tan their own.

A sale such as "1 piece shoe leather" was probably to a farmer who was making repairs on his own family's shoes, whereas a sale such as "4 sides upper" must have been to a shoemaker, upper leather being for the upper portions of shoes.

"Whang leather" usually meant lower-quality leather that was going to be cut into strips for shoelaces, bridle laces, etc.

Items that the tannery bought, or listed as credit on accounts appear in a separate section of the ledger. A sampling follows:

35 pounds dry hides	[$]4.20
Deer skins	1.75
1 hog skin	.50
1 small deer skin	.25
Tan bark	3.37½
1 kip skin and hog skin	2.00
1 buck skin	1.00
1 green hide—29 pounds	1.74
1 sheep skin	.40
1 bull hide—75 pounds	4.50
1 yearling skin	1.20
¾ cord [of] bark	2.25

Such a list brings an additional dimension of reality to stories contacts have told us about those times when just about the only money to be made came from going to the woods, cutting down chestnut oak trees, stripping off the bark, and hauling it to area tanneries for sale. The tanneries, of course, made an ooze of the bark by crushing it and mixing it with water in large vats. The tannic acid released played a vital part in the tanning process.

A small tablet of lined paper found in the ledger and dated January, 1902, contains the following selection of entries handwritten in pencil. Unfortunately, we do not know who made them:

Tea Cake

1 cup of sugar
1 tablespoon of butter
1 egg
1 cup of buttermilk
½ teaspoonful each of soda, nutmeg and lemon
A cup of flour

Ginger Cookies

Put 1 teaspoonful each of ginger, soda, a pinch of salt and three tablespoons of sugar. Fill the cup with [molasses] syrup. Stir well. Turn out into bowl. Put into the cup three tablespoons full of each of lard and hot water. Flour enough to roll out.

Lemon Cake

Cream together 1 cup of butter, 1½ cups of sugar, three eggs, ½ cup of sweet milk, grated rine and juice of one lemon, ½ teaspoonful each soda and cream of tartar (or sour cream and soda), 2½ cups of flour.

Cheap Cake

Two eggs, 1 cup sugar, two of flour, 1 cup of sweet cream, 1 teaspoonful of baking powder, 1 pinch of salt and flavor.

Corn Gems

One cup of cornmeal and 1 of flour, teaspoonful of soda, two of cream of tartar, ½ teaspoonful of salt, a tablespoonful of sugar or molasses.

The same tablet also contains a listing of remedies, handwritten in pencil, as follows:

Ringworm

Teaspoonful of vinegar. Drop a little soda and rub on while foaming.

Sprains or Bruise

Wormwood boiled in vinegar.

Bedsores

Eggshells. Brown and pulverize. Take a teaspoonful three times a day. Make a tea of clover blossoms dry or green and drink at mealtime.

Salve

Fry mutton tallow. When cool, stir turpentine in it until white.

Toothache

Tincture of benzoin on cotton. Good for cuts, burns, and chapped and cracked hands.

Iron Rust

Rub cream of tartar in the spot and boil in clear water.

* * *

The same tablet also contains a set of computations for construction of a house. We have reproduced them here as they appear. "Box in" must refer to the boxing-in lumber needed for walls, floor, and ceiling:

```
House 12 × 8 × 16 × 28
Box in 50 feet long 12 feet high    [$] 600
  "   "  22   "     "   10   "    "       220
  "   "  16   "     "    8   "    "       128
Box in 24 p   8 feet 1 × 3                 48
        75 " 12   "   1 × 3               225
        33 " 10   "   1 × [?]              75
Framing                                  450
Roof                                     540
Sleepers 13                              108
Joist 12                                 124
2 × 12 by 48 feet                         64
Porch 7 feet                             225
Stringers 6 × [?]                         96
Shelves                                  350
                                  [$]3,089
```

The accounts for the Fort Hembree store were maintained in two parallel ledger books. One book was simply a daily log, listing every customer for that day, his or her account number, and his or her purchases or payments on that particular day. The second was organized by customer accounts, the name of the customer and his or her account number written in large script across the top of the facing left and right pages, and beneath the name, the left hand page showing a running total bill by date, and the right describing payments. When the account was credited a certain amount on the right-hand page, the amount owed the store would be altered accordingly.

The whole operation was typically straightforward and simple, and the journals reflect predictable buying patterns: some customers, for example, bought far more than others. McCravey himself was the biggest customer (see photostat of his account), and people like Grove Lemond (who made only one purchase in all of 1846: 18¾¢ worth of tobacco) were the smallest. Some bought fine cloth, others bought only flannel. Some bought books, some none. Some bought no tobacco; others bought almost nothing but tobacco. Some ran up bills of almost $100 before making a single payment on their account; others paid as they went.

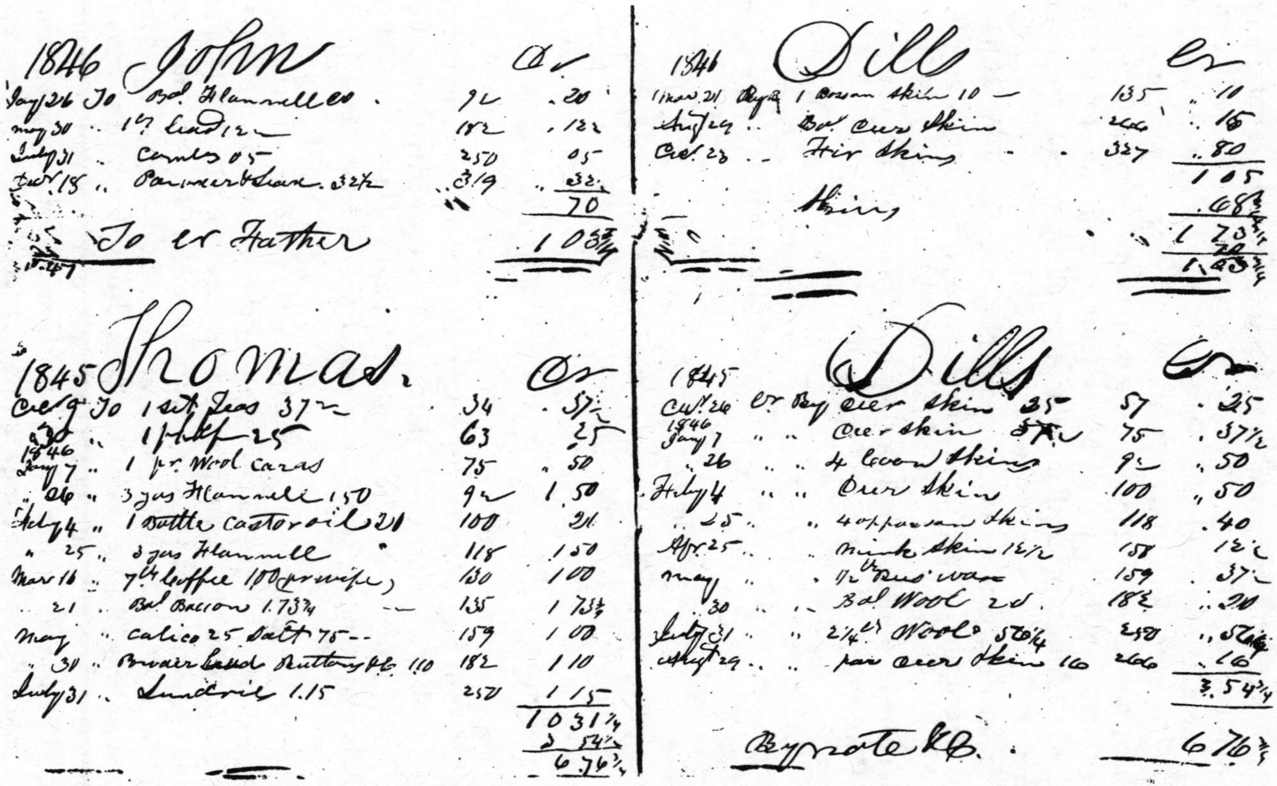

PLATE 38 One of the ledgers for the Fort Hembree store showed a running total of purchases (on the left page) and payments (on the right page) for each customer.

Buying also, as could be predicted, was seasonal. For obvious reasons sales of powder, lead, and gun flints for flintlock rifles went up in the fall; sales of flannel went up in the winter.

We anticipated finding changes in holiday spending habits; however, we found almost none. A coat purchased for $9.00 on December 13 when no other purchase was made all year that cost over a dollar looks suspiciously like a Christmas present. Likewise some December purchases of shawls, bonnets, hats, plates, some lace, and some ribbon. But these were relatively rare, and in most cases the arrival of Christmas caused no change at all in general spending patterns.

Other surprises emerged as we spent more and more time with the ledgers. From what we were able to determine, for example, over the course of an entire year, most of the customers of the store never purchased over ten dollars' worth of goods *total* for the year. The breakdown of the 201 accounts is as follows:

Total worth of purchases for one year:	Number of accounts in that category:
$ 0–10	150
$11–20	19
$21–30	9
$31–40	8
$41–50	6
over $50	9
	201

Fifty-three of the accounts had to be sued—mostly for sums of less than ten dollars. In most cases, the accounts were settled "by judgment," and in most cases the people had paid at least a portion of their bills before being sued. They were *trying*, at least, to pay their debts.

One of the biggest surprises was how little cash actually changed hands. When William Skewbird's indebtedness to the store amounted to $2.50, for example, he gave the store a bushel of corn for which his account was credited 37½¢. Jesse McClure assumed the balance [probably in return for some service Skewbird performed for him] and so the $2.12½ owed was taken from Skewbird's account and showed up on McClure's debt to the store as "Cr. Wm. Skewbird 2.12½." McClure, in turn, paid off his indebtedness by getting $15.79 in credit for "hauling" and $4.50 credit for "wagon and steers" (probably the fee for their use in the hauling job). No cash ever changed hands.

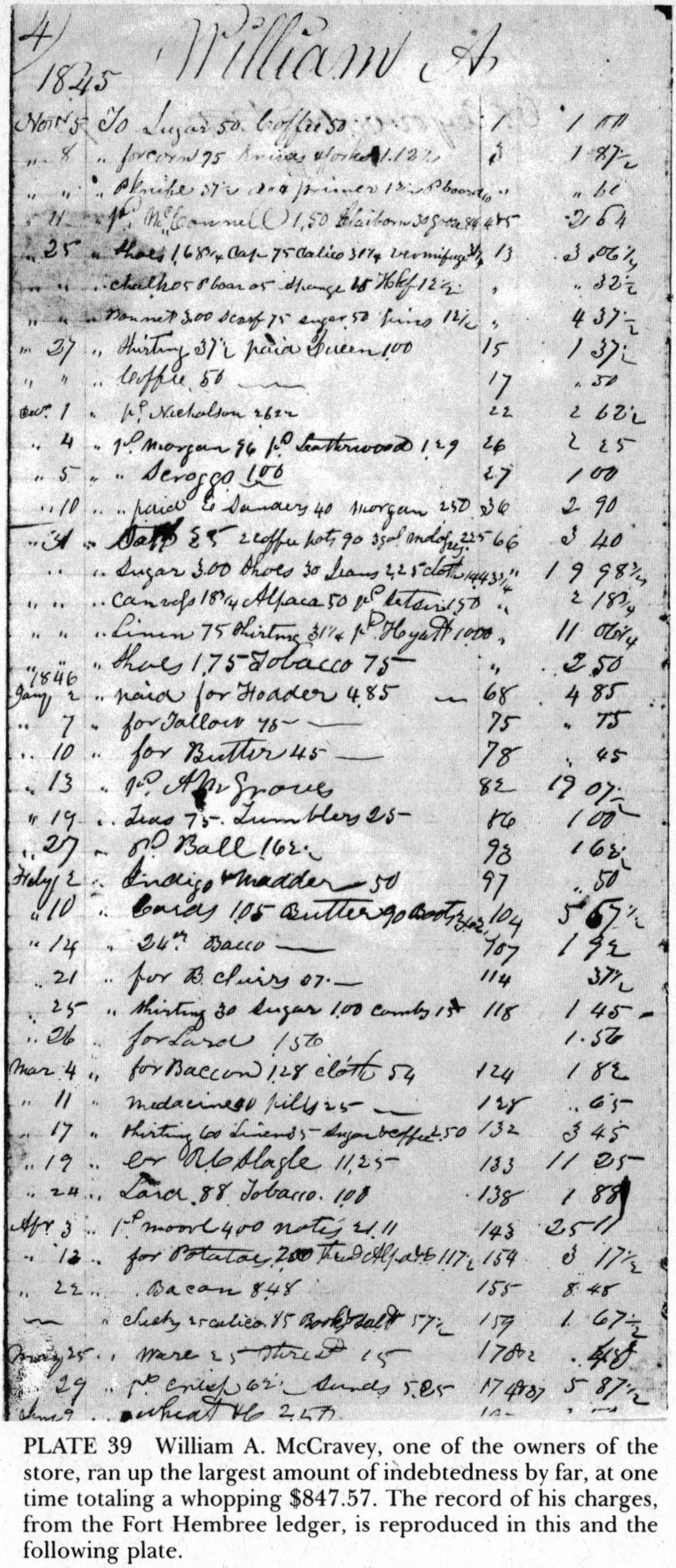

4)
1845 William A.

Nov 5	To Sugar 50 Coffee 50	1	1 00
.. 8	.. for corn 75 knives & forks 1.12½	3	1 87½
.. ..	.. Chalk 37½ a primer 12½ board	..	.. 62
.. 11	.. pd. McConnell 1,50 Claiborn 30	4 85	2 64
.. 25	.. shoes 1,68¾ Cap 75 Calico 31¼ vermifuge 31¼	13	3 06¼
.. ..	.. chalk 05 board 05 Orange 10 Hdkf 12½	..	.. 32½
.. ..	.. Bonnet 3.00 scarf 75 sugar 50	..	4 37½
.. 27	.. Shirting 37½ paid Green 1.00	15	1 37½
.. ..	.. Coffee 50	17	.. 50
Dec 1	.. pd. Nicholson 2.62½	22	2 62½
.. 4	.. pd. Morgan 96 pd. Leatherwood 1.29	26	2 25
.. 5	.. .. Scroggs 1.00	27	1 00
.. 10	.. paid E Sanders 40 Morgan 2.50	36	2 90
.. 31	.. 2 coffee pots 90	66	3 40
..	.. Sugar 3.00 shoes 30 jeans 2.25 cloth 14.43¾	..	19 98¾
.. ..	.. Canvass 18¾ Alpaca 50	..	2 18¾
.. ..	.. Linen 75 Shirting 31¼ pd. Hyatt 10.00	..	11 06¼
..	.. Shoes 1,75 Tobacco 75	..	2 50
1846 Jany 2	.. paid for Fodder 4.85	68	4 85
.. 7	.. for Tallow 75	75	.. 75
.. 10	.. for Butter 45	78	.. 45
.. 13	.. pd. A McGroves	82	19 07½
.. 19	.. Teas 75 Tumblers 25	86	1 00
.. 27	.. pd. Ball 1.62½	93	1 62½
Feby 2	.. Indigo & Madder 50	97	.. 50
.. 10	.. Cards 1.05 Butter 90	104	5 67½
.. 14	.. 24 lbs Bacco	107	1 92
.. 21	.. for B. chairs	114	37½
.. 25	.. Shirting 30 Sugar 1.00 combs 15	118	1 45
.. 26	.. for Lard 1.56		1.56
Mar 4	.. for Baccon 1,28 cloth 54	124	1 82
.. 11	.. medacine 40 pills 25	128	.. 65
.. 17	.. Shirting 60 Linen 35 sugar & coffee 2.50	132	3 45
.. 19	.. Cr R.C. Slagle 11,25	133	11 25
.. 24	.. Lard 88 Tobacco 1.00	138	1 88
Apr 3	.. pd. Moore 4.00 notes 21.11	143	25 11
.. 12	.. for Potatoes 2.00 thread Alpaca 1.17½	154	3 17½
.. 22	.. Bacon 8.48	155	8 48
	.. calico 85 Books salt 57½	159	1 67½
May 25	.. Ware 25 thread 15	170	.. 40
.. 29	.. pd. Crisp 62½ Sunds 5.25	174	5 87½
June 9	.. wheat		

PLATE 39 William A. McCravey, one of the owners of the store, ran up the largest amount of indebtedness by far, at one time totaling a whopping $847.57. The record of his charges, from the Fort Hembree ledger, is reproduced in this and the following plate.

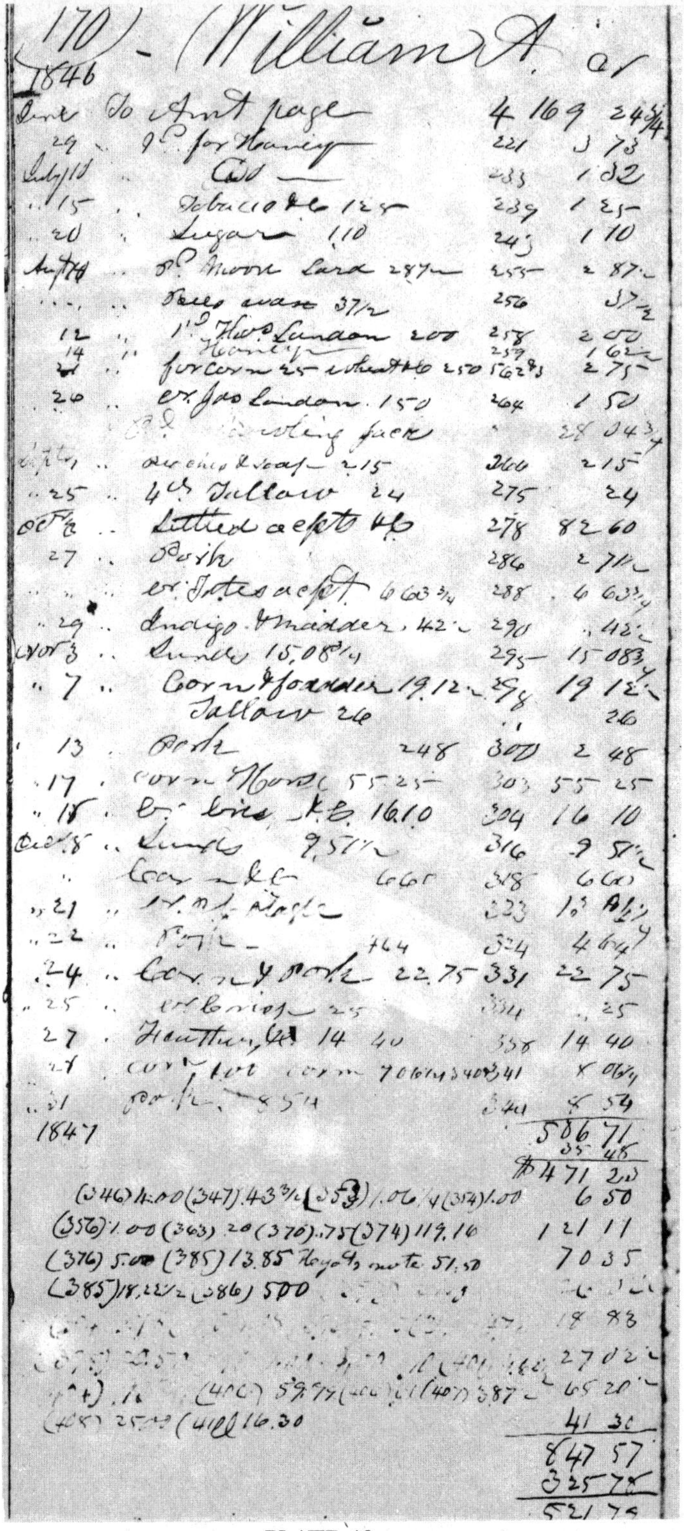

(170) - (William A. ?)

1846
Dr. To Amt page ... 4 169 24¾

29 .. 9 ? for Hominy ... 221 3 73
Jly 15 .. Cost ... 233 1 82
.. 15 .. Tobacco &c 125 ... 239 1 25
.. 20 .. Sugar 110 ... 243 1 10
Aug 10 .. 8 Moore card 287½ ... 253 2 87½
.. .. .. Sees wax 37½ ... 256 37½
12 .. 1 Thos Landon 200 ... 258 2 00
14 .. .. Hominy ... 259 1 62½
.. .. for Corn 25 & wheat &c 250 ... 562½ 2 75
20 .. .. ex Jas Landon 150 ... 264 1 50
.. .. ? rling pack ... 28 04¾
Sep 1 .. ? & soap 215 ... 266 2 15
.. 25 .. 4 Tallow 24 ... 275 24
Oct 6 .. Settled acct 46 ... 278 82 60
27 .. Pork ... 286 2 70
.. .. ex Totes acct 6 03¾ ... 288 6 03¾
.. 29 .. Indigo & madder 42 ... 291 42
Nov 3 .. Sundry 15 08¾ ... 295 15 08¾
.. 7 .. Corn & fodder 19 12 ... 298 19 12
.. .. Tallow 26 ... 26
.. 13 .. Pork 248 ... 300 2 48
.. 17 .. Corn & Horse 55 25 ... 303 55 25
.. 18 .. ex bill ? 16 10 ... 304 16 10
Dec 8 .. Sundry 9 57 ... 316 9 57
.. .. Corn & ? 6 00 ... 318 6 00
.. 21 .. N. ? ? ... 323 10 ?
.. 22 .. Pork 464 ... 324 4 64
.. 24 .. Corn & pork 22 75 ... 331 22 75
.. 25 .. ? 25 ... 334 25
27 .. Feather? & 14 40 ... 338 14 40
.. 2? .. corn ? corn 70 6¼ ... 340 341 8 06¼
.. 31 .. Pork 854 ... 340 8 54
1847 ... 586 71
... 35 48
... $471 23

(346) 4.00 (347) .43¾ (353) .06¼ (354) 1.00 ... 6 50
(356) 1.00 (363) 20 (370) .75 (374) 119.16 ... 121 11
(376) 5.00 (385) 13.85 Hoyt's note 51.50 ... 70 35
(385) 18.12½ (386) 5.00 ... ? ?
... 18 83
... 27 02
(40?) 5 9 7½ (40?) 387 ... 65 20
(408) 25 (410) 16.30 ... 41 30
... 847 57
... 325 78
... 521 79

PLATE 40

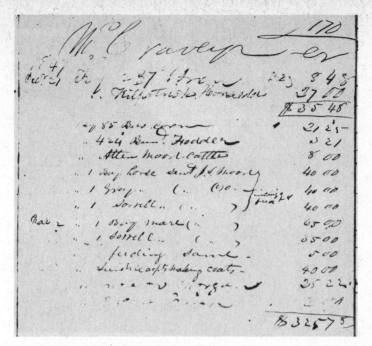

PLATE 41 McCravey made the first payments on his account in 1847. The ledger shows he was credited here with $325.78, mostly through horses he turned over to the store, probably from his own farm.

PLATE 42 For many years, Frank Moore ran a general store in this building.

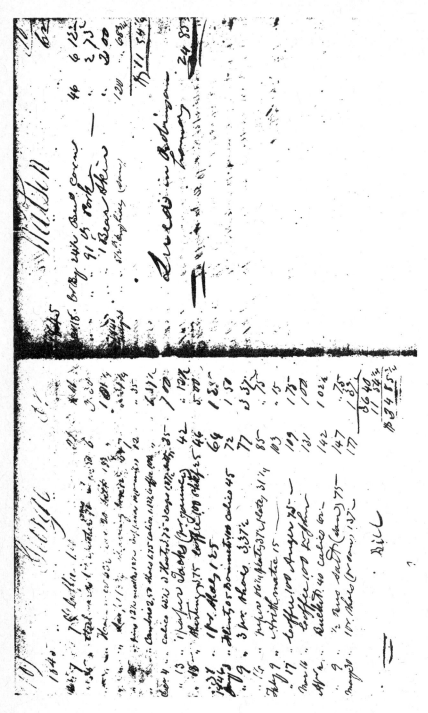

PLATE 43 The account reproduced above is an example of one that was sued for payment. Before being sued, George Watson had paid part of his indebtedness with 24½ bushels of corn, 91 pounds of pork, a bearskin, and hides.

Intrigued, we made a list of the types of goods customers turned over to the store in payment for their bills, and the amount of credit they received. The list:

	Paid	Credit
By beef		[$] .96
" 9 pounds tobacco		1.12½
" 1 bushel Irish potatoes		1.00
" deer skins		.50
" ½ bushel onions		.50
" fur and feathers		.50
" bacon		1.56¼
" 2½ pounds wool		.62½
" 1½ pounds beeswax		.37½
" 24½ bushel corn		6.12
" 91 pounds pork		2.75
" 1 bear skin		2.00
" socks		1.75
" 7½ pounds tallow		.45
" 1 calf skin		.50
" deer skins		1.75
" 5 steers		43.50
" corn		1.00
" shucks		1.00
" 1 bushel corn		.25
" 54 pounds pork		1.62
" iron		2.87½
" 1 coat		5.25
" 4 bushel oats		1.33⅓
" 50 bushel corn		10.13½
" flax seed		.46
" 15½ bushel salt		21.70
" 5½ pounds butter		.45
" cow and calf		9.00
" 19½ pounds wool		4.87½
" 10 bushel salt		15.00
" work on room		2.00
" 3 days work by John		1.50
" 26½ pounds green hide		1.59
" 1 venison ham		.37½
" 6¾ pounds feathers		1.68¾
" 3 opossum, 1 cat and 1 coon skins		.62½
" 20 rabbit skins		.20
" 81 pounds bacon		6.48

	Paid	*Credit*
"	4 opossum skins	.40
"	1 hog skin	.75
"	1 cow	8.00
"	1 steer	9.50
"	driving cattle to Nantahala	1.00
"	1 coon and 1 ox skin	.25
"	wagon and steer	4.50
"	50 head cabbage	1.50
"	work on chimney	3.00
"	oats	1.75
"	65 pounds green hides	3.90
"	hide [sheepskin]	.50
"	mink skin	.12½
"	4 opossum skins	.40
"	cutting wood	.50
"	going to mill	.25
"	4 cords wood	4.00
"	driving cattle	5.33
"	11 pounds lard	.88
"	dope	.10
"	gloves	1.50
"	5¾ pounds cheese	.57½
"	1 coon skin	.12½
"	19 pounds flour	.57
"	cow and steer	15.00
"	14 pounds tallow	.84
"	yearling	3.00
"	2 bushel Irish potatoes	.80
"	1 pair shoes	1.50
"	1 pair boots	4.50
"	1 pair blankets	5.00
"	22 pounds mutton	.66
"	services of wife	- - -
"	8 yards flax cloth [wife]	3.00
"	digging well on half	11.84½
"	2 bushel flax seed	1.35
"	2 bushel wheat	2.00
"	3 bells	3.00
"	bedstead	1.50
"	chairs	.75
"	fruit	1.50
"	oats and gold	1.12½
"	whiskey—sold 7 quarts	.65
"	1 bay horse	40.00

Paid	Credit
" hauling 2 loads from Augusta	100.00
" sow and pigs	10.00
" gold	.45
" 2½ bushel peaches	2.12
" 46 pounds green hides	2.76
" 12 plug tobacco	1.80

Yet another surprise came in the realization that virtually none of the accounts bore women's names. One of the few exceptions was "Miss Mary Brown" who bought some calico, some peppermint, and a shawl, and $1.00 of whose debt of $1.75 was paid by Mr. McCravey himself. Another was "Miss Rachel Scroggs" who bought only shoes, calico, ginger, muslin, and one pocketknife, and who paid off her debt of $4.05 with three bundles of feathers and $2.98¼ "work of iron." Another was Jane Hyatt, who must have been quite a woman, as she paid most of her debt off with green hides and sheepskins.

And as we looked through the pages, accounts began to tease us into conjuring up stories and activities behind the bare facts and figures. What was happening in the lives of the Scroggs family, for example, on November 8, 1845, when both Enos and John came in and bought one Holy Bible and one hymnbook apiece? And who was Amos Curtis, who, on December 18, 1845, opened his account with the purchase of one pair of shoes (75¢), ribbons (37½¢), lace (30¢), and a saddle ($10); paid for the goods with one steer ($8.50 credit) and "by settlement" ($2.92½) and then closed the account?

At times, it was fairly obvious what was happening. On November 6, 1845, for example, Enoch Beach bought chisels ($1.75), augers ($2.25), a handsaw ($1.50), a "drawing knife" (75¢), and some nails (20¢). On November 13, 1845, he returned to the store, the job obviously nearly finished, and purchased hinges (50¢), screws (25¢), and a gimlet (56¼¢). He also picked up 75¢ worth of molasses.

But what was happening in the life of Madison Curtis, who, on November 24, 1845, came in and bought one saddle ($12), stirrups (87½¢) and boots ($3). He did not come in again until May 25, 1846, when he brought in 134¾ pounds of bacon and received $12.12¾ credit on his account. On July 31, 1846, he made his second purchasing trip to the store, buying seventeen pounds of nails for $1.70. On August 11, R. C. Slagle paid $4.95 on the Curtis bill, leaving a balance due of fifty cents. On the same day Madison Curtis came in, paid the fifty cents in cash, closed the account, and disappeared from the record.

Obviously we can only speculate, and entertaining as that is, it remains speculation. And so we have confined ourselves primarily to the presentation of several accounts to give you an idea of the kinds of purchases people made from the only store around this part of the mountains in 1845–46.

The first account is that of Bennett Kirkpatrick. It spans November 12, 1845, to December 24, 1846. We do not know who Mr. Kirkpatrick was, but we selected his account because of the unusual variety of goods he bought. If one wanted to go further and engage in some speculation, it would be tempting to think he was a schoolteacher because of the books and paper he bought, the number of pocketknives (prizes for his better students?), his comparatively refined tastes, and the fact that he could pay part of his account in cash.

The account follows with spellings, capitalizations, etc., maintained as they appear in the ledger:

1845 Bennett S. Kirkpatrick

Novr.	12	To	1 pair wool cards	[$]	.50	[$] .50
"	15	"	1 dictionary		.50	
"			1 pocketknife		.25	
			1 Life [of?] Marion		.75	
			P. board [?]		.05	
			needles		.10	
			Life [of?] Franklin		.75	
			Testament		.37½	
			Primer		.06¼	2.83¾
"	18	"	file		.12½	
			sugar		.50	
			pitcher		.50	1.12½
Novr.	20	To	All blades		.12½	
			shoe knife		.20	.32½
"	22	"	molasses		.15	.15
"	24	"	buttons		.25	.25
"	25	"	file		.12½	
			No. 6		.25	
			chestnuts		.06¼	.43¾
Novr.	26	To	brimstone		.10	.10
"	28	"	½ bus. salt		.75	.75
Decr.	5	"	tallow		.43¾	.43¾
"	6	"	shawl		1.25	
			coffee		1.00	
			bonnet		.62½	
			pocketknife		.12½	3.00

"	9	"	cash	.40	
			shirting	3.64	
			osenberg [osnaburg]	1.35	
			flannel	.50	5.89
"	11	"	coffee pot	.62½	
			calico	.50	
			powder	.40	
			lead	.12½	
			tin cups	.10	
			dipper	.10	1.85
"	13	"	tin bucket	.62½	
			chestnuts	.05	.68¾
"	15	"	vermafuge [vermifuge]	.25	
			tacks	.10	
			pepper	.12½	.47½
"	24	"	buttons	.12½	
			calico	.25	
			crilling	.56¼	
			osenberg [osnaburg]	.42	1.35¾
"	31	"	coffee	.28	.28

1846

Jany.	3	To	shirting	2.17½	
			No. 6	.25	2.42½
"	9	"	1 bucket	.87½	.87½
"	10	"	1 pocketknife	.25	.25
"	11	"	1 pocketknife	.25	.25
"	13	"	molasses	.20	
		"	gimblet [gimlet]	.15	.35
"	17	"	candle moulds	.15	.15
"	22	"	peppermint	.10	
			rhubard [rhubarb]	.10	
			[?] cordial	.12½	.32½
"	28	"	bears oil	.15	
			cash	.05	.20
Feby.	2	"	sweet oil	.25	
			hammer	.20	
			mustard	.20	.65
"	5	"	1 fine comb	.10	.10
"	9	"	1 comb	.10	.10
"	10	"	½ pound ginger	.12½	.12½
"	17	"	coffee	1.00	
			salt	.75	
			sugar	.25	2.00
"	18	To	order Miss S. Brown	1.50	1.50

"	26	"	fish hooks	.10	.10
March	7	"	2 Godfrey's cordial	.20	.20
"	12	"	calico	.45	.45
"	19	"	ink stand	.15	.15
"	20	"	½ yard muslin	.25	
			edging	.15	.40
March	25	To	E. grammar	.37½	
			sugar	.25	
			file	.12½	.75
"	27	"	1 pan	.50	.50
Apr.	7	"	fish hooks	.10	
			calico	2.10	2.20
"	18	"	P. book	.12½	.12½
"	22	"	cup and thread	.15	.15
May	23	"	sugar	.28	
			coffee	1.00	1.28
Carried to page 149					36.05¾
May			Amount from page 20		36.05¾
"	25	"	coffee	1.00	
			salt	.75	1.75
"	"		spice	.12½	
			tobacco	.30	.42½
"	27	"	thread	1.00	1.00
"	30	"	vial B. oil	.10	
			calico	2.50	
			comb	.06¼	2.66¼
June	11	"	sundries	1.92½	1.92½
"	12	"	cambric	.06¼	.06¼
"	16	"	nails	.10	
			mug	.06¼	.16¼
"	20	"	tobacco	.18¾	
			½ quire paper	.12½	.31¼
"	23	"	calico	.12½	.12½
June	24	To	cambric	.25	.25
"	26	"	calico	.25	.25
"	27	"	cash pd. Hubbard (paper safe)	.25	.25
"	29	"	1 jar	.18¾	.18¾
July	3	"	sundries	.56¼	.56¼
"	8	"	cash	2.50	
			knife	.75	3.25
"	21	"	calico	.30	.30
Augt.	15	"	1 bottle No. 6	.25	.25
"	16	"	wire	.06¼	.06¼
"	26	"	tumblers	1.10	1.10

"	27	"	salt (Saunders)	.18¾	.18¾
Sept.	8	"	1 pr. B. Bits	.37½	.37½
"	8	"	Gun flints	.06¼	.06¼
"	23	"	teas	.62½	.62½
"	25	"	1 box pills	.25	.25
Oct.	27	"	sugar	1.00	
			madder	.10	1.10
"	28	"	salt and shirting	4.62½	4.62½
Nov.	11	"	1 hat	3.00	3.00
"	16	"	1 horse	33.00	33.00
Decr.	4	"	1 umbrella	1.00	1.00
"	12	"	½ quire paper	.12½	.12½
"	18	"	bucket	.50	.50
"	24	"	fine comb and purs [purse?]	.22½	
			11¾ pounds flour	.35	.57½
					$96.73
					−34.21½
					$61.51½

By the end of the year, Mr. Kirkpatrick had managed to pay $34.21½ on his account. This amount was made up of $9.00 credit for a cow and calf, 97¢ for twelve pounds of butter, $1.35 for two bushels of flaxseed, $11.84½ for helping to dig a well, 50¢ for a well bucket, and the balance in cash.

The second account is that of Hiram Crisp—selected, again, because of the variety it offers.

1845 Hiram M. Crisp

Novr.	5	To	1 shoe knife	[$] .20	
			shaving box	.20	
			frying pan	.40	.80
"	8	"	1¾ pounds coffee	.25	
			1¾ pounds sugar	.25	
			molassas	.18¾	.68¾
"	15	"	¼ pounds powder	.12½	
			lead	.05	
			1 box p. caps	.25	.42½
"	20	"	4 pounds coffee	.75	.75
"	"	"	1 yard calico	.37½	
			1 pt. molasses	.10	
			7 yards calico	2.62½	
			tobacco	.10	3.20
"	29	"	2 pkkf. [pocketknife]	.25	

			1 shaving brush	.12½	.37½
Decr.	3	"	flax thread	.10	.10
"	6	"	boots	1.00	
			molasses	.18¾	
			1 pound tobacco	.20	1.38¾
Decr.	19	to	1 shawl	1.25	1.25
"	26	"	1 plug tobacco	.10	.10

1846

Jany.	1	"	paid cornet [?]	.50	.50
"	5	"	1½ yards flannel	.60	
			1 vial B [Bear's] oil	.12½	.72½
"	24	"	tobacco	.15	.15
"	31	"	1 comb	.06¼	.06¼
Feby.	4	"	½ pounds copperas	.05	.05
"	10	"	1½ yards cambric	.20	
			10 buttons	.10	.30
"	14	"	½ pounds bacon	.96	.96
"	16	"	coffee	.30	.30
"	24	"	file	.12½	.12½
Mar.	2	"	[?] for eggs	.20	.20
"	5	"	tobacco	.25	.25
"	7	"	¼ bus. salt	.37½	.37½
"	12	"	2 yards calico	.50	.50
Carried to page 130					13.57¼
Mar.			Amount page 1		13.57¼
"	12	"	2 paper pins	.20	.20
"	16	"	tobacco	.25	.25
"	18	"	bacon	1.50	1.50
"	19	"	coffee pot	.60	.60
"	21	"	coffee	.50	
			bucket	.40	
			8 yards calico	2.00	2.90
"	27	"	sugar	.10	.10
Apr.	2	To	tobacco	.10	.10
"	3	"	turpentine	.25	.25
"	3	"	14 pounds alum	.06¼	.06¼
"	4	"	1 razor	1.25	1.25
"	11	"	1 coat	5.25	5.25
"	16	"	5 pounds tallow	.35	
			coffee	.25	.60
May	16	"	1 cake soap	.10	.10
"	18	"	1¾ pounds sugar	.25	
			1¾ pounds coffee	.25	
			1 ax	1.75	2.25

"	21	"	No. 6	.25	.25
"	22	"	1 sheet sandpaper	.05	
			sugar	.10	.15
"	29	"	1 hat	.50	
			linen	.10	
			bol. cloth	.12½	.72½
"	30	"	1 bonnet	1.50	
			1 veil	.75	2.25
June	12	"	powder	.10	.10
"	15	"	sugar	.25	.25
"	16	"	No. 6	.25	
			calico	.20	.45
"	20	"	2½ pounds cheese	.25	.25
"	22	"	cakes	.10	.10
"	29	"	tobacco	.10	.10
July	4	To	tobacco	.10	.10
"	7	"	tobacco	.15	.15
"	13	"	1 pipe	.06¼	.06¼
"	15	"	tobacco	.75	.75
"	18	"	shaving soap [?]	.06¼	.06¼
"	28	"	1 yard col. cam	.12½	.12½
Aug.	22	"	sundries	3.02½	3.02½
"	27	"	[?] for making vest	1.02	1.02
Sept.	3	"	1 pound soap	.12½	.12½
"	25	"	salt	.18¾	.18¾
"	28	"	thread	.10	.10
Octr.	3	"	making pants	.75	.75
"	13	"	1 vial B. oil	.10	.10
"	15	"	1½ pounds soap	.18¾	.18¾
"	24	"	shirting and coffee	4.00	4.00
"	27	"	salt	.75	.75
"	28	"	powder and lead	.18¾	.18¾
"	28	"	tallow and beeswax	.17½	.17½
"	31	"	tobacco	.25	.25
Novr.	6	"	tallow	.28	.28
"	?	"	1½ yards flannel	.60	.60
"	15	"	thread and cheese	.16¼	.16¼
"	18	"	for apples	.50	.50
"	21	"	flannel	1.63¾	1.63¾
"	24	"	salt	.75	.75
"	25	"	sundries	3.10	3.10
					$52.74¾

On the credit side of the ledger, it shows that between the dates of
June 25 and December 25 of 1846, Mr. Crisp brought in shoes and

boots he had made to pay off portions of his account. On December 25, 1846, he paid off the balance of $39.21 by an entry that appears to read "By Moore & shoes." We're not sure what that means unless Mr. Moore—presumably the Moore who owned the store—paid off part of the account for him (or forgave it) in return for something not listed. The amount credited to his account for the shoes he brought in was hardly significant. One credit line, for example, reads, "14 pr. coarse shoes, $4.90; 5 pr. shoes, $3.12½." He also got $4.50 worth of credit to his account for one pair of boots.

A survey of the books shows other types of goods that could be purchased at the store:

padlock	[$] .37½
curry comb	.20
5 pounds nails	.50
2 blank books	.60
1 bar lead	.10
smoothing iron	.30
pencil case	.62½
steelyards	2.00
overcoat	7.00
thimble	.06¼
bobinet	.62½
1 bridle	1.00
suspenders	.12½
chains	.87½
1 sythe [scythe] blade	1.75
½ gallon jug	.37½
1 frying pan	.40
1 gallon tar	.37½
1 girth	.25
ropes	.87½
soup plates	.50
scissors	.31¼
turkey red	.25
hymn book	.25
candlesticks	.40
1 sponge	.10
1 dictionary	.37½
1 shovel	1.12½
1 butter plate	.10
stirrup irons	1.25
pocket handkerchief	.70
1 bunch plow lines	.25

1 set teaspoons	.15
1 mill saw file	.40
spectacles	.50
saltpetre	.12½
castor oil	.25
1 mackinaw blanket	6.00
leggins	.75
mustard	.20
12 yards bed ticking	2.70
1 saddle	12.00
1 oz. red precipitate	.25
assafoetida	?
indigo	1.25
1 horse collar	1.25
lady's saddle	11.00
coffee mill	.75
hartshorn	.10
2 woolen cravats	.87½
pepper box	.05
bone buttons	.25
ribbon	.12½
camphor	.10
gun lock	1.50
whip	1.00
3 yards jeans	2.00
saddle bags	3.25
gloves	.15
quicksilver and pan	.97½
1 toothbrush	.12½
shoe brushes	.25
ink	.10
vest pattern	1.00
sifter	.50
wafers	.10
1 hand saw	1.50
1 spool thread	.10
matches	.06¼
1 Baptist Harmony	.75
1 Panama Hat	3.00
1 box hook and eyes	.12½
Borax	?
paregoric	.10
1 vial laudanum	.10

William Patton Moore

"In Grandpa's day, Grandpa Captain's day, he and his wife were great friends to ever'body. They wadn't nobody that they didn't recognize and . . ."

So begins Frank on William Patton Moore—Captain Irish Bill as he was called. He was probably the most flamboyant of the Moore family, and most noted for his rank as a Rebel captain during the War Between the States. This section, as told by Frank Moore, starts with his background so that you can get a feel of life at that day and time:

The Gashes are my grandmother's side of the house. Her daddy was Tom Gash and her name was Hattie. They lived out in Henderson County, North Carolina. The Gashes were prominent people.

There was five or six children. When Grandma was a child, something got wrong with her parents and one of them died, and just in six weeks, the other one died. So them kids just had to be scattered out. Grandma, she was raised by the Silers at Franklin, North Carolina. They was prominent people of Macon County—some of the wealthiest people over there. They kept slaves.

She was well raised, and when she married Grandpa, they moved over here. She never had had to work. They built a log cabin right up yonder. They just had two windows in it. She went to raising children and housekeeping, and I've heard her tell she washed on a washboard and she was real tender. She just busted blisters and her hands would bleed. She made one of the finest women in the world. Raised ten children and, brother, they wanted for nothing. She worked day and night. She could knit faster than a dog. She'd just knit and talk a subject and go right on, just a-knittin'. It was a sight.

They gave Irish Bill his nickname in the army. He joined the army back when that Civil War started. They was a-callin' 'em in, and one day they called him. At the time, he was a-buildin' a road. He had a contract and was buildin' it across Tusquittee Mountain going to Buck Creek. That road went straight across there. Him and Herbert had a contract on that road, and they was a-buildin' that when the war started. And he was workin' a great bunch a' men on that Tusquittee Mountain there, and they come up and told him that he'd been called to the army. And he told his men on the road, so they took their tools around under the crook of the mountain there and dug a hole. They had a big hole in there that they kept their tools in and they just went

and stored all the tools in there thinkin' that he'd get back, or somebody would, you know, but he never did get back to the road.

He joined the army and he stayed a year, and they liked him and
they sent him back into the county here to enlist a regiment. He come
back here and he got up a big regiment of cavalrymen, and he went
back and he stayed in the war with his men till the war was over. And
when the war was over, he paid his men off. He was down in Tennessee a-fightin' the Yankees and they didn't have no telephone or
nothin', and two weeks after they'd done declared it over, he was still
a-fightin'. He hadn't got the word that it was over. He was still
a-fightin'. They told him that the war was over. That they was defeated. And they said, "Now you'll have to muster your men out any
way you can get 'em out." Says, "We've got no way of takin' 'em
home, no finances of no kind. You'll just have to muster 'em out and
let 'em go any way they can."

He finally come on in home hisself. He brought his horse and his
saddle out of the army, and he had 'em here.

The war was just over and they hadn't set up no law and order, and
they was roughriders. The country was just full a' people a-goin'
through robbin' each other and takin' whatever they could get. And
my granddaddy and some of the boys was up towards Tusquittee
Bald, deer huntin'. Them roughriders come down the road here just
takin' stuff at every house as they come, and they come down by here,
and stopped at my grandma's and they took a lot of things out of the
house. He had a gold watch and they took it. Went down to the barn
and they took his horse and saddle out of the barn and took it on with
'em and went on down in the country.

Well, he was gone a day or so, and when he come back, he found
out about what had took place—roughriders. Well, he got on another
horse then, and he decided he'd overtake 'em. He went way into
Georgia somewhere, and when he got there, they captured him. They
just took him too. And they held him for a week or so. They just took
him in the crowd. And he said after so many days he persuaded them
to give him back his army horse and his saddle and he brought it back.
He never did get his watch, though.

Now when Hattie and Irish Bill first come in here, they had built a
little log house up behind this one [that I live in now]. And then they
built this house later. They built the log house to live in while they
were building this one. The date when they built this house is on the
chimney out there. Actually, I think the house was built maybe a year
before he built the chimney. I believe it says 1870. Jim Dodd built the
house. He went through the country building houses just like this

PLATE 44 Irish Bill on his horse, Dixie, in front of the Macon County, North Carolina, courthouse.

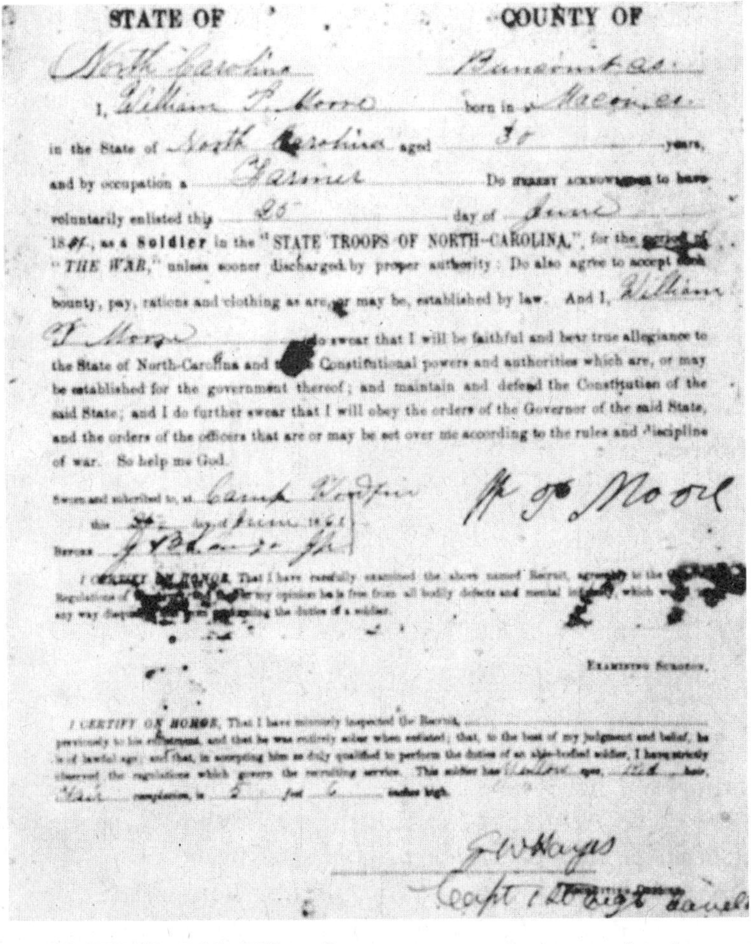

PLATE 45 Irish Bill's enlistment papers, drawn up when he joined the State Troops of North Carolina on June 25, 1861.

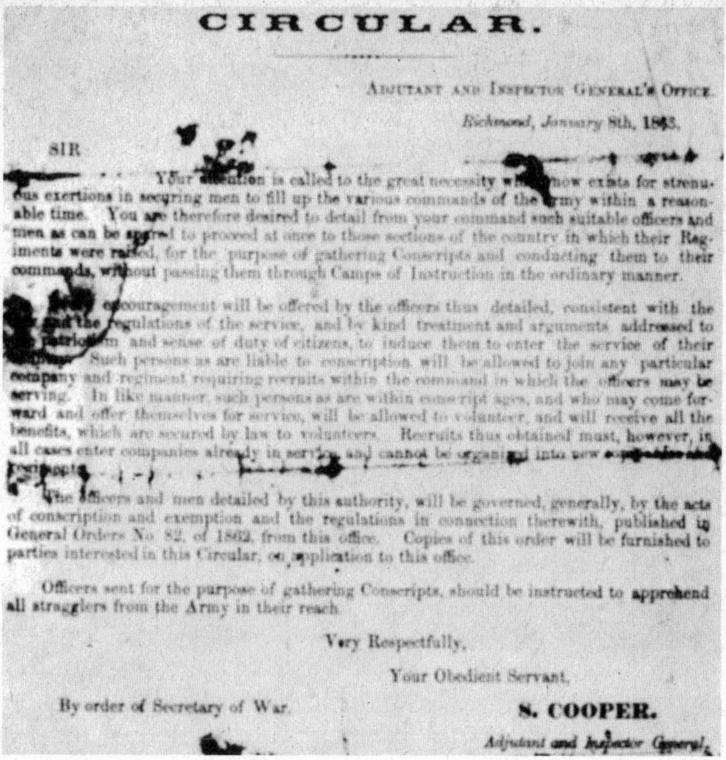

CIRCULAR.

ADJUTANT AND INSPECTOR GENERAL'S OFFICE.

Richmond, January 8th, 1863.

SIR

Your attention is called to the great necessity which now exists for strenuous exertions in securing men to fill up the various commands of the army within a reasonable time. You are therefore desired to detail from your command such suitable officers and men as can be spared to proceed at once to those sections of the country in which their Regiments were raised, for the purpose of gathering Conscripts and conducting them to their commands, without passing them through Camps of Instruction in the ordinary manner.

Every encouragement will be offered by the officers thus detailed, consistent with the law and the regulations of the service, and by kind treatment and arguments addressed to the patriotism and sense of duty of citizens, to induce them to enter the service of their country. Such persons as are liable to conscription will be allowed to join any particular company and regiment requiring recruits within the command in which the officers may be serving. In like manner, such persons as are within conscript ages, and who may come forward and offer themselves for service, will be allowed to volunteer, and will receive all the benefits, which are secured by law to volunteers. Recruits thus obtained must, however, in all cases enter companies already in service, and cannot be organized into new companies and regiments.

The officers and men detailed by this authority, will be governed, generally, by the acts of conscription and exemption and the regulations in connection therewith, published in General Orders No. 82, of 1862, from this office. Copies of this order will be furnished to parties interested in this Circular, on application to this office.

Officers sent for the purpose of gathering Conscripts, should be instructed to apprehend all stragglers from the Army in their reach.

Very Respectfully,

Your Obedient Servant,

By order of Secretary of War.

S. COOPER.

Adjutant and Inspector General.

PLATE 46 A document found among Irish Bill's papers which asks officials and enlisted men to help recruit additional men from their home areas for the South.

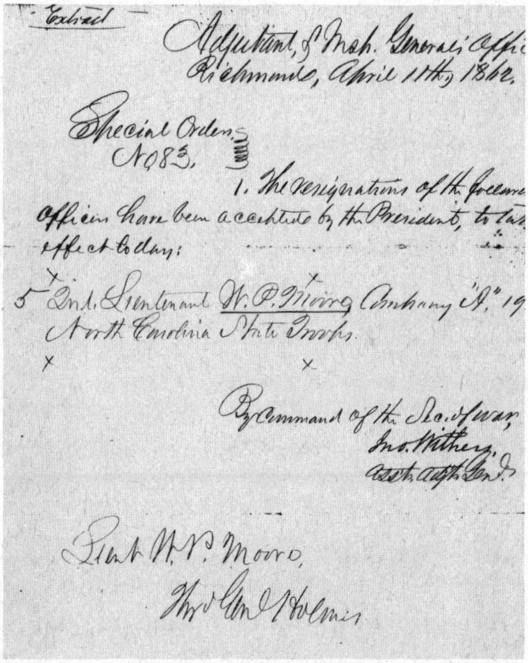

Extract

Adjutant & Insp. General's Office
Richmond, April 11th, 1862.

Special Orders
No 83.

1. The resignations of the following officers have been accepted by the President, to take effect today:

5 2nd. Lieutenant W. P. Moore Company "A" 19 North Carolina State Troops.

By command of the Sec. of war,
Jno. Withers
Asst. Adjt. Genl.

Lieut W. P. Moore,
Thro Genl Holmes

PLATE 47 Irish Bill's resignation from his North Carolina troop.

one. Later he went on into town an' built the Poss house and then went on into Tennessee building.

Jim Neal built these rock chimneys. They're beautiful chimneys, you know. Built out of pretty rock. You just don't see such chimneys in the country anymore. Just as straight as a shingle. Looks like they've been carved. They'd just come through here and build them for whoever wanted them to. I remember when my granddad got it built. I heard my daddy tell about it. And when he went to have it painted, he had a man come from Asheville. He gave the man a horse as payment.

[As I was saying before, Hattie really started a different kind of life when she first moved in here.] Lots of women would've just thrown up their hands and quit but they say she'd wash till the blood came out of her hands and was happy with it. All through the years she never allowed that she knit all the socks them days. She even knit socks for the doctors.

Grandpa had two hundred head of sheep and two hundred head of hogs in the mountains. He'd keep the sheep in the summertime, but the hogs stayed in the mountains until the fall of the year. Then they'd come in here with bells on 'em. He had his hogs well trained and in the spring of the year they'd leave; at that time they was worlds of mast—chestnuts and acorns—and them hogs would leave out and they'd go to Fines Creek across the mountain and they'd stay all summer. In the winter, then, it would get rough, and then one day you'd hear bells a-coming and they'd come right back in here.

I don't remember his mark but our [stock identifying] mark was a crop and an underbit in the left [ear]. That was put on record at Hayesville. If you caught anybody with your stock and your mark, you could go and bring the law on them. And any stock in the mountains over six months old with no mark on it, you could go and shoot 'em down and catch 'em and bring 'em in. But if they had a mark on 'em you had to watch 'em 'cause that [meant they belonged to someone].

They were pretty prominent. At that time there wasn't but one road out of here and they called it the turnpike back in that day. When they came in here for court at Hayesville—lawyers, judges, solicitors and everything—they would come this way with oxen. There wasn't any cars. They'd come across Chunkie Gal Gap, and when they came by here they'd spend the night. This home was pretty nice then. Captain Irish Bill and Hattie didn't turn anybody down. They kept everybody that came through for court. They would stay all night and go back to Franklin. And when I bought this house, the front of it was literally covered up with prominent names. Judges, solicitors, law-

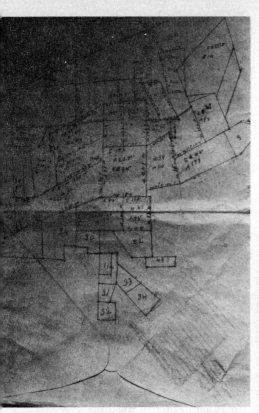

PLATE 48   An old land plat, drawn on the back of a manila envelope, shows the piece of land (Lot 38) on which Irish Bill and Hattie built their house.

PLATE 49   The house Irish Bill and Hattie built was inherited by Frank and Nannie Moore. She still lives in it today.

PLATE 50   The date 1887 is still visible on the chimney.

yers, surveyors: everybody in the world had signed their names there. There was hundreds of them. Sometimes they'd come in here and survey land and maybe stay here for a week too. People like that would all stay here. Had fireplaces upstairs, you know, and bedrooms.

Irish Bill had one stud horse called Crockett that was noted all over this country. Since Irish Bill was a captain in the cavalry, he was a great rider. He'd go to Hayesville to the hotel there and stay all day. Then, of the evening when he'd go to come home, he'd get that ol' Crockett out and he'd ride through town just as hard as that horse could fly. Sometimes they'd put a handkerchief on the ground there in the square and he'd come down with that horse at full speed and swing off and pick that handkerchief up, and that horse just a-running as hard as he could run. Then he'd come on into Tusquittee. He was a noted rider. He was born and raised with horses. That's all he knew.

Grandpa also had a whaling big barn down there and he kept a lot of race horses. He kept stock. Had a jack and a stud horse. He'd breed all over the country. He'd go to Nantahala, to the flats and everywhere, and stand a stud horse and a jack. Found the license the other day. You have to have a license to stand a jack. He kept a big fine stud horse.

People them days all rode horses, and he had room for their horses and stock. They'd put their stock up and stay a week at a time.

One time him and Doc Ledford got into it up in the cove over the line. They fell out over that line, and Doc was a big man. He was a fighter and liked to fight. Granddaddy, he was a little feller and he wasn't afraid of nothing, but he knowed Doc would get the best of him if he tried to fight him.

So there was this fence that Granddaddy'd move back over the line, and then Doc'd move it back, and then Granddaddy would move it back over. He went up one day and Doc was a-movin' it back over, and Granddaddy was a-ridin' Crockett, and he tried to run Crockett over Doc, and he was just a-makin' Crockett run all over him too. He had a Jacob's staff with him to hold a compass. They stick it in the ground and put your compass on it, you know. For land measurin'. And the lower end was sharp, you know, and he got to gougin' ol' Crockett in the side with that! They didn't never get that line settled. They had one line up there that they *did* get settled but that one line there they never did. And then Doc finally left here. They was neighbors right close to us there. They left here and went into Tennessee.

Another time they brought in a bunch of Western mares here into Hayesville, and Tom Streamer bought one of 'em. It was an outlaw,

PLATE 51   Standing, left to right: William Patton "Irish Bill" Moore;
his daughter, Hattie Virginia ("Jennie"), who married Frank Nolan of
Macon County, North Carolina; his youngest daughter, Nannie Elizabeth Kate, who married Clarence Smith; his daughter, Marthey Adelaide
("Addie"), who married Burt Slagle; Henry Moore (brother of J.V.A.
Moore, a historian of Clay County), who married Irish Bill's daughter,
Margaret Roxanna Moore; Minnie, who married Irish Bill's son, John,
who became a lawyer in Miami; Jim, one of Irish Bill's sons, who died
with fever at the age of eighteen; Caledonia Ledford ("Donie"), Frank
Moore's mother; John Moore, the lawyer married to Minnie; an uniden-
tified person not part of the family; May Rosebud Moss who had married
Irish Bill's son, Allie Gash Moore.
    Middle row, left to right: Harriet ("Hattie") Naomi Gash, Irish Bill's
wife; John Allen ("Jay") Moore on Hattie's lap, son of Margaret Roxanna
and Henry Moore; Margaret Roxanna Moore with her daughter, Hattie
May, on her lap; Irish Bill's son, Lawrence Richardson Moore, Frank's
father; Hubbie Ruth Moore, Lawrence Richardson Moore's daughter;
Edna Sallie Moore, another daughter of Lawrence Richardson Moore;
Allie Gash Moore with his daughter, Gialia Belle, on his lap.
    Seated on the ground, left to right: Ira William, Mattie Ellen, and Paul
Henry, all children of Margaret Roxanna and Henry Cornelius Moore.

and there wasn't nobody in this country that could ride it. It was the
awfullest outlaw you ever saw. So Grandpa told Tom to bring her
over. Says, "I'll ride her." Tom, he lived across the creek, and they
came up the road with her and a great crowd had gathered to see him
ride that Western mare. French Cabe lived down on the hill with his
wife Mary. Somebody told Mary that they was bringing the horse for
Grandpa to ride. He was fifty or sixty years old then, getting on up
there, but he was going to ride her. Mary saw what was going on and

sent one of the kids up here and told Grandma what was taking place. Grandma met them out there and she run 'em off! She wasn't going to have him get killed on that old Western mare. So instead they tied a sack of turnips on her with ropes as tight as they could get 'em, and she pitched and she bucked till the juice run out of them turnips, just like water! As long as that horse lived she never was broke.

The race horses Granddaddy raised was all so high-strung he couldn't work 'em well. My daddy had a team of mules, and Grandpa had a garden near here, and one day he wanted to plow his garden. He didn't work too much then as he was in his eighties by now, but he wanted a mule and he come t' get one of our mules. We just had to step out of the field and give him the mule, and he brought it out there and worked an hour or two and put it in the stable in his barn. The barn had racks in the back end of it to feed the horses, and it had a big trough. You had to go in by the horses to get to the trough and he had rows of race horses that he'd raised. He'd move in by 'em to feed 'em in the troughs behind.

[When he came over], we had tried to get him to take our gentle mule. The other mule was mean, and if he thought you was going to whip him or something, he'd kick you. But Granddad wadn't afraid of nothing. He said, "I want that mule," meaning Old Rubin, the mean one. The other one was Kingbolt. He brought Rubin down and went down in the field and plowed about an hour. Then he tied him up to a tree and went over to the creek and fished. He took an old sheepskin with him, and he laid down on the sheepskin when he finished fishing and took a nap.

Along about dinnertime, he come back and fed the mule in the stable, and he always carried his corn in a big half-bushel split basket —the kind that you used to hang on your arm—and he carried his corn in that. He went in by that mule to feed him the corn, and when he got in even with him, it scared the mule and he just whirled around and went to kickin'. Kicked Granddad into the trough and broke his ribs and he took pneumonia and died. He was as strong as he could be, though, and probably would have lived way up into the nineties if he hadn't gotten killed then.

Grandpa lived through some rough times. After the war, he used to carry the mail from Hayesville to the Wayah Gap. He carried it on a horse and met somebody from Franklin at the Wayah Gap, and they'd take the mail on and he'd come back. He said sometimes he'd cross the mountain and run up on big bears and his horse'd try to run away with him. He couldn't do nothing with it. There'd be bears across the road and his horse'd be afraid of 'em.

Macon County was home for Grandma and him too, and sometimes he would take the children and they'd go across Tusquittee Mountain and through the Wayah Gap to Macon County to visit their people. He was very much of a daredevil. He wadn't afraid of nothin'. And the Nantahala River is a river that's clear—even when it's up, it's clear. You can't tell hardly when it's up, for it's just clear all the time. He was a-comin' across this way one time from Macon County, and he come over there to the Monday Place where you had to ford the Nantahala River. It was a big wide ford and I've forded it many of a time. It had come a awful hard rain on the head of the river and he didn't believe it was up that high. He knew it was up, but he thought he could make it anyhow. He drove his wagon into the river and he got about halfway in, and it washed one of his horses under the tongue, and the other'n fell back over the tongue and they both drowned right there in the middle of the river. He was settin' there, water about to take his wagon down, and the horses both drowned there. He had to cut 'em out of the harness and just let 'em go on down the river.

Tryin' times he had in them days. That was way back in the days when it was wild.

Below we have reprinted, as written, a letter that Frank has in his collection. It was sent to Irish Bill while he was serving in the War, but because the letter is incomplete, we do not know who it is from. Since it was sent from Tusquittee, however, it must have been from a member of his family.

"Tusquittee Mar 10th /62
"Dear Will:
I will now answer yours of the 28th Jan, which I recd. some days ago. I am a slow hand to write letters, and it may take me two or three nights to finish. Your Pa & Addie has been over to see us. Staid nearly two weeks, went home last Saturday. When I wrote you before I stated that I had sold 8 head of Hogs at 9 cents gross, 1084 lb, which amounts to $97.56. Henry Brown paid me $50 when he got the Hogs, and promised I should have the balance in a few days, in the mean time your Pa called on me for $20, which I of course let him have, which left me $30, and which I still have. Henry Brown did not pay me the balance as he promised to do, but give it to Frank Brown, and he seemed disposed to retain it on a note he holds against you; it run on so, till week before last, when he paid the money to your Pa. So your Pa had $67.56 of your Hog money. You see then it will be but

little stock I can buy with $30, even if it was in the county to sell, and I tell you it is very scarce. Hogs & cattle are remarkably high for this county. If I had had any idea the Browns intended to act as they did, Henry should have paid me the money before he drove the Hogs off, but I thought he was a gentleman and would do what he said. I am satisfied now that it was an understanding with Henry & Frank, to retain the money on that debt. I was a little mad about it, but as the fellow said, I had a "poor way of helping myself," but as the money has been paid to your Pa I suppose it will all be right, enough on that subject.

"We had the coldest weather last week that has been this winter, rain wind and snow plenty. This week begins a little warmer, but still wet, bad weather on farmers, as well as soldiers, but I guess it is worse on soldiers. I have plowed some, would have been nearly done braking up, but for the rain. Your Pa sold Chaimbers 15 Bu corn & 10 Bu oats on your debt. Paid I. Alexander also in corn.

"Excuse my awkwardness, for you will observe, the 3rd page is the fourth one in this letter.

"All your stock looks well. Ben & Marge are mean as ever and fat enough for beef. There is only seven Hogs left, including the spotted sow. She has seven pigs. The Teauge sow was about on the lift when I came here, and I put her up fatened and sold her. She brought 12.96 by weight. We lost two sheep, one died and the other is lost strayed or stolen. The rest are up, and have 5 lambs. They are very troubelsom won't stay over the creek, nor any where else long if they can help it. I have hauled them over the creek twice this winter, and they came back, both times. I have to side line them to keep them off the rye. Gramp wont stay with us at all lately he has took up quarters at J. C. Moores.

"As for making the saw-mill pay, that is out of the question, while Rose has controle of it. He is not the kind of a man to make any thing pay, but I can tell you what he can do, and will do, he will swindle you out of many dollars, worth of plank. The Mill is in fine order now Rose got a man to fix it up, by the name of Woods, and he fixt it right.

"I have not paid any more tax money nor don't intend to untill the matter is investigated, instead of geting it scaled down from $25, (which we thought was too much,) they have increased it to 31 or 2 Dollars, we will have it attended to at June Court, if they don't try to force collection before then. Believe I did not tell you in my last letter that Sir Walter Teauge had moved back to Nantahala. Hiram Sisk is living where Teauge left, he is good sort of an old fellow, a good hand to work, he has one son & two or three girls able for the field and I think if he can get enough to live on will make a good crop, but he has nothing only as he works for it, he is plowing old Darkey and I am plowing old Ray. Marion has been with us all winter but your Pa talks like he will have to take him home, this Spring, if he does I will have it all to do, for I tell you there is no body to hire, that I can hear of. Sisk will help me some but he can't help much and tend his own crop. I will do what I can though and the balance must ly over."

Below, we have reprinted a newspaper article which Frank has in his scrapbook. Since it was cut out, we do not know what paper it appeared in or the date.

> "Capt. William Moore's Indian Fort
> Of '76 Stood on Present Enka Site

By Rachel Dyas

"What do you suppose the spirit of Captain William Moore would say if that intrepid old Indian fighter and Revolutionary soldier could rise from his solitary grave on a ridge near the Sand Hill school, stand overlooking his beloved Hominy valley and see the snorting steam shovels and panting engines scooping out and leveling the valley where his Indian fort, the first west of the Blue Ridge stood, and which will soon be covered by the gigantic buildings of the Enka rayon plant?

"From Indian fort to vast industrial development in less than one hundred and fifty years, is the history of the Hominy valley, one of the oldest cultivated spots in this section. The first Indian fort, the establishment of which made possible the settlement of Asheville and a dozen other communities, really stood where the new Enka rayon plant will stand.

"The great plant which will really cover the exact spot where the fort stood, by the old Indian trail. And will cover many another fair acre beside for its vast buildings are expected to spread over 75 acres when completed in about 18 months.

"Captain Moore is really buried on a ridge of land overlooking the valley where men and mules, engines and steam shovels now make a moiling hive of activity. Captain Moore has rested there since Nov. 6, 1812, as his headstone above the grave records. He was 86 years old, a Revolutionary soldier and six years older than George Washington.

"Perhaps the old pioneer would not have been so shocked at the boiling activity in Hominy valley. He was himself a man of great enterprise and courage as his exploit in transporting himself, his sons and his daughters and their husbands and wives and children, slaves and cattle into a hostile savage land, and subduing it despite the rigors of nature and the attacks of the Indians, proved.

"It is reported by legend that taking part in the campaign of Rutherford in 1776 against the Indians in which a number of the savages were captured, Captain Moore purchased the unfortunate Indians, and kept them as slaves. The auction was said to have been somewhere near Candler as the party was returning.

"When Captain Moore drove the first wagon that crossed the French Broad river up the old Indian trail into Hominy valley that was the main route between the settlements to the east and the country that later became Tennessee. It was only an Indian trail, but it was the only road, the highway, and all the important men of the day, who later went into and conquered the west stopped there for a visit with Captain Moore. It was the last outpost in civilization, the last frontier, for many years.

"The grant for Captain Moore's land was signed by North Carolina's first constitutional governor, Richard Caswell. A descendant, Mrs. T. P. Gaston, who lived always on the farm which has descended through the family to her and which was sold to the Enka rayon plant, now has that grant. It was the first grant of land west of the Blue Ridge dated 1787 and was made when what is now Buncombe county was a part of Burke county.

"Captain Moore's descendants in Buncombe county can probably be numbered by the hundred, for he was twice married and had many children. Mrs. Gaston, and her brother, Judge Walter Moore, William G. Candler and Mrs. Mal Lindsey, of Candler, are among the descendants and there are many others.

"A most picturesque figure of Buncombe history was one of Captain Moore's sons, Billy Moore, who was a famous prize fighter, never defeated in the rough and tumble contests of that day, and for whom the creek that runs directly beside the rayon tract is called "Billy Moore creek."

"The first fort in this section stood there. In eighteen months or more a great industrial plant covering 75 acres will be humming with the roar of business, where not more than 150 years ago only the stealthy Indian trod. But that is America."

Lawrence Richardson Moore

Lawrence Moore was especially interesting because, toward the end of his life, he wrote down what he knew of his family and Tusquittee. The map reproduced here is one fascinating example of his record. Drawn on a manila envelope, it locates the 125 homes in the Tusquittee Valley. As was typical then, he knew most of the families. Occasionally, however (as in space 31), the word "strangers" appears —apparently someone who moved in from the outside. Frank told us about him:

William Moore's second child, Lawrence, was my daddy. He was a farmer, a merchant, and a blacksmith. That was the way he made his living. When he was first married, he didn't have nothing. Started out with nothin', and he borrowed his daddy's scissor-tailed coat to be married in. Didn't have a dime and he married in his daddy's long-tailed coat. Then they went to housekeeping. I've heard him tell it. They didn't have dishes to eat out of. They just eat out of what dishes they could get. They just didn't have anything.

And along at the time, they began to build a little house up on the hill. They didn't have it completed. It was just a two-room boxed house; they had the top on it, and they had it weatherboarded and the windows in, but they didn't have no partitions in it yet. He was a great church man, and the Methodists was havin' a big quarterly meetin' and my daddy invited 'em, you know—not thinkin' that they would go with him—to come over and stay all night with 'im, and they just took him up on it. And when he got up where him and Momma was buildin' their house, they had no partitions between the rooms, so they took quilts and made a partition so that he and Momma could stay in one part and them in another. Now they done that. That was how poor they was when they started.

And then, through the years, he began to make it all right. He farmed a long time. Raised cattle. And then he put up a store, and he run a store for fifteen or twenty years. He was runnin' a blacksmith shop with it, and he shod horses for all the boys. The doctors of the county'd come and he'd shoe their horses, you know, and he accumulated land and become one of the biggest landowners nearly in the Tusquittee Valley. In other words, he prospered all through the years, and he was one of the biggest landowners, nearly in the Tusquittee Valley, when he died.

He was a great man for education. He believed in education. He schooled his children as far as he could. And out of fourteen grandchildren, twelve of 'em finished college with a B.S. and some of 'em with a masters. Twelve out of fourteen of his grandchildren finished college. Nobody in the county'd ever had a bigger record'n that of children that finished college.

The following is a list of names accompanying the map:

2 David Shelton
3   Dean
4 Bill Daley
5 Bell Evans
6 Crocket Evans
7 John Chubs
8 Jim Moore
9 John Moss
10 New Moon
11 Lucy Stamey
12 Butler Stamey
13 Cress Moss
14 Baptist Church
15 Will Ledford
16 Henry Garison
17   Garison
18 Elmer Nichols
19 Ben Philipps
20 Walter Sannons
21 Charlie Cane
22 Denman Cothren
23 Frank Moore
24 Virge Eller
25 Lenard Smith
26 Methodist Church
27 Billie Moore
28 Carl Chubs
29 Paul Truell
30 Odell Parker
31 Strangers
32 Lawrence Moore
33 Tila Carter
34 Cliston Parker
35   Parker
36 Harley Daley
37 Osker Ashe
38 John Mosteller
39 Elee Stillwell
40 Ray Stillwell
41   Cothren
42 Pet Daley
43 Peck Mosteller
44 Bud Mosteller
45 Ray Mosteller
46 Shunk Mosteller
47 Pat Paterson
   Nair Mosteller
   Lura Allison
   Henry Mosteller

PLATE 52   Frank told us about the plat above:

"My father drew this map in 1950. He was interested in everybody in this [part of the] country and he kept it up. He was natured that way.

"This map is a record of the early families of Tusquittee. He's showing you where all them people lived back in that early age, don't you see? And he's telling every house on every branch. It starts with the Hiawassee River [bottom right], and Tusquittee Creek branches off of that, and the houses he's marked are on the branches that run into Tusquittee Creek. You see, that would all be a lost thing if it wasn't for this map. That's history. It's gone without this, don't you see?

"Now the first creek setting in here, you see, that'll be Downing Creek. Then this next one will be Sandy's Branch here. Then you come on up and this is Good's Cove. And here's Peckerwood, and Perry Creek, and this branch here is named the Moore Branch, and . . ."

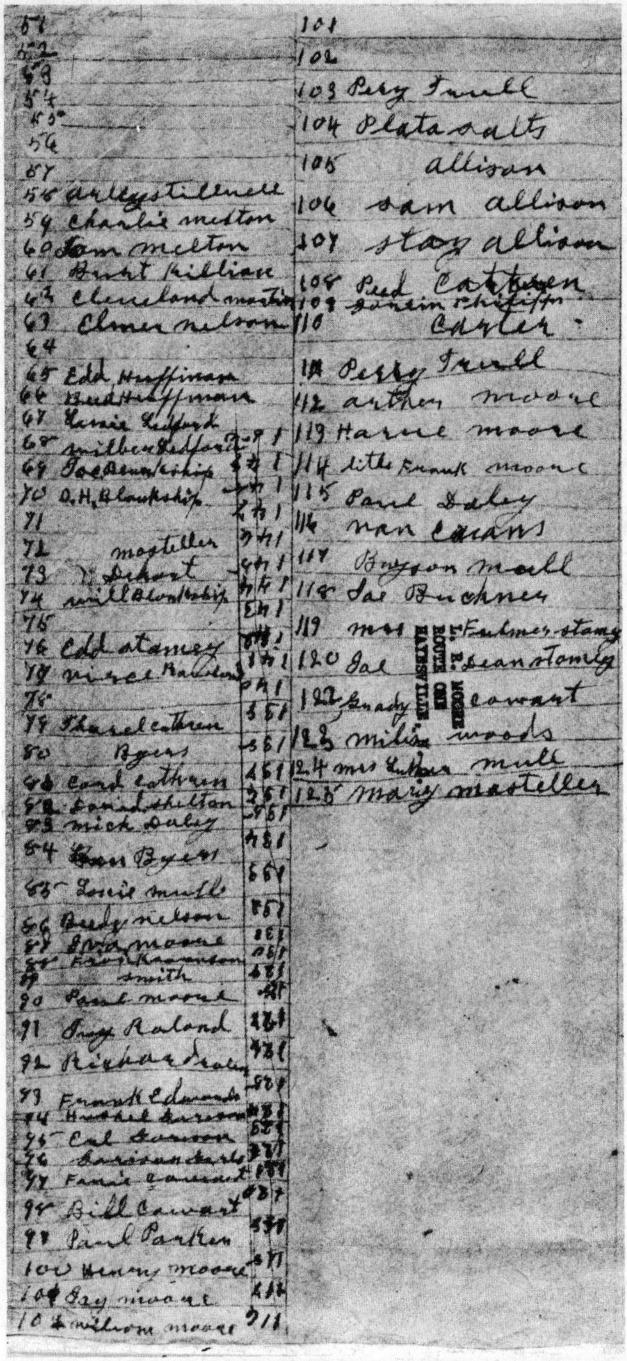

52	101
53	102
53	103 Perry Twell
54	104 Plata salts
55	105 allison
56	106 sam allison
57	107 stay allison
58 arley stillwell	108 Reed Cathren
59 charlie melton	109 garvin shelton
60 tom melton	110 Cayler
61 burt killian	111 Perry Twell
63 cleveland martin	112 arther moore
63 elmer nelson	113 Harvie moore
64	114 litle Frank moore
65 Edd Huffman	115 Paul daley
66 bud Huffman	116 nan cavans
67 Louie Seffort	117 Bryson mull
68 wilber Seffort	118 Joe Buchner
69 Joe Blankenship	119 mrs Fulmer stang
70 O.H. Blankenship	120 Jal Bean stang
71	122 grady cawart
72 mosteller	123 milia woods
73 J Sehort	124 mrs Luther mull
74 will Blankenship	125 mary mosteller
75	
76 Edd atarney	
77 virse Bailey	
78	
79 sharel cathren	
80 Byers	
46 cord cathren	
88 David shelton	
83 mick daley	
84 tan Byers	
85 Louie mull	
86 bud nelson	
87 Iva moore	
88 Frank harrison	
89 smith	
90 Paul moore	
91 Guy Raland	
92 Richard daley	
93 Frank Edwards	
94 Hushel Burson	
95 Cal Burson	
96 Burson charle	
97 Fanie cawart	
98 Bill cawart	
98 Paul Parker	
100 Henry moore	
101 Guy moore	
102 william moore	

PLATE 53

PLATE 54   Frank Moore told us about the barn in this photograph, in the process of being torn down when the picture was taken:

"That's my daddy's barn. He got Doc Groves to help him build it. Doc was an old-time carpenter, and he knew how to handle logs. He helped notch them.

"That was the prettiest barn when I was a boy that you ever saw. It was a beauty. It had a stall in each corner, a door at each end, and a space in the middle of each side, between the stalls, for storage. Then logs went on up about four feet above the stalls to make log bins upstairs for feed. Then a peak roof with a little vent house went on top. We kept pigeons up there."

Unfortunately, the barn passed out of the Moore family and was destroyed.

PLATE 55   A portion of one of the barn's sides.

Franklin Charles Moore

Frank Moore, my grandfather, here talks about his own life, as well as his concern for history. His son, Jerry, has inherited his interest in the family to the extent that he has had many of the more important documents carefully framed and hung safely on the walls of his Century 21 office in Conyers, Georgia.

PLATE 56   Frank Moore.

I went to school here at Tusquittee. The first school over there was a log hut with split logs for seats. That was where J.V.A. Moore started teaching. After he taught there, they built another one. I didn't go to the first log school, but the next school they built was the one I went to for years. Then they did away with it and built an improved building, and I went to school there till they disposed of it.

Back in them days, we would get up 'bout five or six grades and there wouldn't be no more grades, so Daddy sent us to town then; me and Charles went down there and batched and we'd come home on Friday evening. It was a two-story house, seven rooms upstairs and two downstairs. I quit going to school there after the eighth grade. I started the ninth grade and got into algebra and it got too much for me. Not long after I quit there, I married, and have been married fifty-six years. Started with almost no education, no nothing. Raised a family and sent four kids through college, and we've made it so far. Three of them teach and one of them is a pharmacist.

As a boy, back in my time when I was first growin' up, they wadn't no money hardly. We'd work for fifty cents a day. And when I got up big enough to begin to want money, you couldn't find a job or nothin'. I'd trap for fur. You could sell fur. It was low, but you could sell it. And I trapped a good long while. I learned how to grade fur by size and color. Opossum was three sizes: small, medium, large. Skunk was graded by color: black was the highest price of any polecat. Then there was what they called a "short stripe"—a white stripe right behind their neck down to the shoulder. Next grade of polecat was the "broad stripe." The white stripe ran plumb down to their tail. That was the cheapest. Then came the civet cat. The coons were graded by size like the opossum. They're number ones or twos or threes. You had to learn all that. Then we'd ship them to a company and they would grade them again and pay you accordingly. They would send out fur prices through the mail and we would buy them by that.

I got into fur business pretty big and finally got to be a pretty good fur buyer. Herbert Kitchens wanted me to go in with him. He came to see me and he said he would furnish the money to buy and let me do the buying. We would go in cahooters. We got into fur business pretty big. Then I would take them to an old fur man and he would ship 'em in sacks through the mail after they were stretched and dried. I worked with him till he got old and finally we quit.

After I was married, that was the only thing I had to accumulate any money to live on. I'd go coon hunting of a night. Sometimes I'd go for two or three nights. I'd come in and we'd have fifteen to twenty-five dollars' worth of coon hides. At that time it was big money, you know. They used to trap mink or muskrat with a deadfall. They'd just raise up a big rock that would fall and kill 'em. The coons lived in cracks in the mountains. The way to trap 'em was to leave a big hole in the log with a auger. Then take and drive horseshoe nails from all directions. Next take and put honey and butter in the hole. A bear loves honey and so does a coon. Then they'd come and eat and keep sticking their foot on in deeper. Finally, they'd raise it up and that would hang their foot and they couldn't get it out. Then you'd come up and shoot 'em.

I also loved to fish back before the Nantahala dam. I'd go to the river and I'd take some friends with me who were great fishers. I remember how they'd look down at the water from up on a ridge about a mile away and they'd tell whether the fish would bite or not. They could tell by whether the water was clear if it was gonna be good fishing time. They'd say, "Hey, we'll get 'em. That water's right." You could go down of an evening and that sun would go down and that water would be just speckled with trout a-jumpin'. I fished in there right up until they built the lake.

Before they built the lake, Andrew Melton came in here and tried to build a dam over there. He came over there on the Nantahala and tried to build a tunnel where it is now, and he got a way under there and somehow died or got broke or something. Didn't amount to anything. A few years later, they came in here and went through the same tunnel. It's the one that Andrew Melton started, but it's called the Nantahala. And that messed up our fishing in the river.

Frank C. Moore, my grandfather, has seen a lot of years. The wisdom he's acquired and the kinship he's shared with the settlers of Clay County has earned him a good name throughout the county. But this wisdom was no match for glib outsiders who again and again took advantage of his belief in his fellow man. Here he relates a couple of stories and leaves us with his feelings about living today:

I had one big pharmacy book, and away back somebody come along here and give me ten dollars for it, and I'll bet it was worth fifty. It was a great ledger from back years ago. Some feller come and just said, "All right, what'll you take for that book?" and I never thought much about it. He says, "I'll give you ten dollars," and I just let him have it. No tellin' what it was worth. That was somebody just out a-pickin' up stuff like that that knew what he was a-doin'. I sold a lot of things like that that I didn't know what I was a-doin' and Jerry just cleaned me up! That's my boy, you know. He found out they was a-takin' advantage. And I had a bunch of Indian relics that was worth a fortune and I let a feller just take 'em for nearly nothing. They've been in the Smithsonian Institute about ever since they left me. Finest collection of Indian relics you ever saw. And they sent a group of men here from Smithsonian Institute one morning—drove up right there and I was a-milkin', and they wanted to excavate my garden because they had those relics in the Smithsonian Institute up there. And I'd just sold 'em one or two at a time you know and never thought about keepin' 'em. Had a peace pipe, prettiest thing you ever saw. C. E. Curtis is the man that bought 'em, but he took 'em to Smithsonian Institute and displayed 'em, you know. He was over here when they was buildin' the dam and he found out I was a-gettin' some along, and he'd just slip in here and buy 'em as I'd find one every now and then. If I had 'em back, I wouldn't take a fortune for 'em. I had a spear that was awful long, and one side of it was flat, and the other side was kind of on a bevel, and it was out of right *slick* black flint and you could nearly cut [with it] like a knife blade, it was so sharp. I found a big Indian pipe, you know, that had a bear cut off at his shoulders here and his head was turned down and his nose and shoulders made the bowl of the pipe. Down at the point of it they was a hole in there that they'd swung something in at the lower end. Up here the stem come out and on top of that stem was a bar with three holes on each side of the bar. Prettiest thing you ever saw. And then I had one pipe that I found then that had a stem back here that had a big lizard a-layin' on there. Prettiest thing you ever saw. And I just let 'em go. They gimme about thirty-five dollars apiece. I guess you could plow it up and find more. At least that's what [the Smithsonian] men thought but it was in the spring of the year and I had my garden out. They'd a' really moved it if I'd a' let 'em.

Now last summer I was a-plowin' over yonder in the field and I got a big piece of pretty pot about as big as my hand where my plow had hooked it and jerked it off. Back when I was a boy, in the fall of the year when we'd plow these bottoms and it'd rain through the winter, you could go in there and they was just beads everywhere. You could just pick up every kind of bead, and they found a carved camel, you know, and all kinds of things. But you don't hear of much being found any more.

[The reason I've kept all the books and papers and photos I have kept is that] the old resident people have meant more to me than anything. I know of these people that Lawrence R. once spoke of, but they're gone to everywhere else. If it wasn't for these records here, they'd been a forgotten race of people. Grandpa told about all of them—how many children they had, their names and who they married. That means a great deal to my age, but to children under me it don't mean anything to them. To people my age and to people all over the country my age, that's the most important thing of the whole outfit is to remember these old people. It's just a background of the county here. Of our township.

In other words, if it wasn't for these writings here and the history of these folks, the age behind us would be gone. This here just keeps it brought up. It's important for the simple reason that that's the his-

PLATE 57   John Singleton took this photograph through the back of a rocking chair of his grandfather and Wig looking at some papers.

PLATE 58

PLATE 59   The Tusquittee Valley as seen from Frank's front porch.

tory of what went on. That's our county as it was, and without some of us knowing about it, why, the early part of the history of the creek is a dead issue. This keeps it alive to people of my age.

Back when I was a little boy, my daddy sold goods and they all come to the store; all these people he's talkin' about, I knew. I was just a little kid, but I knew them.

Now years and years from now, people that you'd heard about from all of my generation won't amount to anything if somebody doesn't keep a record of it for your children. Someone's gotta keep it alive.

I love to preserve history. It means so much to me now. All my childhood life—without preserving it—it's gone. I'm living in a new age. I'm living in a age now where I'm nearly a stranger in my own county. People's moving in here by the hundreds, and not twenty or thirty years ago I knew everybody in Clay County by name. Used to serve on the school board and every committee that's ever been in the county. Sold goods for twenty years right here and round about. But now I go out and I'm a stranger.

Without this history, you're losing out. If someone doesn't keep a record of it, you'll know nothing. These things have to be passed down or you lose out.

THE PATTON D. QUEEN STORE

During the early 1900s when the town of Mountain City, Georgia, was still called Passover, a tiny general store was owned and operated in that town by Patton D. Queen. This fact was brought to our attention by Jack Queen, a local resident who is the grandson of P. D. Queen and who owns several of the old store ledgers.

The store was no longer standing when Jack was born, so he could not tell us very much about it. He referred us to his aunt, Mrs. Ollie Queen Glore. Mrs. Glore was a young girl when her father, P. D. Queen, ran the Passover store. Her descriptions, along with a number of photographs she had and the store ledgers, helped us to piece together a short history of the store.

She told us: "My dad owned a little store at the foot of the hill where we lived at that time. The store was stocked with food and other items that the average family needed. Candy, gum, and soft drinks sold good."

The store itself was of wood construction. The interior consisted of

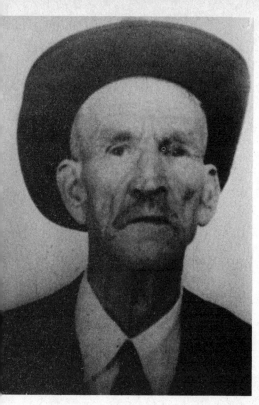

PLATE 60 Patton D. Queen, the owner of the store in Passover [now Mountain City], Georgia.

PLATE 61 The Queen family. Front row, left to right: Lamon, Hattie, Gervace, Annie, and Ollie Queen Glore.

Back row, left to right: Cecil, Ernest Glore (Ollie's husband), P. D. Queen, his wife, Ada, and Lizzie.

DEALER IN

DRY GOODS NOTIONS,
FINE GROCERIES
AND GENERAL MERCHANDISE.

Passover, Ga _____ 190__

Lamar & Rankin Drug Co,
                    Atlanta, Ga,

Gentlemen,

          Please send me by

mail 1 Doz Lamar's Mayapple

Liver pills,

          I enclose stamps

to pay for the pills   75 cts

          For postage   5

                              ──

                              80

and oblige

          Yours truly

          P. D. Queen

PLATE 62 A letter, showing the Passover return address, written by P. D. Queen to a supplier in Atlanta. The letter reads in part, "Gentlemen, Please send me by mail 1 Doz Lamar's Mayapple Liver Pills. I enclose stamps to pay for the pills . . ."

one large room. The store closed at dark because there was no electricity.

A ledger was used to keep account records. There was no cash register. What cash came in, Mr. Queen kept in his pocket. Mrs. Glore said, "Sometimes people would say, 'I'll pay you Saturday,' and Saturday never came."

Since money was scarce, there were several other ways of paying up one's account. Trading goods between store owner and customer was one option. Items traded included: hogs, wool, manure, syrup, rye, lumber, loads of wood, and coffee. Coffee was bought at the store green. If one's account needed paying one could resell green coffee to the store owner. Peaberry was the most popular coffee then.

Working for the store was another way of paying up an account. People received fifty cents for a full day's work. Jobs included: hauling logs, gathering corn, digging ditches, plowing, and planting. Sometimes people also bottomed chairs and received credit for that. These jobs were listed in the person's account as credits.

We went through each account in both of the ledgers that Jack gave us, and made a list of all the items sold in the store and their prices. By far, the most purchased item was tobacco. Other popular items were things that could not be grown or made, like candy, soft drinks, sugar, flour, and hardware.

The dates of both ledgers extended over nine years. In this time period there was little or no price change. Also, another sign of the times, very few women held accounts at the store.

Master List of Items Sold in the Store, as Written in the Ledgers.

January 26, 1898–October 10, 1907

chicken frye	[$]	.10
window hinges		.10
crank rollers		.40
stove chimeny		.35
cow and calf		23.00
elbow for stove		.20
hand saw		1.00
roping		.07
wagon tire		1.51
water bucket		.20
plow stock		2.25
turnip seed		.10

box sprigs	.05
butter (1 lb.)	.12
hog	2.25
shirt buttons	.05
jelly (2 glasses)	.25
comb	.05
pills	.25
union buttons	.20
grinding stone	.98
bought stove	10.00
fodder (1 bushel)	.01
whetrock	.25
brace and two bits	.84
drawing knife	.75
vermifuge	.20
gingham (1 yd.)	.06
diamond dyes (3 packs)	.30
coffee pot	.10
cane seed (2 bushels)	1.37
coppers (copperas)	.02
honey (2 lbs.)	.10
collars (2)	.15
tincture	.10
ball thread	.05
sulphur	.05
soda	.05
lamp oil	.13
shirt	.85
mutton	.50
potatoes (1 bushel)	1.80
meal	1.82
lard meat	.50
corn (1/2 bushel)	.40
flour (sack)	.75
sheeting	1.02
planking	4.25
pepper	.05
gun	4.00
oranges	.20
vassanater [fascinator]	.50
cabbage (17 lbs.)	.17
flannel	.60
spool thread	.05
syrup	.10
caster oil	.05

crackers	.05
sole leather	.27
soft drink	.05
tomatoes	.10
turpentine	.03
matches	.05
chamber pot	.35
bucket	.10
Japanese oil	.50
baking powder	.05
tobacco (1 box)	3.00
paper envelopes	.10
chewing gum	.05
Beau's caster oil	.20
sardines	.05
canned peaches	.10
dope drink [Coca-Cola]	.05
clock	1.00
oysters	.10
shoe polish	.10
stockings	.10
knife	.25
starch	.05
box candy	.25
hop ale	.10
pie pans (2)	.15
pins	.05
dipper	.18
needles	.20
worm syrup	.25
kerosene (1 barrel)	.85
Ramon's relief	.25
bluing	.15
mill file	.15
canned beans	.02
axel [axle] grease	.05
medicine	.10
pants	1.95
calico	.25
meat	1.35
shoes	1.50
paper	.05
cotton seed	.35
flour (50 lbs.)	1.50
wool	1.00

dressing plank	2.15
soap	.05
suspenders	.30
handkerchief	.10
seed corn (2 gal.)	.20
suit	10.50
bleaching (2 gal.)	.20
ham meat	1.00
snuff	.05
lard	.13
socks	.10
beans (1 peck)	.90
smoking tobacco	.05
potted ham	.05
ax	.70
healing oil	.25
goobers	.05
ginger ale	.10
carteridges	
[cartridges] (5 shells)	.10
wash pan	.13
gritter	.10
root beer	.10
dish soda	.35
soda crackers	.25
sweater shirt	.75
spice	.05
pencil holder	.10
log chain	2.25
chestnuts	.05
leather	.55
string leather	.03
rice	.15
salmon	.25
cologne	.10
pepper sauce	.10
tin cup	.07
scissors	.08
medicine powders	.25
cook stove	12.00
Batesman drops	.05
sheep	2.50
hoe	.40
cigars	.25

sifter	.10
knives, forks, spoons	1.10

We also made a list of the various items we found listed in the ledgers that were accepted as payment on accounts:

ham	[$] 1.53
mutton	.35
pork (23 lbs)	1.72
eggs (15 dozen)	1.05
corn (1/2 bushel)	.35
onions	.10
turnips	1.75
potatoes (1 bushel)	.50
beans (1/2 bushel)	.25
peaches (1/2 bushel)	.35
chestnuts (1/2 gallon)	.10
sauerkraut	.15
biscuit	.25
cabbage plants (2,000)	2.00
onion buttons	.30
tobacco (1 bushel)	.25
flour (1 sack)	.70
rye (1 bushel)	.60
fodder (20 bushels)	.30
butter (2 lbs)	.70
syrup	.15
oxen (1)	25.00
calves (3)	13.80
rooster (1)	.15
hogs (8)	10.00
wool	2.35
cloth (6 yards)	1.50
socks (2 pair)	.50
boards	.57
wood load	.50
work (1 day)	.40
work in ditch	.15

We made these lists straight from the P. D. Queen ledgers. There may be some discrepancies due to smudged handwriting, misspelled words, and lack of knowledge of how the ledgers were kept.

Some of the items sold in the store were things that we had never heard of. After we made the master list, we asked Mrs. Glore what they were:

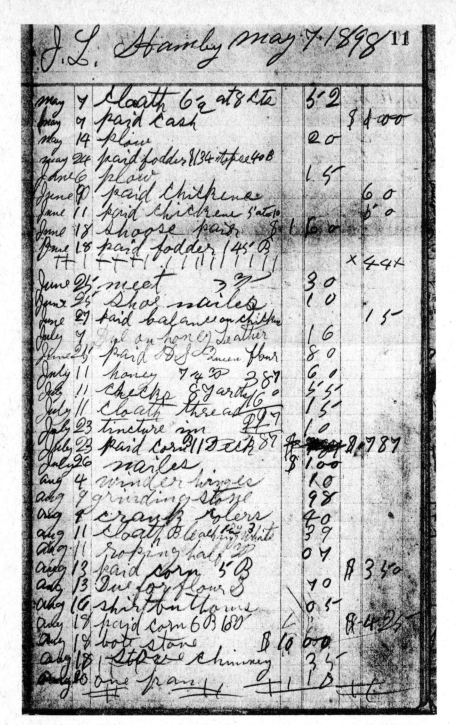

PLATE 63 This is J. L. Hamby's account. It was opened on May 7, 1898. The presence of nails, "winder" hinges, a stove, a stovepipe, a stovepipe elbow, a brace and two bits, a handsaw, a drawing knife, a whetstone, a plow, a shoe nailer, a grinding stone, some crank rollers, some rope, a pan, two tin plates, chickens, hogs, a coffeepot, and oil indicate that Mr. Hamby was probably setting up a homestead.

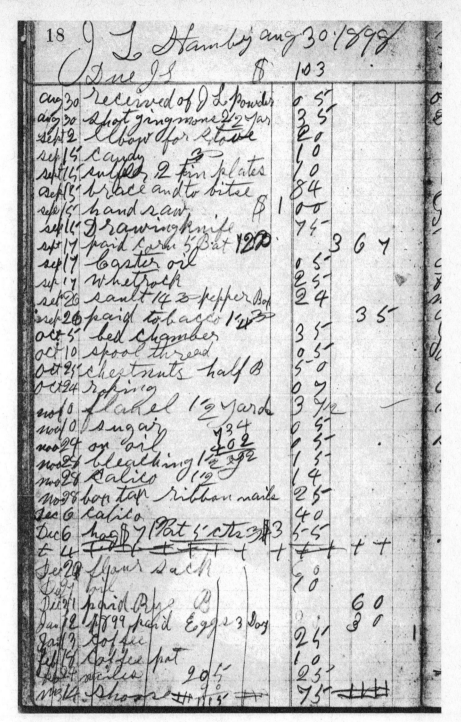

18   J L Hamby aug 30 1898

Due J S $ 10 3

aug 30	received of J L Powder	0 5		0 5
aug 30	shot gingmons 2 1/2 yar	3 5		
sep 2	Elbow for stove	2 0		
sep 15	Candy	1 0		
sep 16	sulfer 2 tin plates	1 0		
sep 15	brace and to bitse	8 4		
sep 15	hand saw $ 1	0 0		
sep 16	Drawing knife	7 5		
sep 17	paid corn 5 Bu	12 00	3 6 7	
sep 17	Caster oil	0 5		
sep 17	Whetrock	0 5		
sep 20	salt 14 3 pepper Box	2 4		
sep 20	paid tobacco 1 28		3 5	
oct 5	bed chamber	3 5		
oct 10	spool thread	0 5		
oct 2	chestnuts half B	5 0		
oct 24	raking	0 2		
nov 0	flanel 1 1/2 yard	3 7 1/2		
nov 0	sugar	0 5		
nov 29	oy oil	0 5		
nov 28	blealking 1 1/2	1 5		
nov 28	calico 1 19	1 4		
nov 28	bon tap ribbon nails	2 5		
Dec 6	calico	4 0		
Dec 6	hog 7 Pat 5 cts 3	5 5		
t 4		t t	t t	
Dec 20	flour sack	2 0		
Dec 21	mil			
Dec 21	paid Rye B		6 0	
Jan 12	1899 paid Eggs 3 Doz		3 0	
Jan 2	Coffee	2 5		
feb 6	Coffee pot	1 0		
feb 4	nailes	2 5		
nov 14	Shoos	7 5		

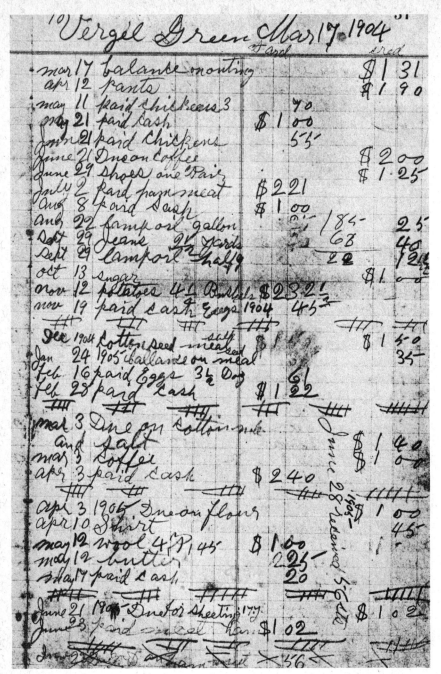

PLATE 65 This account, opened by Vergel Green on March 17, 1904, is more typical. It shows purchases primarily of coffee, sugar, salt, flour, lamp oil, and some clothing such as shoes, a shirt, and pants; and it shows payments made primarily with meat, chickens, eggs, and butter.

Japanese oil—a liquid medicine for headaches. "It came in a flat extract bottle. People would either rub the oil directly on their temples, or they would drink minute amounts with sugar water."

Vermifuge—a liquid medicine for worms. "It had a strong odor and a harsh taste. People never ate anything greasy after taking vermifuge because the grease would counteract the medicine."

Diamond dyes—a cloth dye. "It was poisonous and was used strictly for dyeing cloth."

Gritter—a snuffbox-shaped object with ragged holes punched in it. "It was used to grind spices like nutmeg and cloves."

Box sprigs—sprigs of rooted boxwood.

Fascinator—a crocheted, triangular shawl covering the head and shoulders.

We have included several pages from the ledgers to give some idea how the accounts were kept. One can learn things about a customer through his account. For instance, it is safe to assume that J. L. Hamby was building a house because of all the hardware, the wood stove and its fixtures, recorded in his account.

We learned another thing from the ledgers. If a person who did not have an account in this store came into the store to buy something without any money, he could charge it to a friend's account. It would be recorded like this: "coffee by Dellah Bets." Then this person would pay either the account holder or the store owner. Also, the store owner would lend cash directly to the customer. Then the loan was recorded in the ledger as a regular debt.

Article by Sarah Wallace

MARTHA AND ED ROANE'S STORE

Learning about the P. D. Queen Store made us curious about other stores of that era in Rabun County. We asked Martha and Ed Roane about the store they owned during the Depression in Tiger, Georgia. Martha began by telling us a little about her family, her childhood in the Persimmon community in Rabun County, and how she met her husband, Ed. [For the complete interview with Martha, see Foxfire *magazine, Winter 1983, pages 238–47.]*

Interviews by Tammy Jones, Tracy Speed, Sarah Wallace and Ronnie Welch. Photographs by Chris Crawford and Sarah Wallace.

We don't know much about this, but I think way back [my ances-tors] settled in Virginia. My father has always said that my great-grandfather Isaac then moved to Waynesville County, North Caro-lina, and then came on into Rabun County and settled in the Germany community. People didn't call that little valley up there Germany then, but some Germans later settled there and it was called Germany. My great-grandparents came in there and they built log houses with chimneys. They had I don't know how many children, and my grandfather was one of them. My great-grandfather bought one of the big land lots [that were available when Rabun County was opened up for settlement].

My grandfather, Andrew Jackson Justus, and his brothers and sis-ters divided the [land lot] up. Then later my grandfather went over on Persimmon Road and bought a land lot. He had eight children, four girls and four boys. My father was the oldest one.

I was born in Persimmon [community] on November 11, 1901. I had three brothers and one sister. I am the oldest. My brother-in-law's gone, but we were very lucky. Our family's all [lived to be] in their seventies. I'm beyond that now, four score and one, if you know what that means.

I was raised over on Persimmon in a nice log house. We had two big fireplaces, four rooms downstairs, and two stairways. They took these big wide planks and hewed them out and put them on the outside [when they built it]. Then they had to dress the big long planks and seal [the house] inside some. We had white oak floorings. We cleaned those floors with cornshuck mops and sand. [To make a cornshuck mop,] we'd pull tough cornshucks through a board with holes drilled in it. We'd just scrub with that sand and then sweep it out with brooms made out of straw. I remember when I was a little girl sweep-ing that house out.

We had a big old springhouse and troughs you could set your milk in. [There was a shallow trough for little dishes] and then a deeper one and a still deeper one for jars of milk and pickled beans and kraut. I never did care too much about pickled beans, but some of them liked them.

We had chores to do. [My parents] taught me and my sister to milk. Every one of the boys already knew. My daddy owned a mare and he'd raise colts. We had a gang of sheep. We sheared them for the wool [to make our clothes] and sold what wool we didn't need. We also sold sheep. Mother would wash the wool, card, spin, and weave

PLATE 66   Martha Roane.

it. She had a loom over the kitchen and I always wanted to do a little
[of the weaving], but she thought I'd tear it up. I would run the reel or
the spinner to make the hank. I have even worn the little homemade
skirts. [We wore homemade clothes] till about when we went to
school and then we got to where we could buy clothes [at the store].

Our family never was sick very much, but I had an earache a lot of
the time and it still bothers me some. My mother would make a hot-
water towel and put it on my ear and lay me in front of the fireplace
on a pallet. [That treatment] would help a lot. We did have some kind
of medicine drops for my ear but we didn't use them much, because
they were hard to get.

If you had a bad cold, they'd give you a dose of castor oil. That was
the meanest stuff I ever tasted. When we had the measles, and nearly
every child had 'em, my father would move a big bed in the living
room in front of the big fireplace and make us lay there. He made a
tea and he wanted us to drink that tea. I'd put it in my mouth and
when he got gone, I would raise up and spit it in the fireplace. I don't
know what kind it was, some kind of tea that would make us break out

[with measles] faster. My sister got *so* sick. She finally broke out with them measles and it was bad. We had to blind the windows because they said it would hurt her eyes for the light to come in. I said, "Oh, no, I don't want to be sick like her," so I finally drank that tea.

I first went to school over there [at Boiling Springs] on Persimmon. We weren't allowed to talk in class. Of course, there was still a lot of talking that went on. We had a recess about ten o'clock and then we'd have our lunches around twelve. We had to carry our lunches in little buckets. Henry, my brother, wanted to carry his alone, but my sister and I put ours together. We always had a lot of meats because our parents raised it. We'd take meat and a biscuit, and sometimes when sweet potatoes were in, we'd take them. We'd take milk along, too, and we could go in the springhouse and set our little jars of milk in there. They had built a great big springhouse over the Boiling Springs right there near the Presbyterian Church.

After school we had to walk home and we made it up not to eat much lunch and we'd have a picnic up where the roads tear (fork). One day our parents said we didn't get in at the time we should and they complained to the teacher. He decided to follow us one day and said, "I know now why you don't get home on time."

January the tenth, I never will forget. There was snow and ice on the ground. We moved in up Germany [community]. We left a good house and didn't find one as good as we had been used to, but anyhow we made it. Six or seven neighbors with wagons and all [helped us move]. There was snow and ice on Devil's Branch Road. [I know some of you have heard of it.] They'd get out with their mattocks and make little places for their horses to attach their feet and pull the load. I didn't know whether we'd get there or not, but we did.

I was in about the sixth or seventh grade when we moved up there and we went to Mount Grove Church for school. When I got ready for high school, we couldn't go to Clayton because it was too far to walk. There was no way to go except ride a horse. There was a preacher from Habersham County that came up to our church and he told us we ought to get in up at Rabun Gap School. They didn't have any room at that time but I was able to get in at Nacoochee Institute in White County [where students could board, and pay their expenses by working on the campus].

[After graduation, Martha studied education at the A & M School in Habersham County and received her teaching license.]

I started teaching in 1924. The first school [I taught at] was over by the Germany community out from Clayton. They called it Mountain Grove, and it was in a small church. We had desks for school, and on

PLATE 67 Martha Roane being interviewed in the Foxfire classroom. To her right is her grandson, Charles Dennis.

Friday we would just push them back out of the way and leave it for church on Sunday.

I was the only teacher. It was one room and it was heated by a wood stove. I had to come in and start a fire every morning. The boys would come in and help me. In the afternoons they would get everything ready for me to make a fire the next morning. There was just six months of school each year. School would start the latter part of August and went on to completion in December. We would have about twenty minutes for each class.

I went to Betty's Creek in 1925. There was a schoolhouse in the church there like in Mountain Grove. I think we had thirty-five or forty kids over there. When one of them got old enough and didn't want to go to school anymore, they could just drop out and they didn't have to go back. We would start about eight in the mornings and stay till about three-thirty in the afternoons. If it came a snow, we took off early because everybody had to walk home. The students wore heavy shirts in the winter. The boys would wear pants and those old wool stockings up to their knees and heavy shoes. The girls wore heavy wool skirts or dresses and they too would wear those old heavy stockings up to their knees. The girls wore laced-up boots. [All the children] pretty much had shoes to wear. If they didn't have shoes in the winter, they wouldn't come to school.

We had spelling bees each month, and we had tests on spelling. They had to pass a test with spelling on it to go on to the next grade. We had our lunch outside if the weather was good. They each had to bring their own lunch. They would bring milk with their lunch and would go down and put it in Betty's Creek to keep it cold. That year, 1925, was a very dry year. It got so dry the creek dried up and we didn't have any water to put the milk in to keep it cold. We had different people each day to carry water from way over on the mountainside. They would go get two or three jugs, or whatever they could carry, and bring it back to us. We had a big tub we would put the waste water in, and we would use it to sprinkle on the floor so it could be swept. That's how dusty it got. A lot of people were out of water. The timber on the tops of the mountains just turned brown and died. It was just terribly dry.

PLATE 68

Next I went to Tiger School in the middle of the year 1926. The school was located in the Cannon Hotel in Tiger. I was a third-grade teacher there. Mostly I taught third-grade reading. Sometimes, though, the teachers would want to change around—like, I might take the third and fourth grade math for a while. Ethel Williams and myself are the only two teachers left living [who taught at Tiger School]. She lives in California now.

None of the schools I taught at had inside bathrooms. Tiger School got running water and bathrooms before I left in 1928. At the other schools, we always had to build little outhouses for the students.

I remember when they were making the road through Tiger. They did it with horses and mules and big old scoops. Well, my third-graders would just be turning their heads out the window and saying, "They won't get that dirt out." I would have to try to keep them quiet.

You know, way back you could have prayer in school, and we had a large prayer group that would pray in the mornings.

I had a few students who were as old as I was, and some of them couldn't even read or write, no matter how hard I tried to teach them. They just couldn't learn it.

Cheating in school was bad. If they got caught cheating, it was marked off their grades and I had a conference with them and their parents.

When I taught up at Tiger, Ed had the store there and we'd go over there but I never thought anything about it. Then one day I went over there and he gave me a box of candy. A whole box. I thought, "Hmmm." I had to go to Center, Georgia, in 1928 to teach for a while, and when I got away he started writing to me. So there I was. The first of June, 1931, was the wedding. It wasn't a big wedding, just a little home wedding. Homely. I didn't want a big wedding. All that was there was the family, his close friends, and the preacher and his wife.

Our house was across from the store in Tiger.

We had five children, four boys and one girl. After they got up big enough, they'd work when they got home from school. When it was mowing time in the yards, they'd clean the yards. [When the corn was ready,] they'd go to gather it. During haying time, there wasn't hardly ever school. [They worked all day then.]

[Our children fed the cows and milked them.] Our son Louis would get up in the mornings and get his lantern and his bucket, and go out to milk. Then he would come in and get ready for school. Said he never would forget it [because it was hard work] but he was glad he did it. It made him strong to get out there and get the exercise.

We had a separator and we separated the milk and sold some of the cream and some of the milk to Nantahala [Dairies]. [They're now called Biltmore Dairies.] We would save some of that cream and put it in the refrigerator and have whipped cream. That separator was a mess to wash if you didn't get it before it dried. Whenever the boys got a little older [it was their job to wash it] and they dreaded that, but they did it anyway.

I quit teaching in 1934, although I substituted for teachers some in the 1940s and '50s. I guess the last time was in 1954. [I spent my time raising my family.]

But I've been around these stores all my life. My Grandpa Justus started running his store during the Civil War. He never even had a cash register. Just a strongbox. We didn't have banks until about 1903 and everybody had a hiding place for their money. He hid his money in a sealed closet in the chimney. He'd put it in there and you would never know it was there. Half the family knew about the closet, but I didn't. One day somebody wanted to change some money. Of course, Grandpa didn't let that man come in. He told him to come back later. I happened to go into the kitchen and I saw him getting the money out. Then I knew where it was, but I never dared touch any of it.

When I was a girl, the Tallulah Falls Railroad ran as far north in Rabun County as Tallulah Falls. That's how the store was supplied. People could trade eggs and live chickens. They'd take [only live chickens] and put them in coops since they had no way to keep the chickens refrigerated. If there were too many chickens to sell locally, the store owners would send them to the train at Tallulah Falls in crates and ship them somewhere else. My grandfather, and later my father, hauled crates to Tallulah Falls in a wagon pulled by horses or mules. Then they'd haul barrels of goods back for the store. The railroad brought everything. Later, it came on up to Tiger [Georgia] and that made hauling easier.

ED ROANE: When they brought the railroad farther north, to Tiger, that's when I opened my store. That was 1927.

When I first opened the store in Tiger, the [Tallulah Falls] railroad turned around right up in that valley [in Tiger]. The railroad had a switch right there and that's where they turned the engine around. [That was the end of the line at that time.] The depot was [right in the center of Tiger near the little church there], and I built my store right up from there, and opened it the first day of June, 1927.

There were three or four more [stores] here in Tiger when we built and then a barbershop and a little ol' restaurant where you could get a barbecue. Our store was one of the biggest stores there was in the county. The others were smaller, didn't carry near the amount of stuff that we did. Now up in Clayton, the Cannons had a big store. Ours was a general run store. We sold hardware—wire, fencing—and any-

PLATE 69   Ed Roane in the living room of his home.

thing I could buy in the way of cheese, sugar, salt, coffee. It all usually came in sacks and wooden boxes and barrels. Everyone from Towns County and all around would come here and get their food. Since this was the end of the railroad line, we got all kinds of fertilizer, food and such shipped in on the train.

MRS. ROANE: Ed would order cookstoves and sell them to people who wanted them. They could put an order in and the store would get it for them. Things like that all came in on the train, too.

ED ROANE: To pay for them, people brought in corn, peas, cane, twisted-up tobacco, hogs, cows, sheep, goats, tanbark, ties for the railroad—anything they had we could take in trade. I'd buy everything they had. I don't know how many hogs or cattle I had—a lotful. And I could sell them! Why, law, I reckon I did! I put in a meat market and went to killing hogs and cows. I would wake up at three o'clock [in the morning] and light a lantern in the smokehouse and cut meat till daylight.

MRS. ROANE: Hotel owners bought some of that meat. They also bought great numbers of chickens. Most stores didn't have phones back then, but the hotels could send word that they'd buy so many when available.

ED ROANE: And hogs and chickens went out of here by the [railroad] carloads. There'd be eight or ten cars full of cattle. Folks brought them in from Towns County [Georgia] and all back through

North Carolina—Clay County, Macon County, and Highlands—to be shipped out on the train.

MRS. ROANE: Then the Depression came along. During the Depression, Ed and I fared okay. He always had work—in the store and on the farm. He did a little bit of everything, because a dollar was a dollar then and you had to work for what you got. But the Depression was very bad because lots of people who owned homes couldn't even pay their taxes and some of them lost their homes. Some people would have to sell their cows and other animals to pay their taxes. [If they couldn't pay the taxes,] the government would just take the houses and sell them.

ED ROANE: We helped a lot of people so they wouldn't lose their homes. Now we never lost anything by it. [During the Depression, we just made sure their houses weren't taken by the county because they couldn't pay their property taxes.]

MRS. ROANE: People couldn't get the money even to buy food and clothes with. There just weren't any jobs to find, and back then they didn't have welfare to help out. Most everyone had a garden if they had the land to put it on. We had several people to work on our farm and they were paid a dollar a day. That was a good bit then. Some people would come in the store and get flour and other necessary stuff and put in fifty cents a day on it. It was just real bad all over. We gave [credit] a lot then. Some were forced to go somewhere else [to live] because they couldn't find work. They would leave without paying their bills, not even their rent. Years later, a few came back and said, "Do you remember how much I owe you?" Well, Ed couldn't remember, but they did and they would pay their bill. We had no hard feelings by it. They needed it.

ED ROANE: Our property was the best bond of anything we had, because we could borrow money from the bank. We had nothing against our property. We were able to keep our store stocked up so people [who couldn't pay us during the Depression] could charge at the store. Many families didn't have flour or anything to go on. My mother would ask me just a lot of times how much longer I was going to give a man a boxful of food, and I said, "I don't know. I can still borrow money from the bank if I need it." So I borrowed money to stock the store and fed the people, as many come, and they came from as far as North Carolina. But we were blessed in it, because we had a lot of people that trusted us. I say we were lucky because we had a lot of friends. If a fellow needed a loan—twenty, fifty, or five hundred dollars—instead of his going to the bank, he might come and borrow that money from me. If I knew his father was a good man, a businessman from the county, I never took a note on it, but I never lost a dollar. I wouldn't charge nothing [for interest]—just told them to take the money and use it. Martha knows—for the last twenty years I was in business, I never hardly lost a dollar on loans.

MRS. ROANE: To help pay their bills with us, some people cleaned up creek banks and things like that. Most [store owners] owned big gardens and they needed tending, and lots of cattle. They had to keep the cows fed and the garden looked after [and people would help with these chores to pay off a bill].

ED ROANE: And we had a sawmill, a syrup mill, and a gristmill, and some people would work there in return for credit at the store. Up until World War II [when he was drafted], my brother done most of the farming and seeing about [the sawmill and gristmill]. He'd be gone for a week at the time during the Depression, taking the thrashing [threshing] machine around from farm to farm, thrashing wheat for farmers in the area. We thrashed up through here in the [Rabun Gap] valley. Why, them folks *farmed* up there. I've thrashed many a day way 'long into the night—after dark. When our four boys got up big enough, they went along. When we were far away, we'd camp overnight, didn't come back home. Like if we were way back over on Persimmon, the farmers' wives would cook for all the thrashers. We'd have people to help us and get credit at the store.

MRS. ROANE: When World War II came along, things started picking up. Someone started a sawmill up in Mountain City. People went to work there, and they would go to cutting those big old pine poles. People got to working and started buying cars and homes. It got to where there were more jobs coming into Rabun County and the county started growing.

Jim Ramey had two big hotels in Mountain City and Ed Holden had a little hotel right where Dillard Hotel is now. Later on, Jim Bleckley opened a big hotel. There were some little stores up in Clayton. They weren't big stores. Clayton had board sidewalks and so did Tiger. The roads used to be rocked. I believe they started paving them in the late thirties. There were hitching posts to hitch your horses to. Finally, in the early fifties, the shirt factory came in and then Rabun Mills came.

ED ROANE: By then I also had a store in the town of Washington, Georgia, and we'd move stuff we had here—apples, cabbage, potatoes—down there and then I'd put a load on and go on to Florida sometimes, or have a truck coming from Florida bringing oranges and sweet potatoes back up here. We kept two or three trucks running all the time, trading back and forth. I had to be down there [in

Washington] for a week or so ever' so often, but I had good men down there working for me.

Next we asked Mrs. Roane to tell us about the most popular products and how they were stocked. Here is a summary:

Candy: We usually got stick candy, and sometimes we got this little round, all-flavored candy. Chewing gum was one cent.

Cloth: They would sell bolts of cloth. There were so many yards of cloth on a big bolt. People bought that for sheets and pillowcases. They also sold something called "outin' " [outing flannel], which we call flannel now.

Clothes: They'd sell these loose shirts, work shirts, you know, for men and boys. Sometimes they'd be blue or striped or checked or diamonds. Usually, though, people bought the cloth and made their own shirts. [The stores] sold khaki pants.

Coffee: When you bought coffee out of the store, it was green—in little beans, I'd call it. They took it out of the barrel and weighed out so much. I think it was ten cents a pound. Then the customer who bought it took [the coffee beans] home and parched them.

My mother had a great big ol' biscuit pan and she'd put the coffee [beans] in that pan and put the heat on it. She took a spoon and stirred all the time, so they wouldn't burn. She baked them till they all turned brown. [Then we ground up the beans as we needed them for coffee.]

Flour: Flour came in barrels. I think a barrel had a hundred pounds in it and we bought a barrel at a time. We didn't buy flour by the pound.

Grain: They sold corn for hog feed. People raised wheat and rye and would take it to a mill in Franklin [North Carolina] to be ground. If they had any extra, they could swap the grain at the store. Then, someone who didn't raise their own could buy it there.

Kerosene and lamps: Back then everybody bought kerosene for their lights. They didn't have any electricity. Kerosene came in barrels or drums.

Lamps didn't cost but about thirty-five or forty cents, and that was for lamp, wick, globe and all.

Meat: They sold all kinds of meat, but it was local meat. People would cure the meat and take it into the store and sell it. Most everybody had their own meat, but there was a few that didn't. If someone had some meat left over from where they had butchered, they cured it and put it in the store for those people that needed it. When it's cured, it'll keep a long time in a cool place.

Our family never had to buy meat, because Dad had hogs, cows, and sheep.

People would bring in livestock to Ed's store [during the Depression] for trade. He had a lotful out there, couldn't keep count. So he started a butcher business. Supplied the work camps for the Georgia Power people when they were building these power dams [Lake Rabun, Lake Burton, Tallulah, and Tugalo dams]. He peddled fresh meat from our store. He would butcher on Thursday and either [the customers] would come and get their meat or he would carry it to them on Friday. He had customers all around Tiger and Tallulah Falls.

Medicine: There was no such thing as aspirin, but they did sell pills. They also sold liniments for anybody that thought they had rheumatism, what they call now arthritis. There was a Rosebud Salve. You could order it, but you couldn't buy it in the stores. We'd order a big order of that salve and went around and sold it.

Then there were peddlers who came through [the area] with all kinds of stuff. They would have just bagsful [of patent medicines] and they'd sell a lot of that.

Oil: I think [cooking] oil was ten cents a gallon, maybe fifteen cents. And oooh, now it's two dollars a gallon.

Postcards: Postcards were a penny. You know, they had scenes on them, like mountains and rivers. I used to see those pictures and I'd want one [of those postcards]. So I'd save my pennies and go to the store and buy some.

Rope: It seems like rope was seven cents for so many feet of rope, but I don't remember how many feet it was.

Salt: Salt came in big one hundred-pound sacks. Later, it came in fifty pounds. We didn't have little box salt. It came loose and there were paper sacks to put it in after it was weighed out on the scale.

Seeds: There were people who had extra [vegetable] seed. A lot of times they would divide with their neighbors. When I was ten or eleven, people started ordering seed from Sears' catalog. The seed [bought from the store] came in thick, striped cloth sacks and they sold them by the pound.

Soap: We could buy soap in the store [although many people made their own]. We bought Palmolive. It was a hand soap, we called it. It was green. That's what we always got for a hand soap and to take baths with.

There was another kind of soap, lye soap. It was a kind of reddish color, but I can't remember the name.

Soft drinks: Uncle Johnny had a little store and he sold drinks. He had grape and orange and strawberry Nehi. But now, way back when I was little, I don't recall seeing Coke. That came later.

Sugar: Sugar came in big white, one hundred-pound sacks. If you didn't want to buy a hundred pounds of sugar, they would measure out what was needed. It was so much for a pound, but I've forgotten what it was. I think you could get a hundred pounds for a dollar and a half.

Syrup: Syrup cost a dollar a gallon then [if you went to the store and bought it]. I think it is about four or five dollars now.

We had a big [sorghum] cane patch to make syrup. We had about ten to twenty hands to work it and [when the cane was ready to harvest] they would get out there and strip it and cut off the heads. [This was when Ed had the store in Tiger.]

There was a [syrup] mill in Tiger where you could get your syrup made. People would come around from other counties, hauling their cane in to make syrup. [When syrup was being made from our cane patch] I have even got out there and helped to stir the skimmings. I never could [eat the juice when they were cooking it into syrup]. It would just make me sick. I liked it after it cooled off, but not that hot stuff. I just didn't like that.

ROY ROBERTS

We discovered Roy Roberts purely by accident one summer day. Wig and I were taking another Foxfire contact up into North Carolina so he could visit some friends he had not seen for years, and we had all stopped for lunch at the Old Mill Wheel Café outside Marshall. One of the customers recognized Wig as the editor of Foxfire, *and he said he knew someone we should meet. "Wait just a minute and I'll go get him. He lives right behind here because he owns this café." A few minutes later in walked Roy, and we started our first interview right there on the spot.*

Roy is a man of average height and build. His snow-white hair is cut close to his balding head. The glasses he wears cannot hide the twinkle in his eyes which goes perfectly with his constant grin.

I used to consider eighty-two as being old, but there is nothing old about Roy Roberts. He does not stoop over like most eighty-two-year-olds, but stands erect. He does not shuffle along as one would think an eighty-two-year-old would, but takes long strides and moves quickly. He is not frail. His big hands are powerful and strong, as are his arms and legs. Roy radiates energy; he is in constant motion.

When asked how he has stayed so healthy, Roy replied, "The Lord's been good to me. I quit drinking and smoking and chewing and all that back in 1929. I think not doing that kind of stuff and living a reasonably clean life has helped me to stay so healthy."

Raised on a farm in the North Carolina mountains, Roy went to Detroit during the Great Depression. There he worked checking the inventory of railroad cars for a factory that produced ice cream and refrigerator cabinets, and later he served as a security guard for the families of some of the automobile plant executives. After the Depression, Roy returned to the mountains and has since done just about everything from running a general store and making charcoal commercially in kilns he designed and built himself, to serving as sheriff of Madison County and raising skunks.

On our first visit with Roy, we were interested in the charcoal he had made because we had never interviewed anyone on that subject before. Roy could remember things so accurately and relate them in such detail that he made an excellent contact. As we talked with him, we found that he had done more than we had imagined and we went back to interview him two more times during the summer.

On one visit with Roy we stayed overnight in his cabins. We arrived in the afternoon and stayed until late afternoon the next day. We took eight rolls of film and made four hours of tape recordings. When we first got there, we made a couple of hours of tape and then took a break for supper. Roy's wife made some hush puppies and fried some trout which Roy had raised in the pond beside the café. We ate outside under an open-sided picnic shelter which he had built.

After the meal, he showed us around his place. Behind the café stretches a long, narrow flat sandwiched between the banks of the Laurel River and the side of a mountain. Down the middle of this flat runs a gravel driveway. As one looks down the driveway, on the right side there is a row of small log cabins which he rents out to summer tourists. Beyond these cabins is an unpainted, two-story cement-block garage. Next to that is a rock springhouse that he built. On the left side of the driveway sits Roy's house—a silver two-story cement-block structure with the river running directly behind it. Beyond the house is the picnic shelter, and there is a small lawn with a swing between the two.

While he was showing us around, we found out about his sense of humor. Roy is almost never without a smile and is always looking for a laugh. As we were walking around, he was demonstrating a sling he had made. We marveled at how far he could sling a rock, and I ventured to question his accuracy. Without the slightest hesitation, Roy directed me to stand on a stump. I unknowingly did so, thinking I was going to have a good view. Then Roy placed a rock on the top of

PLATE 70   Roy Roberts on a pair of Tom Walkers he makes for the children who stay at his cabins.

PLATE 71 The Old Mill Wheel Café at the intersection of the Laurel River and Hurricane Creek highways (25-70 and 208).

PLATE 72   Looking from the picnic shelter toward the café and highway, the row of cabins is visible on the left.

PLATE 73   From the highway across the Laurel River, spread along the opposite bank, are Roy's picnic shelter, garage, the cabins, and his home.

PLATE 74

PLATE 75　A closeup of the front of one of the cabins. On the porch is a chair Roy carved out of a solid log with a chain saw.

PLATE 76   Roy shooting the water gun he made for us.

PLATE 77   Roy demonstrating the fly gun he made while we stayed with him.

PLATE 78   The rock springhouse Roy built.
Three poles run from the roof to a nearby hemlock tree so squirrels can feed on the roof.

PLATE 79   Detail of the rock sculpture on
top of the springhouse.

my head and stepped back confidently, saying, "How much you want to bet I can get that rock off your head?"

In an instant I had snatched it off and was down, saying, "You're crazy!"

By then he was almost in tears from laughing so hard. "See? It works every time!" he said. Throughout the rest of our visit I watched him closely, and he had fits of laughter as he recalled the incident.

Then we went back to the shelter and sat around the cement picnic tables, and he began to show us how to make some of the toys he used to play with when he was a child. That's when the fun began. As he would remember things, he would get excited and his eyes would light up. Once he had found the right wood, he sat and whittled while he reminisced until late in the night. After showing us how to make two different kinds of whistles and a popgun, he decided he needed a different stick of wood. So off he went, romping through the woods at ten o'clock at night with no flashlight in the pitch-black darkness. He left us sitting there, dead tired and sleepy-eyed, wondering what was going on. We could hear him thrashing around and breaking branches. By the time we had figured out what he was doing and had started out after him, he was already back with a satisfied grin on his face, holding a perfect stick for his next toy.*

We were ready to call it a day, but he was just getting started. We finally got to bed after he showed us how to make a fly gun.

Roy was waiting for us when we woke up the next morning. He had been up for hours and had already fed the squirrels that come every day to the roof of his springhouse on wooden poles he has running from a nearby tree. He had even made another toy that shot little wooden pegs.

We made some more tape recordings and a water gun. Then we drove ten miles over the mountains to see Roy's abandoned charcoal kilns and his old stores. He had us struggling to keep up with him as he pointed out different features. After that, Roy took us to some land he used to own and showed us a lake and a dam he had built himself. We straggled behind him as he marched up and down hills and through the woods.

Finally all of our film was used and our tapes were full, so we packed up and headed for home. We were all worn out and slept on the way. They say time flies. Well, I don't think even time can keep up with Roy Roberts.

—KYLE CONWAY

Interviews and photographs by Kyle Conway, Al Edwards and Chet Welch. Edited by Kyle Conway and Chet Welch with help from Al Edwards, Allison Adams, Greg Darnell, and Cheryl Wall.

* Directions for making these toys and scores of others appear in *The Foxfire Book of Toys and Games:* E. P. Dutton, 1985.

I know that everybody that comes through here [looks at these mountains and wonders] the same thing. A few years ago we had a vanful of people come by and stop. They was from Michigan and they was going over here to camp for the summer. One of the girls, she seemed to be the spokesman, and she kept looking around. She said, "Mister, I'd like to ask you a question."

I said, "Okay."

She said, "I want to know how you people live around here."

"Well," I said, "I'm going to tell you. Most of us make liquor!"

She didn't say a thing. She got kind of distant. She didn't smile or nothing.

"Was you born around here somewhere?"

I said, "Yes. I was born right over the hill there twenty years ago!" She smiled then.

But anyway, I've wondered myself how we made a living. That time was different than it is now. Everybody tended these hills and made their own corn. There were corn mills that they could take their corn to and grind it. They made their own vegetables. They canned those vegetables. Maybe they had a tobacco crop. And we used horsepower to plow our gardens. They had their own cows to milk. They had their own hogs, and maybe they sold a calf from that cow. We didn't have gasoline. We didn't have no telephones. We didn't have no televisions. A gallon of kerosene would last you a month and cost you ten cents. What did you have to buy in the first place? All you had to buy was your clothes—maybe thread—and your coffee. If you had any cereal, oatmeal or rice, you bought that, or sugar. A few things like that you had to buy. Besides that, all you had to do was pay your taxes. You can see what I'm talking about. Everybody got by. We were poor, but we never did go without something to eat. Always had plenty to live on.

One time my dad bought a farm on credit. I believe it was eighty acres. It had a house on it, and we had to finish up the house and clear [the land up]. We just fixed it up so we could live in it. We had to go out and we had to peel chestnut oak bark, and we paid for that place cutting chestnut oak bark for a tannery. We'd peel around the tree and we'd cut the tree down and we'd stack the bark with the sap down —lean [the strips of bark] up against the tree. In the fall we'd come back and carry that bark out. If we couldn't get our sled up to where the bark was, we would pile it on top of brush and pull it down the mountain with horses to our wagon. Then we'd haul it to Barnard, which was ten miles, and pile it up there until we got a [railroad] carload. Then we would load that car up and ship it on. We paid for that place like that.

[But even with as little as we were making, some people would try to cheat us.] My dad sold [that tanbark] to a middleman. I remember one time my dad sold it to this man. Dad was pretty good estimating weights and whatnot. So [after we were paid], he said, "Boys, we didn't get [credit for] our full weight on that." So we went to the agent at the depot and Dad got the name of the company [the agent had] sent it to, and the [actual] weight on that certain car. [Turned out] the man had took us for I don't know how many ton of that bark. Well, Dad confronted the [buyer] and he wouldn't pay [the balance]. So what he did, he got judgment against the buyer. This man was buying and selling telephone poles also. My dad found out about it and ran an attachment on [a shipment of poles] till he paid off. It's hard to make an honest living, but the results down the road is sure.

[Though we didn't make much], we didn't miss things because we didn't have [them] and didn't know about [them]. I'm going to say that it brought your family closer together because of the fact that you stayed together and talked your problems over. You loved each other better and so when you got to thinking about that, I think it's a better living than it is right now. Our parents, now, they loved us and we loved our parents. We obeyed our parents and we did what they wanted.

[Of course, there were some disadvantages then, too. In those days] if you needed a doctor, the doctor would call on you at home. You wouldn't go to a hospital. Never heard of a hospital. [If] you needed a doctor, you'd have to send someone to get him. It'd be eight or ten miles away. Take you half a day to go and get him. So you better not get sick. It ain't like it is now.

[Since it was so hard to get a doctor in there], my grandfather and my father and all of [the other men of the community] went ahead and made a horse path across the mountain and called it the Doc Woody trail because the doctor was Burnett Woody.

You should have seen that doctor when he come across there. He was a big cutup. This fellow was the first fellow I ever saw wore a pompadour haircut. But I was on that road one time and he come by. I had heard that he would catch boys and he would get him a limb and wear the boys out just for fun. All the boys were scared to death of him. I was up one of those serviceberry trees and there he come along. [He] looked up there and saw me and tried to get me to come down. I wouldn't!

PLATE 80   A view of the land Roy used to own. The sign in the right corner reads: "These fields, locally known as Mill Ridge, were once used to grow tobacco and hay. They were purchased by the U.S. Forest Service in 1970, and now are important brood areas for turkey and grouse. Fruiting shrubs planted along the road provide food and protection for many wildlife species. Wildlife habitat management of these fields and surrounding forests is a cooperative effort between the U.S. Forest Service and the N.C. Wildlife Resources Commission."

The way we did our teeth, there was a fella that had a pair of forceps—or tooth pullers, they called it. If you had a bad tooth, you'd go up to his house and he'd get you down and take your tooth out. (That's) what we did in the dentist business. The last'n he pulled for me, I went to his house and he was hoeing corn in the field. He sent one of his children to the house to get his pullers. He got me down between the cornrows and took my tooth out.

[We took care of a lot of our own problems and didn't even call a doctor.] One time we was peeling tanbark and something stung me on the foot. I thought it was a bumblebee sting. After a while, it wouldn't quit hurting. I looked down and there was two [punctures]. I told my dad I believed that I was snakebit. He looked at it and said, "I believe you are." So I went down there [where the snake had bit me] and I looked and there was a copperhead laying there. "Well," he said, "you go to the house but you take your time and don't get hot." The house was down the hill, and in about five minutes, I was [there]. I told Momma a snake bit me. She went and got the turpentine and held the bottle to that place. Then she got a gallon of kerosene and set my foot down in it and soaked it for a while. Then she made a poultice out of a soggy paste of hot water, meal, and salt. She mixed it up and got it real hot and put it on there with a cloth around it. She left it on there till the next morning. That was it. My foot swelled up, but I never did get sick.

During the Depression, many people left the mountains and went North to the big industrial cities like Detroit in search of jobs. Roy was one of these people. This is what he told us about his experience:

[I went up to Detroit in] 1927. I had a neighbor that [had gone] up there before and I heard from him. I went up there and stayed with him. I went up on a train out of Marshall. I borrowed twenty-five dollars from my grandma to go up there. [My grandma] didn't say nothing about me going to Detroit. She just let me have the money. I've thought about that a lot of times. I think she thought this big store in Barnard was going to come up for sale and she had a little money. She said, "Roy, I'll let you have the money to buy that store." But it didn't come up for sale. [That] was the same store I bought several years later.

So I went up there [to Detroit] and went to work with a corporation [which] made ice cream cabinets. Later that company combined with another company and they started making refrigerators also. I was a checker in the receiving department checking the inventory of the [railroad] cars.

After that I worked for a private detective agency for six or seven years. I guarded the vice president of Chevrolet Motors for three years. I was guarding that old boy when the Lindbergh baby was kidnapped. After that, times got pretty hard and he discontinued our services.

Then I started guarding the man that financed Fisher Brothers when they went into Detroit and started making bodies for General Motors. I guarded his house for four years. He had a gate there and I would close it at night. Sometimes he would come in scared to death. A lot of times, Edsel Ford's wife would be down there. I knew Edsel Ford's wife personally [I also knew a] fella who was with Chrysler. I knew all of them. They visited there, you know.

[Lots of mountain people had gone to Detroit the same time I did.] Generally they tended to live in the same neighborhoods. They lived in a place called River Rouge. That was a suburb south of Detroit. It was really all the same town. You would never know you was out of Detroit when you got into it. Most of the people in River Rouge were from the South. They even had a chief of police that was a Southern man.

That was probably the first time some of [the mountain people] had been in a town any length of time. Of course, I had never been in town either. I was out of the country straight into the city. To me it was quite a change. The numbers of people and the way they lived, of course [were different]. I guess some of them hadn't been to a theater before. I don't guess I had. [Indoor plumbing was new to me.] I just couldn't get used to that. There was no indoor plumbing in our community. Most of us didn't even have a outhouse. We had lots of woods. That's it. Young boys would sit on a stump. Be sure to get on one as high as you could get!

[And where I came from] we didn't have electricity. We didn't have a telephone. I guess at that time we didn't have a radio. I remember the first automobile and the first radio I ever saw. I remember the first airplane that come over. I just had to guess that it was an airplane. I was hoeing corn for ten cents an hour, and that airplane came over and somebody said, "What's that?"

Somebody else said, "I believe it's an airplane." We didn't know. We just said it was an airplane.

During the Depression, I worked every day. Couldn't hardly get off a day. Everybody was kind of afraid of people robbing. Robbing was starting to get pretty rank back in the Depression days. They was pretty desperate. I seen people going down the alleys eating out of garbage pails. Eating out of the garbage pails! I saw that. People were losing their homes. Maybe they had been paying on them for years. People were desperate.

While I was in Detroit, I was making more than the average person, but finally this little store come up for sale back at home and I decided I could make a go of it. So I come home [and the owner] told me what he wanted for it. I said, "All right." I decided to buy it. I hadn't ever sold anything. I didn't know anything about selling anything. I had a little money—not too much. I believe I had about eight hundred dollars.

My daddy said, "I'll sign a note with you for the balance of the money." That was in 1935. We inventoried the stock in the store and the stock was worth $1,356. I had a 1927 four-door Chevrolet sedan that was in good shape, and I decided I would sell that. I sold that car for one hundred dollars. I had a little farm over there that I believe I had paid five hundred dollars for, and I sold it for about eight hundred. And with that money, I bought the business—the stock—and I rented the building. The rent on this store building was five dollars a month. The rent on my house, which was a two-story frame house immediately behind the store, was seven dollars a month. That was twelve dollars a month I was paying for rent. And the store was a good brick building.

There were actually two stores in town. After a year, my business got going good and I tried to buy the store I was renting, but the man wouldn't sell. The other merchant had a nice brick building, and he *was* willing to sell, so I bought his building and stock and moved out of the first store. The post office was in there, and when I bought that second store, I moved the post office. We put the mail on and off the railroad mail cars, and we served two post offices, so everybody in the area came for their mail there. Some of them walked from a mile or two miles back on the other side of that mountain. The woman that was postmistress, she didn't pay anything in rent for that space. I figured it was good advertising if people had to come to my place to get their mail. If I made the store attractive enough, I would get their business, so I tried to make it attractive with the goods and with the prices.

One of the passenger trains was called the 101. It came about seven in the morning and it had mail on it. The other two trains that had mail on them were the number 11 and the number 12. The number 12 ran about one o'clock and the number 11 ran about three o'clock. We had to meet every train. I still dream about missing one of those trains with the mail on it—get there and the train would be pulling off about the time you got there! We had a room in the back of that store and I stayed in the back at night to keep somebody from stealing. One night there was a terrible storm, and I thought it was the mail train coming. We had stock in the back there, and I jumped up and hit my head on a big old tub. When I hit my head, I laid back down. I knew where I was then. It was a storm coming and I had thought it was the mail train.

That postmistress was a neat-looking woman, but she was pretty sensitive. She was a widow. I used to kid with her all the time. There was an old man come in, and he was looking for a woman. He told me, he said, "I like the looks of that postmistress up there." He said, "Could you speak to her for me?"

I said, "Yes, sir!" It just tickled me to have some fun with her. I told him, I said, "I'll talk to her for you."

In the meantime, there was a man that lived back on that gap yonder. He said, "Roy, I have a sow over there. I'd like for somebody to take this sow and raise the pigs." He said, "I'd give 'em half the pigs if they'd just take her and raise them."

PLATE 81   The railroad tracks and the siding that served Roy's stores.

PLATE 82   The store Roy started out in. Roy said, "See, there's a railroad siding down here. Everything was handled by rail. All of my shipments—hardware and dry goods, even tobacco and hogs—come by rails."

I said, "I don't know. I might locate somebody."

The old man spoke up and said, "Roy, I'll tell you what I'll do. If you get me and that woman fixed up, we'll raise those pigs for you."

I thought, "Now I've really got it fixed up shore 'nough."

So I went back up and I told the postmistress, I said, "That old man down there told me to talk to you about him." I said, "He's interested in a woman." Then I told her about the pigs. "He told me if I could get it worked up, you and him could raise those pigs."

Oh-h-h, she turned red, but she didn't say much.

In about a week or two, I said, "Have you ever decided about that?" I said, "That pig situation can't wait much longer . . ."

She said, "Listen here now, Roy. I've heard enough about that old son-of-a-bitch!" *(laughter)* Oh, she was mad as a wet hen!

But we had a lot of fun. And the business kept getting better. Finally I was able to buy that first store out. I also built a seven-car railroad siding built up level with a railroad car floor that we could load and unload railroad cars from. Then I built another store. It was a two-story building thirty feet wide and eighty feet long.

And then I built a tin building for a warehouse, and I kept my tractors and tools in that. So things really got busy around there for a while. There's a little story about when I was building this tin storage building that I'll tell you. I was up on top there doing some work on it. I'd had a cyst on my vocal cord and I went suddenly hoarse. I went to the doctor. He said, "When I take this cyst off, you can't talk for two weeks. Give it a chance to heal. Otherwise it won't heal."

After the operation, my brother wanted to know how the operation went, and I had to write on a piece of paper to tell him what the doctors said. He got a pencil and paper and wrote back to me! [He wasn't the only one who did that, either.] I came over to the depot one day to bill out a car. I wrote out the number of the car, type of car, where it went to, and so on and so forth. The agent grabbed his pencil and started writing back to me.

Anyway, I was up on this building after the operation. I could work with them, but I just couldn't talk. There was a fellow that come down here and wanted to know if he could have a job. I wrote and told him that I needed him, and I told him that when lunchtime come, he could go up to the store and the wife would feed him up there. So when lunchtime come, he went up there and said, "I'm so and so. I'm working here, and that deaf and dumb man down there said to come up here and get something to eat!" *(laughter)*

There was lots of funny things like that, but of course there was hard work, too. When I bought things for the store, I had to be pretty

PLATE 83   Both stores and the warehouse Roy built.

PLATE 84

sure that there was going to be a call for them. I remember one time
—I don't know if you've ever heard of the Ball Band people or not.
They made rubber footwear. They were the first ones to come out
with the composition soles. Before that, they had leather. The shoes
had a red ball in the bottom there [as their logo]. They'd come in the
early part of the season and the money wasn't due until October.
When I had just built that store, I believe I had borrowed $1,500. I
lacked a little having enough to pay that Ball Band bill. I had ordered
this rubber stuff and I was afraid I wasn't going to make it. So I
decided I'd better write them. I wrote them about two months before
the bill come due, and I told them I didn't know if I was going to make
it or not and could my time be extended if I couldn't pay them on
time. What tickled me was their answer. They wrote back and said it
had never been their policy to extend credit before it come due! I
thought that was a pretty good answer; but I made it all right. I just
wanted to know what I had to do. There's nothing like doing it in
time.

The stuff that I got stuck with I just had to sell at a loss and forget it.
There was nothing you could return. We had trouble with women's
shoes more than anything. If you didn't sell out a pair of shoes this
year, you'd get stuck with them next year. We tried not to get that
fancy stuff. Get staple stuff, you know. We sold more of a heavy work-
type shoe for men. We sold good brands of all kinds of tool handles,
stovepipe, dampers. All kinds of plow parts, bolts. We had paints. We
had a line of used clothing. We made more off that than anything. You
could sell a nice-looking dress for a dollar and maybe it cost you fifty
cents.

Then we'd get lined up with some wholesale people and we'd buy
our sugar wholesale, and a lot of canned goods wholesale. And I'd
buy a couple of railroad carloads of shucks each year from Michigan
and out West, and solid truckloads of cottonseed meal—I remember
the price of that meal was ninety cents for a hundred-pound bag—
and soybean meal. I bought all that for people who didn't put up
enough feed for their stock for the winter. Some of them just never
did *make* enough feed.

When I bought flour and stuff for the store, I never bought it in less
than twenty-five-pound bags. I usually bought solid truckloads of
hundred-pound bags of flour. Later they put those hundred pounds
of flour in print bags, and people used those for making clothes. [The
company did that] to help sell flour, I guess.

We sold gas for twenty-one cents a gallon. Kerosene was ten cents a
gallon. All our drinks were seventy-five cents a case—ten cents for the

crate and sixty-five cents for the drinks. Later we started hauling our own drinks [instead of having them delivered] and we got another fifteen cents off of that. When I first went there, we never had a refrigerator. We had an icebox. The man that brought us our drinks also brought us our ice, and we ordered ice by the hundred pound. If the ice was used up before the man got back, we'd just sell hot pop, and we'd sell it like that lots of times. The icebox had a hole down through the bottom and that went to a hole drilled in the floor so the water from that ice would just leak out down through the floor of the store.

We also started buying pulpwood and selling and shipping it. You were never sure you were going to get rid of it when you bought it. You just bought it on your own. Then when a paper company wanted a load of wood, they would write me a letter and tell me to ship 'em a railroad carload.

At first we had to load all that by hand into boxcars. I bought it in five-foot lengths with a diameter of a maximum of twenty inches and a minimum of four inches. Most of it was hemlock, poplar, gum, maple and all that, and most of it at that time had the bark on it. So we'd buy it, pile it off, separate it into piles by [variety], and peel the bark off because there wasn't no wood sold at that time with the bark on. Then we had to load it all by hand to ship to Champion Fiber Company or International Paper at Canton or Columbia or Knoxville or Kingsport. If one wouldn't buy, the other would, usually, so it kept us busy.

Finally we got busy enough that I had to build that seven-car siding I told you about, and we got some mechanical means and started loading it mechanically. And we loaded *thousands* of carloads of wood. Not just one thousand, but *thousands*.

And we bought crossties and sold crossties to the railroad. Anything we could buy and make money on legally and aboveboard, that's what we did.

[I also built some silos near my store, and] I raised enough corn on the bottoms over there to fill those silos full. I kept thirty to forty cattle over the wintertime and fed 'em myself and sold 'em in the fall. We kept a surplus—mostly brood cows—and we sold the calves as stocker cattle or baby beef cattle. We always sold them for cash through livestock markets.

And then, back in the forties, I decided that being in a rural county, we would buy a truck. I had some brothers that were unemployed, so we put a trailer behind that truck and we had a rolling store. We traveled all over the county, and we would swap with people. After

PLATE 85   Wig, Al Edwards, and Roy around a table under his picnic shelter during one of the interviews.

they got to know us and we got the route established, when we stopped at their house they'd be watching for us. And if we couldn't get to their houses, [we'd go to a crossroads, or go as far up their road as we could go, and sometimes several families] would be there waiting when we got there. If they wanted something we didn't carry in the store, then when we went to Asheville we'd pick it up for them and that would save them a trip to town. What we did, since we had the post office in our place, we had a bunch of cards made up. The postcards at that time cost a penny apiece. Well, I had some postcards printed up with our name and address on them. We would take these cards and distribute them to the customers. If they needed a pair of shoes, a pair of overalls, a shirt, plow, plow point or whatnot, they would mail that card and we'd bring [the item] on the next trip. We got a lot of orders by mail that way.

And we [routinely] carried kerosene, snuff, tobacco, flour, meal, coffee, sugar, rice and oatmeal and whatever. Just anything we could fit in that truck. We even had thread. Anything we could get our hands on, we traded. We sold fruit in the fall. We sold a lot of toys at Christmastime.

All that stuff we would swap. People would bring chickens and eggs to swap. We swapped for a lot of potatoes. One time I guess we had five hundred bushels of potatoes at one time. When we'd come back in from a round, we'd have that trailer behind our truck loaded to the top with what we'd taken in trade. We'd get twenty-five or thirty cases of eggs in one day. We'd have chickens, geese, herbs. We'd be eight or nine o'clock getting home at night. I had a hole down through the floor of that first store with a big coop boxed up down there, and I'd just open the door in the floor and drop the chickens down in there. The coop was pretty high off the floor and I'd go down there and feed 'em and water 'em. Then we candled our eggs. Sometimes we would have several dozen out of a case that were bad. When we was out on the road, we'd just have to buy 'em because there wasn't no way to candle 'em out there. But back at the store I had a box with a light in it and two holes cut in it and I'd stick the eggs up to those holes two at a time. If they were good and clear, I would stick them back in the carton. Some of them would be just as black as they could be and they'd be just plain rotten.

Then we'd have to take all that to the city and sell it to get our money out of it. We never got more eggs than we could sell. We always sold them out. Sometimes we'd get too many potatoes and we'd have to take them in the springtime and peddle them out. We always took them to Greene County, Tennessee. I had some boys that would go with me. One would go down one side of the street and the other would go down the other side. Both would have a half bushel of potatoes. The other man would drive the truck, and we'd sell forty or fifty bushels a day.

You'd be surprised at the hams we bought to sell. Sometimes twenty-five or thirty hams a week. We took them to Asheville and sold them to a wholesaler. When I bought a ham, I could tell right away whether it was bad or not. There's a place in a ham that you can stick a pencil plumb through, and all you do is stick that pencil in there and smell of it. If it smells good, it was a good ham. If it smells sour, don't buy it.

I had train engineers that would stop at my place right quick and pick one up. One would call ahead and tell me to have a ham there. I'd have one and put it on his engine and he'd take it on. One of my brothers was loading up a load of hams in the store one time. We had a set of steps that come up from back of the store. This engineer come up there and got a ham and just turned around and took off. My brother said, "What's he doing with that ham?"

I said, "He's taking it."

He said, "He ain't been waited on!"

I said, "When he gets to Knoxville, he'll send me the money back."

PLATE 86

My brother thought he was stealing it, but he had just stopped the train for a second to pick one up and he was just in a hurry!

We also bought herbs to sell. I had started collecting herbs when I was a little boy. I bought 'em and sold 'em even then. I remember one time that we had these elders. They have a white blossom. I collected the blossoms off them and had a twenty-five-pound bagful, and I walked, I guess, five miles across a mountain to a store and sold that bag of flowers for a quarter. When I had my store, we'd go out and buy roots and herbs and botanical drugs that the customers had to sell. We'd buy those and then take them to a wholesale drug company in Asheville and sell them. Before we would pay the customers, we always had to check on the prices the wholesale company was going to give *us* because they would change every week. If they got a surplus of one kind, why they'd lower the price on it. We'd buy ginseng—I still buy and sell ginseng—witch-hazel leaves, cherry bark, wahoo bark, yellowroot, poke. We'd just buy hundreds of different things like that and sell them.

Take all that stuff in solid truckloads to town, and when we got done, we'd bring the money back. My two brothers helped me operate that rolling truck store, you know, and we divided up the profits. That was a pretty big operation to load that stuff and check your stock in the evening and take inventory and unload the chickens and eggs and empty the coops and load them back on the truck late that night ready for the next morning. It was a big job.

When the war came, my brothers had to get a defense job or go to the army, one, and so they worked in the atomic energy plant down at Oak Ridge making those atomic bombs that bombed Japan; so we had to close down the rolling store. We had a good business with it until then, though. We traded anything the customer wanted to trade —anything we could use or sell.

And, of course, with a business in the country like that, you had to give credit. I wish I *could* have sold everything for cash. Right now I figure I've got out on credit from forty to sixty thousand dollars coming to me. Two years ago, I had a woman call me from up in West Virginia. She said, "Roy, we owe you some money, don't we?"

I said, "Yes, you do."

She said, "It's something over a hundred dollars, isn't it? I'm going to send you a hundred dollars." She did, and that was to pay on a bill they had run up in 1940. Every year I get money like that, and I haven't run my stores for over fifteen years.

But you'd trust a man until you'd find out [that you couldn't]. A lot of times, these people that will beat you—they'll beat you and you *a-lookin'* at 'em. He'll beat you and you'll swear he's a good man. A fellow owes me for five gallons of gas—a dollar and five cents—from the first day I was in operation. I haven't forgotten.

I had an experience with one fellow. He came in there and lightning had hit his house. His wife was at the sink washing dishes and lightning went through the sink and busted one of her legs up. He owed me for fertilizer, and he always paid me. So when he come to pay me that fall, I said, "If you're hurtin' now, you can pay me later." He's never been to see me yet. He still owes me that bill. And he was a preacherman's boy. That hurts more than anything when you trust a man to that extent—try to help him out and then he beats you.

A lot of fellas don't *intend* to pay you. Did you ever notice? A man of that nature is always in hard luck. He's never got money. He finally gets in a place where he *can't* get no credit and people won't trust him, and if he gets in a hard place then, he's a-hurtin'. An honest man can go out there and get more credit than he'll *ever* pay back any time he wants it. If you prove that you have credit, anybody that you ask will hand you money. That's been my experience. I remember one boy—I sold him thirteen hundred-pound bags of flour and that kept his family over the whole year. He was a good boy. The same boy came to me and said, "What's your fertilizer going to be next year?"

I said, "I don't know. I haven't got the price on it yet."

"Well," he says, "here's three hundred dollars. You keep it until I get ready to get mine." That's the way I like to trade.

But when you deal with the public, you'll have trouble. Even if you do the very best you can. A few times we went to town and the trailer would be loaded up to where you couldn't hardly *see* the trailer for the roots and herbs and things. We'd get to town and there would be a big rock in the middle of our roots and herbs. I had one man who sold us a case of fresh eggs every week. Then the wholesale man began to complain. He said two or three layers in the case were missing every time. So we had that kind of stuff. You just wait and expect it in the future. The customer is always right. You're not right, the customer is right. I've made up stuff that I knew good and well was right, but it was wrong [according to the customer]. If you argue with a man, you'll lose him. Naturally he can't come back and face you. You just lost him as a customer.

[But we did pretty well, all in all.] Just kept trying new things and figuring out ways to make one business support another. Like I was talking about those rotten eggs? Well, back in '39 or '40, they was a boy brought me a couple of young skunks. I guess he was drunk when he got them. He was pretty bad to drink. Well, I said I'd just keep 'em. I began to pet 'em, and later I decided just for the fun of it I'd raise me some. So I got hold of some more. A skunk makes a good pet, but you've got to get 'em when they're young and work with 'em. A big skunk will eat you up. He'll eat you up in a minute.

So at one time I had about forty of them. I built me a lot up on my daddy's place to keep them. I built it out of wire, and on top of the posts I put me a piece of tin, so if they climbed that post they couldn't get out. I had little hollow logs that went back into the ground and they could be back in there in a box where it was dark. I had a place where I could take my lid off so I could get at them. It was a pretty good setup. I could call them skunks and here they'd come!

But they weren't descented. When a skunk is going to discharge, he'll look at you, and to scare you off he'll turn his tail towards you. He'll turn around here and throw his tail up and keep going sideways. What I learned to do is just to back up and you didn't get sprayed. He will turn around and start going the other way. If they do decide to throw that scent, they will turn around. They'll bow up and pull that tail wrongside out and those tubes will be exposed and he'll press that muscle back there like a little syringe and out comes the fluid. You had to get used to being sprayed. You have to learn to sleep by yourself and things like that! When I was around them, I always wore some old clothes. Baking soda is the best thing to get the smell out.

Whenever I would get someone to help me with them, I'd have to change men the next time because they would only do it one time and that was all!

I decided that I needed to deodorize 'em. I kept studying and studying and finally I got onto some stuff that showed me how to descent them, and I learned to do that myself. The word got around and people in California heard about it and they contacted me and said they would like to come and make a newsreel. They came and made a newsreel of my skunks. That was back in, I guess, 1940 or '41. Well, I got letters from Panama, England, Michigan, and everywhere. I got letters from people wanting to know about them. At that time, I sold them for five dollars apiece.

We saved all the eggs that we candled and discarded to feed the skunks. That's what they liked the best—them old eggs. It was funny how they would break an egg. They would catch it in their front feet and they'd throw it behind them between their back legs. If it didn't hit something behind them and break, they'd turn around and throw it in a different direction. They'd keep on until they heard a crack. If they missed several times, they'd get impatient, and boy they'd get in a hurry then.

I had two of them that would follow me around. They liked insects of all different kinds—particularly little black bugs that would be under boards. I'd turn boards over, and boy those skunks, here they'd come, and hunt for those insects. I'd go and hunt another board and they'd follow me over to get those insects out.

I would experiment with 'em. I'd catch a mouse and tie a piece of thread to its legs and turn him loose, and boy you talking about a time now. The skunks would have a time trying to get ahold of it, you know. They were quick. They loved those mice, but they wouldn't eat a rat. Nothing will eat a rat!

Then, since I had a wood business anyway, I decided to try charcoal. We had a man who came down from out West somewhere. He wanted to get a bunch of people to make charcoal, so he contacted me and I decided I would make some. I had seen one or two [kilns in use]. There was one in Buncombe County around the Asheville area and I went over and looked at it. I talked with them and saw some of the troubles they had, so I designed mine differently and improved on theirs. I never saw any [kilns] constructed exactly like [mine].

I think it cost me $10,000 to build those kilns. I done my own construction. I guess it took four or five months—maybe more—[to build them]. Incidentally, the sides and back was underground. It was a steep hillside, so we hauled a lot of dirt out to make those kilns. We had a couple of dump trucks, and I rented an air compressor, hammers, and drills. The back part was fifteen foot of solid rock, and I had to drill and shoot all that rock out.

When I was moving this dirt, I came across some dark-looking dirt in the clay. I kept watching, and after a while I came across some bones. Well, one of the Forest Service men was acquainted with bones and he said it was human bones. I had run into a grave. I kept all the bones and I buried them again in a different place. I asked an old man about it. I said, "Did you ever hear of anybody being buried there?"

He said, "No, but I can tell you my opinion. I think my opinion is correct." He said, "When they built this railroad here, it was built by slave labor, and wherever a slave died, that's where they buried him." He said, "I'd say that was a slave buried there." I'd say the man was right.

We made three kilns. [Each kiln]was twenty-four feet wide by thirty and a half feet long. They each had an arched ceiling [that was] fifteen feet high from the floor to the complete top of the arch. It was twelve feet high to where the ceiling began to arch. The kilns were made out of steel and concrete. I believe it took two [railroad] carloads of cement, and I don't know how much gravel. We ordered the gravel from South Carolina. We tied steel reinforcement rods on one-foot centers. Then we got plyboard forms and a vibrator to vibrate the cement down as we poured it in and made the walls. We got timbers and supports underneath a plyboard form to shape the ceiling. We welded steel and then poured a foot of concrete on top.

We also had to put these [six-inch-in-diameter] terra-cotta pipes along the sides and back of the kilns at the base. There are seventeen of those [in each kiln] and they are placed four foot apart all the way down both sides and across the back. They are placed about one inch above the floor and they go through the walls. Then they turn up in an "L" shape and go all the way to the top and extend three foot above the top of the kilns. Those pipes were my flues.

Then at the top of each kiln's arch are three two-foot-square openings—one in the front and one in the center and one in the back—and each one has a little bit of a recession to hold a quarter-inch steel plate. When the kiln was burning, those plates sat down over the three openings. The idea was that if you had spontaneous combustion in there, it would blow these plates away and save the kiln from blowing up. They were like safety valves [on a boiler]. I've had them blow up with me and blow the double metal doors on the front of the kiln completely off. When that happened, I would have to get a tractor to lift those three-thousand-pound doors back. If you didn't

PLATE 87 Roy's charcoal kilns. Roy is explaining to us how the doors of the kilns worked.

PLATE 88

do it in a hurry, that fire would get out of control, so I learned how to control my spontaneous combustion by putting those relief holes up there on top to let the pressure off.

Those doors were made of quarter-inch-thick steel, reinforced with

PLATE 89:   On top of the kiln, Roy lifted the lid off one of the square openings. "If you were experienced, you knew what was going on down there."

heavy angle iron to keep them from buckling. That was part of my invention. Each door was ten foot high and ten foot wide—big enough when they was opened so that we could back our trucks right into the kilns and unload the wood right in there. The doors were on rails so they would slide open or shut, and when they were pushed together, we'd fasten them down with quarter-inch-steel iron buttons that were spaced eighteen inches apart. Then we had a smaller sliding door made in the bottom of each of the big doors so we could get through the door to start the fire. It also acted as a little vent, and you could give the fire a small amount of air or give it a lot.

Then the floor of each kiln was slightly tilted toward the front because when I was making charcoal, there was a liquid that came out of that wood—it was moisture that would come out of the ends of the wood and sizzle. With the floor tilted, that liquid would run to the front. It took almost a two-inch pipe to carry that stuff out. When it first started coming out, it would be kindly brown; then the next day it would be browner; then after a while it would turn black, then tar would come out.

We also had the kilns spaced apart from each other and we put rock in between our kilns and filled that space with dirt so that the kilns would be insulated and would stay hot from one operation to the next. You wouldn't lose much heat that way. And I had about a foot of dirt piled on top of them. I never saw it done before, but I figured if we didn't put some dirt on the top and it come a sudden rain with those kilns red hot up there, it would ruin them. That dirt turned into solid clay, you know? In front, you could feel the heat way out away from them, but on top it didn't get too hot because of that dirt. Sometimes we even cooked up there. I would just take a place and beat that clay up into dust and I would put green corn and potatoes under that dust and cook dinner that way.

We used hardwood to make charcoal. If you didn't have a hard wood, you didn't have a heavy coal. The more dense your wood, the heavier your coal and the more tonnage you had. There would be more profit and less work. I also found out the smaller the wood you had, the less tonnage you had because you had more bark. The very best wood for making charcoal was hickory, ash, oak, apple or sugar maple. I liked to use green wood over dry wood because the burning process was easier to control.

It took one week to load one of those kilns up. Each would hold seventy cords, or 8,960 cubic feet of wood. What you would do when you started packing your wood in there was to go back to the back and lay an eight-inch stick of wood down facing the front so that it wouldn't obstruct one of the flues in the back. Then you would do the same with another one. You would lay them about four foot apart all the way across. Then you would come back and lay three sticks across each four-foot section—one stick in the front and one in the middle and one in the back. Then you would come back and do the same thing again, making a rick about twelve inches high. [This would provide an air space for the flues.] Then you would do the same thing along the sides. From then on, you would stack your wood solid all the way to the ceiling.

We had a road built up to the top of the kilns so when the wood got up past the doors and you couldn't load any more from the bottom, we would drive up there and finish loading the wood down through those two-foot holes on top of the kiln. We would put our smaller pieces on the bottom and their size would increase as you went up. You could use wood two foot [in diameter] at the top because your heat was greater at the top than it was at the bottom and your big wood wouldn't char if it was at the bottom.

For starting the fire, in the third rick from the back we'd have a core of dry wood built in there two and a half feet wide by three feet high. That dry wood would start out pretty readily.

In the front of the kiln, the wood was stacked straight up away from the door, not up against it. If a fire got up against the door, the door would get red hot and start buckling. Sometimes it would buck anyway because burning wood would fall up against the inside bottom of the door. We had a lot of trouble with that, so I invented a shelf-like stand that stood against the door and when wood fell down, it kept it away from the bottom.

When we got it all loaded up, we would close the door. To seal it, we tightened the buttons on the sides and at the top. Then we mixed clay dirt and put it all around the door. That sealed that. We had to have it completely airtight. If it developed a crack in it, we had to watch it and seal it to keep the smoke and heat in. After we sealed it, I'd open that center thing in the door and take the center plate in the ceiling off to give it a draft while the fire got started.

To light it, I had a twenty-one-foot reinforcement rod with a burlap sack saturated with kerosene wrapped around the end. Then I would set that afire and run it through that hole to where my dry wood was. I would hold it there until I felt like I got it lit, and then take it out. Maybe ten minutes after it got started, we would put the center plate back and put dirt on it.

One little old boy one time said, "How do you light that thing?"

I said, "Well, I get a boy to crawl back under there to light it." I was just kidding.

He said, "Ain't you afraid he'll get hung?"

I said, "No. I tie a rope around him, and when he gets hung, I pull him out."

He said, "How much do you pay for a job like that?"

I said, "I pay five dollars."

He said, "Do you pay him every time he comes?"

I said, "Well, in his case I don't. He owes me money and I just give him credit when he comes out."

He said, "Hell," and turned around and walked off!

After it got going good, it got red hot and you could look down in there and it was like looking into torment.

When you lit that back in the kiln, after four, five, or six days that fire would burn to the front. When the fire came to the front, then you had to close the vent in the front door and seal everything. Then, instead of controlling the air intake from the front, since you didn't have no more control down here, you had to do all the operation from the top. [You did that by controlling the air intake through the vent pipes that went around the sides and the back—the terra-cotta flues.] I had a little metal dish that went over the top of each one—they were just like two half-moons joined with a rivet—and you could look down in those holes and you could see the sparks coming up. When you saw the sparks down in there, you'd know that your wood over to that hole was charred. Then you would take your dish and put it over that flue pipe and put dirt over it. That would close that one off [and the kiln would start drawing air through a different flue].

See, the kiln would have lots of different degrees of heat in there. One section over here would be cold and one over here would be hot. The smoke would come out the flue where the heat was the greatest, and air would intake where it was the less. So when we stopped the front up, it would start the intake from one of those cool spaces at the top. It would go to sucking air down through one or two of them. So I could open it up and give it air as I wanted to and control the burn from the top.

After two weeks, you'd open it up and you'd start to load the charcoal out. It would be settled down three and a half feet, and it would still be in sticks ranging in size from your finger up to two foot. Sometimes you would find out that it wouldn't be completely out. You would see smoke and you could feel the heat coming off the hot spot. The fire would always be in the center of a big stick you didn't have completely out. It would start building up, and after a while, it would get afire. I learned how to put that fire out. I would have everything closed off, and I would come up to the top and take one of those plates off and take a water hose and flood that where it was hot. It would build up steam and in turn the steam would put the fire out. Steam was a greater fire extinguisher, I found, than anything. It would put a fire out when nothing else would.

It took two or three days, or sometimes a week, to unload it. Under normal conditions, a seventy-cord kiln loaded with good wood should have from thirty to thirty-five tons of coal. I had a front-end loader with a big dipper that we used to load it into a truck. Then we would haul it to Asheville and dump it. We had two trucks that we used to haul it in. I thought it was a pretty good operation. The Forest people brought some people from Siam to see it. I thought, "Well, it must be pretty good for them to bring those people over here."

The briquetting people would take the charcoal and process it into briquets. They would run it through a hammer mill and turn it into

PLATE 90 "I had a little dish that I would lay on top of the flues. They were just like two half-moons put together with a rivet in the center. I could open it up and give it air if I wanted to."

PLATE 91 Inside one of the kilns, one realizes how large they are. Note the arched ceiling and a part of one of the three square openings in the top.

dust. Then they would mix it with commercial starch and water and drop it down into a press and press that. From that it went on a conveyor to a furnace to dry it. Then they weighed it and bagged it.

When the briquetting people closed down, I had a kilnful of charcoal with no place to sell it. So I decided I was going to get rid of it somehow. I started to bag it and put it under my own name. I put it in ten-pound bags and sold it all out, but it took me three or four years to do it. At that time, we sold it for thirty-two dollars a ton delivered in Asheville. When I started bagging it, I sold it for $180 a ton bagged, so I come out on it.

But overall I lost money on the operation. I didn't make enough to pay for the construction of the kilns.

I had my store from '35 to '69. At the time that I sold it, we were selling $70,000 worth of merchandise a year. The boy that bought it from me just went out of business recently. The place grew up. Somebody told me the other day the roof was falling in. It sure has changed since I had it.

But I tell you right now, it was a busy place.

EARL GILLESPIE'S PRODUCE MARKET

My papa [grandfather], Earl Gillespie, has sold produce most of his life. He first peddled cabbage and apples from a horse-drawn wagon and later opened a produce store in Clayton. I got involved in this article because I was interested in what he used to do. I had heard some things about the way he used to run the store but I had never heard the whole story. So when Wig brought up the idea to do the article, I was more than willing to interview Papa.

This article is based on Papa's store, how it was run, what it looked like, how he shipped his produce, etc. I remember when I was younger, I used to stay around the store much of the time after school and during the summers. One thing that sticks out in my mind is the wooden floors covered with a light coat of dust. I also remember the old cash register and how I would just sit in front of it opening the drawers with the lever and then closing them again. There was also the potbellied stove in which coal was burned, and the shed filled with tables high enough for me to walk under that had sacks of fertilizer and seed on them.

Today my father and uncle are partners in a large cabbage business. They have hundreds of acres of cabbage in Dillard and Moultrie, Georgia, and Hastings, Florida. Papa got them interested in the business as boys. Every now and then, he would let them sell a load of cabbage. When they first started, he would loan them the money to buy the cabbage and they would keep any profit

PLATE 92

made off the sales. Then when they were about in the tenth grade, he took them to
the bank to get their own loan.

In the summers, I work for my Uncle Jim in Dillard; I have been working for
him and my father since I was seven and have learned how to drive a tractor and
how to raise and sell cabbage. This summer my uncle is planning on letting me
and two of my friends who work with me have our own field. So who knows?
Maybe he is starting the third generation of Gillespies in the business.

RANCE GILLESPIE

EARL GILLESPIE: Old man Frank Earl was one of the first builders
we had. He was the best builder we had back in those days. I was
named after him. He tried to get my father to go into business with
him, but Dad said that he was going to spend most of his time with his
boys. My father's name was James Brabson. Dr. Brabson of Macon
County was the one that delivered and named him. Back then Dr.
Brabson had to ride a horse from right this side of Franklin.

Our house was up in the valley toward Rabun Gap. Like most people around here, we lived pretty hard. When I was growing up, they used to make our underclothes out of fertilizer sacks. They were rough. Our hand towels came from them also. Finally they got stuff made out of cotton. An old man down here one time said he didn't know what to think about these new drawers!

We raised all our own food, and we gathered some stuff from the woods. When Daddy would bring the chestnuts in the house, we would scald them in the shell. We had a big vat or a big tub and we would pour four or five bushels of chestnuts in that hot water and stir them up. Just keep stirring them that way and the chestnuts would get hot enough to kill the germs in them. That would keep the shell and the meat of the nut soft. It wouldn't get hard then. Then we would put salt on them. I've seen upstairs at the old homeplace as much as five hundred bushels of chestnuts at one time. We could have made bread or something with them but we never did. All we did was just eat them.

We had rail fences on each side of the road and we also used rail fences to keep the livestock up, and to keep people from coming in on your land. I remember our first rail fence down at the old homeplace. We had locust stakes, two of them in each place where the rails crossed, and we put them down in the ground and put a wood cap over them. You couldn't tear it down; you could hardly shake it. The locust stakes went straight down in the ground where the fence crossed and you put them on either side. Then you put the cap on top made out of chestnut or locust, either one. It is made out of just one big slab of wood. You bore two holes in it and just slide it down over the top of those two stakes. There wasn't any use to put a peg in it but we sometimes did if we wanted extra support.

We had horses, mules, cows. I've known my daddy to have twenty-five head of horses there at one time, and you know you have to have a very substantial place to keep a herd of horses. They will fight and run into that fence.

And everybody raised cabbage. My uncle Bob had about twenty acres, and that was a lot of cabbage back in those days. I'd say it would be equivalent to two hundred acres today.

Even when I was little, my father was dealing in produce—picking it up from farmers and taking it to cities to sell it for them. My father and I would go up to Scaley Mountain and haul produce out in a mule-pulled wagon. I first started going with my daddy when I was six years old. Then I started buying it by myself when I was about fourteen. Daddy just turned me loose. He said, "You're gonna have

PLATE 93   Earl Gillespie.

PLATE 94   The old National Cash Register. Sara said, "Earl got it from the richest merchant in Elbert County. It was made in 1898. I would say a lot of money has been passed through it."

PLATE 95   When Wig was in college, he spent a summer in Rabun County, got to know Earl and Sara and their family, and drew this pen and ink sketch of the market in Clayton as a gift to the Gillespies.

PLATE 96   Earl Gillespie recalling humorous memories.

PLATE 97   Earl in his living room with his son Jim, Wig, his wife Sara, and his grandson Rance.

to get up there and buy your own. Take the wagon up there and get me a load of cabbage." And after I would buy the cabbage, Daddy would sell it. We were kind of in the business together. We would go up on the mountain and bring the cabbage down on a wagon. If there wasn't enough cabbage we'd finish out a load with any type thing we could, like chestnuts and apples.

One time we went up to Cartoogachaye and bought apples from Ed Battle. They were the best apples you ever ate. Coming through Gapple Mountain, me and Lawrence were driving the team. Dad said, "We will just spend the night here." [Dad] was up in the wagon, me and Lawrence built up a fire, and a panther came so near you could see him in the light of the fire. The mules got to braying and everything. They could smell him, you know. We just stood there, me and Lawrence did, and watched him go loafing off down the hollow.

We hauled the produce to towns like Athens and Washington and Thomaston and Elberton to sell it. Elberton was a good market. One time Dad and my brother had shipped a load of apples down there, and I went to help them finish selling those apples, and I decided to open a little store down there. That was in about 1925. Some of my brothers and I ran that store, and my father and the other brothers would stay in Rabun County and do the buying and keep us supplied. I have had as much as eight thousand bushels of apples in there at one time; and oranges, grapefruit, and tangerines brought up from Florida. We carried all that stuff. I would say we had one of the prettiest stores in Elbert County.

Then the Depression hit and we lost it. I don't like to think about that! And when some government jobs opened up in Rabun County, some of us left there and came back home. Not long after that is when I started my store in Clayton.

I first remember coming to Clayton with my daddy. Daddy was on the jury. I saw the walkway and it was built out of plank then. The jury men were laying all over the sidewalk drunk. I asked my daddy what was wrong with them. I said, "Dad what are they doing?" He said, "Oh, they're just asleep." I went with my daddy on over to the courthouse and the judge was about as drunk as the rest of them. He about had to call court off, he got so drunk!

When I came back, it still looked about the same. It was just a big mud hole. There still weren't any paved streets or sidewalks. The sidewalks were board. I have seen mules mire up to their bellies there where the drugstores are now and up that hill there. The first time they tried to make an improvement on the streets they laid slabs, such as they have at these sawmills, on the street and that is what the wagon had to roll over. They laid them crossways slightly on top of each other.

Just before the Depression, there wasn't but about four or five stores in the whole town. Louie Young had one up on the corner, Leon Bleckley who was the mayor had one up there below the bank, Marcus Keener had one above Louie Young's, and Bryant Hill had one. When the Depression came, some of those stores had to go out of business. Leon's was a grocery store. It wasn't the first grocery store in Clayton. Marcus Keener had the first grocery store. When I say grocery store, I mean they sold coffee, flour, dry goods and all that too. They kept their produce under the counter. Then the rest of the stuff was the coffee, flour, hardware, and cloth. Almost all those general stores had a little produce back under the counter. They kept tomatoes and cucumbers and squash, and so forth. They didn't have it out on the main floor because there wasn't enough room. They had to keep it under the counter. On the main floor they had stuff like shoes, dry goods. The old stores kept canned goods, salmon and stuff, back under the counter.

But I was the first real produce store in Clayton, and I was the only store in town that also sold wholesale. I started with produce about 1932—rented the building for seventy-five dollars a month. Then I moved into wholesale about 1934, and borrowed the money to buy the building. It cost three thousand dollars. I got five hundred dollars from Tom Hamby and the rest from T. A. Duckett at the bank. And I paid it back in four or five years. They didn't want me to pay them off that fast. They wanted to keep getting the interest from the loan. But they didn't pull that stuff on me. I was about as slick as they were! I went ahead and paid it because I wanted to be in full ownership.

When I first got that store, it was just an old empty framed-in building. It used to be a blacksmith shop. It didn't have a ceiling in it, no weatherboard or anything like that. The studs showed and everything. The outside was covered with clapboard. The inside had nothing in it. It was just gutted out. I've had hay and cottonseed meal packed to the ceiling. The first thing I did was put in a ceiling. And I had a shed put on. My brother and I built that shed, and then on the inside Harmon Deal and I put the ceiling in.

It was pretty rough, but it worked out. Customers would come and tie their horses and mules up right in front of the store when the streets were still mud. And I sold a few things besides produce—not many: some hardware, clothing, Pittsburgh Paint. I was the first to sell that in Clayton. The paint and flour and stuff like that would carry me through the winter months when there wasn't much produce. But we made it a policy that when a man called for an item that we didn't have, we wouldn't order it until three customers requested it. It just wasn't worth buying something that wouldn't sell, and I couldn't afford it.

I had a coffee mill that I would parch coffee in. I would parch it, then I would put it in a grinder and grind it up. I had me a grinder that I would pour the parched coffee in and grind it up. I parched it in a skillet on a potbelly stove that I had there at the store. Some customer wanted it blended, and I'd take Luzianne and Teaberry coffee and mix it for them.

But the Depression hit us hard. I could tell a difference. The demand for the stuff that I was selling just was not there. People just were not able to buy it. They couldn't pay for it. I used to take in corn, potatoes and stuff like that for exchange. That was the way I kept my stock up. And me and Leon Bleckley used to walk home at night. Leon would say, "Earl, I had a good day's business today. I did $3.75." He was honest in it, too. And maybe I done $1.25. That's a fact. That's all I made some days. [What kept me from going out of business during the Depression] was, I had a lot of guts. That is the big thing. I took chickens and eggs [in trade]. I never did say no to people. [One time] George Darnell brought me seven two-hundred-to three-hundred-pound hogs. I gave George a little cash and the rest of it he took in flour. I took the hogs and cut them up and salted them down and sold them.

Then when a train would wreck and maybe the cars were off the track or off down in a holler, I would go down there and look at what was in the cars. I would say "I'll give you so much for this." I bought the stuff at a big discount. They almost gave it away. Down in Elberton was a good place for that stuff. Seaboard railroad went through there. You will always hear about when a train wrecks. Somebody is going to tell you about it. Then you go down there and you don't say anything to them when you first get down there. You wait maybe three or four hours for everybody to settle down. Then you ask them what would they take for that car out there. We salvaged groceries, flour, lard, coffee and all that stuff. It wasn't even hurt. The people that owned the stuff on the train, the insurance would pay them off.

But the big thing that kept us going was hauling that produce wholesale to markets like Atlanta. By that time I had a truck. The first truck I got was from Uncle John Howard. Of course, it wouldn't haul but about thirty to forty bushels of apples. A pickup truck these days would haul more than it could. It was a T model. I got it in 1919. By the time I opened up in Clayton, I had a much bigger one.

What we'd do is go around to the fields and pick up the produce. The farmers would pick it and I would come by and pick it up. Like we might go up to Jackson County, and all there was were these little narrow, muddy roads. It would take us all day or two days, sometimes, to get loaded and get back.

Back then those farmers would cut all the cabbage and put them in tubs. Then they would weigh each individual tub. Then they would put the tub on a sled and slide it off the mountain behind a mule. Then we'd load it on the truck. Then, coming back off these muddy roads, we sometimes had to tie a log behind the truck. That was the only way we could slow ourselves down. One time me and A. L. was coming off the mountain with what we thought was a heavy load—it would be no more than a good pickup load now—and our brakes were just about out. The roads were just wide enough for just one car. So coming down the mountain we cut a log down and hitched it behind the truck with a chain. I mean it wouldn't stop us, but it kept us from speeding. If another car came we would just have to work our way around it. Sometimes they had places along the road to where you could pull over and get out of the way.

Then we'd bring the produce back to the store and grade it and pack it. Pack the beans in hampers. Grade the potatoes and pack them. When I graded potatoes I would just run them through the warehouse behind the store. The grader was a frame with a wire cable doing the rolling. It was sized to drop out the small potatoes. I had people standing at the sides to pick out the bad ones. Then I bagged them in burlap sacks, a hundred pounds to the sack. So I took beans, tomatoes, peppers, cucumbers, and all that to Atlanta. I insisted that [the farmers] grow a lot of different things so when I took it to Atlanta, I would have a market for it. I would take the produce down to Atlanta, even during the Depression, and I still got a market for it. People had to have something to eat, you know. All I would take were just vegetables and apples and anything that would sell.

Back before we had trucks, it was pretty hard to get stuff to market. From the time we picked the produce up and took it to wherever it was we were going, it took us about two weeks. We would sleep under the wagon, camp out alongside the road or in the woods. Lots of times while we were camped out, people would come into the camp and buy stuff. Then after we sold out, we would try to come right back with the wagon. Lots of times they had a little campground or somewhere for us to camp and get water and stuff like that. I came in a snap of getting shot one time. We camped on this guy's land and I went to his house and I said, "I'm camped up here and I want to get some water." He came out there with a gun. I had a little short gun that I always carried with me and I pulled it out. He came to the camp to see if I was telling the truth. He said, "Well, young man, you told me the truth, but you came close to getting hurt." We had to haul all of our feed for the horses. We grew most of the horse feed. We just packed the fodder or whatever kind of feed it was on top of the produce.

But even after we got trucks it wasn't much easier because the roads weren't paved. It was dirt road all the way to Atlanta. Now there was one little strip of pavement in Habersham County. That was about sixty years ago. It was just a one-way drive. You couldn't get but just one car on it at a time, and if you ran off the side of the road, you were in the mud. That stretch of pavement started over here at Dick's Hill Road. Burnell Wilbanks, who has worked for us fifty years, used to carry water over there when the people were working on that road. It started just as the road starts down the hill and it went down there for less than two miles. That was a state project. I think it was a CCC deal. Burnell said they would go around in a truck and anybody that wanted to work they would put them on that road project. Burnell was about twelve years old then. He started hauling water. That was his first job. He just got a big five-gallon bucket and lugged that thing around with a dipper and started giving everybody water. He got ten cents a day.

The reason they built it there was because ever'body was complaining about the road. According to Burnell, that used to be a big throughway where they used to bring all the apples and stuff through. They had to pave it because coming up that hill, ever'body was spinning or bogging down. It was paved out of brick, like Atlanta was first paved out of when I first started hauling produce down there.

When you finally got to Atlanta, the market was located on Piedmont Avenue. The first market I carried a load down there to was a curb market. I would have to drive the truck in there. All they had was a simple market space in toward the sidewalk. The sidewalks were made out of plank. And you never knew what you were going to get for what you'd brought down. Sometimes we got caught in a bind. The market would clean out and we might get maybe two dollars a hundred for the cabbage. Then we would go buy another load based on the price that we got last, and we would come back and the market might drop down to say fifty cents a hundred. So you might lose like fifteen to twenty dollars plus your gas, and that was a big lick back then. The gas alone back then was twelve to thirteen cents a gallon.

Then it started jumping up and every time the price of gas would go up I would raise the price of my cabbage. I had to, to make it work out for me.

But there was no communication over the telephone or anything. Didn't *have* phones. There was no communication at all. You had to take a chance. Whatever the market was the day you went down is what you got. It was a big gamble. You might lose thirty to forty dollars a load. That is like losing four hundred today.

But they were taking a chance, too. You just had to work together or you were all in trouble. One of the buyers in Atlanta was W. W. Lowe, and he came to me one time asking for two bushels of beans. I said, "W. W. you don't even take enough to advertise."

He said, "No, to tell you the truth, I don't have the money."

I said, "Do you want me to change that?"

He said, "I would appreciate it." I unloaded all my beans. There were a hundred to a hundred and twenty-five bushels there. I just took his word that he would pay me back for them later. I'd let him take the responsibility for them and just pay me when he sold them. I said, "Just pay me for part of them and keep your capital to buy some other people's beans if they come in here."

We were both taking a chance, but it worked out. Everybody was in together. Farmers took a chance on me, I took a chance on the market. Everybody risked.

Jim, one of Earl's three sons, got into the produce business through his father and is still in it today. He added a fitting conclusion to this article:

Daddy's big customers later on were Kroger, which used to be the Rogers Company, and Winn Dixie which was Dixie then. I still sell to them.

The shelf life of the cabbage that Daddy used to work with was maybe two or three weeks without refrigeration. Now the cabbage will hold up two days without refrigeration. The cabbage now is grown for speed. Back then it would take at least a hundred and twenty days for it to mature. It grew nice and slow. Now we have seventy-five-day cabbage. Back then every head was placed in the truck by hand and done very slowly and carefully with every head pointed one way and the stalks pushed down. It made them look better. Now we have harvest crews just dumping it into a cart, then dumping it into a box, then loading it on a truck. Now, that's handled three times. Then it goes to a chain store. Then the chain stores deliver it to the outlet store like Winn Dixie. Then it goes on the shelf.

So you go in the store and say this produce stinks, but it has been handled four to six times. Back then everything was slow and easy and they took pride in their produce. You still try to take pride in it, but it's just such a fast-moving thing now. That is the change in the produce Daddy was working with. He had time to work with it and market it. Now you have a matter of days to market it.

One of the most interesting things is that the produce business is one of the last big businesses where still today there are no signed contracts. You phone the people from, say, Kroger and a price is agreed on. It makes no difference if the price goes up between the time that you make the deal and the time you sell them. I mean you readjust for your *next* load, but you get the agreed-on price for the last one, no matter what the market does. It is still just one of the old businesses where nothing is in writing. It is all your word over the telephone.

"QUILTING—THE JOY OF MY LIFE"
Aunt Arie Carpenter

On many visits to our contacts, the subject of quilts often eases its way into our conversations. Though we have not published much on quilts in a long time (see *The Foxfire Book,* "A Quilt Is Something Human"), we have continued to gather information on quilting and some of the traditional quilt patterns of this area. What follows is only a sampling. We have an ongoing collection which includes examples and patterns for at least fifty quilts. Here we include a few that are unusual or visibly striking even in black-and-white photographs, but truly vivid when actually seen in color.

For several years I have been aware of the many picturesque quilt patterns seen in homes around here. However, I had never realized the effort put into the actual sewing of those quilts. I have now begun to observe the quality of the tiny, hand-stitched rows of quilting. We have been told that traditionally the care and skill with which the stitches were made and the variety of embroidery stitches used by a young woman indicated that she was a good seamstress and considered very eligible for marriage.

Several women we have talked to specifically for this quilt collection who are knowledgeable on the subject are Lassie Bradshaw and Mary Franklin, who operate the Georgia Mountain Arts Crafts Co-op in Tallulah Falls; Mrs. Harriet Echols, who has made quilts most of her life; Mrs. Clyde English, a retired high school teacher, who is actively involved in the Tiger [Georgia] Homemakers' Club, which makes several quilts a year to raise money for community projects; Stella Burrell, who earns her living making quilts; and her daughter, Andrea Burrell Potts, who is a former Foxfire student and proprietor of the Tryphosa Craft Shop in Otto, North Carolina, specializing in the sale of handmade quilts made locally, Mrs. Esco Pitts, Mrs. Robert (Edith) Cannon and her sister Mrs. Rose O'Neal, Mrs. Isaac (Ver-

PLATE 98   The monkey wrench quilt on the frame the day we visited the Tiger Home-makers' quilting was an old top, bought by Mrs. Clyde English from someone in Hiawas-see, Georgia, that was being quilted for her to give to a member of her family. The eight to twelve ladies would finish this quilt in two to three days. They meet whenever it is conve-nient for them. Whenever they are quilting, they bring their lunches and quilt for however many hours they can work into their own schedules—sometimes only an hour or two, but usually four to six hours a day. When this quilt is finished, another member may bring one of hers to be quilted, or the ladies may donate a quilt top and quilt it to be sold and the money used for a community project.

From left to right: Mildred Stroud, Rose O'Neal, Marian Gregory, Vernice Lovell, Mrs. Clyde English, Dot Parkman, Edith Cannon, and Myrtie York.

PLATE 99   Mrs. Harriet Echols still makes quilts to sell and to give to her own children, nieces and nephews, grandchildren and, now, great-grandchildren. Here she is showing Shane Holcomb a quilt she has in her quilting frame and pat-terns of other quilts.

nice) Lovell, and Mrs. Ruth Holcomb all shared their time, expertise, and love of quilting with us on cold, snowy days when we would spend three and four hours at each of their homes photographing, measuring, drawing diagrams, and asking questions. They allowed us to photograph old family quilts, giving us the histories of them and of new quilts that are copies of quilt patterns known to have been owned by people around here fifty and a hundred years ago.

MELINDA HUNTER

Students who worked on quilt articles: Melinda Hunter, Shane Holcomb, Karen Lovell, Kim English, and Teresa Cook. Additional diagrams by Oh Soon Shropshire and Joseph Fowler.

CRAZY QUILTS

My project for the quilts article was to find out all I could about quilts called "crazy quilts" in our county, or friendship quilts if they are signed or personalized in some way and presented to someone as a gift.

I started by following up a phone call from Mrs. Isaac (Vernice) Lovell, a member of the Tiger Homemakers' Club who was present at the quilting we attended with Mrs. Clyde English. Mrs. Lovell allowed us to study and photograph a quilt that has been in her family for more than sixty years.

Two outstanding examples of fine stitchery on crazy quilts were hanging right on the walls in our Foxfire classroom. They had been donated to us by Aunt Arie Carpenter more than ten years ago. When some Foxfire students were visiting her one time and admiring some of her quilts, she said:

"I enjoy quilting the best of anything in this world. Get your cloth and get whatever design [you want to make]. How I wish I could quilt and do like I used to. This is Uncle Fred Childer's wife's scraps. All these is. Now I'd piece her one and me one, and she'd get her half and I'd get my half. That's how come me to have so many quilts. Of course, I never had no such dresses as this. We wasn't able to have it.

"But quilting was the joy of my life. Working with that. Ever' little piece."

Mrs. Sue Pennington, a charter member of the Rabun County Historical Society and an avid quilt collector, helped us identify the various stitches in the crazy quilts we had photographed, and gave us information that helped us ask the right kinds of questions of our contacts about crazy quilts.

KIM ENGLISH

REFERENCES

Handbook of Stitches, Grete Petersen and Elsie Svennas. New York: Van Nostrand Reinhold Co., 1970.

Quilting Manual—Now! Designer's Boutique, Delores A. Hinson. New York: Hearthside Press, Inc., 1970.

PLATE 100   Shane Holcomb, left, and Kim English hold a quilt given to Foxfire by Aunt Arie Carpenter, which now hangs on display in our classroom. Aunt Arie told the students at the time she gave it to them that it was made about the time of World War I and she called the pattern "fishtail."

There are only five primary pattern pieces for this quilt. Seam allowances should be added to the dimensions shown. (Note the use of dark and light choices of fabrics to create a striking pattern.)

The overall dimensions for this quilt are eighty-two by sixty-one inches. There are twenty blocks in the quilt. The piecing diagram (Plate 102) is for center block, sashes, and corner blocks. The strips between the finished squares are called sashes, sashings, or slipings. Mary Franklin told us she had heard a woman years ago use the expression "sliping the quilt blocks." Sliping is an old British expression used in quilting.

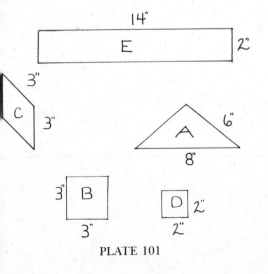

PLATE 101

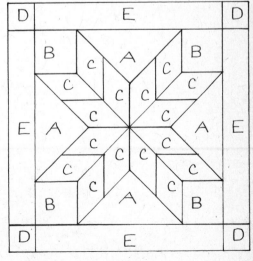

PLATE 102

PLATE 103   Even more interesting than the design on the front are the varied, intricate quilting patterns on the reverse side. The quilting patterns used for the outer blocks are elbow, straight, and diagonal. The six inside blocks have a common pattern in the center (note Plate 104) but have different corner designs (squares on left in Plate 105) and a variety of triangular designs along the four sides.

PLATE 104

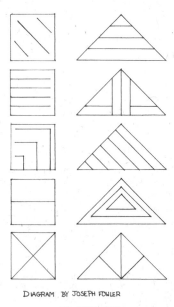

DIAGRAM BY JOSEPH FOWLER

PLATE 105

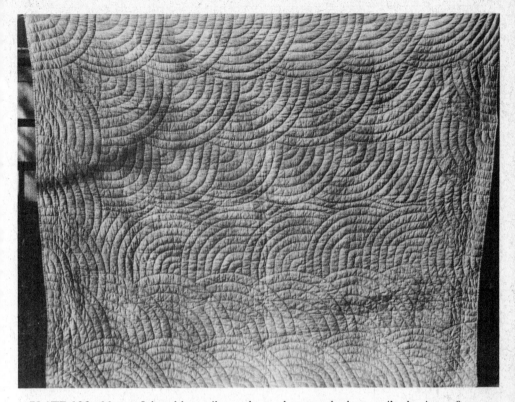

PLATE 106   Many of the older quilts we have photographed are quilted using a fan or shell design. Mrs. Mary Franklin told us, "The fan is the first method of quilting that I remember seeing used. The way the people used to lay the fans or the shells off was, they used string tied to a piece of chalk or something else to mark with. If they wanted a shell six inches wide, they'd tie a six-inch piece of cord to the chalk. Then they held the end of the string and drew off a fan shape. They moved it up as much as they wanted [for the space between each row of quilting]. But the lines of stitching had to be real close together to hold the cotton padding in place. That was just the way they liked to quilt. They liked a lot of quilting. That was a sign of good workmanship, you know. If they made big, far-apart lines, they were considered sloppy quilters."

Mrs. Stella Burrell added, "I've seen quite a few quilts quilted in the shell pattern. You start in one corner. My mother used to always do the fan. They are almost the same. The fan is just bigger than the shell.

"You always quilt on the pattern side. You put the lining on first, then the cotton batting, and then you put your top on. That's the only way I've seen it done. Generally, the lining is basted to the quilt with thread to hold it tight. The top is pulled and stretched all the way around."

The lining extends three to four inches beyond the quilt top on all four sides. The batting, usually made of cotton bats but sometimes of wool, is laid over the lining. The top is laid over the batting. The three parts are basted together. There are tiny nails protruding at short intervals all along the quilting frame, and the outer edges of the lining are pushed down onto these.

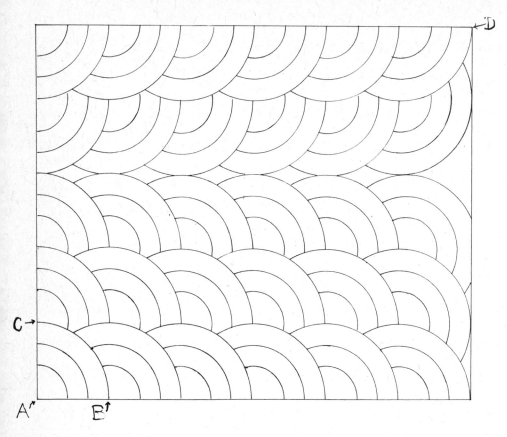

PLATE 107 Diagram of shell or fan quilting technique:

A person quilting using the shell design may choose any distance she wishes between the arcs of each shell. For the one we measured, there was a distance of one inch from the corner (A) where the quilting was started to the first arc. Then there was a distance of one-half inch to the next arc and a distance of one-half inch between the second and third arcs. The pattern repeated itself: one inch, one-half inch, one-half inch, one inch, for a distance of twelve inches or eighteen arcs.

The second shell is begun by placing the twelve-inch length of string at point B on the diagram. The lines are drawn for it as they were for the first. This procedure is followed all the way across the quilt.

For the second row of shells, the twelve-inch length of string is placed at point C. The same procedure is followed across the quilt. The third row of shells is done from this side of the quilt. Then quilter goes to point D, and works from the other side of the quilt. The reason for this is that usually no one can reach farther across the quilt than three rows of shells. Of course, when there are four or more people quilting at one time, the shells are usually all marked off and each quilter works on a shell most convenient to her.

After the quilting is completed, the edges of the lining are folded over the top's edges and a hemming stitch gives the quilt a final touch.

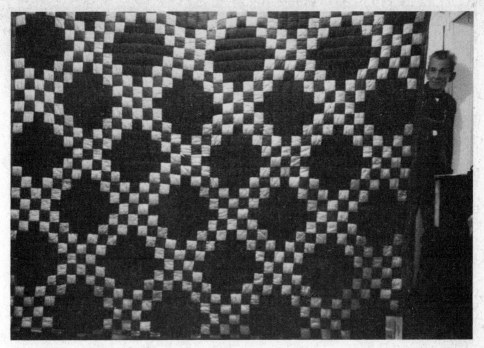

PLATE 108   "Mama made all six of us girls a double Irish chain quilt. She reversed the colors, so they were all different. This quilt was made in the early 1930s," Edith Cannon told us.

The double Irish chain is made by cutting all ten-inch squares from one color. For this quilt, they are navy blue. The two-inch squares are from solid colors of red, blue, and white fabrics. The pattern for the quilt is developed from: (A) alternate ten-inch squares of blue with a white two-inch square sewn on each corner, and (B) two-inch squares sewn into ten-inch blocks. The small squares are put together as indicated in the diagram (Plate 109). R = red; B = navy blue; W = white.

Mrs. Cannon showed us the back of the double Irish chain quilt and told us, "They had sheep and sheared them and washed the wool. Mama carded her own wool. She laid the lining out, then placed the wool bats on it. She put the quilt top over them and began quilting. The back of this quilt is made of feed sacks dyed navy with Rit dye." (Plate 110)

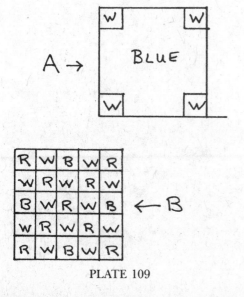

PLATE 109

PLATE 110

PLATE 111   This quilt was made about 1920 and is now owned by Mrs. Isaac Lovell. The fabrics vary from heavy menswear to velvet and other delicate dress fabrics. There are one or more different flower patterns in varied stitches on each square and the squares are connected with assorted embroidery stitches. Close-up views of the quilt are shown in Plates 112, 113, and 114.

PLATE 112

PLATE 113

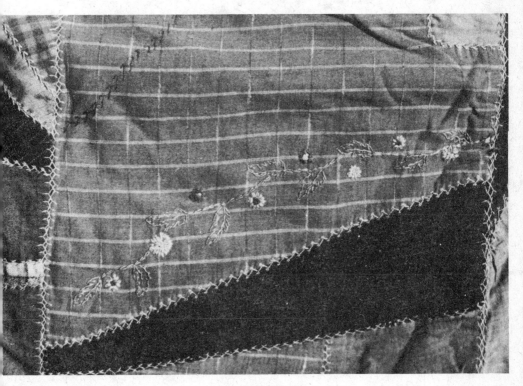

PLATE 114

PLATE 115   This friendship quilt belonged to Mrs. Nan Powell, a lifetime resident of
Rabun County, Georgia. It was made about 1898 and, judging from the names embroidered on it, was made by the young people in the Wolf Fork and Germany communities as a
wedding gift for Mrs. Powell's father, Dock L. Justus, and his bride, Lula Mosley, who were
married January 4, 1899.

It has been a long-standing custom here for young people to make, as wedding gifts,
friendship quilts. They may be in a standard quilt pattern (as this one is, but the name is
unknown) or may be a "crazy quilt." Each person will make a square for the quilt and
embroider her name and perhaps the date on it. Then all the women friends, and sometimes men, will meet together and quilt the top and present it to the bridal couple.

A close-up of one section of the worn quilt (Plate 116). There is a flower embroidered on
one corner, "Friendship and Remembrance" on another corner, "Laura Dickerson, Wolf
Fork, Ga." on another corner, and "Quilt Piece for Mr. D. L. Justus" in the upper right
corner.

Another square in the same quilt shows someone's initials (Plate 117).

PLATE 116

PLATE 117

PLATE 118   This quilt was made by Aunt Arie of scraps from fine dress materials, mostly silk. The pieces were assembled into large squares basted together with tiny stitches. Then decorative embroidery stitches in red, light blue, dark blue, yellow, orange, light purple, dark purple, green, aqua, and pink embroidery thread cover the basting. This quilt is tacked to its lining (made of bleached flour sacks with some of the lettering still visible) by embroidery thread of the colors used in the embroidery stitches plus black. She sometimes combined two colors in the tacking knot. There is no filling or batting in this quilt, so I have called it a "summer quilt," or perhaps it was used as bedspread because of the pretty and delicate fabrics of which it is made.

Aunt Arie was born in 1885 and spent her young adult life caring for her ailing mother, so we have assumed that she made many of her quilts from 1905 to 1923 She married in 1923 and probably did not have as much time to do quilt work as before. By the time she was introduced to Foxfire in 1970, she had a paralyzed arm and could no longer do the fine hand work that is demonstrated in her quilts. (Plates 119 and 120 show close-up sections of the summer quilt.)

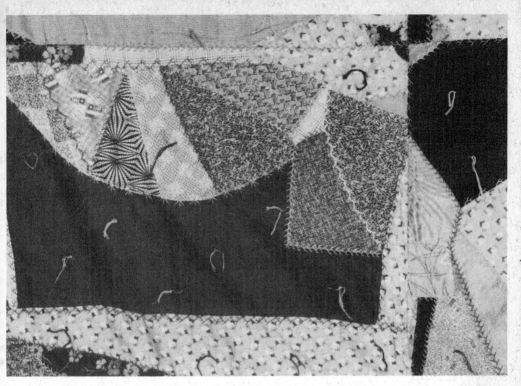

PLATE 119

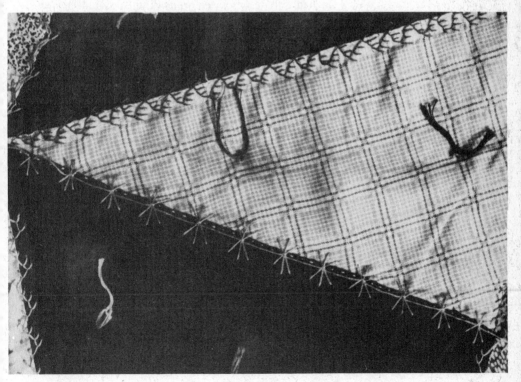

PLATE 120

PLATE 121 This quilt was made of scraps that were probably from Aunt Arie's cotton dresses, and shirts and pants worn by her husband. The materials are printed and solid cottons, worsted wool, and cotton flannels. They appear to have been basted together with tiny hand stitching and then stitched with decorative embroidery stitches of black, white, and red. Note that several pieces have flower designs embroidered on them.

Since there is a filling in this quilt, I have called it a "winter quilt," or perhaps it was used as an everyday utility cover since it is made of hardier fabrics than the "summer quilt" made of lightweight, less durable materials. (Plate 122 shows the arrowhead stitch (A) and the feathered chain stitch (B). Plate 123 shows the herringbone stitch (A) and the multiple feather stitch (B). Plate 124 shows the chevron stitch.)

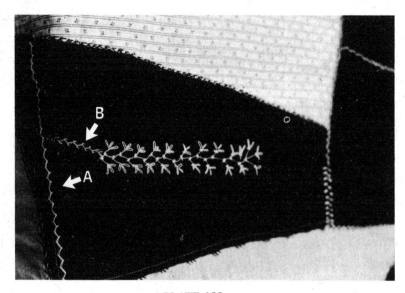

PLATE 122

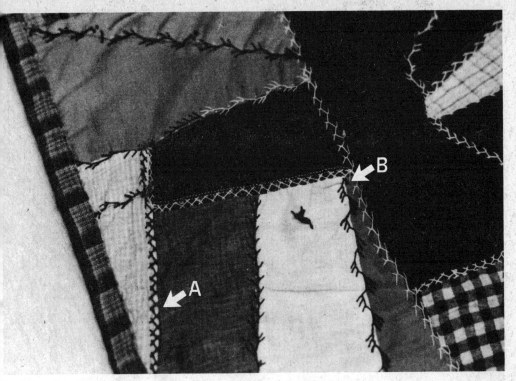

PLATE 123

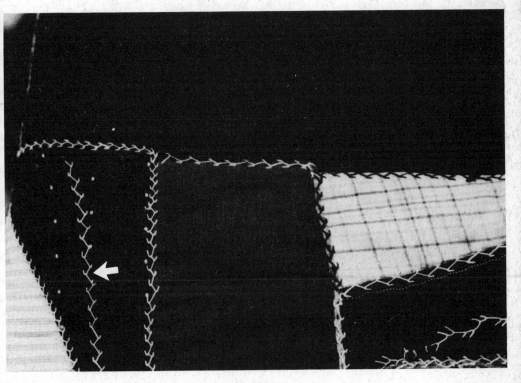

PLATE 124

PLATE 125   Kim English, left, and Karen Lovell are holding the "winter quilt," which is backed with a batting of wool or cotton and lined with a plaid cotton material. It is not quilted but tacked with black embroidery thread.

PLATE 126 Edith Cannon's "churn dash" quilt. "My mother helped me make this one when I was ten years old. We called it the churn dash, but now this pattern is sometimes called the monkey wrench." Plate 127 shows the pattern for the churn dash or monkey wrench. This is the same pattern being quilted in Plate 98.

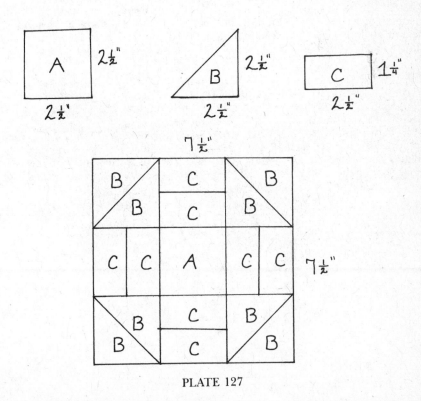

PLATE 127

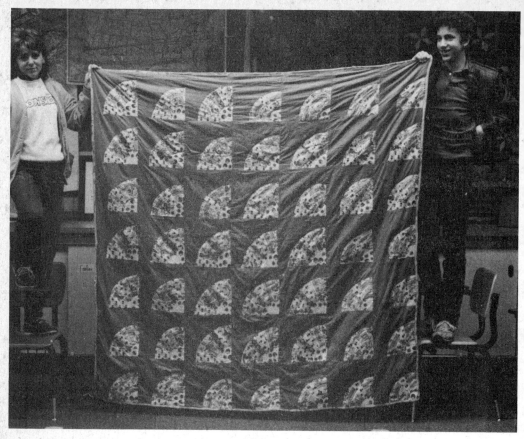

PLATE 128 Kim English, left, and Shane Holcomb holding Mrs. Clyde English's quilt, "grandmother's fan." Mrs. English told us, "This is an old pattern. Everybody's made them through the years. You can make the 'Dresden plate' pattern by putting four of the fans together."

PLATE 129 Diagram for the grandmother's fan quilt: (A)-Quarter circles are cut of contrasting fabric, (B)-Six pieces of varying printed fabrics for ribs of fan, (C)-Ten-inch squares of a solid fabric onto which the fans are stitched.

Directions: B pieces are first stitched together to form the ribs of the fan. A is then placed over the narrow ends of the B's as illustrated in the diagram. Turn the raw edge of the circular side under as it covers the ribs' ends. The fan is then stitched onto C, turning under the raw edges of the wide end of the B's. The squares are then stitched together as shown in Plate 128.

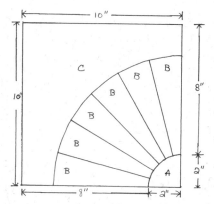

PLATE 130 A "Dresden plate" quilt made by Mrs. Cannon. Plate 131 shows the principal pattern pieces. Cut seventeen to eighteen A's for each plate. Sew them together in a circle. Cover the center hole with a circle (B), turning under the edges of the circle as you stitch it onto the "plate." The completed plate is then placed on a fourteen-inch square of a solid-colored fabric. The squares are then attached to one another with strips of a contrasting fabric.

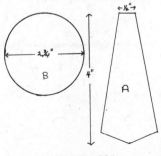

PLATE 131

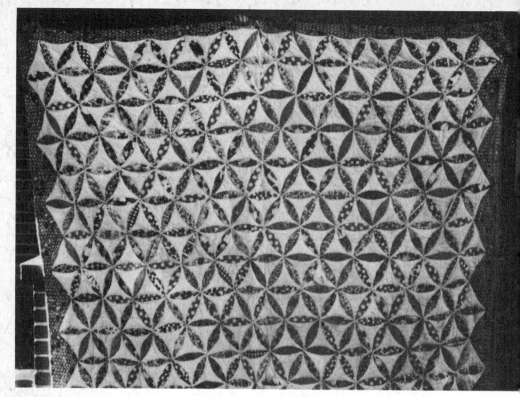

PLATE 132 "Joseph's coat of many colors" is a quilt made by Mrs. Harriet Echols and very few other people in our community. She is the only one we could find who still had the pattern pieces for it. She remembers this pattern being made when she was quite young. This particular quilt was made many years ago but the colors are still brilliant.

There are only two pattern pieces in this quilt. Plate 133 shows the shape and dimensions. The A pieces are made of various colorful prints and the B pieces of one solid color, in this case white. Mrs. Echols warned that if they are not cut precisely and joined carefully, the quilt may pucker.

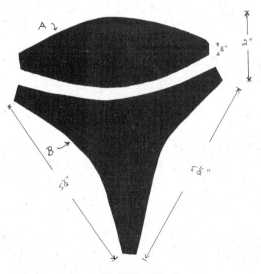

PLATE 133

PLATE 134   The "grandmother's flower garden" is a popular quilt. The hexagon-shaped pattern is the only piece in the entire quilt, and may vary in size from quilt to quilt. (See Plates 135 and 136.) We have seen tiny pieces carefully stitched with a myriad of colors truly representing a well-tended flower garden in spring, and other quilts with the hexagons as large as one and one-half to two inches on each of the six sides. You can create the effect you want the quilt to give by carefully choosing and placing the fabric colors.

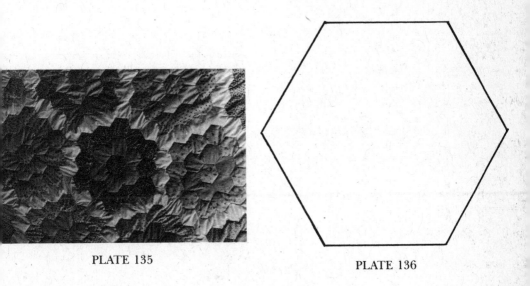

PLATE 135

PLATE 136

PLATE 137   The "drunkard's path" quilt. A close-up view of this quilt shows how pieces must be arranged for the effect (Plate 138). Only two types of fabric are used, but equal numbers of each pattern piece must be cut from the solid fabric and from the coordinating print. The two pattern pieces (Plate 139) may be arranged in several ways to give the drunkard's path as shown here, the "snail's trail," and "falling timbers."

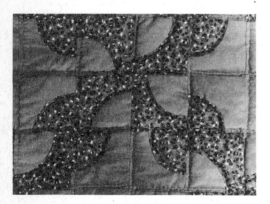

PLATE 138

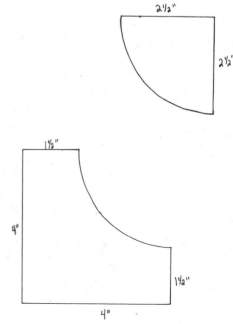

PLATE 139

PLATE 140   The "bear paw" is a quilt pattern that several ladies have talked about being made here since quite early in the 1900s. Mrs. Edith Cannon showed us one her mother had made before 1930. The one pictured here was made by Mrs. Ruth Holcomb. Plate 141 shows the three principal parts of the square for the bear paw quilt. Plate 142 shows a whole square in the quilt. "L" and "D" indicate light or dark fabric. The squares are joined by strips of a matching or contrasting fabric.

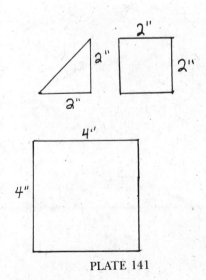

PLATE 141

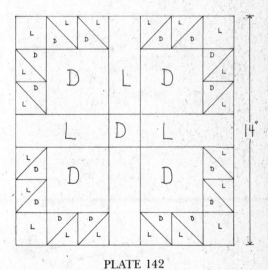

PLATE 142

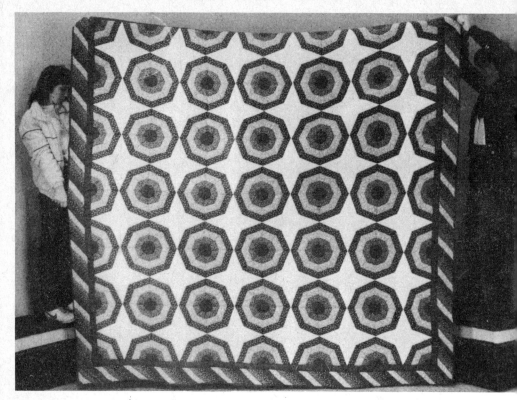

PLATE 143   The "spiderweb" quilt is an intricate design we came across in several places. Varying the design of the patterned pieces in the "webs" produced different effects. Also, at first glance one may see "stars" instead of webs. Note that the stars are quilted to enhance their shapes (Plate 144).

Plate 145 shows the pattern pieces for the spiderweb quilt and plate 146 shows how the pieces are assembled.

PLATE 144

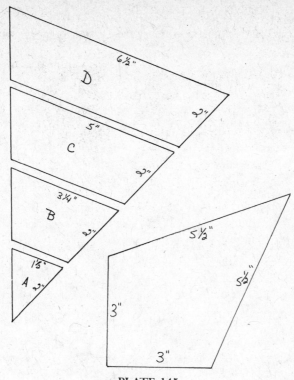

PLATE 145

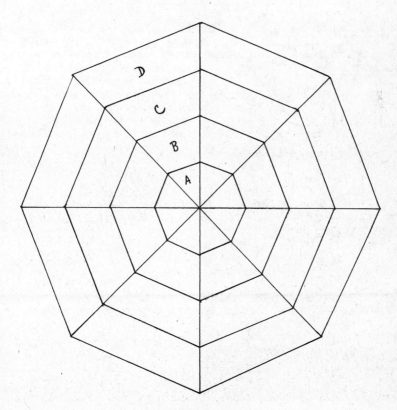

PLATE 146

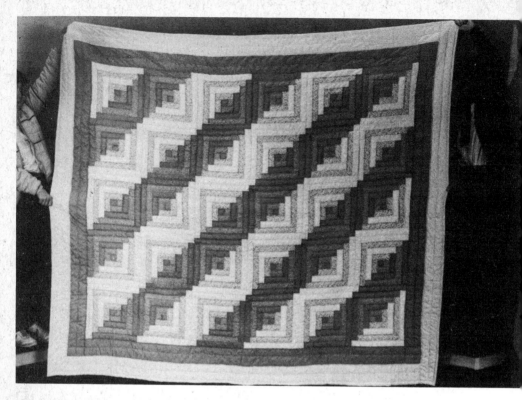

PLATE 147   The log cabin pattern is an easy one to follow, and leaves itself open to many various designs, just by the choice of fabric colors and prints. Plates 147, 148, and 149 are only three of a multitude of effects. To get the effect shown in plate 147, place dark fabrics on two adjoining sides of each square and light colors opposite. Then join the large squares, matching light to light and dark to dark.

PLATE 148

PLATE 149

PLATE 150 This diagram shows the procedure for putting the squares together.

Many people traditionally use red as the center of each square to represent fire and then add the strips around it "like logs stacked around the fire."

After deciding on fabrics to be used, you may make long, two-inch-wide strips and then cut them into lengths according to the pattern. Add the strips clockwise in the order designated in the diagram. The center block "1" is two inches square; "2" is also two inches square; "3" is two inches wide and four inches long; "4" is also two by four inches; "5" is six inches long; "6" is six inches long; "7" and "8" are eight inches long; "9" and "10" are ten inches long; etc.

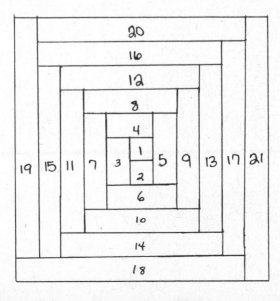

PLATE 151 "Dutch doll" quilts are always favorite gifts for new babies in our area. There are several variations, including "little overall Jims," a mixture of the Dutch dolls and the "overall Jims," and, for teenaged girls, the "umbrella ladies" (Plate 155). Mrs. Esco Pitts makes all three for her daughters and grandchildren.

Plate 151 shows a Dutch doll quilt made by Mrs. Edith Cannon for her granddaughter, Cindi Nix. The Tiger Homemakers helped Mrs. Cannon quilt this one for Cindi, now a Foxfire student. Plate 152 shows the pattern for the Dutch doll. The dolls are usually twelve to fourteen inches high. Plates 153 and 154 show the overall Jims made by Mrs. Pitts for her grandsons. These quilts have been made for new babies in this region "as far back as anyone can remember."

PLATE 152

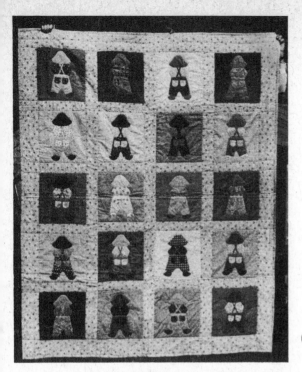

PLATE 153

PLATE 154

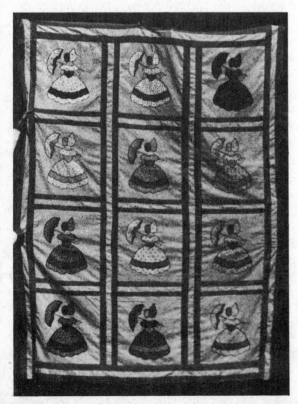

PLATE 155 This plate shows an umbrella ladies quilt made by Mrs. Pitts. As a child, she had one made by her mother, so she assured us that all these patterns have been known around here for a long time.

NOLA CAMPBELL
CATAWBA INDIAN POTTER

*S*ince the publication of **Foxfire**
8 with its emphasis on folk pot-
tery, we have been able to lo-
cate and document yet another potter—one whose technique is completely differ-
ent from any we have met previously.

The story starts with Teresa and Adam Wilburn, both students in Foxfire
classes. Their grandmother, Nola Campbell, who lives in Rock Hill, South
Carolina, makes traditional pottery following the style of the Catawba Indians.

Adam and Teresa were finally able to get an initial interview on a weekend
visit to their grandparents in September 1983. They brought back a tape full of
interesting information, and a complete set of photographs on the firing process of
the pots Mrs. Campbell makes. However, we still needed more photos of her
actually forming the pots, and we also needed some more taped instructions of
how to make them. We realized she was a gold mine of new material for us, and
we wanted to go back for more.

Soon after the tape was transcribed and the photographs printed, the Wilburn
family moved to Rock Hill themselves. A second interview couldn't be conducted
until summer when more students could go over and spend a day or two.

Cheryl Wall and I, two students working full-time for Foxfire during summer
vacation, scheduled a visit with Mrs. Campbell soon after the summer program
got under way. From the directions given us by Mrs. Campbell, we easily located
Neely's Store, an old-fashioned general store with an antique Coca-Cola sign
and old gas pumps outside. Someone at the store directed us to go "just down the
road a piece" and we were soon driving up to her house.

The one-story white house sits a short distance from the road and was easily
visible as we approached. Mrs. Campbell later explained that this was land that
she and her husband own, but that it was adjacent to the land owned by the
Catawba Indian Reservation where Mrs. Campbell, half Catawba Indian, was
born and reared.

She had been sitting in the living room working on a pot and watching
television when we came to the door, so she switched off the television with no sign

PLATE 156   Nola Campbell

PLATE 157   The Campbell home in Rock Hill, South Carolina.

of reluctance. After we were seated, she returned to scraping the newly made piece of pottery with sure, deft strokes as we explained what we needed on this interview. We brought the tape recorder, camera, and other equipment into the living room and started in on our questions.

Mrs. Campbell's house is a cheerful, homey place. There are photographs of her and her husband and their family, as well as the usual pictures of scenery, hanging on the white painted walls of the living room. There is a big, comfortable overstuffed chair in one corner, and along one wall is an antique sofa on which we sat.

Mrs. Campbell, even though she has a solemn, strong expression about her, with her coal-black hair tinged gray at the forehead, and her high, characteristically Indian cheekbones, is a happy person who flashed occasional smiles throughout the interview. While she was talking about her Indian father, she commented on her features, saying that her skin color was more like her white mother's. "I'd rather be darker than what I am." We prodded her for more information about the Catawbas, and she told us about her first husband being chief for a period of time and related both funny and sad stories of her youth and young adulthood.

The method of making pottery used by Mrs. Campbell, handed down to her from the other Catawba women, does not utilize a potter's wheel; instead, the pieces are made from coils of clay and shaped without spinning. This technique is perhaps the oldest in the history of pottery. The clay is rolled into long coils and these are stacked on top of one another for the desired shape. The coils are then clinched together and rubbed to produce a smooth surface. After they are air-dried, Mrs. Campbell starts the firing process by heating them in her cookstove. Then she places them in a hole in the yard and builds a fire over them. Her pottery is not glazed, as she cannot get the fire she uses up to the 2,000 degrees Fahrenheit or more necessary to melt most glazes. Although foods were cooked in this type of pot by Indians in ancient times, she makes her pots for decorative purposes.

The process of making them is fascinating, and we're glad, thanks to Nola Campbell's generosity, to be able to share it with you.

ALLISON ADAMS

OH SOON SHROPSHIRE

My uncle married my grandmother—my mother's mother—and he brought her down here to the reservation. My mother was from Chesnee, South Carolina. Her first husband was mean with her, and he didn't provide for her like he was supposed to do, so she upped and followed her mother here to the reservation. My mama and daddy got together after she left her first husband. Her name was

Maggie Price, and when she married my daddy she became Maggie
Price Harris. She was full white. I took back after my mother's side of
the people. I'd rather be darker than what I am.

My daddy's name was James Davy Harris and he was full Indian.
There's not many [full-blooded] Indians anymore. He didn't go to
school, but he was a Sunday school teacher. Everything he learnt, he
learnt in church. We're Mormons—Church of Jesus Christ of Latter-
Day Saints.

Our church was established on the reservation before I was ever
born in the world. I grew up and joined the church when I was eight
years old because my daddy belonged and therefore I wanted to. He
wanted us [children] to be baptized there, so I was baptized where he
wanted me to be. That's where I'm at today. I grew up in the Mormon
Church and I'm proud of it. We use the same Bible [as other
churches] and we've got a Book of Mormon to go along with it.
There's a lot of people that don't know the teachings of the Mormon
Church, but [the Book of Mormon] is the only thing that's different, I
think, and it's referenced to the Bible.

I was born down here on the Catawba Indian Reservation in York
County [South Carolina] in 1918, May second. I was raised around
here and I've been living here almost all this time. My uncle come
after us to take us over there to Fort Mill [South Carolina] to work for
awhile. So I guess if he hadn't done that, we'd a' just lived right down
there on the reservation all [my life]. There wasn't no place for the
[Catawba] Indians to go but there.

There were seven of us children. I had two brothers. One of 'em
died when he was quite young, 'bout the year I was born. He had the
flu and then he took pneumonia with it and he died. My other
brother, Douglas, has been dead about ten years now. I have one
sister dead, Ruthie, and three a-living. My oldest sister, Verdy, is
seventy-six. My twin sisters, Reola and Viola, must be sixty-three.
They're about three years younger than I am.

[There's a story about the time when the twins were born.] Mama
sent us over to my uncle's the night they were born. I didn't know
what we was going over there for, but we went to stay all night with
Mama's sister, Randy, and her husband. I wanted to be rocked to
sleep that night, and she wasn't going to. I cried and I cried, but she
said she wanted me to go on and lay down and go to sleep myself. I
told her that if she didn't rock me to sleep that night, I was gonna tell
my daddy. So she rocked me to sleep. [There was a room in their
house where cotton was stored after it was] picked before they got
ready to take it to the gin and have it baled up. That was the room

where we children slept that night. She throwed a quilt over that cotton and left me on the cotton pile. Next morning, my brother Douglas came after me and said, "Sister, now Mama's got two little ol' babies in the bed with her over there, and I don't want you lookin' at 'em." So I done what he told me, and we went to the house. Reola and Viola had took my place and I didn't like it one bit. I reckon I was petted when I was little. I'd cry for someone to carry me; I didn't want to walk.

I didn't get to go to school my first year at (age) six because they said I was too little. I had got ready and went, but they said I was too little so I was sent back home. That was all right. I didn't care about having to go back home.

[When I got home], Mama fixed me a cotton sack to pick cotton in [because] Daddy said I had to pick cotton. I was gonna pick cotton on the row he was picking on and he didn't like that. He put me out in front of him because he didn't want me goose-picking. That's where you leave the cotton in the burr. "You ain't gonna be goose-picking it now! You got to get it all out of the burr or you're going to have to go back and pick it," he said. Ruthie and Verdy was pickin' behind me and oh, they was just laughing and talking! I was tryin' to look behind to see what was going on back there and my daddy snatched a limb off the cotton stalk and just whipped me good across the back. "That'll learn you how to look back. I put you out here to work!"

I said, "Well, I was working."

He said, "You wasn't working. You was looking back at what Ruthie and Verdy were doing. You're not supposed to be looking at them." They weren't talking to me, but I wanted to hear what was going on. I was nosy!

The next year I went to school. We went on the reservation. Daddy wouldn't let us go if it was bad weather. He'd keep us there at home 'cause he said we had too far to walk. We had about a good mile! I went through the fifth grade, but that's as far as I went. Indians could not go to high school in the early 1930s, so I never got to go. I got out in the fifth grade.

I wouldn't smoke, but one time I watched for the other girls that was secretly smoking and that smoke was just a-boiling up. I was [pretending] to break pine tops to build a little playhouse but was really watching for teachers so that I could warn the other girls and they could put out their cigarettes [if the teachers came near]. The boys went and told the teachers that we was all down there a-smoking. Honey, that schoolteacher didn't come the way I was a-looking. [Instead of coming] straight down from the schoolhouse, she went around through the field up from behind us. Well, she caught 'em smokin' and she washed my mouth out with Octagon soap because I wouldn't tell on them. I stayed there at the pump for half a day that day. I said, "No way you going to get me in that schoolhouse after she done washed my mouth out."

We caught the boy that went and told on us. We was jumping rope on the south side and he just come a-flying around that way. I said to the girl I was turning rope with, "He's the one who told on us. Now if you'll help me to wrap him up in this here rope, then I'll whip him right good." So she went one way around him and I went another and we got him wrapped up in that rope. Then I pushed him down and jumped on him and just went to beating him for dear life. I had to write, "I must not fight on the school grounds" one hundred times. [My teacher] asked me to apologize to him and I wouldn't. He didn't have to do anything because I'd done beat up on him!

One morning, my mama went to carry my daddy's breakfast to the field. When she left, they wasn't nobody there [at the house] but Ruthie, Viola, Reola, and me. We knowed where our mama kept the snuff so we decided to go get us a dip of snuff. I gave Ruthie a spoonful and she put it in her mouth and Reola and Viola got them a dip and I got mine. They was all spitting theirs out and I was eating mine. I was the one that got sick! It was my idea to get the snuff and then after I got it, I got sick. Mama didn't know what was wrong with me and I didn't tell her till many, many years after that.

[One time] Mama sent me and Ruthie to get my daddy's and my brother's axes. So Ruthie said, "I'm gonna get Daddy's ax."

I said, "No, you're not gonna get Daddy's ax either. I'm gonna get it!" I run out there and I beat her to it and I got the ax.

Ruthie said to me, "If you'll just put your foot up on this chopping block, I'll cut your toes off." I always was a little daredevil, so I set my foot up there and she cut my toe off, sure 'nough! There was just a little skin holding [the tip of it] on, so [when my mama found out what we'd done] she went to the woods and got some soft pine resin. She got some spiderwebs down with a broom. Then she got some soot out of the fireplace and she put all of that on [my toe] and glued it on there with paper tape. I've got my toe yet!

I was picky 'bout what I ate. [I still am.] I had one hen that I called mine. When she was layin', I didn't eat eggs from other hens. I had to have the eggs *that* hen laid. If she didn't lay till about dinnertime [noon], I didn't eat breakfast till then, till I got *my* egg. If I didn't have one to cook that she laid, I didn't eat!

My brother raised game chickens. One time, when I was less than seven years old, I was gonna get me one and take it in the house and raise it in the house. I got a little dib [from its mother], and that old [mother] hen flogged me! I threw that little chicken down and climbed a peach tree, but she was right on my back. [Someone in the family] had to knock that hen off my back.

I wanted Verdy, my oldest sister, to carry me all the time and she didn't like it, so one day she said, "I'll fix you! I'll fix you up good!" She carried me right close to a rock pile and she fell down with me. She done it on purpose. That broke me from wanting her to carry me —right then and there.

It was hard times back [when I was a child], and when Christmas came, people enjoyed it. They really loved to see Christmas come. I'd get a new pair of shoes every Christmas and I'd sleep with 'em on the first night. Since we didn't get but one pair a year, they had to do us. We could tear 'em up if we wanted to, but if we did we went bare-footed. If we took care of 'em they lasted us all winter. When the first day of May came, I was tickled, because Mama'd let us go barefooted.

But we just didn't have the money to buy other things for Christ-mas. We would get fruit: apples, oranges, grapes and raisins, maybe five or six English walnuts and some Brazil nuts [we got very few of those]. We didn't get much candy because Daddy didn't believe in us eating sweets like that. He didn't want us to have it, but we'd slip around and if we got a dime or a penny, we would get us some candy anyway.

We didn't have [store-bought] baby dolls to play with then. We would get us an old torn-up dress or a piece of cloth and make a head for a baby doll. Then we'd get another piece of good-sized cloth and we'd [put the center of that over the head]. We'd tie a string right under the head and that'd make a neck and the rest of the cloth was the body. That's what we played with for baby dolls. It was many, many years before I had a real baby doll to play with.

My daddy and brother would go hunting, but they didn't go very often. When they did, they'd bring back six or seven rabbits. I've seen them clean them things, dress 'em, and Mama'd dry 'em over the fireplace. They just kept 'em turning like they were cookin' 'em over the fire.

My daddy died before I turned ten years old. When my daddy was sick, we [were living] in just a two-room house down next to the river. About every hour I'd run to the spring and get fresh water for him. I carried a half-gallon fruit jar to the spring and got him a drink of water and carried it back to him every hour, and I would just run for dear life. He died in April and I was ten on the second day of May.

The day they took him away from home to the hospital, he was real bad sick. The Red Cross women came down and got him, carried him to a hospital in town and that's where he died after about a week. I was crazy about my daddy. We missed him after he was gone. Mama had to put us out on a farm over there off the reservation to work after he died.

I can remember back when we moved down out of the reservation to that farm. We had to go to work on the Sutton farm and pick and hoe cotton, or anything they had for us to do. The Indians always farmed, and they raised their children up to help. That's how I learned to pick cotton. I picked cotton before I was ever eight years old.

So Ruthie and I both worked on that farm. We didn't finish elementary school like other children did. In the fall while school was going on, the owner of the farm said he wanted four or five bales of cotton done a day. It doesn't bother me to work. I like to work, but I didn't think it was right for him to do us like that. It was because we was Indians. That's how come we had to work like that.

I never will forget this. Me and Ruthie were picking cotton. Mama sent the two twins to the field where we was at. I don't know what they was doing out there, but they started crying up a breeze. They said, "Oh, I'm sick, I'm sick, I'm sick."

"What's wrong with you?" I asked.

"My head's a-hurting," they just kept it up.

So I told 'em, "If I give you something, will you take it?" Yeah, they'd take it. So I went through the cotton rows and I picked up little rabbit droppings. I got six—two for Reola, two for Viola, and two for Lillian, my uncle's little girl. I gave 'em to 'em and I said, "You take these and your heads'll quit hurting." So they took 'em and they chewed 'em up and I gave 'em some water to swallow. After a while they were walking around out through [the field] and they wasn't crying. I said, "Has you'ns heads quit hurting?"

"Yeah."

"Do you know what you took?"

"No."

I said, "You'ns took rabbit pills!"

"Oh, we're gonna tell Mama!" So they went running to the house and told Mama and I got a good whippin'. I always was a little devil!

One time we children didn't get our pay for working in the cotton fields. I tried to get my mama to go and collect our pay for what work we done, but she wouldn't do it. So our uncle went and got our money that we worked for. He was my mama's brother and she didn't want me telling him [about us not getting paid] but I did anyhow.

We moved off the Sutton place in September of 1930. My brother, Douglas, told Mama she was going to have to move us back home [to the reservation]. He came and got us hisself. Mama didn't want to move, but I had told Douglas [about us not getting paid] and he said, "Well, I'll bring y'all back home."

When I was about sixteen years old, we moved off the reservation again to do some more farming. We went to work on the Kelly place. Guy Ballard was the man that was [in charge] of the farming. When he moved off, he was replaced by a man named Smith. Now, that man was mean! We'd go up to his house and he had close to an acre of peach trees right out beside the well house. He didn't want us to pull any of those peaches, but his wife would tell us to get down there back of the well house so he couldn't see us and we could get all the peaches we wanted. We would have to throw the peach seeds where he couldn't find 'em, so we'd run off and eat those peaches.

I was a Harris back [before I married] and when I married the first time, I married another Harris. We was maybe fifth cousins, something that's distantly kin. When my husband was in the service, I got my check as Nola Harris Harris. I said that if I marry again, I'm gonna change my name! Raymond, my first husband, must have been about pretty close to full Indian because his dad was full and his mother was an Indian too. He was also born and raised on the reservation and his father was chief at one time.

Raymond farmed. He raised corn and vegetables. I canned what I could of blackberries and different fruits and vegetables. That helped out. Raymond also cut pulpwood for different people. He didn't get but about fifty cents a cord for it. If it was cold out there and was going to snow, I'd get the ax and I'd go to the woods and I'd cut down firewood and carry it up. Then when my husband came home, he didn't have no wood to get. I'd done got it. Using an ax and cutting wood—I guess that's how come my hands are so big. I guess I do have the strength of a man, not a woman.

From farming, Raymond went to work at the Goldtec Mill. Then he went to the Blue Buckle Industrial Mill. That's when he [got drafted into the service] and had to go overseas. The Blue Buckle people told him that they would give him his job back when he got out of the service. He was discharged from the service in '45.

He served as chief [of the Catawba tribe] from '48 until he resigned in '51 when he got sick. [The tribe] wanted him to [remain chief] for two more years and he told 'em he just couldn't do it. He had been the youngest to serve as chief down there.

He went to the veterans' hospital when he got sick. He felt like the doctors down there weren't doing anything for him, so after he stayed in the hospital about eight days, I took him back home. He died at [the age of] thirty-eight in January of 1952—a young man. I wasn't but thirty-four.

Now just before Raymond died, he told me to take care of Grady. I was thinking he didn't know what he was talking about. He said, "That little boy of ours."

I said, "Yeah, I know—Grady."

"I want you to take care of him," and that was the last thing he ever said to me before he died.

One day [shortly after Raymond died], I whipped Grady. That night, Raymond came to me in a dream. Just seemed so real, like he was there in person! I was in the kitchen and had my back turned to the little hallway, just a little square place where the doors went into each room. He was standing in that doorway into the kitchen. I don't know what I was doing, but I had my face turned to the window in my dream. He spoke to me. I turned around. I said, "I thought you was a little skinny man."

He said, "No, I just gained a little bit of weight."

I asked him, "Well, what do you want?"

"I don't want you whipping Grady like you whipped him the other day."

"Well, he deserved it."

"If you whip him, don't whip him that hard." [And then he went away.] Now, Grady was the only one of our children that he was concerned about before he died, 'cause Grady was sick all the time.

I had ten children, five boys and five girls. Betty was born in 1934, Carl in 1937 [he was killed in Vietnam], Grady in 1939, Martin in 1941, Della in 1944, Leon in 1946, and Deborah in 1948. Then Raymond, their daddy, died in 1952. I stayed single two years and about two months and then I married Willie Campbell in 1954. Edwin was born in 1954. Rita was born in 1956, and then my last one was born in 1963. [She was born dead and I had carried her for nine months.] So that's the family.

[When I was a child], the Indians did love to dance. I can tell you that because I seen a lot of dances. Before I was ever eight years old my oldest sister, Verdy, would want to go to these square dances. Way back then [there were no Indians] that could play square dance music, so we had a black man who played a guitar, a banjo or something, and was a friend to the Indians. He'd come down there in his mule and buggy and just sit in the corner and play music, and the Indians would dance all night long. The dances would be at a different house each weekend and they'd have to tear down everything that was in the room and set it somewheres else so they could have a square dance. The houses weren't all that good but they had big rooms to 'em. Maybe they didn't have but two or three rooms to a house, so they had to be big. Daddy never did have any [dances] at our house, though. I had to go with my sister [to the dances]. Most every house had children so I'd go and play with the children while the big people was dancin'. I'd sit and watch 'em dance many a time.

There was one Indian, Davis Harris, who liked to dance. One time when he was sick in bed, my brother asked him, "Oh, Davis, you goin' to the dance they're having this weekend?"

"Where's it gonna be at?" And [my brother] told him, and he said, "Yeah, I guess I will." Even though he was sick, he'd get up and go to that dance! He loved to dance, and he'd dance the whole time. Chief Belew had an Indian suit and a headdress that would hang way down in the back. He would go out and demonstrate the Indian dances and he would sing, just put on a show for people.

One day when I was at work [as a blanket inspector for a corporation], some of the people [I worked with] asked me to do the rain dance. They knew that the Indians believed in rain dances, but I couldn't help but laugh. Well, I got into some kind of little dance, and behold, it rained that day! I don't know if what I done had anything to do with it, but those people thought it was really true. Several times after that, they wanted me to do the rain dance. I'd say, "I don't want it to rain," but they kept on and kept on after me so I'd do some kind of little dance and it would rain and it would tickle them to death. I didn't have anything at all to do with it. It was the Lord's work.

The Indians were superstitious. I know my daddy wouldn't let us sweep a floor and sweep [the dirt] out the door after the sun went down. You could sweep the floors, but if you didn't have something to sweep the trash up in, you had to leave it. I have never, to this day, known what that meant. Daddy just said it would bring you bad luck. If I sweep after dark, I'll sweep it up in my dustpan. I won't sweep it out the door. It was just something I was used to doing as a little girl and I'm still following the way I was taught.

I can remember this—when a little baby was born, they didn't want you to leave his clothes out on the line at night. If you washed and put the baby's clothes outside during the daytime, you'd better bring them in before night. They said the wild Indians and evil spirits would bother 'em. I didn't believe in that one or try to follow it. If something on the line didn't get dry, I left it out till the next day.

The Indians didn't want you to put a baby's feet on the ground. They said it'd make the baby restless at night and bring the evil spirits about 'em. I just can't believe that evil spirits really bother little children. They are a child of God and are holy until they get old enough to be accountable for their own sins. I never did care about [this superstition]. I'd put mine down just to see their little ol' feet. They'd just kick. But the Indians didn't want you to do that.

I've heard tales about people coming back so many days and nights after they die. They come back after midnight and wander around where they had lived. I'd be so scared to go to bed, I didn't know what to do. But if [the spirits] ever did come back [nobody I knew] never seen none of 'em. It was just something [people] talked about. When the spirits go back to our Father, that gives 'em death here on earth. They'll be put in the spirit world until the day of Resurrection. Then the spirits will pick up their bodies and we'll come forth to be judged by what we done in the flesh while we were here.

A lot of people believe that if a black cat crosses the road, you'll have a wreck or other bad luck if you cross where that black cat had been. [Some] would make a cross on the windshield or something or other like that.

Well, I really don't believe in superstitions, but there's a lot of these things [if you pay attention to them] does mean something to you. If you hear something and you get to thinking about it, after a while you'll believe things like this.

I should have learned more about the Indians when I was small and when some of the older Indians could tell me [our history], but I didn't think about that. I didn't think that it would someday be valuable to me to know all these things. I didn't care about it. When I was in school, I didn't like history. I said, "Well, now, I ain't gonna study about something I ain't never seen and I never will see, and I don't want to learn about people I don't know nothin' about."

They say that at one time [the Catawbas] were branched from the Sioux tribe. Then my forefathers came to settle down here and it came about that they were called Catawba Indians and I think the Catawba River was named after the Indians.

[To choose a chief], the tribe would have a meeting and they would talk to the ones that they wanted to put in [as chief]. They voted, and the one with the most votes got chief. The person elected chief don't

have to be full-blooded Indian. Every two years, a chief is either
reelected or a new chief voted on.

[There is an old Indian burial ground] on the other side of the
river. Some of the [modern Indians] heard that they buried their
valuable things in the grave with [the dead] so they got to thinkin',
"We're gonna go over there and dig in them graves." So they went
over there and went to diggin'. It was told that they found different
little things in the graves and brought them back to the boat that they
had crossed the river in. When they got into the boat, something
jumped in with them. It wasn't something they could see, but it was
with 'em. They could hear things. Several of 'em [got so upset they]
just throwed the things they had got into the river and didn't bring
'em home.

There ain't many tombstones down there [at the old cemetery].
[The families] just didn't have the money to buy tombstones for their
dead, so they'd just bury 'em and put a rock at the head and one at the
foot. That's where my first husband is buried, but he does have a
tombstone. [Just Indians are buried there], and people who married
Indians.

This [land] where we're a-livin' now is part of what was the old
reservation at one time. It's no longer owned by the reservation. I
happen to own it myself. There ain't but 632 acres on the reservation
now. There's less than five hundred [Indians living on the reserva-
tion] that's on the tribal roll, but there's children born since [that list
was made up], so they'll be adding them. [The reservation] has been
there from the 1840s when the Indians leased their land to the state
of South Carolina for ninety-nine years. When that time was up, the
Indians never got their land back. South Carolina had leased it for
these years. They just took it away from the Indians. [The Indians]
are tryin' to get a lawsuit started, and I don't know whether they'll
ever get anything out of it or not, because by the time they [get it into
court], I guess just about all the Indians will be dead. Their children
coming along have not got much Indian in them at all. They just keep
marrying out. They can't hardly marry back into the tribe because
they are too close kin. The people that's livin' today ain't the ones
that was living back when all this [land leasing] was done in the 1840s.
These people now, it's new to them and they're fightin' it, and I don't
blame 'em.

I personally don't hold nothin' against the white people 'cause my
mother was white. I love the white people, and I love the Indians. I'll
fight for the Indians quicker than I'll fight for the white people,
though. If somebody stands up there and cusses the ol' black Indians,

then they're gonna have me to whip if I can fight 'em, and I'll try! I've got in more fusses about [the mistreatment of the Indians] than anything in the world. I might get whipped, but somebody will know I was there.

I don't think that I'm any better than any white people, but I'm as good as they are. My mother was white and I loved her, but my daddy was Indian and I thought more of him than I did my mother. I guess maybe the Indian part was what kept me hanging in here because I really loved my daddy. I really did.

The Indians ain't never had nothing. They have had a hard time. It ain't been too long ago that [Indian students] have been accepted in the high school up here in town. Then people says, "Indians are dumb." Why are they dumb? I can see why they're dumb—'cause the white people wouldn't let them go to school. That's why they're dumb. But they've got more sense than [white] people give them credit for.

There are some people living down on the old reservation now that don't even have running water in their houses. The state don't give 'em nothin'. When I was a little girl, we did have a doctor for the Indians. And back then they did appropriate a little bit of money, about thirty-five dollars to a head. That wasn't much money at all. They couldn't get jobs. I guess that's why the Indian women made pottery. That's how they made a living.

They was a lot of people living on the reservation, and they was a lot of people having to live with each other because there weren't enough houses or money along there. There was maybe two families in a two- or three-room house. That just wasn't enough room for all the families to live in. In the thirties, there was several people around that had cars. The Indians wasn't able to buy nothing like that. They just barely did have beds and chairs to sit in and a stove to cook on. That was [all the furnishings], just about, in the houses.

I was proud to be poor and it didn't bother me. I worked hard for everything that I've got. I try to be honest with everybody and I don't try to tell lies about what I do. I just try to be honest. It doesn't take a whole lot of money for me to live on. If I can have groceries and stuff in the house and have the little things that I need and I can provide for myself, I'm happy. I really am.

Back when I was young, there were a good many people that made pots, just about every little place you went. But they don't do it now because they have jobs that they can get outside [of the reservation]. You know, pottery making is hard work and many people don't like it.

I thought [as a child that the Catawba language] was silly. I thought, "Well, now, that just don't sound right." Looked like every word sounded the same to me. I said, "No, I don't want to learn that 'cause it don't sound good." I didn't care about it and I don't think any of the rest of them cared anything about it either, 'cause they ain't none of 'em that can talk it.

Same way it's gonna be about this pottery-making stuff. If some of our younger people don't want to [make it], they ain't gonna fool with it. But someday they're gonna say, "Well, I wish I'd a' learned it while I could." It's gonna be gone, done away with after a while. They ain't gonna be nothing the [modern] Indians ever learned to do [to preserve their heritage].

Georgia Harris and Doris Belew are two other older Indians who still make these pots. They have samples of our work at the museum in Columbia [South Carolina]. I sent one up there [to the Smithsonian] and it got broke. It was valued at seventy-five dollars, and the insurance didn't want to pay it. They just don't know the value of anything and how much trouble it takes to get these pots fixed up and what you're going through to do it. They think, "Well, now, it's not worth that much." But anything handmade nowadays, you really pay for it, pots or anything [when you're buying].

Georgia Harris is the best pottery maker of all of us. Lot of 'em say that I am and I say, "No, not me. I learnt from her, so she's gotta be first." I give her credit for that. She still makes a few, but she's not making like she used to. She's in her eighties, anyhow. She's still going good, but she's not as active as she used to be.

Georgia's married to my brother, and her son, Floyd, asked me one time, he said, "Make me some little pots. Mama is makin' pots. You make me some."

I said, "I can't."

And Georgia said, "Yes, you can. If you want to learn, you can learn."

I was about twelve or thirteen. I never did think I'd be interested in making pottery but I started off [and she encouraged me] but she wouldn't help me. She'd tell me, "Now, you watch me and do what I do, and the way I do it, you do it." So that's the way I learned. Nobody took my pot down and shaped it for me. I had to shape it up and work with it for myself, y'know. Sometimes Georgia made the pots and I got to rub 'em. While she would be building and scraping, I would be rubbing.

What I made then was just little tiny things. Now I can make anything I want and I make all kinds. I make loving cups, pitchers, vases, ducks—just anything I put my mind to, I can make it.

My sisters, Viola and Reola, make it too, but none of our children make it. They don't want to get the clay on their hands. Lot of people will say, "What do you do when you get that mud up under your fingernails?"

I say, "Work right on. It don't bother me." Lot of people don't want that mud on their hands, and I think that's why my children never did like to make it, and they just don't like sittin' down makin' pots. Leon's little girl says that she wants to learn to make 'em. She's about eight. Whether she ever will or not, I don't know. You have to want to do something before you can and you have to pay close attention if you are going to learn anything. Stay right with it. It'll take several years to learn to do this. You just don't learn overnight.

Doris Belew and I went to Washington, D.C., back in '76 to demonstrate pottery making up there. I think the Smithsonian had something to do with it. We made [pots] in the Hilton Hotel in Washington, and I laid 'em up on the heater in the room and they dried out that night. I rolled 'em up [in towels] and brought 'em back home with me.

I've also been to Greenville, South Carolina, and a place near Union, South Carolina, to demonstrate [making] pots. Each time I [made a trip to demonstrate], I had to be gone five hours but I made a hundred dollars. I went to Ebenezer School [in Rock Hill] when they were studying about Indians. They wanted me to come demonstrate the pottery. I also demonstrated to the Girl Scouts over here in Mount Holly. When the girls were getting ready to go home, I went and broke all my clay up into fourteen little pieces and give it to 'em. They really had a time out of it after that; they got real messy with it.

They also had a pottery school down here on the reservation and were giving lessons. I had the privilege of teaching one day a week to Indians that wanted to learn to make pots.

The Catawbas never did make nothing like baskets. The Cherokees does. Somebody was gonna teach the Indians down here to make 'em, but I never did see anything made. We did beadwork in school, though. They got beads and learned to make rings; they took a wire and [looped it], put the beads on them wires and just kept a-going through. Then they'd weave them on the end some way or another. I didn't care about making beadwork.

I don't know how far back this pottery [making] goes, but I've heard the story that pots were the utensils [the Indians] cooked in. I've never seen that myself, but I've heard it from way back.

I get good prices for my pots now—anywhere from five dollars to a hundred and fifty. At one time I was making quite a few, right after my first husband died. My brother and his wife would carry 'em to the mountains to Cherokee [North Carolina]. After a while, we got to where we couldn't make nothing off of 'em, so I quit making for ten or fifteen years.

Then I started back makin' 'em again. My [second] husband took a load up to Cherokee and they wanted to give him ten cents apiece for them. They thought that we were desperate to sell them. So my husband said, "No, I'm not gonna sell her pots for that because they're worth more. I'll take 'em back home first." If I'm gonna give 'em away, there ain't no point in me makin' 'em.

People come here. They'll drop by and want pots. If I've got 'em, I'll sell 'em to them. If I ain't got 'em, they'll come back later for 'em. This is usually people that's out enjoying their vacations and come by in passin'. Sometimes I'll set up a booth and sell. Georgia has sent people up here several times because she didn't have any to sell. And Jack Punk, up here at Neely's Store, he's got pots in there but he said that when they want the good pots, he'll send 'em down here to me. And he has sent a good many people down here to buy 'em. He's a nice man.

Different things sell better than other things. The ducks that I make sell good. Peace pipes and little vases and pitchers sell good, too. I don't ever keep any [pots that I make]. I don't think they're pretty. I just don't like 'em after I make 'em. I imagine there's a lot of people that would, but I don't. I don't think Georgia keeps any of hers either! Course, if she's like me she'll give her children and grandchildren her cracked ones. I don't like to sell 'em cracked, but there's a lot of people who like to buy 'em 'cause they're cheaper than if they're good.

I get tired of making pots sometimes, if I work for a couple of weeks in a row. Just sitting still is what is the trouble. You have to just sit down and work. There's no jumping up and down. You just sit there. [Since I don't make one from start to finish all at one time,] it's hard to say how long it takes, but [it's] about eight hours apiece.

I'm telling you, this ain't no easy job. There's a lot of people who think that it's easy made. But they're not easy made. They'll say, "Oh, I could do that." And when they start doing it, they can't do it like they thought they could. I heard one man say one time, "Oh, that looks easy. I'm gonna go get me some clay. I'm gonna make me one." I don't know what kind of clay he got, 'cause he didn't go over to the river and get it. He sure didn't know nothing about where we get [our clay] at. He went and got some of what *he* called clay. He sat down to make [a pot] and said, "Shucks, I can't make that stuff. It looked easy, but I can't do it." He throwed the clay away!

Getting good clay is the main thing. You just don't get good clay hardly anymore because [it's almost all been taken]. We get the clay in the [Catawba] River bottoms. We've been getting it in the same place for years and years. Two kinds of clay, blue clay and pipe clay, are mixed together. You've got to dig real deep to get the pipe clay and it comes from a different place. And we do not tell; we don't give the secret away of where we get it. And we don't show how we mix that clay.

That stuff is hard to dig out. A woman just couldn't hardly dig the clay. It'd take a good man to get down there and dig. [My sons, my son-in-law, and my husband] have all went and helped. Sometimes maybe there's two or three different families might go. We dig the hole [for the clay] and then when we've got all we need, we fill that hole back in with dirt. Then we bring home five or six bushels, lay it out in the sun and let it dry, so when we're beating it up, see, it'll be little small chunks. When we put water in that dry clay, it's going to melt up. Then we can just work with it in a tub and it'll get real thick like syrup. Then pour a little more water to it so it will run through a screen wire onto a cloth. Then I let it dry [until the clay is a workable texture]. Then I've got to put the clay in a plastic bag or plastic bucket to keep it damp so I can work with it.

PLATE 158   Tools Nola uses to shape and burnish her pots and to etch designs.

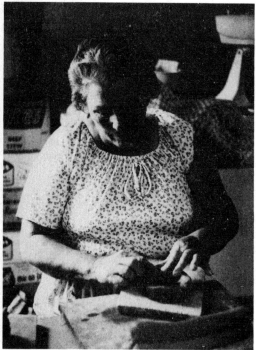

PLATE 159   Nola rolls the clay out into long cylinders and sets them aside. The base of the pot is then prepared from a ball of clay pressed into the shape of a saucer.

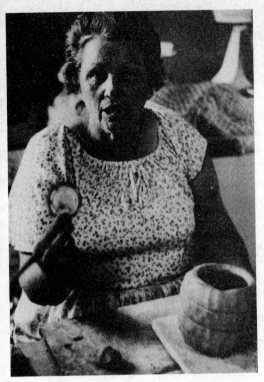

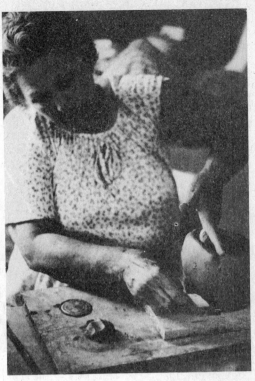

PLATE 160   The cylinders are added to the base one row at a time until the desired height is reached. She secures the rolls together with her fingers by a process she calls "clinching," and uses the lid of a tin can dipped in water to smooth the inside of the pot.

PLATE 161   She uses a rectangular piece of tin to smooth and shape the outside of the pot.

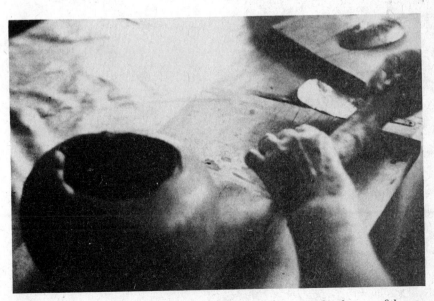

PLATE 162   Now she makes another cylinder of clay to use for the rim of the pot. She fastens its ends together to form a ring and then works the ring to fit the diameter of the mouth of the pot.

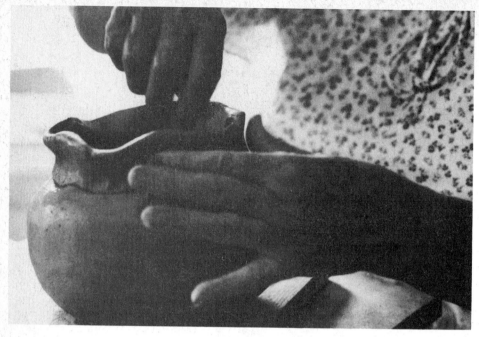

PLATE 163 She clinches the rim to the mouth of the pot, shaping it into waves and curves if desired. Then she sets the pot aside to stiffen before burnishing.

PLATE 165 The other is solid.

PLATE 164 She also makes two varieties of ducks. One is hollow, its wings and tail shaped by trimming the clay with a dull knife.

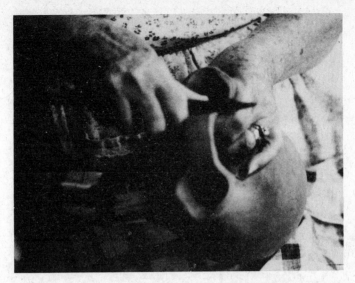

PLATE 166 After the clay has dried and stiffened somewhat, the surface of the jug or pot is scraped. Here, she works on a wedding jug. "I'd rather make them than scrape them and rub them and finish them up. That's the part that's tiresome to me. I have to scrape a few and then do something else.

"I scrape my pots with old wore-out kitchen knives or pocket knives. Then after I scrape them, they sit and dry some more. Then I wash them down with a cloth."

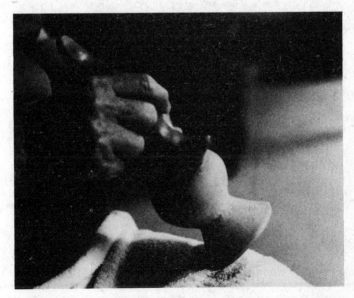

PLATE 167 "Then I take a rock or something else smooth and rub them. Rubbing makes the pots slick. I also use a little piece of deer antler that my husband cut for me. It's real slick. I rub in all the little places and up under the handles of the pots with it."

Here, she burnishes the handle of a small Rebekah pitcher.

PLATE 168 "I make peace pipes, ducks, turtles, pitchers, wedding jugs, crimped bowls, vases, Rebekah pitchers, gypsy pots. These styles are traditions that the Indians have made up from history, way back. They tell me that in the olden days, they made the pots and other utensils they cooked in. The ones that I make can be used to put flowers in or just set up to look at and have around. They're pretty."

These pieces have been scraped and burnished and are now drying before being fired.

PLATE 169 Before firing, Nola bakes the dried pots in her oven to make sure all the moisture is evaporated out of the clay. She said, "I put them in the stove for four or five hours to heat them so they can stand the fire. They get really dark when they're ready, and you can smell them all over the house. It's just like wet dirt when it rains. When I started making pottery, we had to use the oven of a wood stove."

PLATE 170   While the pots bake, Nola's husband, Willie, removes the debris left in the pit from previous firings.

PLATE 171   Then he splits wood for the firing. Nola said, "I think the wood we use determines the color of the pots. If we throw pine bark in on them, they spot and have (different colors). You don't know what they'll look like until they come out."

PLATE 172   Teresa Wilburn, a granddaughter, helps put the first layer of wood in the pit. Nola explained, "We have to lay four sticks of wood down, and that's where the pots go."

PLATE 173   A layer of newspapers or pine needles is added over the wood.

PLATE 174   Then Willie removes the heated pots from the oven.

PLATE 175 While still hot, the pots are placed on the layer of paper in the pit.

PLATE 176 When all the pots are in the hole, they are covered with a layer of newspapers or pine needles.

PLATE 177   Now the firing process begins. "I take my dry wood and little dry twigs off a tree and put them in there first. Then I set the paper and twigs on fire and they'll catch up. Then I lay my green wood on that and it'll start burning."

PLATE 178   As each layer of oak on top begins to burn to coals, Willie adds a new layer, gently positioning the pieces with a shovel. Nola says, "We just go out there and keep adding wood until I think I've got three good fires burnt down on it."

PLATE 179   Nola and Willie relax as they put the last layer of wood on the fire. "After I burn them three or four hours, I know they're ready."

PLATE 180   "I'll leave them in the hole until after the ashes get burned down pretty low. If I don't, and the air hits them while they're hot, boy, they'll pop in a minute! I let them cool off before I try to handle them."

PLATE 181   After being removed from the pit, the pots are ready to be rubbed with a rough towel to clean off the ashes.

PLATE 182   A fired snake pot and wedding jug.

THE JUD NELSON WAGON

Though we have published several short wagon-making features in the past [Foxfire 2, *pages 118–41, for example], we have never attempted anything about that subject that comes close to being as comprehensive as the following chapter.*

For this section of Foxfire 9, *David Brewin, a young professional blacksmith who was a member of the Foxfire staff at the time, spent three months with Jud Nelson, a master mountain blacksmith/craftsman, and followed him through and photographed the entire process of making a complete farm wagon. David was there when Jud selected the chunks of raw white oak for the wheels' hubs from a neighbor's pile of winter wood; and he was there when a commemorative brass plaque was attached to the bed of the finished wagon prior to its being transported from Jud's shop in Sugar Valley, Georgia, to the Foxfire complex in Rabun County where it is now part of our permanent collection. In the interim, David transported students back and forth between the two locations so they could help him photograph the construction process.*

With over 160 plates, this chapter emerges as the longest one we have ever undertaken in the documentation of the making of one item by a single craftsperson; even at that, it is incomplete. The entire story would fill this book. What's here, however, will give those of you who are unfamiliar with the process involved a rare glimpse into a formidably complicated—and yet once commonplace—task.

Why do we bother?

Well, for starters, the importance of having a man like Jud in a community seventy years ago—a man who could build or repair a wagon—was exactly analogous to the status we would give today, were there no assembly lines, to the only man left in our region who could design and build and/or fix a car.

That's part of the reason. Another has to do with the fact that Jud is one of a rare breed. John Conley and Will Zoellner, his counterparts who were interviewed for Foxfire 2, *are both dead now, and they were rarities when we interviewed them years ago.*

PLATE 183   Jud Nelson standing in front of
his shop.

*And another is rooted in our continuing desire to help young people around
here understand that despite the almost brutal harshness of a self-sufficient
lifestyle, artists lived who lay to rest the stereotype of the insensitive mountain
hick.*

*The chapter begins with Jud telling about his life. The remainder is made up of
photographs and diagrams made, for the most part, as the wagon was being
built. However, a number of the diagrams and some of the information in the
captions were taken from an extraordinary book called* Practical Carriage
Building.* *Should any one of our readers out there actually plan to go beyond
simply appreciating the following material and try to build a wagon, this book
will prove to be indispensable. Instead of being the work of one author, the book is
a compendium of the opinions of a number of different professional blacksmiths of
the time regarding nearly every step in the process of building both wagons and*

* Vols. I and II, compiled by M.T. Richardson. New York: M.T. Richardson, Publishers, 1892.
Reprinted by The Early American Industries Association (c/o John S. Kebabian, 2 Winding
Lane, Scarsdale, N.Y. 10583, 1981).

carriages. It's an invaluable document, and the Early American Industries Association is to be highly praised for reprinting it.

Meanwhile, we hope you'll agree with us in our estimation that the space devoted to Jud and his wagon is richly deserved as a part of Foxfire 9.

My mother was born in 1878, in the month of October. Daddy was born in March of 1875. Granddaddy Patterson and [Granddaddy] Nelson were both born in 1840. They had a standing offer [that the one who was still living] when the other one died would build a coffin to bury him in. That was the deal they had, and Granddaddy Patterson built the coffin to bury Granddaddy Nelson. Granddaddy Nelson died in 1908, and Granddaddy Patterson died in 1911, two months to the day before I was born.

I was born in Cherokee County [Georgia] and moved to Gordon County in 1913 when I was two. I've lived in this county ever since then except for about four years [when I was in the Navy].

Daddy had three brothers. My uncle John Nelson, Daddy's oldest brother, was a blacksmith. He had a shop down below Canton. I never did remember seeing him—he seen me when I was little—but they said he was six foot six inches tall and was a real character.

I've heard a lot of them say that he was a fiddle player from a way ago. Daddy said he knowed of them a-sittin' down at night there—start about eleven o'clock—and he'd still be a-playin' when the sun come up and never play the same tune over. He'd drag that bow! I think he was pretty full of mischief, too. Mean as the devil. Said that some old feller down there—didn't know him—kept on at him to come out to [his house] and bring his fiddle with him one winter night and stay till bedtime. Uncle John went out there about eleven o'clock that night, and that was late then, and he got his fiddle out and started playing and he was still playing when the sun come up the next morning. That old man never did say no more to him about the fiddle playing after that. He had all he wanted! *[laughter]*

And I think he could take a piece of wood and carve anything that he wanted to out of it—animals or anything no matter what it was. I heard my sister and them talking about it.

But he was a real Francis Whittaker [one of the finest blacksmiths in the country] in his days from what they tell me. Him and the other man is all I ever knew that could weld a main leaf for a car spring and upset it and retemper it, so he had to be pretty damn good on it, I think. I haven't tried welding a spring in thirty years. Used to, I'd just try it and think I had it and then it would fall in two. I didn't do no good! *[laughter]*

And I heard a lot of folks say that years ago, gun springs would break, and a lot of other blacksmiths could make [them] but they couldn't temper [them correctly]. And I've heard a lot of them tell me that there'd be *blacksmiths* ride a horse ten or fifteen miles to get Uncle John to temper a spring for them. They'd make it and get it dressed good and then take it to Uncle John. My daddy said he would harden it, and then he used beef tallow, and he'd draw that temper with that beef tallow once it got dry.

Lots of people would try to get him to teach them. My cousin told me once that years ago a blacksmith started out and he went down and told Uncle John that he wanted him to teach him how to forge-weld. Uncle John went down there and the feller had some corn [liquor] sitting there and they got to sucking along on that. Said that old boy got pretty high. He was still pumping that bellows and had [a piece] in the fire ready to weld. Uncle John didn't say a word to him and that boy took it out and he'd done burned it up. Uncle John said, "Well," says, "that's the best lesson you'll ever learn." Says, "You've got to pay attention to what you're doing." Got on his horse and went on back home.

That reminds me of another story! *[laughter]* Years and years ago, in them Prohibition days, the federal court in Rome [Georgia] picked jurymen from eight or ten counties. One of the jurymen they picked was an old man who went from Canton down to Rome there to serve on the jury. He drove a horse and buggy down there. He had a good friend down there at Rome, and that old man liked to drink in the evenings. The friend knew where they could get them a drink.

You've heard the sensible answers a drunk man gives? This old boy was sitting over at the table, his head a-laying on the table. He was done sot. Some man and his wife had separated and everybody was discussing what they'd do if she was a woman of theirs. Said the drunk raised up and said, "It's a strange thing to me that everybody knows what to do with a mean woman but the man that's got her!" And *plunk,* back down went his head. Said that's all he said. *[laughter]* Said that's the sensiblest answer that he had ever heard a drunk say! He never said another dang word. That's all he said.

Alec was his name and they called him "Square" Alec. He was a-coming in from Canton one morning about sunup and he was cold. Said, "You reckon the old man likes whiskey better than a hog likes slop?" He was coming on out and he met two fellers and a big frost was on the ground. The old man had a brick laying in the floor of his buggy to keep his feet warm. These two fellers had just made their first or second run of whiskey. They had a pint bottle full there with them. They told him, "Well, Square, we've been off and made a little run." Says, "Got a little sample here. Just wondering if you'd like to sample it."

Said, "Yes, I'd love to sample it."

They handed him that bottle and he put his thumb down about halfway down the bottle and turned it down and drank till it reached his thumb, and he smacked his mouth. Turned it back up again and emptied that bottle, handed it back to them and said, "It's just a little bit scorched in the bottom!"

But anyway, later in his life Uncle John went down to Plains, Georgia, and put up a blacksmith shop and wagon manufacture there in 1922. He got damp out there building the shop—took pneumonia and died in about two days. He was fifty-two or fifty-four.

Blacksmithing was one pretty good way to make a living back then, and there weren't many others. I know there used to be a lot of logging around here. There was [a demand] for crossties. Course, years ago the railroad would take crossties that were hewed [by hand]. You see, they didn't have to be squared like they're sawing 'em now. They would just hew 'em with a broadax. Uncle Tom Serritt would get down on his hands and knees [with a] gauge. They'd cut the whole tree down and make four, five, or six ties out of it— whatever it made. They had this gauge that was seven inches, or whatever the thickness of a crosstie was, and they'd lay it down and slide it along and mark the log with an ax. Then they'd [score] the sides about twelve inches apart. [After one was scored], this old man would get down on his hands and knees and take that broadax and crawl down one side and shave it right off the bottom, and then he'd get on the other end and come back and shave it off the other side. He hewed enough of them crossties to lay a railroad from here to Atlanta! He was a character, I'll tell you!

I've seen stacks of five hundred or more hewed ties down here. The railroad would pick 'em up. On these "number ones"—thick 'uns— they give a dollar and fifteen cents. "Number twos," I believe they said was ninety cents, and "number threes," they come on down to sixty-five cents. If they got below that, they had to carry 'em back and burn 'em for firewood. And now then a friend of mine and another feller has bought a hundred thousand [used ties] this side of Carter's Crossing. The railroad had replaced about two thirds of the ties and they bought a hundred thousand of them old ones and I understand they're getting five dollars apiece for them! *[laughter]* So I reckon that's a deal on it.

My daddy was a neat kind of man. He was a farmer and a fiddle player and a carpenter. He nailed with his right hand and sawed with his left hand! Later on he did a little blacksmithing. But cotton was where we got our money. Hard work but the price would jump to the bottom. He sold one bale for about seventeen dollars. It was five cents a pound and a bale weighed a little between three and four hundred pounds. Daddy had some people who could pick a bale of cotton a day. Then Daddy and my older brother would load up four bales [of cotton], five hundred pounds [to the bale] on a wagon. It had a flat bed and they'd load up four and they'd go into Rome with it. There was a better cotton market in Rome than there was in Calhoun. [They'd do some shopping for the family while they were there.] They'd come back and [we'd] always line up there and [each get a new pair of shoes]. Mother would give Dad the size of shoes [to buy us] but I never did get a pair that fit. They had to swap 'em a time or two. I'd squeeze my toes up and couldn't get 'em on. I'd get a blister with that. We had them ol' brogans. Did you ever see any of 'em? Had a brass tip on the toe. Anyway, that was it. But I'd listen for that wagon a-comin' in at night. That's when we'd get a hunk of hoop cheese. Cut off a big ol' slab. And maybe get a little something else that'd be different. If they got a pretty good deal on cotton, we got a little more. If it wasn't too good a deal, maybe we didn't get nothing much. Back then, you could buy bacon for thirty-five cents a pound. It come in a half-pound package at eighteen cents. That was *bacon* at that time. Get a good hunk of cheese for thirty cents a pound. You'd dial that cheese cutter around to what you wanted, pull that knife down and cut off fifteen cents [worth]. Get fifteen cents' worth of cheese and crackers in the barrel there and Co-Cola and you had you a good meal.

Daddy and his brothers also were all sorghum syrup makers. Everybody back then made a sorghum patch. That was the sweetener. They cooked different things and sweetened 'em with that sorghum syrup. We had from twenty to sixty gallons of that syrup all the time. Daddy was a good syrup maker. Uncle Jeff Nelson was too. He'd pass for a brother to ol' Will Geer that played on the Waltons. Mustache and everything. Just about his size, and talked like him. Sam Rampley also had a little ol' syrup mill there—one horse—but he didn't know how to make syrup. Him and his boy started makin' it. Uncle Jeff went by and he seen they was getting it ready to make, drawing it off, you know. Uncle Jeff said, "By junk," them was his words, "by junk, he's

puttin' fire under that pan and got it cookin', making pretty syrup."
Uncle Jeff was going to the woods cuttin' cordwood.

He come back that evening late and Sam said, "Done got done
makin' syrup, Jeff. I made two barrelfuls." And a few days later he
come up there and told him, say, "Jeff, I want you to go down and see
what's wrong with my syrup. It's blowing the damn stoppers out of
the barrel." *[laughter]* He drawed some off and it was just ready to
ferment. It'd all soured and went to workin'. *[laughter]* He said Sam
had to pour it all out. He hadn't cooked it long enough.

We was used to that ol' homemade syrup, you know, but George
Adams' daddy come in [one time] with a bucket of that clear maple
syrup. We never had seen none of that. He had a biscuit [with some of
that syrup] at mealtime. And that just bugged him to death. He just
couldn't get that off of his mind. He slipped in the house—there
wasn't nobody in there—and looked for them big ol' leftover biscuits,
big ol' catheads, you know. He decided he'd look around and see if he
could find that syrup. By golly, there was a saucerful of it already
poured out there and that was real handy. He was lookin' over his
shoulder, just like somebody stealing something, you know, and he
busted that ol' biscuit open and sopped it around [in that saucer] and
sopped it good. He got nearly every bit that was in that saucer and
crammed it in. Had to get this done and get away from there, or get in
trouble because they didn't allow the kids running in and getting into
stuff. You was gonna have what was left from dinner for supper! I
guess he had done swallowed a whole lot of it before he realized what
was a-going on. One of his sisters had loaded up that saucer with
castor oil. It looked just like that Karo syrup. He never did find out
which sister it was and that's the reason she's still living! He ain't
found out yet.

Sometimes they mixed that sorghum in with remedies, too. I remember during World War I when that flu epidemic broke out. They
was lots and lots of people that died with it. I never will forget—I was
seven years old. My brother and I was going to the store. It was pretty
cold. 'Fore we left, Mother said, "Wait a minute." Said, "Let me give
you 'uns something here to keep you from having the flu." Now I *like*
sorghum syrup, but she liked to have turned me against it that time.
She stirred up some sulfur in that sorghum syrup and give it to us to
keep us from having the flu. And I cried halfway down that bank.
When I got back I said, "Ma, I might take the flu and die, but," I says,
"be damned if I want any more of that sulfur and syrup. I'll tell you
that!" But that was better than that asafetida some people used.
They'd put a little ball of that around your neck and thought you

never would have the flu. It smells like a wild onion that rigor mortis has done set in. *[laughter]* You buy it at the drugstore. I've seen 'em wear that little ball around their neck and that ball would be just black as that coal in there and you couldn't stay around 'em! Yeah, you couldn't stay where they was at!

But anyhow, back then there was more syrup mills than there was blacksmiths, 'cause everybody had from a half acre to a acre of syrup cane. Maybe one mill [to crush the cane] would be sittin' in one section and maybe eight miles on, someone else would have another one. They were just scattered around, and people shared them. Usually the mill would be mounted on a wagon so they could take it around, but it would want to rock around with you if you was feeding it heavy. So up in 1934, the last year I farmed, we had about three quarters of an acre of syrup cane, and me and my uncle tried something different. We built a wood form, and put bolts in it, and poured a concrete slab that weighed, I guess, four ton. Then we bolted that mill down on it and got it ready and my daddy started makin' syrup as pretty as you ever seen. Hell, they kept haulin' [cane] in from five to seven, eight miles from there. He made eleven hundred gallons that year right there. Never moved. [The mill] was right on the creek, plenty of water. And that mill would flat go, too. It was a big two-horse mill is what it was, and we had a good copper-pan evaporator.

Daddy was also a fiddle player. He didn't know one note of music from the next, but boy, he could drag that bow over them right along, and that man picking the banjo staying right up with him. I was little and I ain't never heard anything on television that beats it to me. Not just because he done it. He had a fiddle and he bought it in 1895 in May, secondhand, and he got the case, the fiddle, and the bow all for $2.75. My daddy's name was Bill and my youngest grandson's Bill, too. Bill will be ten years old in November and my sister and [the rest of the family] wanted Bill to have that fiddle so my daddy had worked on it, put a neck on it, after he'd got up eighty years old. I told the boy I wanted to carry [the fiddle] up to Blairsville to Mr. King, a repairman, and I carried it up there and he reworked it and it looked like new. It was a Hoff made in Germany in the early 1800s. And he told me, "Don't let nobody play it if you don't want to sell it." Give $2.75 for it when [my daddy] bought it and give $215 to get it reworked.

Dad could do anything he took a notion to. He didn't have the education, but he could figure stuff out in his head. He used to make barrels, and he made a good many baskets. When I was nine years old, he bought himself a set of tools and put a blacksmith shop up here on the farm. I was seven years old when I first seen a [blacksmith] shop. Daddy and another feller was doing some work there and it scared the hell out of me—those sparks flyin'. I ran like a turkey! But after he set his own shop up, my job was cranking that blower for him. He didn't run the shop regular for the public—it was mostly farm repair work—but he'd do some work for the neighbors maybe on a Saturday or when it was rainy weather. He'd sharpen their plows, do some mule shoeing; first one thing, then another. But he was smart. I've seen him take a damn piece of cast iron and take a file and melt it a little bit and lay it in the fire and get it hot and put a little borax on it and take a damn piece of brass and braze it together. It was like using a brazing rod, but they didn't have brazing rods back then, sixty-five years ago. I never did try it. Hell, I couldn't a' done it. Never did try it. Don't know whether I could do it or not. I got started in blacksmithing myself when I was twelve or thirteen. I'd make stuff like wagons for me and the neighbor boys to play with on Sunday, and if we tore it up that Sunday, I'd rework it and have it ready for the next Sunday again. Then later on, why all I studied about was [wanting to] build houses more than anything. Back then, if a carpenter made a trade to do a job for people, they had to take two toolboxes. Everything was handmade, planes and all, you know. They'd load up [all their tools] in two toolboxes and you had to go get 'em in a two-horse wagon and carry 'em maybe twenty miles, fifteen, whatever it was. [The carpenters] stayed with 'em while they were doing their job and went home on weekends maybe. They didn't need no greenhorn so I stayed in blacksmithing. When I was seventeen, I started shoeing for the neighbors. I'd shoe a mule for 'em and make a little spending money. I worked with one old man, fifty-one years old, and did all his work during the Depression. His name was Mr. Cagle. He was a tall man but he drew over when he walked. He had done farming before he was a blacksmith. I was twenty-one years old. I came to work when the sun came over the courthouse and stayed all day. He paid me a lot of money. He gave me three dollars a week and my board. I did some tempering of steel for him and helped him shoe. He died of cancer when he was eighty-one.

The year I was twenty-two years old, I bought my own shop. I'd worked a lot in that shop that summer, so Uncle Bob come easing across one morning. He said, "Jud, would you love to buy a black-smith shop?"

I said, "If I did, it wouldn't do me no good. I haven't got the money."

He said, "Ah, God, I've got it." Says, "Dock and them want two hundred and fifty dollars for that," and my daddy said, "Offer 'em two hundred for it; Dock's a-hurtin' for a little money." That was a whole lot—a hundred dollars was—in 1934 and '35. Well, Uncle Bob said he'd pay a hundred for his half and I paid a hundred for my half. So Dock agreed on [the price] and we went down and bought it. I opened up for a year over there and then moved up here the last of 1934.

I got married in May of 1934. Her name was Jenny. We only knew each other for about three years before we got married. She was two or three years older than me. She was a schoolteacher.

I built a log [building for a] shop up here, me and my daddy. I done a lot of work in it for the neighbors there. Some of 'em had wagon work to do and buggy wheels to fix back then. I started on the first wagon work then. My daddy couldn't figure out [the dimensions] in his head, [but] he could do most anything with wood. Most of the neighbors got me to do their mule shoeing. Some people come from two counties [away]. [I also did some carpentry work.] I built my first house that summer. I was twenty-three years old. I worked twelve hours a day and got $2.40. I got twelve cents an hour on it.

I went to Jacksonville, Florida, in '41 to do blacksmithing for the Navy. I stayed there till '45. It was just like a big farm, more than anything. I made a bunch of anchors and hooks and different things. I helped make the lids that went on the underground tunnels there. I bet you we made five thousand of them damn things. Wasn't any trouble to make.

Most of the money I made [blacksmithing] would come in in the fall of the year 'cause ninety percent of the farmers works from spring to the fall, and they'll have their work done in the summer and come in in the fall and pay [their bill]. A few of 'em forgot to pay in the fall. Anyway, it's a pretty happy life, real hard work but I enjoyed it. I didn't weigh but about 165 pounds. It didn't matter though. It never did get too rough.

I could a' been half rich now. I throwed away enough old farm equipment to've sold. I never did think it'd be this way. By gosh, I ain't a-braggin', but when I started out there at first we had so damn much competition we had to be pretty good if we did anything. Course, there was right smart of it to do. I guess blacksmithing was a real important part of the community back then.

PLATE 184   A typical afternoon in Jud's shop will find good friends like George Muse (left) and Wallace King (center) and Sammy Joe Dobson (right) visiting and watching the activity.

PLATE 185   Jud and his friend, George Adams.

PLATE 186   The sign that hangs over the door of Jud's shop.

PLATE 187   Jud begins the process of making a wagon by first making the four wheels. He says, "The wheels take more time on them than any other part. They're the big part of it."

For this wagon, he found the seasoned white oak he needed for the hubs in the woodyard of his neighbor, Wallace King. "I believe this wood will work. It's good oak and it's good and dry. That's the main item on it."

PLATE 188   Using a band saw, he cuts each piece to approximately fourteen inches in length, longer than the final hubs will be, but Jud says, "I just trim 'em off a little long. Got to cut 'em again anyway." Then he removes the bark with a drawknife.

PLATE 189   Now Jud removes as much of the excess wood as he can before mounting the hub in the lathe for the final turning. Here, he prepares to square the block to ten and one-half inches . . .

PLATE 190   . . . cutting off the sides with a band saw.

PLATE 191   Now, with a square, he marks each block to its final length of ten inches . . .

PLATE 192   . . . cuts each squared block to the desired length . . .

PLATE 193 . . . and locates and marks the center of each.

PLATE 194 With a nail set, he punches a shallow indentation into the center of each hub, and then draws a circle eight and one-half inches in diameter on each end with a compass.

PLATE 195 With the diameter established, Jud now can remove additional excess wood from the corners at a forty-five-degree angle with his joiner. It would be extremely difficult to turn on the lathe with the corners left on.

PLATE 196 Now Jud mounts a hub in his lathe, and before starting to turn it, he removes some of the remaining corners and rough spots with a drawknife.

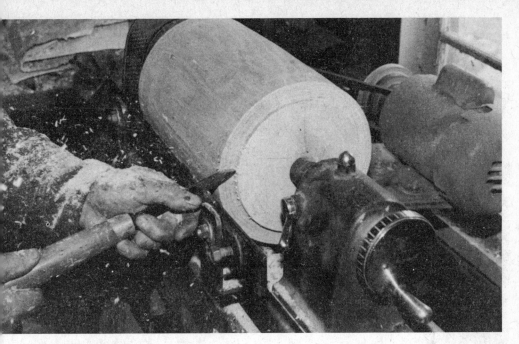

PLATE 197   Because it is nearly impossible to cut off the ends of each block exactly square with a band saw, Jud now uses a cutoff tool to square up the ends.

PLATE 198   The end of the hub that will go next to the wagon and hold the bearing is turned to six and one-half inches in diameter. Note that he has also scribed a pair of lines around the belly of the hub. The mortises for the spokes will be fitted in between these lines.

PLATE 199 With the diameter of the end established, he shapes the ends to hold the iron hub bands, tapers the hub's shoulders, and removes the hub from the lathe.

PLATE 200 When all four hubs have been shaped, Jud paints melted paraffin wax on the ends to try to prevent checking (splitting) since the wood for these hubs had only seasoned for a year.

PLATE 201 The two-and-one-quarter-inch mortises for the hub's spokes must now be cut. He subdivides the space between the scribed lines into twelve equal parts for the front hubs and fourteen for the rear, using a small traveler to get the circumference and dividers to establish the dividing lines. With a center punch, he makes three small holes on each dividing line to guide the drill he will use to cut out the mortises.

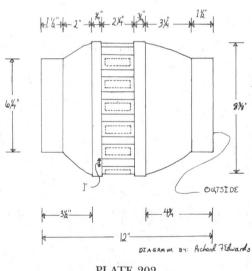

DIAGRAM BY: Richard F Edwards

PLATE 202

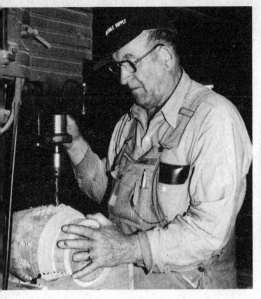

PLATE 203 Now he drills three holes into each mortise, drilling all the way into the center of the hub, which will eventually be hollow. Before machinery, Jud says this job was "started with a brace and bit and finished out with a hand chisel. It was hell, but they done it." Note the box Jud has fashioned to hold the hub steady while he drills.

PLATE 204 After the holes are drilled, he puts the hub back in the lathe to hollow out the end that goes next to the wagon in order to seat the bearing.

PLATE 205 Now, using a two-and-one-half-inch expansion bit, he drills out the center of each hub. This hole will eventually be tapered and enlarged to three and one-half inches in the end that will hold the bearing.

PLATE 206

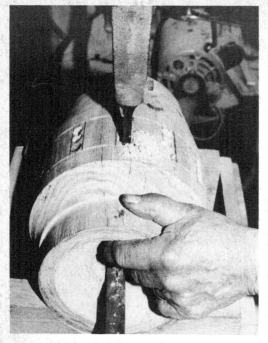

PLATE 207   With a mortising bit, he drills out each mortise to its size of five-eighths inch by two inches.

PLATE 208   At this stage the four hubs are beginning to take shape. The two on the left are for the front wheels, the distance between their mortises contrasting sharply with the distances between the rear hubs' fourteen mortises.

PLATE 209   Jud fashions the inner bands from quarter-inch by three-quarter-inch steel. Using a rawhide string to obtain the circumference of the hub where the band will go, he cuts them just short of the exact length they need to be. Then he scarfs their ends for forge welding. When scarfed and welded, the band will fit tightly around the hub.

PLATE 210   The ends of the inner hub bands are now forge-welded together . . .

PLATE 211 . . . and then driven over a cone mandrel to true them up and make them perfectly round.

PLATE 212 Now the outer hub bands, measuring three sixteenths by one and a quarter inches, are cut, rounded and their ends forge-welded together.

PLATE 213 As each weld is completed, Jud dresses up and rounds each band at the weld's seam before taking it to the cone mandrel.

PLATE 214 The bands finished, Jud heats one of the outside bands to approximately 900 degrees Fahrenheit on a black heat.

PLATE 215 Then he takes it to one of the hubs, partially suspended in a barrel of water by four pieces of scrap lumber, lines it up against the end of the end of the hub . . .

PLATE 216 . . . and begins to drive the heated band onto the hub. As he does so the wood catches fire.

PLATE 217 Lifting the hub out of the water onto a block, he finishes driving it home as the flames surround it. Then he flips the hub over into the barrel of water, where the shock of the change in temperature causes the band to shrink immediately and tightly around the hub's end.

PLATE 218 This process is repeated four times for each hub.

PLATE 219

PLATE 220   Now that the hubs are banded so they cannot split, Jud finishes hollowing them out with a rounding chisel he made for this purpose.

PLATE 221 Jud often has to custom-make the tools he needs to do any particular job. Here, for example, he takes a piece of metal from the coil spring of a car and shapes it . . .

PLATE 222 . . . tempers it to a dark blue . . .

PLATE 223 . . . attaches a handle, and grinds the blade.

PLATE 224 The finished tool was used at the lathe to help turn the inside of the hubs.

PLATE 225 Next Jud fashions the spokes out of well-seasoned white oak. In nearly all spokes, one side of the tenon that fits into the hub is slightly tapered and the opposite side is straight. Jud tapers his one eighth of an inch. This helps ensure that when the metal tire is added and shrunk onto the rim, the spokes will all be pulled toward the outside of the wheel, creating "dish," a feature of most well-built wheels that will be explained in a later caption. Without the sloped tenon, the dish might be pulled to the wrong side of the wheel when the tire is added.

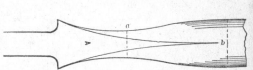

PLATE 226 Most spokes also have two concave surfaces cut in their sides above the hub tenon. This is known as the "throat," its purpose being to create a point in the spoke where an "elastic cushion" is formed that absorbs the effects of a concussion or blow as the wheel hits obstructions before the shock can reach the tenon in the hub and damage or weaken it. (Illustrations reproduced from *Practical Carriage Building.*)

PLATE 227 After checking a piece of stock against a finished spoke to make sure it is big enough, Jud traces the outline of a spoke on the stock using a pattern, and then cuts it out with a band saw.

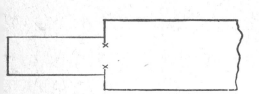

PLATE 228 Common form of tenon and shoulder. (From *Practical Carriage Building.*) Great care must be taken when cutting a square shoulder for the hub tenon to make sure the cuts do not extend *into* the tenon itself (x x on the above diagram) weakening the tenon and affording a place for moisture and subsequent rot.

PLATE 229 Final rounding and shaping is accomplished with a spokeshave . . .

PLATE 230 . . . and a belt sander. Since the diameter of the rear wheels is to be forty inches and the front wheels thirty-six inches, the spokes for the rear wheels are longer.

PLATE 231 With the hub bolted to his workbench by means of a threaded rod through its center, Jud sets the spokes. The hub is sitting on its inside edge (the edge that will face the wagon), and so the spokes are set with their tapered sides down. *Practical Carriage Building* (hereafter referred to as *PCB)* is filled with tips as to how to accomplish this job—boil the hubs in a kettle of water for twenty minutes before driving the spokes; or heat the ends of the spokes first near a stove (to shrink the wood), and then, when hot, dip each end into boiling water quickly (to lubricate the end so it will not rebound in driving) and drive it home—but Jud simply drives the spokes into place with a hammer. It is important here that the shoulders of the spokes' tenons fit tightly against the hub.

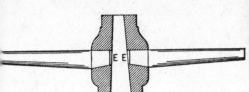

PLATE 232　How the spokes should be driven. (From *PCB*.)

PLATE 233　With the spokes in place, Jud uses a spoke pointer on a brace and bit to shape the ends of the spokes into cones (note the end of the spoke immediately behind the pointer).

PLATE 234　With the cone as a guide for the hollow auger or spoke auger, he can now shape the ends of the spokes into the round tenons that will go into the felloes (fellies). (Since the felloe end of the spoke is the weak end, the trick is to have as large a tenon as possible to hold the felloes on without breaking off, and yet small enough to leave a good bearing surface for the felloes. According to *Practical Carriage Building*, many makers leave half the width of the tenon—a fourth on each side—for shoulders.

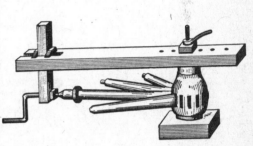

PLATE 235　Various other methods have been devised by blacksmiths in the past for accomplishing this task, as illustrated in these three diagrams taken from *PCB*. Jud shuns such gadgetry.

A spoke-tenoning machine.

PLATE 236　A spoke-tenoning and boring machine as made by "Blue Nose."

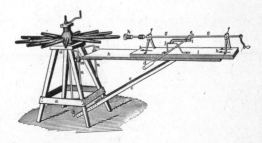

PLATE 237　The machine completed.

PLATE 238   Now, using one pattern for a forty-inch wheel and a different one for a thirty-six-inch wheel, Jud marks off the felloes (also called the "rim" by Jud and many other blacksmiths) he will need on two-inch-thick seasoned oak lumber—seven felloes for each back wheel (one felloe for every two spokes) and six for each front wheel. He also has patterns for rear wheels forty-four inches in diameter but, he says, "Forty inches is plenty tall enough 'cause you haven't got them ruts and ditches to contend with now."

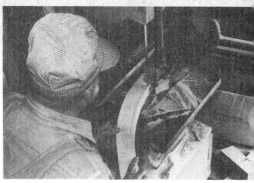

PLATE 239   When the felloes are outlined, he cuts them out on his band saw. Blacksmiths used to have to do this with a felloe saw (See *Foxfire 2*, page 123).

PLATE 240   Placing the felloes on top of the spoke tenons and using a framing square, he marks the location of the holes he will need to drill for the tenons, drills these holes through the felloes from the inside, and then, drawing the spokes closer together with a spoke puller of his own design so that the tenons will hit the holes on the inside of the felloes, he drives the felloes on. As each felloe is driven on, the spokes spread back apart to their original spacing.

PLATE 241   With a hammer and chisel, Jud splits the end of each tenon, drives a wooden wedge into the end of each, and saws it off flush with the outside of the felloe to lock the felloes and tenons tightly together. Some wagon makers, Jud included, cut the ends of the tenons off a bit short so that when the felloes are driven on, the tenons' ends will lack one sixteenth of an inch of being flush with the outside of the felloes. This was so that when the metal rim was shrunk onto the wheel, drawing its diameter down by as much as a quarter of an inch, the metal rim would not press on the tenons' ends directly and risk springing the spokes. Others, however, in *Practical Carriage Building* claim this is not a problem if the felloes are set properly on the spokes' shoulders.

PLATE 243   Now Jud smooths the edge of the wheel and the joints between the felloes with a belt sander. The inside edges of the felloes are beveled or chamfered with a drawknife.

PLATE 242   As all old wagon makers did, Jud "saws the joints" between the felloes to make the faces meet properly and to create a bit of slack space for the metal tire to pull together as it shrinks around the wheel and creates dish. According to Jud, it is also acceptable to saw out a three-eighths-inch space between two felloes and leave the other joints untouched.

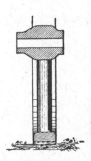

PLATE 244   The finished rear wheels awaiting the metal tires.

PLATE 245   The addition of the metal tire to the wheel is a critical phase, for if not measured and set properly it will come loose and the wheel, without its steady stabilizing tension, will break apart. The tire also "locks in" the amount of dish the wheel will have, and it can either increase or decrease the amount of dish depending on its diameter and the degree to which it is shrunk on the wheel.

The question of dish is a matter of some debate among wagon makers, but most agree that a certain amount is beneficial, as these diagrams from *Practical Carriage Building* illustrate. Section through a straight wheel, illustrating the best form for supporting weight, irrespective of other considerations.

This diagram, for example, illustrates a cross section of a wheel with the opening through the hub exactly horizontal and the spoke beneath it exactly vertical. This works well enough, except when the wheels are called upon to resist horizontal strains caused by uneven road surfaces.

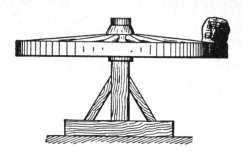

PLATE 246 A wheel with dish, on the other hand, absorbs horizontal strain as illustrated by the weight on its rim. The greater the weight against it, the more the felloes press against the spokes, the more the spokes press against the hub, and the greater the pressure against the tire and the more firmly it will be held in place, thus binding all the parts of the wheel together.

A wheel properly dished, and presenting the very best form for resisting the horizontal strains to which it is subjected in actual use. (From *PCB.*)

PLATE 247 If the dish were reversed, and strain applied, the spokes would fold like an umbrella, the diameter of the wheel would be reduced, and the tire could slip off and the wheel collapse.

A wheel with reversed dish, presenting a bad form for resisting horizontal strains. (From *PCB.*)

PLATE 248 When a wagon is moving on level ground there is no problem, but when one encounters a slope the load shifts against the downhill wheels, creating horizontal strain against those wheels which the dish can absorb easily. The position of a wagon or cart upon a side hill road. The vertical line drawn through the center of gravity falls to one side of the track, thus showing that the lower wheel sustains the larger portion of the load. (From *PCB.*)

PLATE 249 What Jud wants is a tire that will exactly match the circumference of the wheel, minus the three-eighths to one-half inch that the tire must be reduced by to close all the joints and help create the necessary amount of dish. For these critical measurements he used a traveler, measuring the outside circumference of the wagon wheel by counting its revolutions and cutting the necessary length off the twelve foot, three-eighths-inch-thick metal bars that will be rolled into tires. When the tires are rolled, he can also check their inside circumference against the wagon wheel and make necessary corrections.

PLATE 250 After cutting the flat bar to the right length for a tire, Jud feeds it into a tire bender which curves it evenly into a hoop.

PLATE 251 Then he double-checks his measurements . . .

PLATE 252 . . . scarfs the two ends . . .

PLATE 253 . . . heats the ends to a white heat, or approximately 2,400 degrees Fahrenheit . . .

PLATE 255   Upon checking his measurements after forge-welding, Jud found one of the tires to be three eighths of an inch too large.

PLATE 254   . . . and forge-welds the ends together. Though the circumference is decreased slightly by overlapping the two ends, the welding process itself as the ends are pounded and flattened together expands the circumference back out to its original size.

PLATE 257   Then he took a pair of dividers, the legs of which were braced by a horizontal bar to keep the legs from opening or closing during the operation. Since he wanted to shrink the circumference of the tire by three eighths of an inch, he placed one leg of the dividers in the depression made by the center punch and made another mark with the punch three eighths of an inch beyond the second leg of the dividers.

PLATE 256   Using a trick he learned from an old man he once worked with, Jud made a mark on the inside of the tire with a center punch.

PLATE 258 Then he heated a section of the tire, put it in a tire shrinker, and reduced the circumference until . . .

PLATE 259 . . . both legs of the dividers touched the two center punched depressions. Had he wanted to expand the circumference, he would have reversed the process.

PLATE 260 Now Jud sets a wheel on a wheel bench, dish down. Nearby, he builds a bonfire from scrap wood around its metal tire to heat it thoroughly.

PLATE 261 When the tire is hot, George Adams and Sam Everett help him carry it to the wheel bench and slip it down over the wheel.

PLATE 262 Using a pair of homemade tire pullers, Jud pulls the tire down over the felloes wherever it binds . . .

PLATE 263 . . . and then he and George and Sam pound it down into place as smoke curls up around them.

PLATE 264   When the tire is in place, the wheel is immediately taken off the wheel bench and rotated in a trough of water to cool the hot metal and cause it to draw even more tightly against the wheel.

PLATE 266   Four finished wheels.

PLATE 265   Last, holes are drilled through the metal tire and wooden rim at every seam between the felloes, and bolts inserted through felloe clips to bind the tire even more permanently to the wheel. This is a method strongly advocated by one of the wheelwrights in *PCB* who writes, "A heavy wheel needs but one-half to three-quarters dish, when the tire is on, when new [Jud's has three quarters of an inch]. . . . [I am convinced] that [wooden] dowel pins should never be used [between felloes] as when the joints get loose, the pins invariably split the felloe. That felloe plates are much better than dowel pins. That tires should always be bolted on, as bolts are better than nails and are easier removed." (Volume I, page 101.)

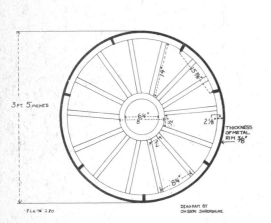

PLATE 267

PLATE 269   . . . burning the old hubs away so he could get to them.

PLATE 268   Jud is now ready to make the axles and mount the thimbles, or spindles, and bearings, also called "boxing," on their ends. Concerning the terminology, Jud says, "When we'd go to the store for these parts, we'd order 'spindle and boxing' for a wagon." He salvaged the thimbles and bearings from an old wagon . . .

PLATE 270   Next he measured and sawed out the new axles from seasoned oak timber.

PLATE 271   The critical part of the operation is shaping the ends of the axles properly to receive the thimbles and hold them at the proper angle. As with whether or not to dish a wheel, and if so how much, here there are also varying opinions. One area of disagreement concerns the amount of taper, or the degree to which the thimble should be tilted on the end of the axle. With a wheel that is dished, the prevailing opinion seems to be that the thimble should be tilted just enough to ensure that the bottom half of the wheel, whether rolling or standing, will always be at right angles to the bottom of the axle—or that the load-bearing spokes should be vertical (as shown in the diagram from *PCB*). The degree of taper, of course, depends on the amount of dish. Here Jud checks one of the axles from the old wagon to see how its blacksmith shaped the end.

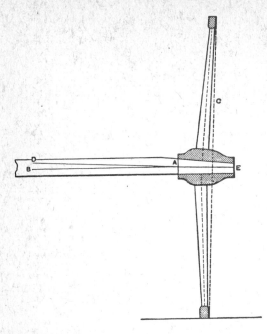

PLATE 272   Plan one.

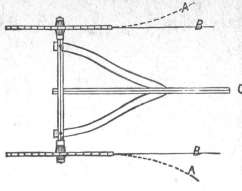

PLATE 273   The amount of taper next calls into question whether or not the wheels should have "gather" or "lead" as Jud calls it, and if so how much, gather being the amount the wheels are toed in toward each other as opposed to being set perfectly parallel. Those who argue for gather, including Jud, say it is not necessary in a wheel that is not dished. But when a wheel with dish is set correctly on the axle, the spokes on the bottom half that are bearing the load will be perfectly perpendicular, while those on the top will be canted out, as shown in the previous diagram. This fact, argue some, will cause the wheels to want to follow path A as shown in this diagram from *PCB*. Toeing them in slightly keeps them rolling straight and reduces the amount of resistance against the spindle's nut. Too much toe or gather, however, and the tire will wear out too quickly.

H. L. C.'s theory. (From *PCB.*)

PLATE 274   Using the old axle as a guide . . .

PLATE 275   . . . Jud carefully marks the new axle . . .

PLATE 276 . . . and begins to remove the excess wood with a drawknife.

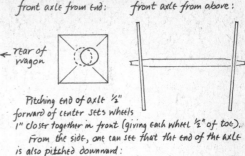

PLATE 277 As shown in this diagram, he removes more wood from the top of the axle than the bottom to give taper, and he also pitches the end of the axle forward one-half inch to set the wheels one inch closer to each other in front than in back, creating the desired amount of gather.

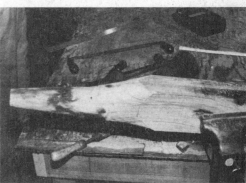

PLATE 279 The effect of this is to char the wood on those places that are still too high and give Jud some guidance as to how much wood still needs to be removed.

PLATE 278 When the end of the axle is nearly finished, he heats one of the spindles and slides it onto the end, and then removes it.

PLATE 280   He constantly double-checks his measurements and the fit.

PLATE 281   When the axle is finished . . .

PLATE 282   . . . he heats the spindle and drives it into place . . .

PLATE 283   . . . as smoke boils up around him.

PLATE 284   Then he clamps the axle to his workbench . . .

PLATE 286 Now, the hardest part finished, Jud cuts and planes the rest of the timber for the wagon's undercarriage. First he assembles the front end, which in this photograph is shown nearly finished. (From *PCB.*)

PLATE 285 . . . and slides on a wheel to see if it will run true. If needed, wedges can be used to eliminate any wobble. To Jud's delight and satisfaction, all the wheels ran true on this wagon, so this step was not needed. Had it been, Jud would have taken the wheel off, split the lip of the hub beneath the bearing and opposite the point of wobble, and driven a wedge into the split and cut it off.

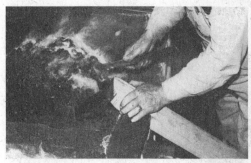

PLATE 288 In making the front end, he cuts and shapes the hounds, and bands their ends with metal for protection against wear.

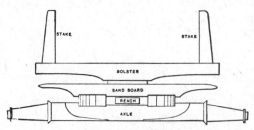

PLATE 287 A diagram of the front end of a farm wagon like the one Jud is making.
Front view of axle and bolster. (From *PCB.*)

PLATE 289

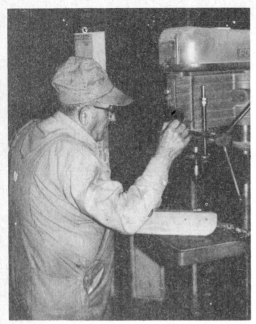

PLATE 290   The necessary holes are drilled for bolts, all of which will be countersunk.

PLATE 291 The crossarm for the front hounds is mortised, and fitted over tenons cut in the hounds' ends.

PLATE 292

PLATE 293   The plate at the opposite end is bolted into place, top . . .

PLATE 294 . . . and bottom.

PLATE 295 The sand board is planed, cut out, and then shaped with a drawknife . . .

LATE 296 . . . and the metal rub plate 1 which the bolster will ride is bolted down.

PLATE 297

PLATE 298   Placing the front axle, hounds and sand board together . . .

PLATE 299   . . . Jud prepares the hole the center of the bolster for the kingp which will allow the front axle and sa board to turn freely under the bolster.

PLATE 300   Then he sets the bolster in place with the pin to double-check his progress. Note that a metal plate corresponding to the plate on the sand board has been bolted to the bottom of the bolster, and mortises have been cut in the ends of the bolster for the stakes that will hold the wagon bed in place.

PLATE 301   The mortises are cut in the t of the front axle for the hounds . . .

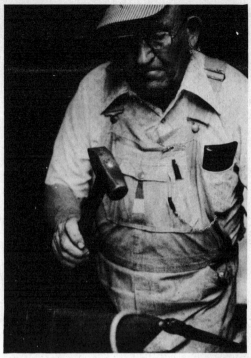

PLATE 302 . . . and metal rods are cut and threaded . . .

PLATE 303 . . . and bent into the shape of U bolts. These will be used in numerous locations to bolt the entire undercarriage together.

PLATE 305 . . . to secure a metal brace for each thimble on the axle's underside.

PLATE 304 Here, a U bolt is bent around each of the thimbles on the front axle . . .

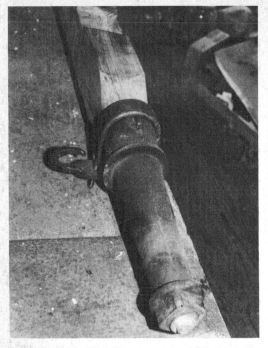

PLATE 306 The plate through which the ends of each thimble U bolt pass is shaped into a hook in front to which the stay chains will be hooked when the wagon is in use. The threads for each thimble's nut are made to keep the nut from unscrewing while the wheel is rotating.

PLATE 307 Now U bolts are made (note that these are flattened in the curve) and holes drilled in the hounds to pin the hounds, sand board, and front axle together.

PLATE 308 On the underside of the axle, using a U bolt puller, Jud adjusts the bolt and plate and . . .

PLATE 309 . . . bolts it down.

PLATE 310   That finished, the front end is ready for its bolster.

PLATE 311   First Jud cuts out the stakes and mortises out channels for their hardware (made of mild steel, three sixteenths of an inch by three quarters) . . .

PLATE 312   . . . and shapes the base of each into a tenon to fit the mortises in the bolster.

PLATE 313   Then he checks to make sure each fits squarely on the bolster . . .

PLATE 314 . . . drills a hole through each for a locking bolt, and bolts each into place.

PLATE 315 He bolts one end of the metal strip that wraps the stake into the top of the bolster . . .

PLATE 316 . . . saws any excess off the tenon . . .

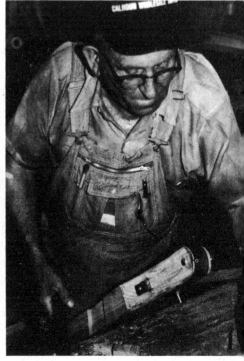

PLATE 317 . . . and bends the other end of the metal band that wraps the stake over . . .

PLATE 318   . . . and bolts it into place with a
g bolt.

PLATE 319   Then a protective wrapping is
nailed to the top of the bolster. The wagon
bed will sit on this surface.

PLATE 320   With the addition of several more
etal braces, the front assembly is finished. The
urved braces keep the rocking bolster from
anging in the sand board.

PLATE 321　The finished front assembly as seen from the rear.

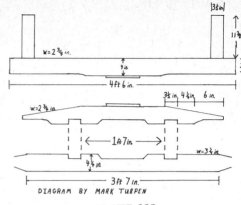

DIAGRAM BY MARK TURPEN

PLATE 322

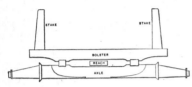

PLATE 323　Using basically the same processes, Jud now builds the rear assembly. Back axle and bolster (Fig. 180 *PCB.*)

PLATE 324　He rounds the ends off, bands, mortises, and sets the stakes in the rear bolster . . .

PLATE 325　. . . and cuts the mortises in it underside for the hounds and the coupling pol or "reach." The reach will connect the front an rear assemblies, and holes will be drilled in it a intervals for a metal pin which, when pulled, wi allow the front and rear axles to be eithe pushed farther apart or brought closer togethe as the wheelbase needs to be changed to accom modate the job at hand.

PLATE 326　Again, U bolts are used to tie the bolster, hounds, and axle together.

PLATE 327　The finished rear assembly.

PLATE 328　The finished rear assembly as seen from behind the wagon.

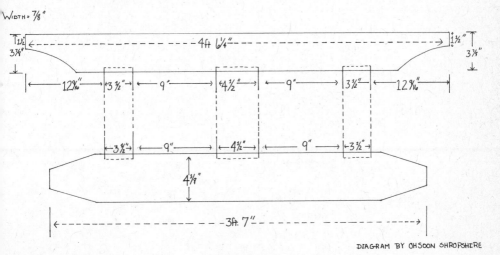

WIDTH = 7/8"

1½"
3⅞"
4ft 6¼"
1½"
3⅞"

12⅜"　3½"　9"　4½"　9"　3½"　12⅜"

3½"　9"　4½"　9"　3½"

4⅝"

3ft. 7"

DIAGRAM BY OHSOON SHROPSHIRE

PLATE 329

PLATE 330   Now the wheels are added,
and the coupling pole, and the two halves
pinned together.

PLATE 331   The brake assembly. The lever used to
pull the brake shoes against the rear wheels can be
seen behind the spokes of the wheel in the fore-
ground.

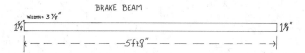

BRAKE BEAM

WIDTH = 3 7/8"

1 5/8"   1 5/8"

—5 ft. 8"—

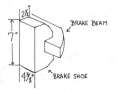

2 1/8"

7"

BRAKE BEAM

BRAKE SHOE

4 3/4"

PLATE 332   Dimensions of brake assembly.

PLATE 333   A view of the brake assembly and the rear axle assembly from above. The hounds are attached to the coupling pole by two metal plates, one above and one below. The metal bolt in the center of the plate can be pulled and reset in any of several holes drilled through the coupling pole to change the length of the wagon.

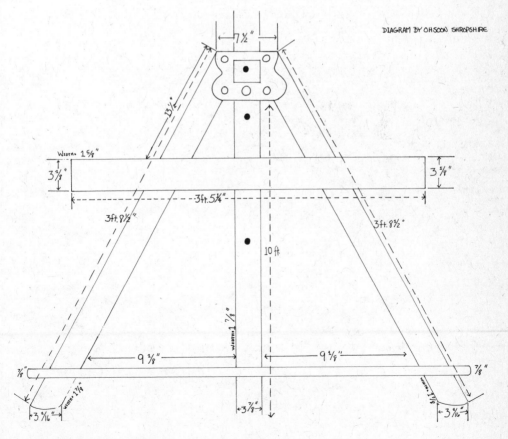

PLATE 334   The dimensions of the brake assembly and the rear axle assembly.

PLATE 335   Last, Jud makes the bed and seat and then places it on the frame between the standards.

PLATE 336   The finished wagon from the opposite side.

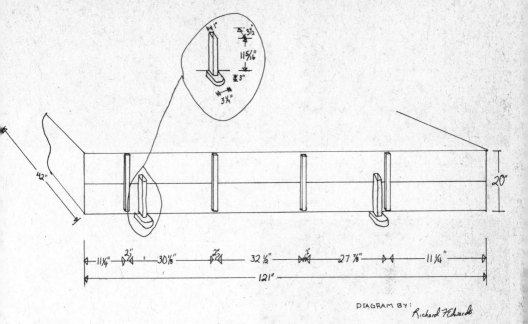

DIAGRAM BY:
Richard F Edwards

PLATE 337   Dimensions of the wagon bed.

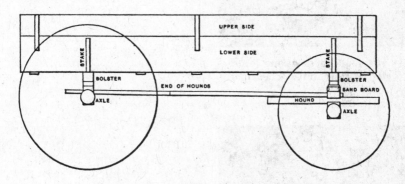

PLATE 338   Side elevation. (From *PCB*).

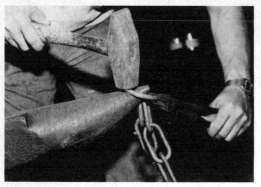

PLATE 339 Jud also makes the chains and hooks he needs, forge-welding the ends of the links together . . .

PLATE 340 . . . for stay chains and tongue chains.

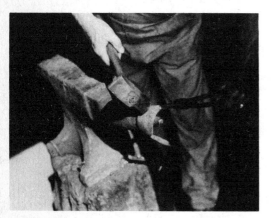

PLATE 341 He also forges out and forge-welds the singletree irons and attaches them to the singletrees.

PLATE 342

PLATE 343

PLATE 344   When Jud finished the wagon, he mounted a brass nameplate on the end of the bed.

PLATE 345

PLATE 346

TWO MEN OF GOD

F oxfire 7 was completely devoted to the subject of religion in the mountains. Since the publication of that volume, however, two remarkable stories have been uncovered that would have been part of the seventh book had we but known about them at the time.

The first was initiated by Curtis Weaver who, as a student in one of the Foxfire classes, found out from his family that his grandfather was a preacher who had used a boulder in the woods behind his home as his personal altar and confessional. The boulder was not only still in place, but so were the pebbles on its flat top that he had used to keep track of the religious status of the members of his congregation. Though his grandfather had been dead for seven years, members of Curtis's family were able to help us piece together the story.

The second came to our attention through Bill Henry, a woodcarver of considerable talent who lives in Oak Ridge, Tennessee, and is one of our oldest friends. Through Bill, we met Henry Harrison Mayes, a religious folk artist whose single-minded obsession is to spread the message of salvation through the universe by way of highway signs, messages in bottles, and cement crosses—highly visible reminders of our mortality.

Together, these two stories add two more pieces to the religious mosaic we have been assembling.

THE PRAYING ROCK

In the spring of 1983, a Foxfire student, Curtis Weaver, came into the Foxfire classroom and checked out a camera for the weekend. He made some photos of a certain rock located less than a half mile into the woods above his home. The reason he wanted the pictures was that the new owners of this property were planning to clear off and bulldoze the land on which this rock sat. The rock had suddenly become quite special to him, for he had recently found out from his parents that his grandfather, Mr. Charlie Bry Phillips, had called it the "praying rock." Mr. Phillips was a preacher, and the praying rock marked the location of the spot where Mr. Phillips went to pray when he was deeply troubled. Curtis also discovered that the small pebbles on the rock had been placed there by his grandfather and represented people for whom he prayed. They were separated into piles to distinguish those who had been saved from those who had not, and they had not been touched since his grandfather's death in 1975.

Curtis showed the photos to Wig, whose interest was thus sparked, for he had never heard of this custom. He and Curtis interviewed Curtis's parents, Joe and Catherine Weaver, and made additional photos resulting in this article.

Curtis remembers his grandfather quite well, even though he died when Curtis was only eight years of age. Before Curtis knew of the significance of the rock, he had passed by it many times but never truly noticed it.

Now that the rock and the area surrounding it are more widely known as a holy place, there is a possibility it will not be destroyed after all. As one of our friends said, "I wouldn't want to be the bulldozer operator who is stupid enough to take his machine onto that piece of ground."

ALLISON ADAMS

Interview and photographs by Curtis Weaver. Edited by Allison Adams and Aimee Graves.

CATHERINE WEAVER: [My father] was Charlie Bry Phillips and he was a Missionary Baptist preacher. He was born in Rabun County and grew up over on [Highway] 76 West in a big two-story gray house sitting back in the edge of the woods. That was my grandpa's old house. Then later he lived down on Warwoman Road, and then over on Chechero. [When I was a child] we lived up on what they called Needy Creek.

He ran that Mountain Rug Company for years when we lived up there on North Valley Street. And then he worked down there at Blue Ridge Lumber Company. He was night watchman down there.

He started preaching after he got married. He was "called" to preach, August 1956. Fact of the business, whenever he got married, he couldn't even read. Mama taught him how to read out of *The Saturday Evening Post,* newspapers, and the Bible. He had no training, no education. He was just called by God.

See, [a person] gets *saved.* And then they feel the calling of God. He's called them to preach. Okay, that person can preach in various churches, but he cannot *pastor* a church. [For that, he] has to be

PLATE 347   The front of the Phillips home. The praying rock is several hundred yards into the woods behind the home.

PLATE 348   Behind the home, several outbuildings still stand.

licensed and ordained. Say he belongs to Black Rock Baptist Church, and Taylor's Chapel wants to call him [to be their pastor], they have to contact *his* church where he's a member and ask them to have an ordination service to ordain him as a preacher before he can pastor a church. Daddy was licensed to preach February 1957, and ordained April 1958.

He pastored several churches in Rabun County at different times. He organized, or founded, People's Baptist. He started that church, and he wasn't a preacher then. He felt God wanted him to raise a church, and he did. We started out in a little tent on a piece of ground given by Uncle Tom Mitchell. The wind tore the tent up several times and then we started building a church. That church is still going.

[He was using the praying rock when he was pastoring] Black Rock Baptist Church. He got the [idea for the rock] straight from God. [He chose that certain rock, because] the Bible says, "Go out in the woods and pray," and that's what he did. He went out and found that rock. The way we understood it, he just felt led to go out that way. He went out to the garden and he was seeking a quiet place away from the noise and everybody. When he got to the rock, God said, "That's it." He just knelt down there and he went back to that place from then on. It's just like God led him to that place.

If Daddy couldn't sleep, he'd get up praying. He'd sit with his Bible, and you could see the light on at two or three in the morning. Dad'd be reading the Bible. He'd say, "I'm awake for some reason. Maybe somebody that I don't even know about needs prayer."

Maybe three or four days later, somebody would say, "Brother Charlie, I *know* that somebody was praying for me the other morning at three o'clock. I was so sick I thought I was gonna die."

He said, "That's my answer."

People called him all times of the day and night, and said, "So and so's sick. I want you to pray for them"; or, "My husband's run away with another woman. I want you to pray that God'll bring him back." He'd go out there [to the praying rock] and he'd put his little rocks up and he'd pray about it. He'd stay until he got an answer. If some man was lost, someone might ask him, "Look, this man's lost and I want you to pray for him." He'd put the rock [for the lost man] in the lost pile and if the man got saved, he'd put his rock over there in the saved pile. If he backslid, he drawed him out of the saved pile. He was out of the will of the Lord. He wasn't *lost* again, because if you're once saved, you can't be lost. Jesus would have to go back to the cross. So he took him out of the saved pile and put him down here *out* of the will of the Lord in neither pile. He wasn't living right, but when prayers were answered, he'd put it back into the saved pile.

He didn't have a rock for everybody in the congregation, just special ones. Just the ones that had problems and asked for help. He chose the rocks by just reaching down on the ground to pick one up, but he knew which rock was which—who it was. He could say, "This is so-and-so, and this is so-and-so." He could tell you what pile they were in and why they were there. He could name every one of those rocks for you. I'm sure he had a rock up there for himself, but I don't know which one it was. That's probably something nobody will ever know.

Preachers from Habersham [County] would come up here and go out to the praying rock with Daddy. They would bring prayer requests of their own, and go out there and pray about it. They wouldn't come back until they got an answer. It didn't matter if it was all night.

A drunk man come to this preacher down there in Habersham, and he said, "I need to talk to a preacher. I need to get saved. I need somebody to pray with me." And [that preacher] said, "Well, we'll pray, but I think we ought to go to Rabun County."

And the [drunk man] said, "Whatever you think." So they come up here and went with Daddy out to the praying rock. Daddy asked Joe to go with him. They stayed out *all* night. It rained all night and it didn't slack. They would pray and rejoice and cry, but they really prayed there until that man made it right with God. That drunk man put his head on that rock and didn't come up till next morning—daylight. When he came up, he came up a saved man.

Now a lot of the neighbors around here heard somebody out in the woods and questioned the noise that they heard. They thought somebody was out there hurt or something, but it would be my daddy out there praying.

There was a little broken blue bottle top left at Daddy's death. The man had been a preacher who had backslid. He was drinking, and as far as I know, still is. His little blue bottle neck cap thing is still between the piles down there. He went back to drinking. Went plumb back. [He had] pastored a church and all that. Sometimes Joe's heard him out in the woods at night with it just pouring rain over on Flat Creek. He's come through there and stopped. Heard somebody a-praying just as loud! That preacher was out in the woods by himself praying. We could hear him. I guess you would say that we're all human. We're all created equal, but a preacher is supposed to be a leader, a shepherd to the flock. He is special to God because he has

PLATE 349   The praying rock from the front. Preacher Phillips would kneel before it, sometimes resting his head against it as he prayed.

PLATE 350   Several piles of small rocks sit undisturbed since the preacher's death.

been chosen to carry God's word. And [that preacher] backed up on Him—kind of like Jonah, you know, when he was supposed to go to Ninevah. As far as I know, [that preacher] is still drinking. He's never started back preaching. That's one that is still out of the will of the Lord now. He's still not back where he should be.

PLATE 351   Curtis's thumb and forefinger rest around the bottle cap that represented the preacher who backslid. The stones to the left of his hand represent the unsaved, those in the middle stand for the people who have backslid, and those on the right are for those who have been saved.

There's this young man right up here that got out of the will of the Lord and quit going to church. Daddy pulled his rock out of the pile and went to talk to him. He said, "You're out of the will of God. Your rock is in the wrong pile. You better get back where you're supposed to be." He and Daddy went out to the praying rock and that man got right again. Daddy put him right back where he was supposed to be. Now that man's walking the chalk line. He's pastoring a church.

Since Daddy died in 1975, everything's been left just the way it was. All the rocks are there. I can go out there and sit down and I can just feel him. I can feel the Lord, like it was whenever I was out there with Daddy. I can just get chill bumps all over me. I can just feel that there's someone there with me.

Daddy was a Baptist, but he did not knock other denominations. He got up and preached the Bible, and he just did not believe in compromising with the devil. If you're going to stand for God, you've got to stand for God all the way. If you don't, then He don't do nothing for you. It can't be half and half. [My dad's] life was lived for God—every day, every hour, every minute. The way he said it, "Put everything you've got on the altar and crawl on with it. Go whole totally out for the Lord. You've got to live it, you've got to dress it, you've got to preach it, and you've got to act it day by day. Because," he said, "somewhere there's somebody a-watching you. And if they're looking for mistakes in me, they're gonna find some, of course. You've got to do your best for the Lord. You cannot get up and use your mouth to preach the word of God and then turn around and curse somebody. You cannot do it. It's not right."

WATCHMAN ON THE WALL

Henry Harrison Mayes, a retired coal miner and devout believer in spreading the word of God to all people all over the earth and even to other planets when transportation becomes available, lives in Middlesboro, Kentucky.

Bill Henry, a friend of ours from Oak Ridge, Tennessee, and the man who introduced us to Alex Stewart [Foxfire 3, pages 369–97], told us about Mr. Mayes. He wrote: "This old gent is someone you must meet soon. He's eighty-five and has had several heart attacks. What a story he has to tell! I love him. He's a lot like Alex. Hope the enclosed material will pique your interest."

With the information Bill sent us was a photograph of a frail-looking man showing Bill a row of cement signs shaped like hearts on posts with the message: "Prepare to meet God" molded into them. We all felt like we had seen these signs before, but we couldn't say when or where.

On the way home from school one afternoon, I saw a similar sign along highway 441 just south of Mountain City's city limits sign. I'd seen it a hundred times, but it was just a part of the landscape. Like the grass and the trees and the telephone poles, it was supposed to be there. That sign is made of corrugated tin, but it bears a strong resemblance to the signs in the photographs. My curiosity was aroused. This person who had erected the sign in Rabun County had made other signs and Bill told us he had distributed them, sometimes alone, along roadsides throughout the entire continental United States.

What Mr. Mayes does is considered a type of folk religion. News articles about him have been published in Newsweek (October 26, 1970, and January 21, 1974), Life (June 9, 1958), and National Enquirer (February 2, 1982).

Mr. Mayes lives a long way off—a six-hour drive from Rabun County, Georgia. However, Bill and his wife felt so strongly about our interviewing Mr. Mayes that they invited us to come spend the night with them in Oak Ridge and drive on up to Middlesboro in the Cumberland Gap area of Kentucky the next morning with Bill and his son accompanying us, having taken the day off from their jobs.

So on a foggy, early spring morning in April, we drove up to Mr. Mayes's house armed with cameras, tape recorders, and a high sense of curiosity. On the way, Bill had us stop several times to make photographs of Mr. Mayes's work— a barn with corrugated tin letters stretched all across the side facing the highway telling motorists to "Prepare to meet God," and then again to photograph a cross and a sign by the roadside on the way to Middlesboro.

Mr. Mayes and his wife Lillie live in a house shaped like a cross along a tree-lined street on the outskirts of Middlesboro, a small college town. They have four children and eighteen grandchildren. He is a thin man, weighing about one hundred and ten pounds now and standing five feet, six inches tall. He has been quite ill recently and so although he was very talkative, his voice was faint as he told us his story, and we realized from the emphasis on the information he gave us that he knows he is doing a very important work and he wanted us to understand that. Even though we knew that he had related his life's experiences to many people, he was patient with us as he explained the details of preparing the bottles he ships to missionaries and others, and as he told us how he had made the signs and gotten them erected by highways and roadsides. [He began putting messages in bottles after his heart attacks because he was no longer strong enough to put out the cement signs by himself.]

Mr. Mayes told us that when he was a young man, he was seriously hurt in a mining accident. He promised the Lord that if he got well, he would dedicate his life to serving God. He felt the best way for him to serve God would be to post signs throughout the continental United States admonishing people to repent of their sins and accept God. He has been doing this for over sixty years in his spare time and for the most part using only money he and Mrs. Mayes have earned.

Mr. Mayes told us: "I run all this work interdenominational. My religion is the good that is in Catholics, Protestants, and Jews. My politics is the good that is in a common Democrat or Republican. There are good people in all [walks of life]. They all mean good; they just misunderstand, misinterpret [God's word]. The essence is, we're all the same. When something goes wrong, we're not gonna talk to Satan; we all know who to talk to—God.

"The cruelest thing on earth is race hate. My wife and I hope to come up with a force to drive race hate from the earth. The black is called dumb niggers, the yellow is called Chinks and screwy eyes, and the white is called white trash. We are all equal. Hitler killed six million Jews in five years; the white man killed thousands of Indians in two hundred years. That's so wrong. The world needs one religion, one language, one nation, one kind of politics, and one race."

Harrison Mayes is a self-educated man. "I went to school until I got to the [fifth grade]. Education is fine. I love it. I'm not against it, but education don't give you the know-how that God wants. I wish I had a lot of education but I

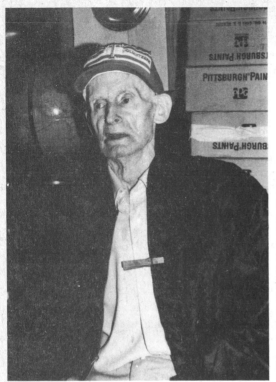

PLATE 352 "You can make fun of me, but when you go to making fun of the sacred work, you'll go to getting in trouble. I asked one doctor to give me a little assistance in buying five of these sixteen-foot boards to make these wood crosses. He just made fun of my work and called me crazy and so on. Thirty days from that day, he never could work another lick. I felt like his making fun of me caused that.

"If you mess with this work I'm a-doing, you'll get in trouble. Now, that's just it."

PLATE 353 Mrs. Mayes.

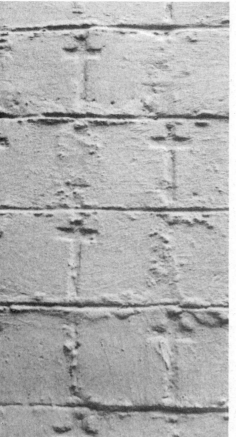

PLATE 354 "I tried to make this house mean everything. I've got eight rooms in this place. That represents the eight people that was saved in the Ark. This house is shaped like a cross. The front end's got twelve windows and represents the twelve apostles. The back part has ten windows for the Ten Commandments.

"I built this place out of concrete because I don't want it to never leave here. I don't never want it sold. I want it to finally wind up with the Salvation Army, using it as a place of their business."

PLATE 355 Note the crosses etched into the concrete walls of the Mayes home.

don't. I don't know English much, but I don't pretend to know. Many highly educated people who've got university educations just don't live up to what they're supposed to. It's just as well to say they're astraddle of the fence [about their religion]. It don't matter how many times you say, 'Prepare to meet God.' You'd better mean it. It's a matter of what's behind it."

Mr. Mayes's philosophy of life and religion is so different from anything I'd ever heard about that I was shocked—I sat up and listened, trying to comprehend all that he was talking about, wondering where he got his ideas, and marveling at the energy and ingenuity he has demonstrated to carry out what he believes in.

I assumed he belonged to one of the many Protestant country churches in this Bible Belt region of the United States. And he had at one time. He told us a story of why he withdrew his membership.

"I heard of a midnight show coming down here [in Middlesboro] in Otto Brown's theater. It was advertised in the paper. All right, you had to be eighteen before you could get in and it was for men only. I knowed about what it would be, but I [wasn't real sure]. It opened at twelve. I got in my car and went down there. I told nobody where I was going. Well, it wasn't fit for cattle to look at, much less humans. Just about all of 'em in there was eighteen-year-old boys.

"Well, I went back to the house at two o'clock in the morning and put my car up. I thought I was slipping out and slipping in but when I come in, my wife jumped all over me. She thought I'd done wrong. I said, 'Now, listen, I know exactly what I went for.' I went to get a petition up to get that stuff stopped. Suppose I'd walked up to one of the businessmen that I know very well, my partners that I trade with, to sign a petition to not let no such a thing come in our city. Not to stop the theater, but to stop that [pornography] stuff. If one of those businessmen had asked me, 'Well, what went on over there, Harrison?' I didn't have to say, 'Oh, I don't know. I wasn't there.' If I hadn't gone and seen for myself, it might have been an evangelistic program, for all I know. But I knowed what went on.

"I took my petition with all the [names] I got up and I give it to Mr. Brown. [I knew he was the manager of the theater.] I never since knowed him of having one [of those type films] because all the leading businessmen of town asked him not to do that.

"The pastor of my church, as good a man as they is in this country, come told me, he said, 'Harrison, you've got to go up and confess it to the church that you made a mistake.' [He was taking care of the church, which is natural for him to do.]

"I said, 'Yes, I did. I'll be right up.'

"So I went up to the church. I got up [before the congregation] and I said, 'Now, listen, listen. I don't owe nobody no apologies.' I told them why I went and what I done and so on. I said, 'Now I'm gonna ask everybody to forgive me, just forgive me. I'm gonna also ask, not that I'm mad at nobody, to take my name off* *of the church record so I can experiment on things I need to know to carry this work on."*

He's waging a one-man war on pornography, sexual violence, abortion, racism, world pollution, overpopulation, and lawlessness. He's done this through signs and in small bottles. The bottles contain messages sealed in them that are distributed to jails and cast into bodies of water throughout the world whenever he can persuade people to launch them.

HEDY DAVALOS

Interviews and photographs by Chris Crawford, Greg Darnell, Aimee Graves, Tammy Carter, and Denise Layfield. Editing by Allison Adams, Hedy Davalos, Richard Edwards, Kevin Fountain, and Cheryl Wall.

MRS. MAYES: I was nearly fifteen and he was nearly twenty when me and him got married. He was painting them [messages] on rocks then. He'd take a paintbrush and he'd go out and paint "Jesus Saves" and things like that on rocks. He would make little signs and tack 'em on telephone poles.

MR. MAYES: Well, here's what happened. I tried everything. I tried preaching, I tried running revival meetin's, and I tried going all over to Florida and different places making music. I never could make a go at nothing until I got into this sign work. That was exactly my calling.

I painted [my first signs] on logs. I put 'em up all over the place. Then I got to putting them on cardboard paper. I'd write whatever I wanted to. I tacked them on telephone poles. I got into bigger stuff, painting messages on rocks and big billboards. I just went on up to bigger and better things. I put 'em on four-foot by six-foot aluminum sheets where they would last. And I put them in forty-four states myself. Then I also got to having tracts printed up to send to the chaplains in the Army and on ships in World War I and II. I had a hundred thousand tracts made to send.

He had shown us his shop where forms were stored for making the huge concrete crosses. And we had already been outside to see and photograph the impressive rows of crosses erected in his yard.

I'd say I've got around sixty to seventy-five crosses set up around the United States. I don't know exactly how many I've got left in the yard out there. I intended to make two hundred, but [my heart attack] happened and I had to cut some short. I intended to make four concrete ones for each state and put 'em around the capitals, out on

PLATE 356 Signs seen in the Mayes's front and side yards and in his workshop, which is in the back part of his house.

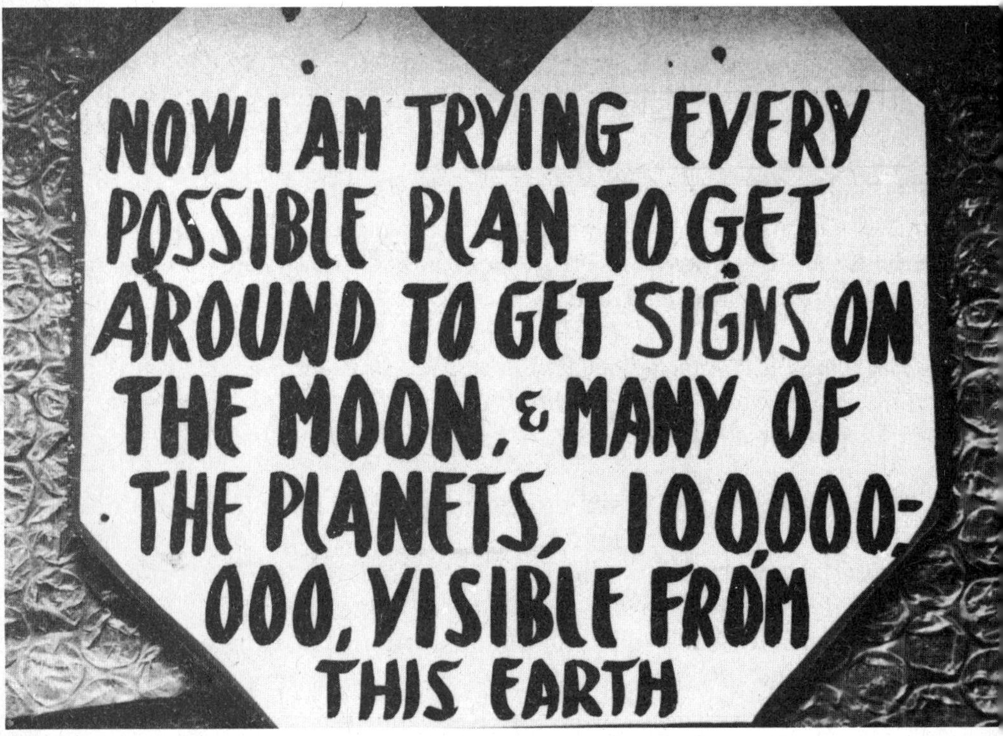

PLATE 357

PLATE 358   A roadside sign erected by Mr. Mayes.

PLATE 359   One of several crosses standing in the Mayes's front yard.

PLATE 360   "When transportation gets available, I want the crosses in the backyard moved to the country or planet they're made for. I made one for the North Pole, one for the South Pole, one for the bank of the River Nile, one for the Suez Canal, one for the Panama Canal where it can be seen by the traffic in the shipping lanes. Others are designated for Germany, France— whatever name is cut on the cross. I made a few for the planets. I've got Venus out there, and Jupiter and several others."

the highways leading into these cities. They will finally crumble away, but I think seventy-five years is the life of concrete. Anyway, that's a long time.

I used to take four or five boys [to help me] to put the concrete crosses up. Those crosses weigh fourteen hundred pounds apiece and my normal weight was 123 pounds then [I weigh 110 now] so I needed help, but you know how boys are. You can't get them in the bed and you can't get them out of the bed. Young fellows are just a public nuisance! One would want to go to eat at this place and the others at another place. I finally decided I was goin' to put the crosses up by myself, me and the [truck] driver.

I loaded them here with a chain block. I'd drive the truck right in under the cross, stack 'em up several on each other. We'd drive right to the place [along the road] where I was goin' to put one up. All I had to do was to dig the hole and in fifteen minutes I was ready to leave. I used posthole diggers. I've got two of 'em—a little one and a big one. When it was raining real bad, the water would be pert' near up at the top before I'd get the hole dug. I had the truck braced so it couldn't get away. I'd pull the sign over to the edge of the truck and just tip it down right over the hole. I'd drop the cross into the hole. Or sometimes I'd dig down and hit rock, tons and tons of it. Then I'd just dig as far down as I could and pack rocks up around [the cross] where it didn't go down in the ground far enough. I had some sacks with me and I'd just go over [to a rock pile alongside the road] and sack me up some of those rocks. I was trespassing but people that was guarding [on some new road project] would say, "He doesn't look guilty. He's got permission [to get those rocks or put up that cross]." I'd pour those rocks out around the cross and tamp 'em down a little bit and that cross would be just as tight as it could be.

[I've put a lot of crosses up] and I've put signs up in forty-four states myself. I don't know exactly how many signs, but I could hunt the files up and tell you. When this [heart attack] happened, I had to quit. [That's when I went to putting messages in bottles and distributing those.]

For the last forty years, hardly no individuals have let me put a sign on their place. I come along wanting to put a sign on a man's farm place. He's got all the room taken up that he can spare [with paid advertising]. He's getting good money out of advertising signs put out on his property. I couldn't pay that kind of money. Therefore he runs me off. Naturally, the highway won't give me permission. They can't, but I've got [my signs and crosses] on all the roads. I trespass and do it. I know where to put 'em so they'll be out of the way. If I were to put 'em in the middle of the road, I ought to be put in jail. But it is my religious right [to put up the signs] even if it is trespassing. I'd pick out [a place] I wanted. I'd get right down across the fence, up on the bank, next to the farmer's fence and put a sign up.

You [have to] put a sign 660 feet from the interstate highways. Nobody but great big ol' companies can make signs that big. I can't. I couldn't stand it. I took it up with President Carter. [He came down to Middlesboro to make a speech and I went to see him.] I said, "I can't make these signs [to be seen] this far. Talk with the interstate [highway] department and get them to give me a right to put my religious signs just across the road." He took it up with them. It come down to my rights. They couldn't stop me nohow because it's my constitutional rights. They [wrote up something] so I could get just off of the right-of-way. In other words, he couldn't say "yes" or "no" so I just went right ahead.

I'll say every newspaper in the United States has got a picture of my signs because all kinds of men's been here making pictures and talking to me. A lady from California come and got pictures of the small concrete crosses, and they're in Washington, D.C. [in the Smithsonian Institution].

Well, in 1975 I decided to quit making crosses and signs, and I meant it! I had this stroke and I had so much trouble out of it that I didn't hear God at this particular point. I was righteously mad. I didn't care if the Lord did kill me. Then I had what you would call a vision. I know that was what it was. It said, "You hurt so bad, you don't need to know what I've got you into. I'm going to let you in on enough. That'll satisfy you. That's all. That's all." *Now* you couldn't stop me [from carrying on this work]!

I don't ever want this work to stop. I can't put no more signs up. I don't make no more. I now put [messages] in bottles. I've got 56,000 of these bottles spread throughout the world. There are twenty languages in the bottles. "Prepare to meet God" is translated in fourteen languages: Turkish, Indonesian, Greek, German, French, Italian, Spanish, Russian, African, Chinese, Syrian, Jewish, Japanese and English. "Jesus is coming soon; get ready" is translated in six languages: Greek, German, French, Italian, Spanish, and English. If you find [a bottle] in Australia, all you have to do is write me the number on it. Then I'll check my files in there [in my office] to see when the bottle was put in the water. I'm sending the bottles to all parts of this earth to missionaries to have them throw the bottles into lakes, rivers, and oceans. If I'm sending bottles ten thousand miles away to the foreign missionaries, who's gonna come here and get me for littering? I'll tell the missionaries, "You be sure and don't let people see you throw these in the water, or they'll call you a litterbug." God's got me doing this and litterbug or not, I'm not trying to hurt nobody.

[When I ship a box of bottles to a missionary], I'll send a brand-new dollar bill to each one in the family for a birthday present *if* they'll tell me the number of children they've got. Four or five years ago I sent a box of bottles to the Church of God missionary from Cleveland, Tennessee. He and his wife had seven children. I sent 'em nine one-dollar bills. I just make it a flat four brand-new one-dollar bills if the missionary don't specify the number of children. [This helps out with their expense for distributing the bottles and shows my appreciation.]

Now here's what happens [when people find the bottles]. Say a man from China opens this bottle and pulls out the message. He reads the message in Chinese. He ain't Christian and he don't know a bit more than nothing what that means, but he's going to start trying to find out. If it wasn't in Chinese, he would never try to find out. [I don't understand these foreign languages, but I had some people at one of the universities do these translations for me.]

One I had put in at Central America drifted to the Philippines. It had to go about six thousand miles. It was twenty-three months from the time it was put in till they wrote me about the time they found it. I had some put in around up in New Jersey. Well, six months later, I got a letter from someone that had found one of them in the English Channel. What had happened was it had gotten into the Gulf Stream.

In the Tennessee waterworks, all these here dams and lakes head for New Orleans. I've put [the bottles] in this little branch over here and they end up in New Orleans, and when they get to New Orleans they get all over the world. I had six of them put in the Tennessee River. Well, some officers come up. They asked me what I was a-doin'. I showed 'em. One of 'em said, "You can't do that. They have boat races here. Somebody might get hurt on a bottle." Naturally it was the truth, so I just said I wouldn't put 'em in. I went right up the river to my mother-in-law's place, got in some bushes where they couldn't see me, and put 'em in there.

I'll tell you one thing. In the state of Washington on the Snake River, there was a man who worked in a lumber business up there. He was walking along one Sunday morning fishing, and he happened to see one of my bottles washed up on the shore. I put 'em in half-pint whiskey bottles then. His eye got a glimpse of that cross. "Aw, some fool's littering up this river," he said to hisself. He went to walking on and he got to thinking about that cross. He said, "I'm going back to

PLATE 361 At his workbench, Mr. Mayes forces the stiff cardboard message into plastic drink bottles. He fills each bottle temporarily with lead shot so that the message will be pressed tightly against its sides. After a few days, he pours the shot out, inserts a cork with glue, and twists on a cap.

PLATE 362 Note the letters hanging from clips above his workbench. People from all around the world find his bottles and write to him. He keeps a record in his files of each bottle with its coded message and where and when he sent it for distribution.

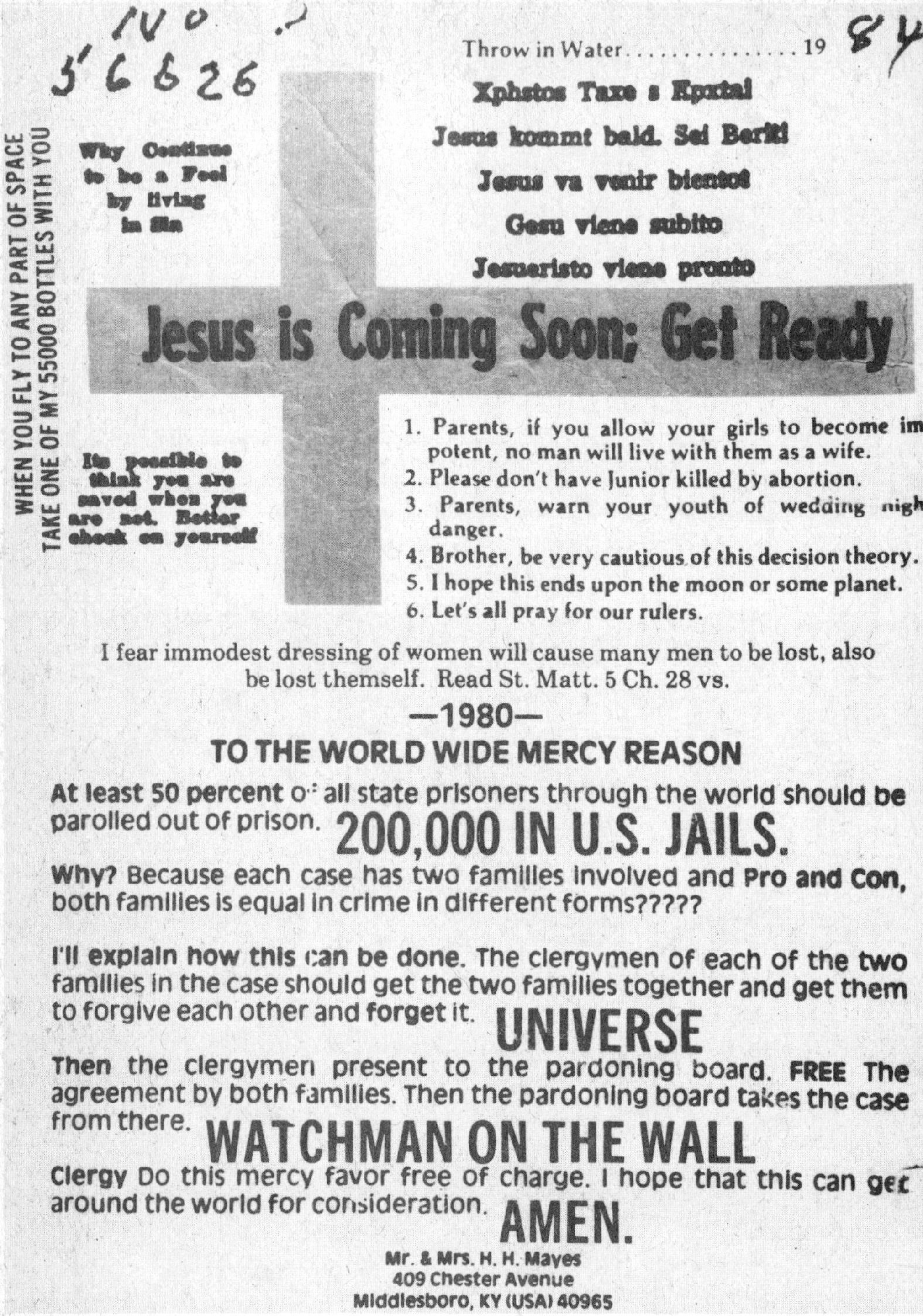

Throw in Water.............19 84

5'6 6 26   NO ?

Why Continue
to be a Fool
by living
in Sin

Xphstos Taxe s Rpxtai

Jesus kommt bald. Sei Bertti

Jesus va venir bientot

Gesu viene subito

Jesueristo viene pronto

Jesus is Coming Soon; Get Ready

Its possible to
think you are
saved when you
are not. Better
check on yourself

1. Parents, if you allow your girls to become im-
   potent, no man will live with them as a wife.
2. Please don't have Junior killed by abortion.
3. Parents, warn your youth of wedding nigh
   danger.
4. Brother, be very cautious of this decision theory.
5. I hope this ends upon the moon or some planet.
6. Let's all pray for our rulers.

I fear immodest dressing of women will cause many men to be lost, also
be lost themself. Read St. Matt. 5 Ch. 28 vs.

—1980—
TO THE WORLD WIDE MERCY REASON

At least 50 percent of all state prisoners through the world should be
parolled out of prison. **200,000 IN U.S. JAILS.**

Why? Because each case has two families involved and Pro and Con,
both families is equal in crime in different forms?????

I'll explain how this can be done. The clergymen of each of the two
families in the case should get the two families together and get them
to forgive each other and forget it. **UNIVERSE**

Then the clergymen present to the pardoning board. FREE The
agreement by both families. Then the pardoning board takes the case
from there. **WATCHMAN ON THE WALL**

Clergy Do this mercy favor free of charge. I hope that this can get
around the world for consideration. **AMEN.**

Mr. & Mrs. H. H. Mayes
409 Chester Avenue
Middlesboro, KY (USA) 40965

PLATE 363   One side of the message put in the bottles that go out to prisoners and
missionaries and others to be distributed around the world. Note the handwritten code
number 56626 and the year '84 at the top.

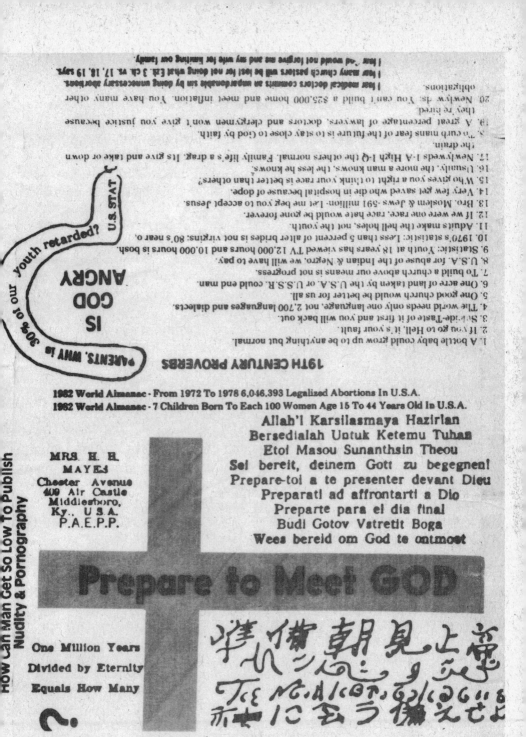

PLATE 364   The other side of the message.

see what that fool's got to say." He picked the bottle up and read the message. My wife's name was on there then instead of mine. He wrote her a letter and said, "Listen, I've never been to church in my life. I've never done a thing in this world for the Lord, and if you ever did pray for a man that needed it, I wish you would [pray for me]."

I wrote him a letter, I did, and I never did hear from him. Now I'm just as confident as I'm a-sittin' here that he never did get right with the Lord and died. When he comes up before the Lord, he'll begin to make excuses, so to speak. "Lord, I've never been to church and I've never heard a preacher," and so on.

"Yes, but I had a man in Kentucky to put a bottle in the Snake River purposely to give you the warning and you didn't take it." Now, the Lord don't have to give you a thousand warnings. If he gives you a special warning, that's enough. Sometimes you may get thousands of them before you leave, but one direct warning is enough.

I also send bottles to jails. I've got to send the messages in plastic bottles to the prisoners. They can fight with 'em all they want to and they can't hurt one another. [I send a box to] the ladies' department and one to the men's. My wife and I are praying for the prison force, the prisoners, and their families. Of course, I send these in care of the jailer. Now he can't accept a bribe, but I've got two brand-new dollar bills in every one of those boxes that goes to the jail. I tell the jailer, "This money's not for you. It's for your father and mother." [That way, though, it shows my appreciation for him getting the messages to the prisoners.]

I am eighty-six years old and I started making signs and putting them up sixty-six years ago. God has helped me to get these sacred messages in fifty states, eighty-two nations, and on the seven seas, all the big rivers and lakes on earth.

I don't want to stop with putting signs up all over the earth. If we don't do something to stop poisoning our air here on earth, we are going to have to go to [living] on other planets. We can go to the moon with the speed that we've got, but I tell you, the moon ain't the best. There are nine planets and I've got nine grandsons. Each of my grandsons [is responsible for placing one of those crosses] on each of those nine planets after I leave.

I want this work to stay here as long as there is people anywhere. I want it in all the universe. I want it everywhere. I'll try every possible plan to get around to set signs on the moon and planets.

Me and my wife, Lillie, had four children and we've got eighteen grandchildren. All but one of the grandchildren are married. I expect my children and my grandchildren to carry on my work. When I leave

PLATE 365 This cross reads, "Erect this
sign on the planet Mars, 1990."

here, when I'm through, my oldest son's daughter, my granddaughter, is to take over the reins of this thing—not to finance it, but to see
that it is financed and that [the family continues to put out signs and
that bottles are still mailed out to jails and missionaries and others].
That my work is carried out.

Nobody pays for me and my wife; we pay for all the postage and
everything we do [making the signs and putting them up on roadsides, and getting the messages into the bottles and the bottles dis-
tributed] out of my paychecks when I worked and now with my
pension. [I have solicited small contributions occasionally from local
businessmen for special projects.]

I'll tell you this. Me and my wife have got $75,000 in our own
money in this business. The Bible says the Lord awards you fourfold.
It don't mean with money—maybe health, maybe everything. [I know
he didn't reward me in beauty, because I'm no beauty.] Make that
$75,000 fourfold, and me and my wife are worth a lot.

I heard Jimmy Swaggart [a radio evangelist] this morning say that
his expense is a hundred thousand dollars every day to carry on the

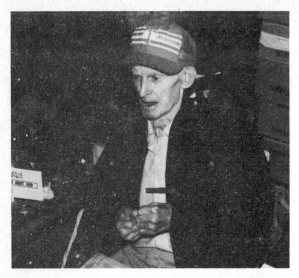

PLATE 366

PLATE 367 The bicycle that Mr. Mayes rode around town before his heart attack.

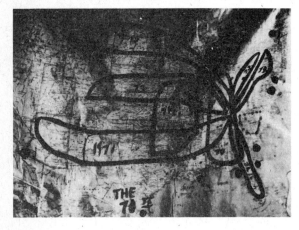

PLATE 368 A U.S. map hangs on one wall of the workshop. The dark heavy lines indicate the routes he took across America to erect signs, along with the years he went.

work he's in. That's a lot of money. He's a wonderful preacher but I'll say not one-sixth of the population of the world ever listens at 'im. Now Jimmy's a-preaching worldwide and costing a hundred thousand dollars a day. Well, my work costs ten dollars a day for all this. That is what it comes up to for paying the postage for [getting] the bottles [out to all the world]. I'm honored to say that just as many people see these bottles as listen to Jimmy Swaggart. And it's costing them nothing.

The Lord has called me to do this work. God has made me a universal watchman of the world. I am nothing except what God has made me. You'll find that story in [the Old Testament of the Bible] in Ezekiel, chapter three. If the watchman posted [on the wall to guard the city] sees the enemy coming, he warns the people. If he don't do it, they'll be lost. He'll lose his own life and the ones he should have warned will be lost with him. We must warn all people of the evils that surround them in this world. All church pastors are more or less watchmen of the world.

I ain't nothing. What God has got me doing is something you better not monkey around with or you'll be in trouble. Thousands on top of thousands of people will be turned away on the last day. The Bible says they'll come up and make all kinds of excuses saying, "I done this. I done that."

[God] will say, "Yes, but I had a little old man to warn you and you didn't heed it."

PLATE 369   One of Mr. Mayes's signs on a local barn.

"LIFE IS GOOD"
–D. B. Dayton

My grandparents are D. B. and Sadie Dayton. They live in Hiawassee, Georgia. They are very close and they've been married for forty-five years. They get along together the best of any two people I know. They mean a lot to me—more than anyone can imagine.

When I first decided to interview Papaw, I mentioned it to Kim and she liked the idea. I wanted to interview him because when I'd go visiting, he would tell me all kinds of things that happened when he was a little boy. I thought that the things he told me would be enjoyable to someone else also.

Papaw and Mamaw live in a trailer that has been bricked over. It has a cement porch with a roof over it. Their yard is very small with shrubs set out along the edge. On the porch, Mamaw has flowers set out in pots and there is a swing on one side. When you are sitting in that swing on a very hot day and the breeze comes and cools you off, it feels so good. Behind and beside the trailer are hives of bees. In Papaw's spare time, he makes racks for bee gums and sells them, and of course he makes racks for his own use also.

Beside the trailer, about twenty feet away, there is a big, long grocery store. Papaw has owned the store for as long as I can remember. When I was a little girl, if I wanted some candy or something to eat or play with, all I had to do was ask him and run in that store and pick me out anything I wanted. On one end of the store are living quarters that Mr. and Mrs. Lag rent from Papaw. On the other end of the store is a shop where Papaw has his woodworking tools and makes his bee racks, washstands, cabinets, and tables. Aunt Bug runs the store now, and so Papaw and Mamaw spend lots of time in the shop. They go out there together whenever they like, but Papaw still enjoys tending to the store whenever Aunt Bug has to go to town for something.

Papaw also likes to go down to Red McKinney's, a little country store in town and play checkers with the other men his age who gather there.

Back not too long ago, he had a severe heart attack and he isn't allowed to pick up anything heavy or work too hard, but both of my grandparents were told by

PLATE 370 Dana Holcomb with her grandfather.

PLATE 371 A view of the Daytons' store with their house at the left. The Lags live in the right end of the store building.

PLATE 372 Left to right: Mrs. Lag, Mr. Lag, D. B. Dayton, Sadie Dayton.

the doctor to walk down the road by their house every day. I've always been told that where Papaw went, I was always there. He reminds me every once in a while how mean I used to be when I was a very little girl. He always got tickled at me because he aggravated me until I'd get mad at him and then would go off and pout.

While Kim and I were over there, we got out the family Bible and looked over the family tree written up in it. There were pictures of the family stuck in the Bible and we looked at them. Mamaw started telling us stories like the one about the time when I was small and the family was visiting in Atlanta, and I threw my little red shoe out the window of the building where we were staying.

When we went over to interview Papaw the first time, it tickled him to death. He was real eager to tell us all kinds of stories. We got almost two tapesful that time. After we came home and transcribed them, we found there were some more questions that needed asking. I went back over there and asked the list of questions that I had made out. While I was there, Mamaw had some sowchy cooked for dinner. I had never tasted of it before and at first I didn't want to. I finally got up enough courage, and it was good. I thought it would taste like spinach or turnip greens, but it didn't. It was better.

In doing this interview, I found that it made me appreciate my grandparents more than ever before. I hope you get as much out of it by reading it as I did by doing it. I would like to thank my parents for making it possible for our transportation over there.

DANA HOLCOMB

On a Saturday morning, Dana, a best friend of mine, and I drove over to Hiawassee to do a personality interview on her grandfather, D. B. Dayton. It rained early that morning but from about dinner time on, the sun was shining. Finally it turned out to be a beautiful day to do an interview.

I met her grandfather, her grandmother Sadie, and her aunt, Elaine Bonner, known to everyone as Aunt Bug. During dinner they got to talking about all of their relatives and other people that I had heard Dana mention before.

During the interview he talked to us about his parents, brother, and sisters, and mischief he had done while he was little, courting, jobs he has had, and things he does in his spare time now. The things I liked and remembered best are his stories about mischief and his daddy at Christmas.

D.B. has the talent of getting you to listen to him even though you've already heard some of what he is talking about. Sometimes he will tell you things that would make you laugh, but if someone else told you, they wouldn't be funny at all.

Sadie makes you feel right at home, just like you were one of her grandchildren. She is the kind of lady that makes you feel loved, and someone you will remember for a long time.

Aunt Bug is very friendly and reminded me of someone between a teenage girl and an older sister. She wants us to grow up and do things on our own, yet have fun and do things the safe way, too. I never did find out how she got the nickname "Bug."

I ate dinner with them and between the fun I was having and not being too hungry anyway, I didn't eat much. They wanted to make sure I had all I wanted to eat, just like when I go to a best friend's house to spend the night.

Before we left we all got told good-bye and to come back as soon as we could. On the way back we were all tired, even though the ride home didn't seem half as long as the ride over there. But for some reason you can't ever get to where you are going quick enough.

KIM HAMILTON

Interviews and photographs by Dana Holcomb and Kim Hamilton.

My parents were Sam and Rosena Dayton. She was an Eller before they married, old man Alf Eller's girl, from up on the head of Hightower.

My parents, they was strict. I don't know how long it was before they ever let me go anywhere unless they went with me. I never did have a dream. I knowed they wasn't no use of it. I knowed I couldn't never go anyway, never did think about going.

My daddy's been dead about thirty years. He had high blood pressure and he wasn't allowed to eat no grease, nothing with grease cooked in it. My wife could always make good biscuits and she put grease to 'em. He'd come up by our house and he'd have to have a biscuit. He'd eat 'em by theirself [plain]. They wouldn't let him have none at home, you know, but he'd slip and eat 'em at our house.

My mommy was crippled most of her life. When she was nine years old she was sitting in a girl's lap, and the girl was sitting thisaway. Mama had her legs up like this and the girl squeezed her up some way. She cried because it hurt her. She never did walk another step. She grew up crippled in one leg. That caused her to go on crutches all of her life. They didn't take her to the doctor when that happened. They didn't know. If they had to go to a doctor, they had to ride a mule ten or fifteen miles, and they just didn't know anything bad was wrong. The doctors here lately say she throwed her hip out of place. That's been a long time—ninety-something years ago. She was nine years old when that happened and she raised eight children and lived to be a hundred and two years old.

My mom and dad got along best you've ever seen till Christmas.

Daddy'd get drunk ever' Christmas. He worked like a slave through all the rest of the time. When Christmas come, we'd have two peppermint sticks of candy, a orange, and a apple in our sock. We hung our socks up then, all of us. That's what we'd have. My daddy went off to the store one time and he got our Christmas that day, and he got him a new pair of overalls. Somebody gave him some liquor—enough to get him drunk. He walked home. It's four miles from town to where we lived, and when we seen him coming, Mommy says, "He's drunk." She could tell just as well when he got drunk. We went out to meet him. He had a box of candy and one leg of those new overalls under his arm. The other leg of 'em was a-dragging in the dirt. He had that candy strowed everywhere. We went back down the road and picked up the sticks of candy where he had spilt it—them long, hard sticks of peppermint candy. Then they wasn't no sugar sticks.

When he got home, Mommy got on him. Just as sure as he got drunk, she'd get on him right then, and make it worse. If she'd just a' waited till he'd got sober, it's been a whole lot better but she'd get on him and they'd quarrel. They'd have a cuss fight just as sure as he'd get drunk. They wasn't a Christmas that passed hardly that he didn't get drunk but through the other times he hardly ever did.

My daddy didn't have no money to pay his tax. We had to pay poll tax back then. He wasn't worth much, but he wanted to vote. You couldn't vote if you didn't pay your poll tax. If he got ahold of one dollar from one year to the next, he would pin it up in his overall pocket with a safety pin. It'd stay right there till tax-paying time. He'd keep it a whole year in that there bib pocket. He'd go pay his poll tax and then he could vote. He was like my granddaddy, a strong Democrat, and he wanted to vote. I stayed with my granddaddy for a while. He told me, "Son, if I'd knowed you'd be a Republican, I wouldn't a' fed you another bite." He's told me that a many a time and just about that strong, too.

When I was old enough, I had to pay a dollar a year poll tax to get to vote, too. Most of the times about a third of th' folks, when they went to election ground, they'd get with the others and get drunk. Somebody, some candidate, would furnish 'em enough liquor to get 'em drunk on. They'd have a fight, somebody would, before they ever left the grounds. They had to stay there till seven o'clock. They had a slow way of counting votes then. They had to count ever' individual's vote. Had three a-counting, so one wouldn't cheat. If one come up wrong and the other two right, they'd have to count 'em over and make it tally out right on the votes.

I had one brother and six sisters. Birdy was the oldest, Dorabelle the next, Addy, Clyn, I was next, Geneva, and Maggie was last. There were two year between all of us but Maggie and Geneva, and they was five year between them. I was born on upper Hightower (in Towns County), April 4, the year nineteen hundred and fourteen.

My earliest memory was when we moved from Hightower to Scataway. We had a bunch of chickens and had to catch 'em after night. I was just a little bitty boy and one got away. She flew away off down in the pasture. I mocked how she flew and Poppy and them laughed at me ever since. They'd mock me. They'd say "Flawk! Flawk! Flawk!"

We moved to Scataway for Vogel Lumber Company. They give us free rent to watch for fires and keep them from burning the fences up. Fire'd get out then and burn the rail fences up. If it got out and burned the fences, we went and asked people in to help us rebuild them. They all come in and built them back and we give 'em their dinner. That's all they got out of it.

Our neighbors at Scataway were Hershal Barnes, John Beck, and Paul Shook. They was real good neighbors.

Our house looked like a twenty-four-foot square. The living room and bedroom was all in together, one big old square room. Then they had a little hallway that run out to the kitchen. It was open, just covered overhead. I guess we had four or five beds. Mommy and Poppy slept in the one right up by the fire chimney. I believe there was four more beds in the back. We kept warm about as good as anybody, I guess. We had plenty of cover but when you got out from under it, you got cold. We had us something like a straw tick for our mattresses. It was sewed up all round but for a little piece in the middle. Mommy would reach under there ever' morning and stir that straw where you laid of a night and had packed it down. She'd reach in there at that hole and she'd stir it up. We got our straw changed ever' fall and used it for a year. When the thrashers come around and thrashed rye, then we'd go get us some new straw and put in the sacks. We'd have us one with one of them sheets on it. I've waked up many a morning, the sheet kicked down and me a-laying in the middle of the bed in a pile of straw. That's right. I'd wake up, awful pitiful, a-laying in that straw.

My mommy swept the floor with a homemade broom that she made from broom sage she'd gathered. She quilted all winter long when she didn't have nothing else to do. She had her quilting frame right in the middle of the old big house. Of a night, she'd take the strings and roll up all four corners of the frame where we could walk under it. The next morning, she'd roll 'em back down and start a-quilting. We was mostly all gone and she had plenty of room then. She'd quilt 'em in fans. She'd start and go around like that, and get a little bigger. They called that fans. She bought her thread for a nickel a spool, a great big spool of cotton thread. She'd get her material from wore-out clothes, the ones we had that had holes in 'em and we couldn't wear no more.

She'd take knitting needles and knit socks, sweaters, and things like that. She had an old spinning wheel. Lord, I've seen her stand on one leg all day long. She'd get started and she'd go to pulling that cotton, not a thing in the world but cotton. She had cards and she'd roll it out in rolls about fourteen inches long. She'd put one end of that cotton to that old spinning wheel. Then she'd turn the big wheel with her finger. She would pull that back and when she got through with that, she'd tie another one to the end of it. She'd keep it a-going all the time. Eventually she'd get a great old big spool of thread wound up. She'd take the thread and fix socks. You talk about something good, now they's good! If she could get ahold of enough cotton, she would put it in a quilt. It was hard to get cotton then. They would put a lining on it and that made it a lot heavier quilt than they make now.

We went barefooted all through the early summer. From this time of year on, we was barefooted. We'd do well if we got a pair of shoes a year—old brogans made out of leather, leather bottoms, leather tops, and ever' time you took a step, they'd skreak. They wasn't thick like they are now. That pair of shoes was the only one you got till spring, but of course they was tough. They was slick and you'd fall down. You couldn't walk in the mountains hardly a'tall with them. I weared 'em till the sole come off. I've seen old men with a hole that was yarned together. I've wore 'em myself that way.

In the wintertime, we had lye gums. That's a big old round hollow log that's set up on boards and we'd take all of our ashes [from the fireplace] and put in that gum. Then in spring of the year, we'd take water and pour it in the gum. The water'd go down through to get the strength out of the ashes and drip into a bucket. That's what you call lye.

We made our soap from that lye, made it kind of like jelly. Now some people made it where they would let it dry and they could cut it out into big bars. We always made it just like jelly.

We cooked our hominy with lye to take the husk off the corn kernels. It'd leave the pure stuff, you know. After supper, we liked to set by the fire with us a saucer and ever' one of us would eat one grain at a time of that hominy with our fingers. Didn't make any difference. We'd eat all we wanted.

Mommy had a washpot setting on some rocks out under an apple tree where it was shady when she'd wash clothes. She had a great old big stump there for a battling bench. She'd boil clothes for a little while and then she'd put out on that stump. She had a great big old heavy paddle that Poppy made for her. She'd beat them clothes, and the dirt and water would just fly ever'where. She'd beat 'em and then she'd rub 'em sometimes. At first she didn't have a scrubboard, but eventually they got one. She had to rub 'em out with her hands. Then she would rinse them through clear water and hang them out on the line. They'd be dingy. They didn't use any bleach. Sheets and stuff like that would look dingy. They 'as supposed to be white. They was made of thick, rough stuff.

She'd get a telephone line and make a clothesline out of that. My daddy went to John H. Corn's to work and they had a telephone. Ever' once in a while somebody'd steal somebody's telephone wire and make 'em a clothesline. We'd have to get the company to come and tie it back together. They'd take the rest down and give it to someone to take home and use for a clothesline.

One time I climbed that apple tree over Mommy's washpot. I fell out of the tree and hit my head on that pot. It had a broke place in it and I hit it right there. Mommy was pregnant with Maggie, so Birdie run out there and she wouldn't let Mommy see the blood. You can still feel the cut, where it dented my skull or something. I didn't know how bad it was, so I didn't go to the doctor. I just bound it up and went on. I was just up there climbing around boy-like and fell out. Maybe a limb broke with me or something. I don't know what happened.

People was a whole lot healthier then than they are now. We never was sick, hardly. When we needed medicine, we had turpentine, castor oil, and salts. I didn't like castor oil—Lord, no! Just as sure as you started taking a bad cold, that's when they give you some. They said castor oil and salts would work colds out of you. If somebody got cut and was bleeding bad, they would reach up in the back of the chimney to get some soot and put on it. We called the soot in the chimney "cobweb." They used hog lard for burns and catnip tea for babies to break the hives out on them. When your stomach is out of shape, your lips are cracked, or you have fever blisters, dig up yellow root and chew it.

Mommy put a poultice or breast rag on my chest in the fall of the year, the first tisic spell I had, and it stayed there till spring. There was turpentine, lamp oil, salve, and different things in the breast rag. I had what they called the "tisics" [phthisis] when I was a young 'un. That's in your lungs, where you can't breathe. I'd have to go,

"Ooook! Ooook!" all night long. You could hear me all over the house getting my breath. I'd pert' near smother to death. Mommy would sit beside me on a straight chair that she'd whittled out rockers for. (She nailed 'em on that straight chair herself.) She rocked that chair all night many a night, sitting right by me.

Well, when I was about nine years old, I caught the whooping cough. They said it would kill me or cure me one. I got the whooping cough and it cured me. Yep! Never did have the tisics no more. I reckon you just cough it all out. You'd cough for three weeks, then you'd whoop for three weeks. You'd whoop ever' time you'd cough. You had it about nine weeks. That stopped the tisics, I reckon. I just coughed it all out.

Way back, they was these little young children that had polio. If they 'as one in the settlement anywhere got it, Mommy'd tie a piece of garlic around our necks. It hung around our necks and it stunk like ramps. Stunk awful, but we wore it till the disease died down—a long time. We thought it kept the disease away. We didn't know whether it did or not, but it sure did stink bad enough.

People don't do nothing now for you when you're sick. Back then, somebody'd have the typhoid fever and their corn would grow up. Neighbors would come in with plows and hoes and weed it out till they got well. It was like building a fence. People'd come in and have a workin'. Build your fence back if the fire got in it and burnt it down. All they got was their dinner. They had a good time, too! When we built the fences, my daddy was plowing these steers. Them steers would drag the logs in close to the fence, where they'd split the logs into rails. They'd split 'em and lay 'em up. Some would be a-splittin', some a-draggin', and some a-layin' 'em up, zigzag like.

We lived hard. We cooked on a wood stove, and didn't have any electricity till about thirty years ago. We'd go to the store and get oil for our lamps. I think the oil was twenty cents a gallon. We'd use pine knots we got from rotted trees to build a fire with and to use as light when we eat supper after dark. We'd stick one in a corner of our old rock fireplace to see by of a night. It was just as rich as it could be. It'd bust into splinters—just like burning kerosene.

We had nothing but an old plow, hillside turner, and a pair of steers and hoes with homemade handles in 'em for the gardens. We didn't have a rake then.

When we were in the mountains for the Vogel Lumber Company, we dug up sassafras trees, peeled the bark off and toted it out in a sack, an' then scraped the rough part off of it. It brought five cents a pound at the grocery store. We'd bake a cake of flour bread, spread it open and put sugar in it, and take that to the mountains with us—eat that and drink water out of a cold spring. That's what we had for dinner while we was digging bark.

We couldn't afford to eat turkey and we couldn't afford to eat many chickens. What few chickens we had, we had to get the eggs they laid. We'd take the eggs to the store and buy sugar, salt, and coffee with 'em. Couldn't eat eggs except only on Easter Sunday. About two weeks before Easter, we'd steal the eggs. When the old hen laid, we'd go get them eggs and we'd hide 'em. By the time Easter come, we'd have a pretty good bunch. We'd boil 'em and we'd color 'em with broom straw. It'd just color 'em yellow-looking. That's all the coloring we had.

In the summertime, we had vegetables. Mommy would make "leather britches." That's dried beans. She'd take a pumpkin, cut round rings out of it, peel it, hang it on a stick, put it out in the sunshine, and let it dry. That was dried pumpkin we had in the wintertime. You could put a piece of fat meat in there, cook it with it, and that meat was just as sweet as it could be. That pumpkin made it sweet. That was the best meat ever I eat.

She wouldn't make jelly as much as apple preserves, and she'd make something else out of apples, like apple butter. We'd go to the creek and get fox grapes and make fox grape juice. If you got some flour bread, you could make you a pie for dinner. We'd pick huckleberries. If the woods was burnt off one year, the next year you never saw the like of the huckleberries in your life that would be there. You can't find 'em now since the woods haven't been burnt. I don't know what causes them to grow. They just kill ever' other thing out.

We had chestnut trees and persimmon trees. When persimmons get ripe, now, they're good. That's what 'possums eat, persimmons. We had those little bitty fall grapes. They was extra good. We made them into some kind of a jam, seeds and all. What we lived on all winter was syrup, molasses. My daddy and granddad made the syrup. My granddad had a mill. Ever'body from Scataway brought their cane there to have it made up into syrup. They'd skin the cane by hand. Then they had an old thing made like a small shovel with holes in the bottom of it. They'd skim that top off the cooking syrup and pour it in a hole in the ground near the furnace, all that old green skimmings. I've stepped in it, a lot of times. We used to sow rye and make rye bread. It was black. We eat cornbread for breakfast. I didn't know what flour bread was for a long time. We'd have it sometimes on Sunday mornings. That was the only time we had flour bread. And we used to parch corn. We didn't have no popcorn. You would take a skillet and parch big grains of corn in it. It got real brown and chewed easy. It was good.

We'd eat poke salad and sowchy. Sowchy comes off the creek banks. It's about the first thing that comes up on the creek banks in the spring. I've got a sister whose birthday is in March. She never has failed to get a mess of sowchy salad for her birthday. I bet she does it yet. We'd go to the creek and pick it. Boil it, and then take it out, put it in grease and fry it. It's extra good.

We had ramps. They smelled rougher than a onion. We'd find them way back in the mountains in what's called the Ramp Cove. We'd eat them early in the spring. They tasted awful good. They was like a onion but the scent! You could smell 'em for two or three days. We'd fry 'em or eat 'em raw, either one. People used to go to the woods, lay out all night and eat raw ramps for supper.

When we moved to Scataway, my daddy walked six miles every day to work. He'd get up of a morning at four o'clock and we'd take a bucket lid and set it in the middle of the table. We'd take rich pine knots, split 'em up, and light 'em up and lay them in that bucket lid to have light to eat breakfast by. He'd leave and walk that six miles, ditch all day for a bushel of corn or a dollar's worth of meat. Never did get no money. It was always corn or meat. He'd bring the corn home and we'd take it to the mill, have it ground, bring it back and eat it.

Sometimes he'd get a pretty good piece of meat. It wasn't very high then—about ten cents a pound. He'd get about a foot-and-a-half-square piece. The old man my dad worked for made lots of corn. He had a lot of hogs and he'd fatten and kill lots of 'em. While we'd kill about one or two, he'd kill a dozen. He paid people off in meat who worked for him. Never got a dollar off him. No way you'd get a dollar.

We had our hogs in the mountain wild. We'd take a good catch dog and he'd go out and catch one by the ear. He'd hold 'im till we got its hind legs and we'd tie 'im and drive 'im in home.

Us children didn't work at nothing, only making a crop. Times were a whole lot worse then than they are now. We didn't have no money, and couldn't get none. If I got hold of a nickel or five pennies when I was a little boy, I thought I was rich! I'd hold 'em between my fingers like that. When I was a little older, I toted rock for an old man up on Bearmeat, by the name of Patrick Coleman. All day long we stopped up holes under the fence with rock to keep the pigs out of his corn and that night he'd give me a nickel. I toted rock all day long for a nickel, right up here on Bearmeat Creek.

I'd go to mill about once every two weeks. Toted a half bushel of corn over there. Sometimes me and Geneva would both go together.

She'd take about a peck and me a half bushel. The miller wouldn't be
at the mill and we'd have to go hunt him up at his house. We'd go out
there and holler at the gate till he'd start toward the mill. We'd go on
back to the mill and we'd see him a-coming around the curve, just
patty, patty. He was a great old big man. It'd take him half a hour to
get to the mill.

The old corn was grinded by water. Every time the old rock wheels
would go around, just a little meal would squirt out. It would take a
half hour or better to grind a half a bushel of corn. Then we'd load it
on our backs and back down the road we'd go. It'd take about all day,
time we got there and back home.

People used to plant whole fields of just solid clay peas. When they
got ripe, they was all to pick. We lived over in the holler, and we went
and picked peas for ol' man Will Holmes. The night before we left,
we'd bake us a whole lot of sweet potatoes and we took them with us.
When dinnertime come, we'd go out to the spring. A woman would
come down there and set us out a jug of buttermilk and give us some
glasses. There we'd eat baked sweet potatoes and buttermilk for
dinner. That's all we had—ever' bit. Now, that's so. Then we'd go
back and pick till night. We'd walk back to home and the next day do
the same thing, till we got all the peas picked. Sometimes we'd pick
two or three days a week. So many would get ripe, we'd have to go
back and pick 'em again, just like beans.

When they got real dry, we'd spread out bed sheets or somethin'-
r'nother, and take sticks and beat the hulls off of 'em. We called that
thrashing seeds. We'd thrash 'em till the hulls would come off 'em.
We'd have to do lots of 'em with our fingers, bust a hole in 'em. We
would get paid a dollar a day.

[People in this area used to gather up turkeys and drive them, just
like cattle, to a railroad station to ship them to market.] They'd drive
'em to Turkey Gap in one day. When it'd get night, the turkeys would
go to flying up to roost. The people'd camp there with 'em all night.
That's the reason they call it Turkey Gap. The next day, they'd drive
'em on to Clayton. There was a railroad over there then, the Tallulah
Falls Railroad. There wasn't a way to ship them from here, but they'd
be a lot of turkeys over here in Hiawassee. And they used to drive
sheep, a herd of sheep, to market and they'd get 'em on the train.
Don't know how much they would bring. Not much, I'm satisfied.

We'd turn the cows out and we'd have to get started off huntin'
them about four o'clock in the evening. We had to hunt 'em every
day. They's some of 'em had bells on 'em, and they was some of 'em
sharp enough to where they wouldn't ring that bell. They'd lay down

just on purpose. They'd be as easy as they could be and they never would ring the bell. Most of the time, though, you could hear the bell a-ringing. We'd have to go for miles and maybe not find 'em that evening. Then the next morning, we'd have to start back, drive 'em in and milk 'em. They wasn't no Jerseys at that time. They come out later. These here was those big red-spotted cows, roans. Jerseys come out way after I was a grown man.

We took three weeks out of school through fodder time. We'd pull fodder. Back then, that's all the thing we had to feed the cows on. Poppy would go along and cut the tops off the cornstalks and lay 'em down in a pile. We'd come along and pull the fodder from the ear down to the ground. We would tie it up with our hands and hang it on a stalk where he could cut it off, right above the ear of corn. He'd have to turn 'em back and tie them tops up in a wad. We'd tote 'em up for him. He'd shock 'em up five in a place and tie 'em. A stalk 'round the top of 'em would keep the rain off.

We pulled tanbark and Paul Foster would haul it. We dug that sassafras root and we'd take it home, lay it out and let it dry. We'd have to turn it over every day, so the sun could dry it. Paul Foster had a store and he'd buy it. He had a old model '28 Chevrolet truck and he'd load that truck up, and it would take him all day to go to Murphy [North Carolina] and back. Me and his twin boys went with him. They's a watering tank right this side of Murphy where people watered their horses. It was a great big tank full of water and it poured off in there just as pretty. We stopped there and got us a drink of water.

Paul sold his bark and he bought some bananas, first ones I'd ever seen or the twins either. Well, we come back to that watering tank and he divided 'em, gave us all one apiece. I didn't know what to do with it. Nary one of us knowed how to eat 'em. I just helt mine around awhile and directly one of them boys just took 'im a big bite off his, hull and all. Paul said, "Oh pshaw, son, you're s'posed to peel that thing before you eat it." It was pitiful at the time. Then I peeled mine and ate it. I was sharp enough to wait and see how it was done. Then we came on home—took us a night to come in.

Papaw told us different things that he and his brother and sisters did when they were growing up—mischief they got into, other experiences they had together and with their friends.

I had a sister that was two years younger than I. My daddy sent her and me after some wood one time. We had to go about a quarter of a

PLATE 373 Mr. Dayton with Kim Hamilton.

mile, way across the creek over onto a hill. When we got there, I picked her out a stick that was little that she could carry, you know. I got me a bigger one. She was mad because she had to go. I never paid no attention to her and when we got back to the house, she had a stick bigger than I did. She told Poppy that I made her tote that big stick of wood. She commenced a-crying, said I made her do that. Poppy kept on till he made her own up that she lied. She got the whupping—I never got one. She was mean. You couldn't touch her—she'd cry every time that you touched her. She was awful.

I never heard tell of any robbing and stealing. They's one breaking-in ever I heard tell of from Paul Foster. He stayed there at his store all of his life and somebody broke in it one time. Now, we lived right over the hill. Paul Foster had twin boys, and me and them twins run around together. We decided one day that we'd go in the window, so I helped 'em up to the window. They went in and got some candy. Paul Foster heard about it and caught us somehow or other. I told my daddy, "Well, I didn't go in."

He said, "But you was there with 'em. You was just as bad to blame as they was. You stood and helped 'em in." That night I got a switching and them twins got one, too. We never did break in anymore.

When I was a little bitty boy, I got what they called a panhandle knife. It was about so long and had a tin handle. My granddaddy called 'em a panhandle. They cost a dime. Now they'd cost at least fifty cents. That's the only one I ever had—was little old bitty. You couldn't cut nothing with it.

Bosh Kimsey gave me the first haircut ever I got and it cost twenty-five cents. My mommy had cut it for ages and that was the first 'un I ever had to pay for. He's still there today cutting hair for a dollar. He's been there sixty years, I'd say. He cut it for a quarter for ages and ages. [Lots of folks] are charging two dollars and a half for a haircut now. Bosh is a good hair cutter. I still go to him. Give him a dollar ever' time I go.

Sometimes I stayed with my granddaddy, and we had to go from Scataway across the mountain over to the highway to get our mail. I had an old mule that I rode across the mountain. Once when I was visiting him his sister, my Aunt Sally, came to see him all the way from Idaho. I remember she took my picture sitting on that old mule—ol' Kate I believe was that mule's name. It was cold and I had an ol' 'boggan cap on.

I went coon huntin' when I stayed at my granddaddy's. And the first year I was there, I went squirrel huntin'. I kept a count of 'em. I'd get up before daylight and be away on the head of Scataway. I was just a boy then and I killed forty-two squirrels that fall and they 'uz pretty good, too.

I hardly ever went fishing as a boy. The lake here comes right down in front of the house and I've fished there one time in the last five years, I guess.

I'll tell you about two dogs we had when we were living in Scataway for Vogel Lumber Company. We had a little yellow feist about two foot long and a big old cur we called Buttons. We'd be out a-working somewhere and directly we'd hear that little old feist go to baying at something. When that old big cur heared him bay, he'd go to him. When he got there, he went in. He'd have a snake—a rattlesnake, any kind, didn't make no difference. He'd kill that rattlesnake. He got bit four or five times. We'd have to put lamp oil on his head and this wild touch-me-not [flower], it's got some kind of milk in it that we'd feed to him. He'd lay around a day or two till he got well. That cur would know just as well when that little old feist barked. It'd trail 'em up and bay 'em by itself. The cur wouldn't trail 'em up but when he heard him bark he went right to him. When he got there, he went in and got that snake—didn't make no difference what it was. He'd shake it and break its neck. It's pitiful at th'snakes they was up in there then. We was all lucky we never did get bit by a rattlesnake. I've seen 'em four inches through, big 'uns.

One time my mommy and brother was out in the fields picking blackberries. It was all growed up and they was pushing through the briars. Mommy looked down and there was a rattlesnake. She said it was quiled up as big as a half-bushel tub in its own quile. It was so big she couldn't kill it. She just eased back out and when Poppy come home, it'd left. Clyn was too little to kill it so they left that snake, a great big 'un. Poppy was off a-ditching. If he'd been there, he'd went and killed it.

Clyn had a little steer just so big, and he had him learnt to pull a sled. Everybody was gone but me one day and I hooked him up. I thought I'd ride the sled. I did—I got on him and away I went! Come down to the creek and had to cross. The bank was kinda steep, and when that sled went off into the creek, I went right in front of the sled, right between the steer's hind legs. He pulled the sled over the top of me and me in the creek, but it never hurt me a bit. All I was afraid of was going home wet. I stayed out a long time trying to get my britches dry. The steer was easy caught. He was tame, you know. He didn't stop when I went off over the sled. He just drug the sled right over the top of me.

Clyn was a lot older than I was and he was breaking little bulls to ride. He'd hold the little bull by the horns till I got on. Then that bull locked down and he bucked me off. I went over his head and one of his horns stuck in right there (below my lip). My daddy was gone to work, a-ditching. Vogel Lumber Company had a telephone so if a fire got out, we could call 'em and tell 'em that a fire was in the woods. They was another one over at John H. Corn's where my daddy worked and my mother called over there. She told him about the bull and he understood that it'd hooked me in the mouth and tore my mouth open. Here he come! When he got there, it wasn't too bad— just made a scar.

I never rode a train in my life. Never rode a airplane and don't never aim to. First airplane ever I seen was so high I could just barely see it. I'd heard about 'em. If one ever passed over here, it didn't get down low like they do now. They was up yonder and we could barely see 'em, but now they're getting down low.

I was about twelve years old when I saw my first car. Me and my brother was walking from the house at Scataway to Paul Foster's.

There was bad curves in the road, and I seen a car a-coming around a curve. I didn't know how in the world he'd ever get around that curve. He made it, though. I thought he'd have to go straight but he come around that curve.

They told this on Max Shook. I don't know if it was so or not. I imagine it was the first car he had ever seen. The old A-Model had a little bitty horn: *"Urrrk, urrrk."* It was kind of like that roadrunner I had. Max seen that car a-coming and he outrun it. The cars had wooden wheels then. Max said it went *hicky, hacky, hicky, hacky, ooork, ooork.* He mocked it a-running. The people in the car blowed the horn at Max. He outrun it to where he got to the end of the road and he turned down to the trail. It was so. I'm satisfied it was so.

Trick or treating was about the worst mischief we got into. We would go get somebody's cow and take it to somebody else's barn. And take their cow to another barn. Swap all the cows around. The owners didn't know we was doing it because they'd be in the bed asleep. They'd go out to milk the next morning and they would have a different cow standing in the stable.

Poor old Horace Parton was courtin' on the head of Scataway. Three or four of us, I don't know how many, decided to play a trick on him. He took his girl home and come back down to the forks of the road, and they was a pretty sandy place there. We took us a wire and tied it from the fence over to the bank of the road, about a foot high off the ground. We run on back up the road and got us some rocks. We got out of his sight. It was after dark and we started rocking him. We didn't rock him to hit him, just scare him. He started a-running and when he hit that wire, he turned a somerset right into the road. It was a wonder we hadn't a' killed him. He got up from there a-running. We never heard tell of him no more. He wasn't even at home. We was tickled to death about him a-falling. We went and took our wire down, then set around and talked awhile. Then we went home. Now, we done all such as that to people. It was fun to us. I wouldn't do it now for no means in the world.

A great bunch of us would get out and pitch horseshoes all day a Saturday and Sunday. That's two days we got to rest. We had a lot of fun. It was a long sandy place where we'd drive up stobs. Four of us would pitch, and if you got close to the stob, you got one point. If you rung it with your horseshoe, you got five points. If you leant the horseshoe up against the stob, you got three points. Two people were on each team, and whichever team lost would set down, and two more would get up and pitch against the winners. If they lost, they'd

PLATE 374   Dana, Dana's mother, Maelane, and Mr. Dayton.

set down. That's the only way you could tell the champions, pitching against each other.

We liked especially to go to revivals. They'd have a revival for two weeks back then but other than that, the preacher would only come once't a month and preach. We didn't go to church ever' Sunday then, just once a month. We'd have two weeks' revival and have some awful good meetings then. They had these meetings in that old log house where we went to school with the chimney to it. We weren't having school in the fall of the year when revival time came around. We had green beans and roastin' ears to feed the preacher when he came to preach.

That old log school was called Pine Grove School House. It was just a big one-room house with a chimney six foot wide. We burnt big wood in it and that's what kept us warm. Us boys would go out and hunt the wood, pick up what dead stuff we could get. It was located on Scataway about four mile from where we lived. They wasn't nothing like a bus; we had to walk. Mad dog tales would get out and we'd have to walk to school, us scared to death. I'd pass Jim Ledford's house and he had an old bull. See, they run outside then. There wasn't no fence law. Ever' time we'd pass his house we'd run, afraid that old bull would get after us.

We used to live right over there in the hollow, and go to school right over there. We'd walk back across the hill home, eat dinner, and come back to school.

The meanest thing I done in school was crooking a pin and putting it down on the bench for somebody to set down on. A lot of people set on them. You'd take a pin and you'd crook it two ways. The flat part is what they set on. That part sticking straight up. When they set down, they didn't stay long. We'd all deny out of all such as that. I never did set on one. I'd do it myself, but I'd always watch. They got to where they would watch where they set. I've got whuppings for some meanness. I don't even know what for, now.

We wasn't real mean to the teacher. We had a stove made out of a barrel. We kept some water on top of the stove. It kept down head-aches, they said. I was putting wood in it one day and she was setting there. I knocked that water off and it scalded her leg. I laughed at her. I didn't know no better then. I believe she was Mrs. Brown. We just had lady teachers. Our school only went through the seventh grade. Ever'book that I got, I had to borrow from somebody else to read in. They would attend school. Then I'd borrow their book. I'd get my lesson that way.

We didn't keep warm walking to school. One time when I was a great big boy, my britches was tore. It'd come a snow and we was coming down the road from the schoolhouse. Me and John Allen each got us a girl. Then we'd push 'em and slide 'em by their feet down the road. I got Eileen under the arms and here me and her went. I hooked my toe in my tore britches leg and I went flat down. She went on down through there on her back. It made her mad! She thought I done it on purpose, but I didn't. I don't remember what she said. She just quarreled me out.

I went to the seventh grade and didn't know it. The only way I ever learnt anything was when I started a little ol' store. It was Frank Duckworth learnt me how to figure corn so much a bushel. We'd buy it by the pound mostly then, fifty-six pound to a bushel.

I don't know why I waited so long to get married. I was bashful, I guess. I didn't get married till I was twenty-four. When I was about eighteen years old, I got to courting. I went from one house to the other, backwards and forwards.

My daddy had a mule and Jess Ormby had one. Jess didn't have no stable for his mule, so he put it in my daddy's stable. Me and Bill Ormby [Jess's son] would go courting together. When it got dark, we'd go and steal the mules out and ride 'em at night. One night my daddy caught Bill getting his, and it liked to have scared that boy to death. Bill would get on that old gray mule and ride him without a bridle. We'd go somewhere and stay till way in the night, mostly to Ernie Parton's. He was about the only one that set up real late.

Up till I was twenty years old, I pulled a crosscut saw, cut logs in the mountains. We cut eight-foot logs for a dollar a thousand on thousand-foot log scale. If they was any over eight foot, we got seventy-five cents a thousand. It took us all day with that crosscut saw to get a thousand foot. We'd make seventy-five cents or a dollar a day. That's all we made.

I put a little store up before I got married. I was about twenty years old and I had thirty-some dollars. I believe I sold a pair of steers for thirty-some dollars and I put a store up in Daddy's barn loft. He had the barn down below the road and the road was just about level with the door that went in the loft. I done real good. I had lard, flour, sugar, and stuff like that. I would trade all week except on Saturday. My brother had that old '28 Chevrolet truck, and I hired him to take me to Hiawassee with my corn. They'd bring corn in about all the time. I'd take in corn and buy my groceries from Frank Duckworth. I wouldn't get 'em wholesale—you had to go to Hayesville to get 'em wholesale. I couldn't go there, but Frank would give me a discount on the groceries. I'd bring 'em back and sell 'em. I hauled in lots of corn that people traded to me. I made good money.

Later I boxed up one end of Mommy's old long porch and had my store there. Then I got able to build me one. I built a store eight foot wide and twelve foot long below the road, had a lot of trade there. Then I rented Frank Corn's house, a big old long house out there. I put a store in one end of it and I lived in the other end. That's where I lived when we got married. That's been a long time ago.

I'd put up that store and I had a little money. My brother had a family and he didn't have any money. He wanted me to go with him to Clayton and buy a truck in halves with him, where he could get my money. He was a little sharper than I was and I did it. Well, it didn't turn out right. I couldn't drive and he kept the truck all the time. He got me out one day teaching me to drive the truck. I run into the bank [of the road] with it and that's the last time he let me drive. I swapped him my part of the truck for two little steers after that. That was the first time I ever tried to drive.

When I got able, I bought me a A-model and Paul Ormby learned me how to drive. He wouldn't get in with me. He stood on the fender and told me how to drive. He was afraid I would wreck so he stood on the fender. He should have been in there where if I had started to wreck, he could have jerked it back in the road, but he stood on the fender. I learned how to drive on that A-model. [The next thing we got was an old '41 Chevrolet truck. I bought it off the county, but they had already wore it out.]

[I learned to drive that old A-model] before we ever got married. I got Frank Burl to go with me to ask for Sadie. He was a way older than I, a great old boy, never did marry. We went in at Sadie's house and set down. The family was all setting around the fireplace, except for Joe, Sadie's father. I had a pretty good come-on. I said to Lonnie, Sadie's mother, "Lonnie, me and Frank come to get us a woman."

Sadie was about sixteen, and she had a younger sister, so Lonnie said, "You can't have both of them." I felt like I come around pretty good about asking for her. [I was twenty-four and still pretty bashful.]

Then I asked Sadie if she was ready to go get married. She said, "Yes."

When we married, we didn't go to nobody else's house. I had me that house rented [with the store on the other end]. I had it already furnished, what little it was—a dresser, a old wooden bedstead my granddaddy had left me when he died, a stove; everything we needed. It wasn't much, but then we didn't have to have much.

We've got four kids living and three dead. When D.L. and Von was born, we had Mrs. Bradley, a granny woman, with them. Mrs. Bradley was with us when Maelane was born, but there was trouble and we had to go get Doctor Johnson. Now he was getting so old I had to drive him up there and back home. He wouldn't hardly come out because he was so old. That cost about ten dollars then. Nowadays it would cost you about a thousand dollars, I guess, if you was to go to the hospital.

Only doctor I knowed when I was a little boy was Doctor Rice. He lived at Hiawassee, about eight miles from where we lived. Doc Rice was a great old big fellow, and he just wouldn't go [way out on calls like Dr. Johnson would]. Dr. Johnson would do a whole lot more than Doc Rice had. He was a little bitty fellow. You'd go after him and he'd come any time of the night. He hardly got any money out of it. Sometimes people had it to pay and sometimes they didn't. He never did do a thing about it.

During the Depression, we lived down here at Paul Foster's. We tended his land on the halves. One time at dinner we had cornbread and that was everything we had. My daddy always said that he never would set down to dry bread, so he got his piece of bread and stood up and eat it. Now that's the truth. You just don't know how hard times was.

Then the WPA started building roads, and all us people would go out and work for ninety-eight cents a day. Then it got up to a dollar and twenty-eight cents a day. Me and my daddy-in-law would walk four miles from where his house was to the highway, and an old dump truck would come and pick us up. We'd set on the back of that truck, and it way down towards zero, and we'd ride to Soap Stone up there and work all day long. Then they'd take us back to where we got on the truck and turn us out and we'd walk back home that night. It'd be about dark when we got back home. We'd eat milk and bread for supper.

Then after that I hauled acid wood. I'd make three trips a day from here to Hayesville. I had men cutting for me, and when I'd get back from hauling a load, they'd have another load ready to go. They was a limb fell on me once doing that. It hit me right on top of the head. I had an old white horse, and I had to ride that horse plumb out to the truck (because) it couldn't get in to where we was at. The doctor cut my hair off and bandaged me up, and the next morning I couldn't turn my head. It come just in an inch a' breakin' my neck. That was dangerous work.

And then I hauled tanbark for a while. We'd take a spud and peel the bark off those chestnut oaks and stand that bark up against the logs to dry out so it wouldn't mildew. Then we'd haul it out to the truck on a sled—hook the mule to it and pull it out to where we could get a truck to it.

But the job I enjoyed most was hauling fence posts. That was back twenty-five years ago. I hauled 'em for about fifteen years to people way down in Georgia. There was one place I hauled to where the boss man would make the colored men unload my truck. Fourteen of them would get on that truck at one time and they'd have those five or six hundred posts unloaded just in a few minutes. One of them asked me who done our work for us up in the mountains, and I said, "We do it ourself."

He said, "White folks down here makes us do it." They'd work from daylight to dark, and they'd be in debt from one fall to the next fall. When they wanted to eat at a café, they had to go to a window in the back and the cooks would give 'em their stuff there. My wife run a café while I was hauling posts, and she let 'em eat inside if they ever stopped there.

I made enough money off those posts to pay for that house we had on Scataway. Then I started selling produce about sixteen years ago. I sold that truck I had been hauling posts in for eight hundred dollars and took the money to Atlanta and got me a load of produce. I'd haul it in a pickup and set up right beside the highway. Times was a whole lot better by then. I was the only one selling produce (in this area), and people heard about me and would come and buy my load just in a few minutes. I'd make three trips a week to Atlanta and get all I could haul on that truck. I could get overripe bananas in fifty-pound bunches for seventy-five cents a stalk, and people would come in and buy them. I made good money on stuff like that. I had a man helping me, and he'd tend to the selling while I'd be gone to Atlanta for another load. That kept me busy till I made enough money to build this store out here.

PLATE 375   Mr. Dayton with some of his beehives behind his house.

One way or another, we always managed to make it. I told an old man here yesterday that this here was the happiest place in the whole world. You can listen to the television and hear of all kinds of floods and snow and [trouble] but right here it never gets too bad but what we can't do something.

And I stay busy. When I have spare time, I go to Red McKinney's store. He sells dopes [soft drinks], crackers, and tobacco. That's about all he sells. And he makes ax handles. He started out making them years ago for a dollar a handle, but now he's got up to three dollars a handle. Any time you go there, they's five to ten or twelve men a-settin' there talking. He's got one of them great big old round potbellied stoves—the only one I know of in the [area]—and he keeps his fire in it in the winter. There's an old man there who plays checkers with me. He's eighty-two years old. Right here lately he's courting somebody so we haven't played in a while. We play rook there, too.

So I do that. And then I stay here and sell some stuff for beehives, and sell some china cabinets and washstands I make. I've got two solid oak china cabinets I made, and four solid oak washstands that are just like these old-timey washstands. And I take care of my own bees. I've had bees off and on all my life, but I don't have but twenty-two hives now. I sold sixty-four hives last summer. I have had as high as a hundred and twenty hives. A super of sourwood honey brings me fifty dollars. My bees are going good. I'm looking for a swarm just any day. They'll settle in a bush, and I'll take a gum and shake 'em off in front of the gum and they go in there with the queen and start a family of their own. That's the way they prosper, just like people.

So that's the way I've lived. I've stayed all my life right back in the mountains. I wouldn't live in a city if they was to give me the whole thing. I couldn't sleep a wink. I wouldn't live in Atlanta if you was to give it to me and make me keep it!

HAINT TALES AND OTHER SCARY STORIES

S torytelling is not an uncommon thing around here. It's a tradition in my family that's been passed down from generation to generation.

When I was a small child, my grandmother, Ruth Holcomb, would always tell me stories—day or night, it didn't matter to her. Whenever I wanted to hear them, she'd sit down with me and tell panther stories or mad dog tales. Those were my favorites and she knew lots of them because she grew up seeing mad dogs in the neighborhood and hearing about panthers (pronounced "painters" by some people around here).

We always sat in the living room when she went to storytelling. She'd tell me story after story and have me so scared there was no way I'd even go into the next room by myself. Somebody would have to go with me.

I was always told if I saw a dog coming up the road, when I was waiting on the school bus of a morning, and it was foaming at the mouth, I was to either lie down in a ditch or stand real still and try not to breathe, so it would pass on by without biting me. I went to wait on the bus one morning and I practiced how to hold my breath and stand completely still. I think it's silly now that I look back on it, but I sure believed it then.

When I began editing these stories, I was at home lying in front of our heater on my stomach. Nobody was around me. Mom was taking a nap and Dad and my little brother were away. The television was off and it was real quiet. The house was popping—you know how a house does when it cools. And it was pitch dark outside. I got so interested in these stories that they were giving me a creepy feeling all over, and I finally decided I'd better put them away till the next day.

Kim Hamilton, Rosanne Chastain, and I collected most of them over the summer. Others had been told to **Foxfire** students over the years but have not been published previously. Tales about panthers and mad animals get inserted into someone's conversation occasionally and don't seem suitable as you're putting together an article that deals specifically with some other subject. So this was *an opportune time to pass along stories we've had tucked away in the files for a long time.*

Every person that told us haint tales or scary stories was quite happy to share them. Each of them had his or her own unique and fascinating way of telling them. Lots of the stories have come from their own personal experiences and from what their parents and grandparents had passed on to them.

I still love for my grandmother to sit down and tell me these stories. I get terrifying feelings of panthers tearing through my skin or mad dogs snapping up at me, but I really know I'm quite safe with Granny.

Put yourself back in time and let your imagination roam as you enjoy these stories. Can you see a panther getting after you or a mad dog biting at you? What would you do?

DANA HOLCOMB

PANTHER TALES

MARGARET NORTON: They used to have real panthers here, but I never have seen one. There used to be one up on the creek here long years ago before I come. There was a trail come up this mountain and they always said everybody was afraid to travel it after night. Said they could hear that panther walking right along with 'em. You'd be in the trail and it'd be down below, and it'd just be pat, pat, pat right along till you stopped to see about it or shine the light on it. It'd stop, too.

I've heard them tell that lots of times but I'm not afraid. I don't go out after dark by myself.

JAKE WALDROOP: Well, I see'd a painter at the Deep Gap. I'd been to Tallulah River and I was coming back. It was in the nighttime and I come through the Deep Gap to the head of Kimsey Creek on an old trail. They was a tree that had fell from right at the side of the trail, and lodged in another big tree. I guess you've see'd them that way, ain't you?

I was coming down the trail and the moon was shining, and I seen this old gentleman [panther] just walk across the trail, and he come to where this tree had fell, and he just went walking out in them big limbs, you know.

I had an awful vicious Plott bitch with me [a dog usually bred for bear hunting]. And I didn't have no gun, but I had a great big old dirk knife. I stopped and I looked at him and I says, "Well, ol' fella, if you come down here, you may get me but I'm gonna get some of you."

So I got my old knife out and I called Con, the dog's name. She had a collar around her neck and I had a great long cord about six or eight feet long in my pocket and I tied that cord in the ring on her collar. I wanted us to both be together if that painter come in contact with us, so I just walked on by him and he laid out there wagging that old tail back'ards and forwards. I went on down a little piece and I looked back. I was about a hundred yards down. I'd keep my eyes on him as best I could, so he just kept laying there. I come to where there was a whole lot of underbrush and I went out of his sight. Well, I went on down a little ways where they was a branch [creek] coming down. And I had some whiskey, so I said, "I'll take me a drink of whiskey." I turned up the jug and took me two or three good swallows and put the stopper back in it. I set it down and laid down to get me some water out of the branch for a chaser. And just as my lips hit the water, Con growled and just jumped the full length of that cord and I heard that thing jump and I wasn't thirsty no more! I got up and got my jug and down that trail I come, and it was a half of a mile to where my brother and another boy was waiting on me. And just as I got down close to the camp, that thing screamed right up on the ridge above me and they opened the door and come out and see'd me a-coming and they said, "What was you a-hollering about?"

I said, "I wasn't. That was a cougar or a painter, whatever you want to call it."

It went right back up over the Yellow Mountains and you ain't never heard no such screaming in your life.

RUTH HOLCOMB: A long time ago, these people sent for this lady who was a midwife. The only way she had of getting to their house was to ride a horse. This panther came up behind her when she was riding to their house. She took off her scarf and throwed it down at him, trying to scare him off. It tore that scarf up and kept on coming. She kept her horse a-running and kept pulling off her clothes piece by piece, trying to stop that panther.

When she reached the house where she was going, she almost had all her clothes off and the panther was still right in behind her.

HARRIET ECHOLS: Now my mother said that when she was young, she knew some people and there was a new baby being born. Back then, they had home deliveries by midwives, you know. This neighbor woman was expecting herself, but she wasn't too far along not to go help out. They had come to tell her they needed somebody to be there to help the midwife with the baby delivery, so she went around to her neighbor's house.

The next morning when her husband got up, he was expecting her to be home for breakfast. He thought she and the midwife would walk back home together. She hadn't come, so he started over there to see if everything was all right.

On his way, this panther was laying on the fence on the side of the road and it jumped at him. I don't remember if he had a dog with him or what, but anyway he got away from it. Then he saw his wife. The panther was guarding her. It had killed her and had tore into her and ate the baby. My mother said that was true. Said all they found of the baby was one little hand and it was just mature enough to tell it *was* a hand. That panther was guarding the woman's body because when it got hungry again, it'd eat her.

JAKE WALDROOP: When I was out in the state of Washington, why they was some Indians living there. And this Indian woman, she had a washplace about a hundred and fifty yards from her house. She had something on the stove cooking and she went from her washing to see about it. She run up to the house to see about her stuff she was fixing for dinner and left her baby sitting in a box down at the washplace. She said she heard a painter scream, and she wheeled and run back, and when she got there she heard it scream again, and it had took that baby off and eat it!

HARRIET ECHOLS: My mother told me this story about a panther, too. People had to ride horseback or go in wagons or buggies in those days, you know.

They were having this revival meeting, and this man and his wife had a pair of horses and they were riding them to church. They had a baby just big enough to sit up and hold onto one of them as they rode.

The minister said he'd eat dinner with them that day, and the woman rode back to the church with him that evening, but her husband couldn't go. He had to do something else, but he knew she'd be safe coming on home without him. So she had a little ol' dog that followed her when she rode off anywhere with the baby. After church that night, she didn't think anything about riding back home by herself. She knew her husband would wait up and look for her.

He was sitting there on the porch when he heard her horse whinny and come tearing in home.

She said she'd come around a bend in the road where there was a big bank and a panther was up on that bank. It jumped down trying to land on the horse, but just missed. The dog had sensed it and kept it from jumping on the horse with the woman. She just wrapped the reins around the saddle horn and told the horse to go home, and she held to the baby. That horse just stretched out, carrying her home.

The man grabbed his gun. He'd felt like something was wrong and he had his hunting dogs at the house. When the horse had got to the fence around the yard, it'd jumped it and her holding to the saddle with the baby. That panther was still right behind 'em. That little dog would jump at the panther whenever it'd jump at the horse.

The hunting dogs run out and scared the panther, and it run up on the haystack and got up on the stack pole. He had his gun and he shot it, and that's all that saved her and the baby.

JAKE WALDROOP: One of my uncles, Millard Cruse, one time had been to a mill over in Tusquittee to get his corn ground. He had loaded up six or eight bushels of corn and went over there to the mill, and when he came back through Tunny Gap, why it was dark. And he said he heard this panther scream up on the ridge.

He had a big yoke of steers to his wagon and he had him a big long whip that he would whip them along with. And he said he began to whipping them steers when he heard that panther hit the back end of his wagon. He said he beat it off with that whip—beat it till it would get off. And them steers a-running! He said it would take a little bit for it to catch back on, but it followed him for two miles, trying to get in that wagon.

I heard my mammy and all of 'em tell me that the whole back end of the wagon bed—said there was his old claws where he had tore out planks and everything trying to get in. I reckon he was gonna eat my uncle. That's all that was in the wagon except the cornmeal. That's the only one I ever heard of attacking anybody around here.

ETHEL CORN: They said one liked to got Carrie Dillard one time, when they lived at the Lloyd's Cove. I think she'd been to Highlands or somewhere. Everybody back then rode horseback and she was on a horse, and a panther jumped and just scraped the horse as he come down. That horse reared and started running, and they said that's all that saved her. She was just a young girl and that horse a-rearing was all that saved her.

HARRIET ECHOLS: This was before I was born, but it's a true story. My dad said one evening he and the children in his community was coming home from school—the whole crowd was together. They all had their lunch boxes and their books in their bags hung across their shoulder. When they separated, going out to different places, different roads, they heard this screaming and hollering. You know, a panther hollers just like a person, and the children answered back. They thought it was some of the other children. It kept hollering and they kept answering it back. He said to one of the other boys, "That's not nobody hollering at us! Look coming down the fence!"

The panther was walking the fence coming down to them. So they throwed their books and lunch boxes and everything down and ran to get to the nearest house. It was a mile from where they was at to the Rogers place and they ran out there and told Mr. Rogers that there was a panther after 'em.

The boys got the dogs and went back but they didn't get the panther that evening. The dogs kept chasing it and stayed out all night. They went back next morning to hunt the dogs, and the dogs had treed that panther and killed it.

JENNIE ARROWOOD: They said there was somebody that used to go across to Shooting Creek—across that mountain over there—and play the fiddle and make music for people.

They said one time a painter got after him and he climbed a tree, and the only way he ever got down was to play the fiddle and scare it away. If he quit playing, it'd go to climbing the tree toward him!

RUTH HOLCOMB: One time this man was out a-hunting and he see'd this panther coming so he laid down on the ground and covered up with leaves. That panther finished raking some leaves up over him and left. He figured it'd be back to eat him, so as soon as he saw it was gone, he jumped up and got away.

And then they was telling about this man that had this little shack built and another man was looking for a place to hide out, to keep from having to go to war or something. He had come to this man's shack while the man was out hunting for something for breakfast, rabbits maybe. So this man that was hiding out crawled up in the top of the house. There was beds built out of poles up near the top of the house. He could peep out from up there. He heard this panther come to the house, and when the man that was out hunting came back to the house the panther jumped him, and this panther tore that man all to pieces. The man up in the rafters on the bed was afraid to come out. 'Fraid that panther would eat him, too.

HARRIET ECHOLS: My uncle Harv was staying at his house by himself one night. He'd been hunting squirrels in the afternoon and had dressed them and put them in a pan on the stove. Because some of the neighbors had been hearing panthers screaming at night, Uncle Harv had kept his hunting dogs on the porch that night. After he fed the hogs and milked the cow, he fixed his supper and got ready for bed. He called the dogs and told 'em to stay put on the porch. See, they trained the dogs to mind and to stay. Maybe he put something out there of his and told them to take care of it.

So he went to bed and said along in the night, all at once he heard the awfullest fuss in the kitchen. He said it scared him to death.

The chimney of his house was built right up against a high bank and the panther had crawled down the chimney and come into the kitchen and found those squirrels. He had pulled the dishpan down into the floor, ate up all his meat, and went back up the chimney.

Uncle Harv got out and put the dogs out after the panther, but it got away from them. Finally he came back, and next morning the neighbors took some dogs and killed the panther. Of course, he said he couldn't swear it was the same panther but it *was* in the area and that's the one they thought it was.

ETHEL CORN: I've heard tell of 'em a-trying to get in a house where people lived. Back then, half the time, they didn't have no glass—only hang curtains over their windows. One night Octy McCall heared a panther and happened to look, and it was a-sittin' in her window.

Back in them days, they used broom sage—they'd get out and get the broom sage, broomstraw, and make their homemade brooms— and she went to throwing that broomstraw in the fire and that run that panther off. That's the way they scared 'em off—with fire.

JENNIE ARROWOOD: Panthers never did come in *our* house, I don't reckon, but I've heard tell of 'em getting into people's houses. People used to have straw ticks on their beds, and they'd take 'em off and put 'em right at the hearth if they thought panthers were around. If a panther started down that chimney, they'd take so much of that straw at a time and burn it, and not let it get in on 'em. They'd try to come down the chimneys if they couldn't get through the boards. I've heard tell of panthers scratching the boards off the house trying to get in, but now I wasn't there to see it.

MAD DOGS, EAGLES, AND OTHER ANIMAL TALES

ADA CRONE: One thing that happened back when I was about nineteen or twenty, I guess, was a circus came through town. We didn't never get to see a circus. We didn't have the money to go to one. But a wild animal got loose. We really don't know what it was. Some of 'em say it was a laughin' hyena, but we really don't know what it was. I'd went to town one day, an' comin' back I had to walk through the mountains a pretty good ways, three or four miles I guess, and this thing started hollerin' at me. It would start hollerin' real low and it'd get louder an' louder. It'd make your hair stand on top of your head, I'm tellin' you. It skeered the daylights out o' me. But I was afraid to run. If I'd run goin' down that mountain, I mighta stumbled an' fell an' it [might've] jumped on me. This is what I had in my mind. I stopped and I looked around an' tried to see it, an' I never could see it. I went on home. When I got home and went in, my mother said, "Did you hear that thing a-hollerin'?"

I said, "Yes, it followed me down the mountain."

She said, "It's goin' to get you one of these days if you don't get in afore dark."

I said, "Well, it's not dark yet."

She said, "It's almost."

And I said, "If it does get me it'll have a good meal, I guess, one time." And I went somewheres a few days after that. I came back another way. And I heard somethin' run across in front of me. It went like a horse with iron shoes, made a big racket. I run around some big ol' rock cliffs down below me. I run around below those rock cliffs an' I seen it! It was a big old yeller thing that was standin' there. It looked sort of like a dog but it had a real slim body and long legs. I was a little bit afraid but I wanted to see it. I just wanted to see what it was. It had mange too. It was yeller and it was a pretty thing. I stood there and looked at it long as I wanted to and it looked at me. Never did try to hurt me. I walked off then when I got through lookin' at it. I told my mama 'bout it and she didn't believe it. She said I didn't see it. But I really did, though. I seen that thing and I don't know what it was.

Finally it just got gone. I really don't know what happened to it. My two brothers and some of their friends would take a dog and go and try to catch it at night. And the dogs wouldn't run it. They wouldn't even track it. They wouldn't have nothin' to do with it. And it would stink. It stunk like a—I guess what y'call a civet cat. It really had a bad smell to it. But it just got gone. I don't know whatever happened to it.

RUTH HOLCOMB: There was a place up on the mountain where the men used to come a lot hunting for 'possums and other animals for furs. They took their dogs with them and when they'd get near that place, the dogs would run off and leave the area. Something would spook them and nobody knows what it was. They've never found out till today. Still don't know what it is, but the people that was hunting with the dogs could hear it.

And one time this woman set her baby out in the yard to play while she was doing her housework. Then there were a lot of eagles—bald eagles, we called 'em. While she was in the house doing her work, this eagle came by and picked this baby up. The folks seen this eagle a-going with it and they went to see what it had done with the baby. It had gone to a hollow tree and had hid the baby down in there. They said all that saved that baby's life was that the eagle babies were eating on a lamb's leg right then. The mother eagle had caught a lamb and the little eagles were eating on that.

The people had to get up in that tree and get that baby down.

HARRIET ECHOLS: This neighbor of mine where we used to live told about helping to take care of a little child that had been rabies-bit.

Said one day the little fellow was out playing, he was four or five years old, and this dog come in the yard and he played with it awhile. After a while the dog bit him and he went in the house crying. He told his mother, "My puppy that come up out there bit me."

She didn't think nothing about it, but the next day word got out that there was a mad dog out. They finally found it and killed it, and they knew that was the dog that had bit the little boy. Back then they didn't have these shots for rabies. There wasn't anything they could do for him, and the little child went mad. This neighbor of mine was one of the men who took care of him. He said the child would say, "Please, don't let me bite you. Don't let me bite you." He just felt like he wanted to bite somebody.

They stayed with him two weeks. These two men just took turns sitting by the bed. They wore rubber gloves when they cared for him. He couldn't eat anything, wouldn't eat, and sometimes he couldn't drink water. He'd want water and they'd try to give it to him, but he couldn't drink it. He said that was the most pathetic thing he ever saw in his life.

It'd take both of those men to hold that child when he would have those fits. Said he would say, "I'm gonna bite somebody. Please don't let me bite nobody."

He died after about two weeks, they said.

ETHEL CORN: Oh, yeah, they was afraid of mad dogs! And there used to be a lot of 'em through here. Only at certain times of the year that they would come through. I never had one to get after me, but there was one to come by the house where I used to live. I heard it and I looked out, and just before it got to the house, I knowed by the way it traveled something was wrong. It had took a fit and before I could run in and get the gun and load it and get out, it was too far away for me to shoot it.

That night it made a lunge at Edward Carpenter's horses. He'd been loggin' and he was late coming in.

Then I heard a fight in the night and it had got my dog. He wouldn't hardly come out to me when I called him the next morning. I never thought of it being my dog in that fight till he went mad. He went mad in about nine days and I had to have him killed.

Another time Poppy had two dogs, and they both got bit. I got 'im to build a pen and put 'em in it. We weren't for sure but we thought the dog was mad that had bit 'em. Poppy put 'em in that pen, and when they did go mad, you never heared such a racket in your life as they was doing. They didn't go mad, though, for about twenty-one days, and every time they'd make a racket, I'd run down there. I wanted to see how they'd act when they did go mad. I always went down to feed 'em, and the first I detected of 'em going mad was one of 'em went to growling at the other 'un when I put in the food. When I scolded him to try to make him hush, he just kept a-growling, and I picked up a stick and stuck it through a little crack like I was going to hit him. When I did that, he lunged at it and I backed off from there. They couldn't get out, though, for the pen was built out of logs and even logs covered over the top.

RUTH HOLCOMB: A mad dog can smell you, can really smell you. I was on my way to school. I had to walk by my grandmother's house and I had just went by the door when I heard somebody holler and tell me to get in the house. A stray dog had stayed at our house all night and was following me to school. It went on up in the settlement and bit some people's dogs. Well, some people up there killed it before it bit anybody.

People couldn't hardly do their work for watching for mad dogs. They'd have to get done before dark. Nobody would hardly go out after dark for the mad dogs would bite 'em. They said if you got bit, you'd go mad in nine days.

Mr. Holcomb had a cow to go mad. He'd just bought it and milked it, and he and all the children had drunk the milk. It didn't hurt them, but the cow went mad and climbed the wall.

BLANCHE HARKINS: My mother told us a story about a boy getting bit [by a mad dog]. They couldn't do anything with him. They put him off in a building. They kept him in there till he acted like he was wild. They put him in a cage just by himself.

MARGARET NORTON: They didn't use to have that vaccine for rabies, and when you saw a dog coming down the road slobbering, all the children got in the house. Your daddy got the gun and shot him.

LEONA JUSTUS and RUTH HOLCOMB: And back then sometimes you didn't know which dogs were mad. Lex was tending Daddy's land and they was out there at the old barn and Daddy was putting up the horse. Lex had a little feist dog and it went mad. It got after Daddy and Daddy run in with the horse in the barn. When he come out, the dog went after him again and he finally jumped up on something and got away until Lex could get the gun and kill it.

They used to say if you saw your dog's eyes looking like glass, looking red, right then it was going mad. And a mad dog'll lay there and then start looking way off. Then they leave home, start running till they come to a branch of water, and then they'll go mad. They'll foam at the mouth and run around in circles.

Their tongue swells out of their mouth. I know that for I saw one in town. It was one they kept penned up till it went mad, and they was showing it in town. That thing would run up to anything and shove its head up against anything. Its tongue was out of its mouth and was swelled out till it couldn't bite. They killed it.

You don't have to get bit to go mad. If you get some of that foam in a cut or a sore place, you'll go mad.

Some people in the mountains believe that a madstone—a stone taken from the paunch or stomach of a deer—can draw poison from the bite of a snake or mad animal. The first one we ever saw was brought to school by one of our students. It was smooth and flat—about the diameter of a silver dollar and one-third of an inch thick. His father had found it in the stomach of a whitetail deer he had just killed and field-dressed, and it was one of his most prized possessions. We asked several of our contacts about these:

* * *

HARRIET ECHOLS: There was an old doctor I've heard about. He didn't live in our community and I can't remember just where he was. A lot of people just thought he was a quack, you know, but they said he had a stone of some kind that he put on the place where these dogs would bite you and that would draw that poison out. Several people went to him and then our neighbor's wife was bit by a mad dog and he took her to him.

JAKE WALDROOP: Well, I've heard of 'em. And ol' man Vance Dills had one. There was an old fellow who lived in the cove over from us, Bill Daniels, and he was plowing his steer up in his mountain pasture, and a copperhead snake bit his steer. He went and got Vance to come with his madstone. Bill said that when he stuck the madstone to where them snakebite holes were, it just stuck there. When the stone finally fell loose, he said the steer was all right. It cured the snakebite.

They said they could get them madstones out of a deer or out of a wild turkey gobbler. They were the ones who carried the madstones in their stomach. Vance Dills killed a white deer and got that one out of his stomach. That one of Vance's was the only one I ever seen. It was the size of a guinea egg, like a small hen egg. It was a little slick grayish-looking rock.

Jake knew of two more instances where that madstone worked. A girl bitten on the breast by a mad cat was cured by the madstone. And a man bitten on the ankle by a snake was cured. The madstone works by being soaked in milk about fifteen minutes. Then it's applied to the snakebite or bite of the rabid animal. It will cling to the bite and fall loose when the poison is all out.

HAINT TALES

LOLA CANNON: My mother's people, the Godfreys, were one of the first three white families to settle here in the Chechero district. Where the cemetery down there is now was where they built their first cabins. A little girl made her a playhouse and played under a tree there. She died and they buried her there.

Later they built their house down the road a little ways. The mother said that on moonlight nights she could see that little girl in her playhouse. Whether that was just her mother's idea or not I don't know, but there was another old building right down there where queer things were said to happen. Back in those days, when people died neighbors came in and prepared and dressed them for burial.

Usually they had to keep the dead person in the home overnight, and then people would come in next day to dig the grave. The neighbors would stay and sit up all night to keep watch over the body. They always said when they set up with anybody at that old place, they would hear things. They would *hear* doors opening and closing, but they couldn't *see* anything. There were fireplaces on opposite ends of the house and they would hear something like the fireprongs and shovel falling on the hearth. Some of the brave people would go look and they would be lying there but nobody was in there. Noises like that. People said they could hear footsteps on the porch.

PLATE 376

I don't believe in things like that, but older people repeated the stories and it built up in younger people's minds and made them think these things happen. I don't think dead people ever come back. It's just in our minds that they come back. They may. Our minds may bring them back to us.

JENNIE ARROWOOD: My grandmother Ferguson told me about this house where somebody was killed and put in the chimney under the hearth, and the ghost of that person would knock four times, knock on every corner of the house. Nobody wouldn't live in that place very long. Yeah—knock on every corner of the house and then leave out. They said they found his arm bones after that—from his elbows down —everything. I reckon it'd knock and scare away the one that'd killed him, lived, you know.

RUTH HOLCOMB: Down on the creek—this was a long time ago— they said a white lady had a Negro baby and she didn't want people to know she had it.

Women used to wear these big long hatpins in their hats to keep them from blowing off. So she stuck that hatpin down in the top of that baby's head and killed it. They tell me now she buried it on the side of the hill down there. I've heard a lot of people say that they can hear that baby a-crying. After she killed that baby, she left here. Nobody knows where she went.

MAELANE HOLCOMB: Back when I was about ten years old, we moved into this big two-story white house right at the edge of Hiawassee. The house had a big set of stair-steps that went upstairs, and there was two big fireplaces up there. That's where Daddy and Mom was a-sleeping and the bathroom was right under the stairs. Me and my sister, Von, slept in one end of the house, and Daddy and Mama slept upstairs at the other end. We'd been living there about three months when one night they woke me up, woke us all up, and we heard something crying just like a little baby. Daddy looked and he couldn't find nothing.

After we heard that, Mama and Daddy got to talking around to people that lived in town and they said nobody wouldn't live in that house no length of time, that it was haunted. We come to find out that this girl had had this baby and she'd got rid of it. She had cut it up and flushed it down the commode. And that crying had sounded just like it was coming out of the bathroom there under the stairs. We all heard it.

It scared Mama and Daddy both. It wasn't but about three days till they packed us up and we moved. That house is tore down now. There just wasn't nobody that would live in it.

RUTH HOLCOMB: They said a long time ago this lady and her daughter went to live way up on some mountain somewhere and nobody would carry them any food. They stayed on the mountain and starved to death. The woman died and the daughter got her buried. Then she died, too. They said after she was dead and buried that people could go near that mountain and hear her screaming. Said now since she was dead, they could still hear her screaming. I don't know why nobody would go near them. Back then they had typhoid fever so they could have had some disease that no one wanted to get.

Grandma Ada Crone used to tell me "haint tales" when I was little. When we interviewed her, I asked her to tell some of those stories to us again and they follow:

CAROL RAMEY

Between Tiger and Clayton, there was a graveyard called the Roane graveyard. Well, they claimed that you could go by there and you'd see a light there at night and it would follow you. It never did try to hurt nobody but it would follow you.

Well, there was a man—I forget his name now—but he went to see a lady that was called Gertrude Rose. And when he left her house, he told her he was scared that that light would take out after him. She says, "No." She says, "I'll fix it where that light won't hurt you." She got a lamp and she lit it and she stuck a pin through the wick. She said that would scare off any kind of a ghost or anything that looked like a ghost. Well, he started home and he went [through the graveyard] and the light took out after him. He throwed his lamp down an' he ran. He fell in a branch an' he was wet all over an' skeered to death. When he got to his house he was out of breath, and his wife asked him what in the world was wrong with him. Was he drunk? He said, "No, that light took out after me and I 'uz skeered t'death." Says, "I'll never go through that way again in my life."

I guess they had some haunted houses [back when I was a girl]. I don't really know. I know of one they *said* was haunted. I really don't know about that though. It was pretty close to where we used to live and we had to turn off the highway goin' through the woods to our house. And there was a log house there and a man had been killed there. One of my brothers claimed when he came through there that he'd see a man a-walkin' 'side of him without a head. He had his head in his arms holdin' it walkin' along. My brother started running and the man without a head would run too, but he'd carry his head in his arms. And my brother was skeered. He said it skeered him half to death. He tried to run off and leave it but the more he run, the more it would run. If he slowed up and walked, well, it would walk too. But it never did try to hurt him. He said he tried to talk to it, but it wouldn't say nothin'. I don't know whether that's true or not, but that's just a tale that I was told.

* * *

Mike Cook, one of the Foxfire staffers, told us a while back that his grand-mother, Mrs. Eula Carroll, had some interesting stories of her childhood. Well, we went to Cleveland, Georgia, and taped her and found Mike was right. This story happened when Mrs. Carroll was about sixteen years old.

We went to a circus in Gainesville—me and my sister and a cousin. My daddy told me if we didn't get back 'fore dark, I'd have to milk. We had a flat tire down here about Clermont, fifteen miles below Cleveland [Georgia]. It was on a T-model Ford. [It was getting late] and it started mistin' rain. Then it was dark as pitch [by the time we got home]. Oh, it was so dark, and my daddy was so upset with us.

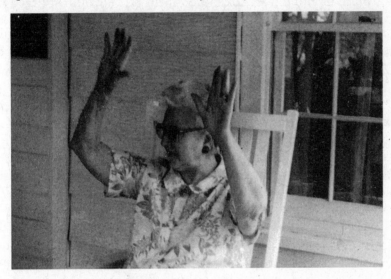

PLATE 377 Mrs. Eula Carroll

He told me I had to go to the barn and milk that cow. He wouldn't let me take the lantern, and he wouldn't let me take the collie dog. So I went on down to the barn and opened that huge door. And honey, it was so wide! It had rollers on it and they needed greasing. [They're like little wheels on the top of the sliding door.] I opened that door and it screaked all the way down. It sounded terrible. Oh, me! It sounded like some kind of haint.

So I opened that door, and I couldn't see a thing in the world. I walked down that huge hall to get the cow's feed. We swept that hall and kept it just like a house. There was what they called a "hack" parked in there. It was like an old-fashioned surrey, except it was larger. It had three seats and you could take out the seats [to haul things in it]. That was what they carried my [mother's coffin] to the cemetery in. It had curtains that came down and snapped, and it had little isinglass windows in each one. I had to walk by that hack and I had a horror of it.

Well, I got on by that and went on to this other huge door. I had to open it to go get the cow in out of the pasture on the other side of that barn. I got the cow and I opened that big door again to come back. The cow knew exactly where to go. [The cow and I] got back alongside the hack and something made a loud noise—sounded terrible. [If you've ever been around stock, they blow when they're frightened. She was just blowing.] She wouldn't move a pace, wouldn't move a step. And every time I'd move, that awful noise would sound again. And just about the time I'd stop a little bit, and she'd quit blowing, it'd start again. And I was standing there, and I was just praying. I was a Christian and I said, "Oh God, help me." I knew something was after me, was gonna grab me any minute. I *knew* it was gonna grab me. So I was praying, "Oh Father, help me. I can't go any further." The cow wouldn't move. She was standing, and she'd back up right against me.

And all at once I saw this halo of light up in the loft. Beautiful light! And in this light was my mother sitting on a straight chair. And she had on the last dress I ever saw her wear. Beautiful! It was a navy with white dots, and it had lace all in it. She'd made it, and it had long sleeves. She just looked lovely. And her hands—I had hands just like my mama—her hands were slipping down out of her lap. She said, "Eula, don't be afraid. I'm here." And I wanted to run up those steps.

The cow went on in then and went in the right stall, and I wasn't afraid anymore. I went on to milk the cow, and she stood just as still. Then I went on out, and that old door screaking didn't bother me a bit. I wasn't afraid anymore.

I [started walking toward the house] and Little Brother was sitting up at the other gate with a big raincoat over him, and had a lantern and the dog. If I had hollered, he was gonna run to me. My daddy wouldn't let him [come to barn with me to milk]. I went on in the house and I told my daddy [what I'd seen in the barn], and he cried. He said he'd never do that again. I said, "I'll go back tonight if you want me to."

Oh, and the noise . . . When I went back by that hack [later], I saw that one of those curtains had come down in the back. See, there were three sections, and one had come loose and it had come down and was flopping against that spring seat in there. And you can

PLATE 378

imagine—well, it was weird. It was just blowing enough to move it and then it'd hit against that seat and then it'd flop. The wind had probably caught it. It had those three tiers of curtains and they came down, and it'd come loose.

I just knew . . . It looked like I would have known they wouldn't have made a noise if somebody was planning to get me.

My mother had been dead around seven years. Now I know that anything that happens to me, my mother's always there.

WITCH TALES

LOLA CANNON: People I knew didn't believe in witchcraft like it was practiced in Salem, but they did have some certain superstitions, I guess you would call them.

My grandmother had this funny belief. I think it was amusing to her. I don't know. She'd make a cross in the dirt with her toe, spit in it, and make a good wish for somebody. Any time she left the house and had to turn back, that was her idea. She would always smile when she did it. I think it was sort of fun to her.

There was one thing she wouldn't let us do. That was what she called "spin a chair." You have probably seen people standing and talking, swing the chair back and forth. She wouldn't let us do that. Said it was unlucky.

And she didn't allow us to walk with one shoe on and one shoe off. That's a habit I still have today. I just don't walk with one shoe on and one off.

People said it was unlucky to set out a cedar tree because when it grew tall enough to cast a shadow the length of a coffin, a member of the family would die. And a great many people wouldn't set them out.

And then there was a man named Mr. Page who lived down near the Chattooga River, in the Warwoman district. I just remember going to his house once. I had suffered with a toothache for a long time and he had a toothache remedy.

There was only one doctor in Clayton back then and children were pretty shy about going to the doctor anyway. Sometimes we'd suffer terribly without letting our parents know.

My grandfather took me down to Mr. Page's and he asked me how long my tooth had been hurting, all about it. Then he got up and went to a chest in the back of the house and took out something that looked like a piece of rich pine kindling. He cut a tiny sliver off of it and sharpened it. He said, "Suppose you pick the gum around your tooth till it bleeds."

Well, I did. Then he wrapped a piece of cotton around the point of this pick and went back and put it in a box.

Well, the tooth still hurt me on until we went home. I was terribly discouraged. I thought it was supposed to stop magically. I went to bed that night and slept, and the next morning my tooth wasn't hurting me! It didn't hurt anymore.

Some people would call that witchcraft, I guess.

David Payne asked his grandfather, John Lee Patterson, if he remembered any scary stories he'd heard or that had happened when he was young and these are two he shared with us.

This here is the story of back in the olden times around 1820 till about 1875, when they claimed they had witches in this county. Some of my grandparents used to tell me about an old lady who was a witch, and she lived over on Bullard Mountain. Her name was Holly Bullard, and the mountain is just after you cross the bridge on [Route] 76 west going toward Hiawassee. On top of that mountain is where she lived.

Her and her father were the only ones. Her mother passed away and she became a witch they claim, now. I don't believe in them myself, but back then they said there was such a thing.

[My grandfather] told me a tale about her that one time she wanted to buy a pig to fatten from one of my grandfather's uncles, and he wouldn't sell one to her, which they didn't sell for much back then. Three dollars, two dollars, maybe even seventy-five cents. I don't know. But she said, "They won't do you no good if you don't sell me one of them." Then he run her off, and she said, "Them pigs ain't going to do you any good. Something is going to happen to them pigs."

So he claims that she went on home, and the pigs quit eating and would run around squealing and getting poorer and poorer until they finally fell over dead—all of them.

So one day she was a-walking down the road and asked him how was his pigs a-doing, and he said that they all died out because of some disease. Then she told him they died because he wouldn't sell her one. And then she just went on down the road.

Then there was another man by the name of Alp Teems, and he was a distant cousin of my granddaddy, and they claimed he could turn himself into anything he wanted to and make you think he was a horse or cow or something or other like that.

So he had a brother who was all the time trying to kill a deer. There was a deer they claim would cross the river up there from one mountain to the other to eat, and they'd shoot at him and couldn't never kill him. So his brother was up in a gap on the mountain waiting for this deer one morning just about daylight, and then they said this big ten-point buck came down the ridge right by him. So he picked up his muzzle-loading rifle he had ready to shoot, and when the buck got up on him he shot him point-blank, and the buck jumped up the hill like a rabbit jumping, and then turned around, snorted a time or two, come right down by him, and he already had his gun loaded again and he shot him again.

He knew he didn't miss it, and he said the deer just kept hanging around there out in the thicket. Then he remembered his grandmother and grandfather telling him that if he scraped some silver off a coin onto his bullet and loaded it in his gun that he could kill any kind of witches with the next bullet. So he pulled a silver piece out of his pocket and scraped some of that silver off of it and packed it in there with the wadding and loaded his gun, and about that time he raised up and there stood his brother, Alp. And Alp said, "You wouldn't shoot me, would you, brother?" And his brother said, "No, I was trying to kill a deer and I have already shot it twice, so I thought I'd try this remedy on him." .

And Alp said, "Aw, that was me pulling a joke on you!"

A SECOND LOOK AT THE LOG CABIN

A major chapter in *The Foxfire Book* was devoted to log cabin building. Since the publication of that book, we have been able to collect additional information that rounds out the log cabin chapter in significant ways. Some of that material follows.

The first section has to do with the Rothell house, a huge log home which had stood abandoned in an adjacent county for years and was up for sale. It was purchased by our organization and moved to Rabun County; its history and reconstruction were documented in the Summer, 1984, issue of *Foxfire*. A portion of that material is published here for the benefit of a number of readers of this series of books who will be interested in specific architectural details that were revealed when the home was disassembled.

Following the Rothell house material are short sections that illustrate a puncheon floor, and the making of a maul and a broadax handle—all things referred to in *The Foxfire Book,* but not actually documented until now.

THE ROTHELL HOUSE

The two primary living sources for the history that we have gathered so far for the Rothell house are Moot Friar of Stephens County and Mitch Anderson of Rabun County. Both were directly connected to the Rothell family.

Before we moved it, the Rothell house was located in Stephens County on Rothell Road, a gravel road that runs parallel to Toccoa Creek not far from the point where that creek enters the Tugaloo River. Before Stephens County was created on August 18, 1905, the land on which the house sat was in Habersham County (and probably would be in Habersham still had not the residents of Toccoa been so incensed at the defeat of their struggle to make their town the county seat of Habersham, instead of Clarkesville, that they decided to form a county of their own). Prior to the creation of Habersham County in 1818, the Rothell house land was in Franklin County—the county formed through various treaties with the Cherokee Indians in the late 1700s.

The last resident of the empty log house was Amanda Rothell, who never married. Her brothers and sisters were named Mae, Lucy, Bruce, Keith, Clifford, and John. Mitch Anderson married Mae, who is now deceased. Lucy was Moot's mother. Born and raised in the log house, she was ninety-four on the third of September, 1984, but we could not interview her as she is in a nursing home and is very ill.

From the courthouse records, as far as we can determine, the house was actually built by James Blair who was born in 1761 in Virginia, moved to Franklin County, and by 1805 had been chosen as one of its commissioners. Aside from serving during the Revolutionary War as one of the Kings Mountain Men under Colonel McDowell, Blair was perhaps best known in our part of the country as the surveyor who surveyed the boundary line between Georgia and the Cherokee Nation known as the Blair Line. He was a state senator at his death in 1839.

Foxfire acquired the house in the summer of 1983. Greg Darnell, one of the students in the program, tells the rest of the story in his introduction to the issue of *Foxfire* that featured the home:

A summer crew was hired by Foxfire to move the house. It consisted of Pat Shields as the foreman, and high school students Chris Crawford, Richard Trusty, Scott Shope, and Anthony Wall. Two former students, Clay Smith and Darryl Garland, helped also. Their main job was to remove the siding, remove the roof and debris, number the logs, and move them to Mountain City where they would be put back together. They also took pictures of the steps as they went along. Along with the photos of the house, the first interviews were done with Moot Friar and Mitch Anderson, two men who knew the Rothell family well. This work continued all through the summer.

In the fall, when school started back, Scott Shope went to work on starting this issue of the magazine. Scott mostly printed the summer photos and continued taking photos of the house in stages as it was being rebuilt. Some other students got interested and helped with the work, taking and printing photographs and going on new interviews.

At Mountain City, George Ensley worked on grading the location where the log house now stands. Pat continued to supervise while Frank Hickox and Roy Carter worked on the construction with him along with Clay and Darryl.

Reconstruction went on until about December when the weather got bad. The roof was put on and the work was stopped. All this time, Scott and other students were working on the magazine. They continued to work on it throughout the school year. Still more photos were taken and printed while others drew diagrams and went on more interviews and began to do research on the land in the courthouses at Stephens and Habersham counties.

I am a student who got hired this summer by Foxfire to work on *Foxfire 9* and this magazine. My name is Greg Darnell. I got started on this magazine at the start of the summer right as school got out. About half of the magazine was done when summer started. I was helped by other students who were also hired this summer by Foxfire. Kyle Conway and Chet Welch helped take additional photos, draw diagrams, and go on final interviews with Moot and Mitch.

Wig and I worked on this issue the day we had to take it to the printer getting the last pages ready. On the day before, we were at the courthouse in Clarkesville still trying to get all the history straight. We went back as far as we could, but because there weren't any land plats, and the boundaries were just described as locust trees and boulders, we never were sure we had it all right. Hopefully some people in Stephens County or other members of the family we haven't met will help fill in the blanks.

The building itself is still not complete. We got the roof on so that it would be kept dry, but it is still a good ways from being complete. The reason for this is money. We did get a donation of $200 from the Belks Stores, though, and we are working on raising the rest. When we do have enough money to complete it, it will be used as offices for the Rabun County Historical Society, a community meeting area, and a museum.

The Farm

Mitch Anderson, who has been retired for twenty years from a lifetime of working with the Georgia Power Company, was raised near the Rothell place, and so he was one of our prime sources of information as to how that part of the country in general and the Rothell place in particular looked when he was young:

* * *

We moved into the settlement up towards Toccoa Creek within a mile of the Rothell place about 1915. My wife and all the Rothells and my four brothers and sisters, we were all kids together, and we were

PLATE 379   Mitch Anderson

together most of the time. We'd get together on Saturday nights, and we all went to school together. That school moved about three or four times. It started out in the woods. Wasn't a road to it. The reason for that was that there were people coming off the Tugaloo River to that school, too, so they took the distance between the Toccoa Valley, you might say, where we were, and the Tugaloo River settlement, and they divided the distance and [put the school halfway between the two].

Then they started having school in the old Tom Scott store—that's where Payne's store now is. The old store had closed out, and so it was just an empty building.

Then they built the Pulliam School, and then they built a school on top of the hill behind the old barn on the Rothell place, back up there on that hill and adjacent to the Rothell place in one corner. Mr. B. O. Yearwood donated that land—deeded it to the school for as long as it was a school, and then that land was supposed to come back to him when it ceased to be a school. It was called the High Point School, and it stayed a school till it was abandoned, I believe.

All those schools were elementary schools. After you finished elementary school at one of them, you either went to school in town or that was all the school you had.

Now the Rothell Road came down by the Rothell house, and the old Clarkesville Road went up behind the house to Clarkesville. That was before my days that that old road was being used, but I've heard my dad speak of it. That road went up past the High Point School and the Murphy family graveyard, which is still there up on the hill behind the Rothell place.

At the front of the house there used to be an early spring garden. They always had a good little garden there—small, but it'd come in real early. It got the morning sun, you know. The little shed behind the house was the smokehouse, and they had their big gardens in back of the smokehouse. They always planted their pole beans back there. Boy, they *raised* them, too!

Then there was a big barn straight on up above the house. Bruce Friar, Moot's daddy, his mules ate it up. That was when he was in the mule-trading business. They ate the bottom log till it almost was set down on the ground. He thought he'd get it built back, but they finally tore that barn down.

And there was a little house right below the main house that a servant named Sarah Elrod lived in. She worked for Mrs. Rothell. Another one named Aunt Millie lived there [after] Sarah. Then there used to be another servant that the boys bailed out of the chain gang. They called him "Old Snook." He lived there a couple of years, I believe. Worked in the fields and helped around the house—got in wood and all. And then he disappeared. Slipped off and they didn't find out where he went.

And right out from the house, behind the kitchen, was the well. It's a hundred feet deep, and it's solid rock in the bottom. When they got down there and hit that rock, they finished it up just like a washpot. That's what they told me—that the bottom of that was just like the bottom of a washpot all hollowed out and smoothed up. That well always had six or eight feet of water in it.

And the house itself was a big house. They gathered in a lot. They all belonged to the Shiloh Baptist Church, and they'd go to church and maybe four or five or a half a dozen would come home with them, you know. Come home and eat. Mrs. Rothell was a good cook.

MOOT: It's a *big* house. I covered it one time in tin. I'm gon' tell you something. I wasn't as old as you [pointing to one of the students], and they throwed a rope over the top of it and I tied myself to the

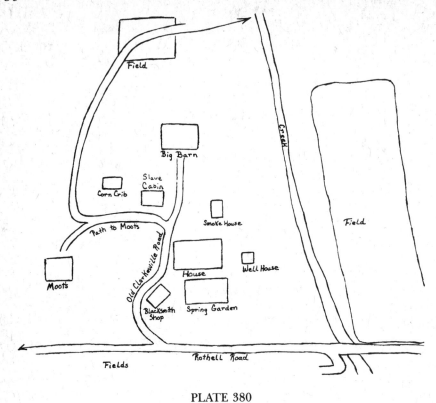

Field

Creek

Big Barn

Slave Cabin

Corn Crib

Path to Moots

Old Clarkesville Road

Smoke House

Field

Moots

House

Well House

Blacksmith Shop

Spring Garden

Fields

Rothell Road

PLATE 380

rope and they let me down, and I'd nail that tin down. I *know* how big that house is.

They had it fixed up nice. Had carpet all over the house. Mitch and I wired it right after I got back from World War II, so it had electricity. I tell you, you should've seen that place when it was actually furnished. It was beautiful the way they had it fixed up—to be an old house. They had more stuff in there than you could shake a stick at. There's stuff scattered all over everywhere that came out of there.

There was always a crowd there, and it wasn't nothing *but* happiness. They didn't have no growling at all. No, sir. I've seen it so full of people that you couldn't get on the porch, hardly, nor in none of the rooms. They'd all be full! And I guess some of them drank, but they done it on the outside. They didn't come in with it!

The Upstairs

The upstairs portion of the house was a full second story that was located over downstairs rooms D/B/E. A boxed-in stairway went from the hall downstairs (B) into room J upstairs. A storage area was located under the roof of rooms F/G. Rooms I and K were divided from J by floor to ceiling partitions that were faced with lapped wooden shingles.

The furniture which was in both the upstairs and downstairs of the house has gotten scattered, and it is now located in various private collections and in the homes of various members of the family. People we interviewed were able to help us find several pieces that the owners would allow us to photograph, however, and they were able to tell us which rooms the pieces were located in when the house was occupied. The photographs on these pages show the results of that quest.

Originally the upstairs rooms were bedrooms. According to Mitch, "They slept upstairs in the early days, before my days, but when the kids were growing up, Mr. Rothell got uneasy about them sleeping up there [the danger of fire in a log house with only one exit out of the upstairs was a very real one] and that's when they changed those rooms up there and turned them into sewing rooms. In one side they had a loom, and I guess they hung hams in the other side."

Moot was able to supply additional details concerning how the rooms were used when he was younger. According to him, one of the rooms (I) was left a bedroom even after the children were moved downstairs. "There was one bed set in there, and two or three big rocking chairs. Then in the center of the room they had hickory splits that hung down [from the rafters] that they hung meat on. I remember all that just as good as if it was yesterday."

In the central portion (J), family and friends gathered to sing.

MOOT: Where you came up the stairs in the middle part is where an organ sat. There was a homemade bench down either side and a bunch of chairs made out of hickory. I've set in them and played with them a thousand times. Then there was a kerosene floor lamp that set right beside the organ. That lamp was just like the ones downstairs. Those lamps have long chimneys and they burn mantles—circular netlike wicks like a gas lantern burns. It makes out the prettiest light you ever saw in your life. That thing burns like—man, it'll light up the whole country!

Then there was a piano, too, that set in there beside the organ. It was so heavy that when I moved it into my house it fell through the floor! My floor wouldn't hold it, and so I had to give it away. John could play them both, and he could play banjos, fiddles, and everything. Every one of them would get in upstairs in the evenings. The Griggses and the Crawfords and the Hunters and all'd come and

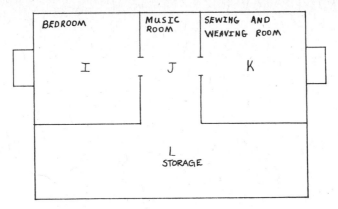

PLATE 381

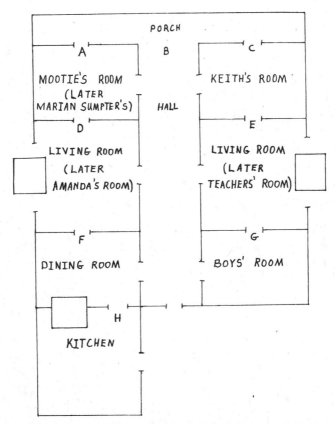

PLATE 381   Mitch helped the Foxfire students draw a floor plan of the house and label the rooms. The original house was only rooms D and E. F and G were then added before either Mitch or Moot can remember. The original house and this first addition are what were moved to Mountain City. A, C, and H were relatively recent additions and, ironically, were in such a state of disrepair that they were not moved.

PLATE 382 Kerosene floor lamps like this one were scattered throughout the house. This one sat beside the organ upstairs.

PLATE 383 This dresser was in the upstairs bedroom.

they'd have big eatings and singings several times a year, and they had a singing *every* night, just about it. Jim Farmer's bunch from up at Clayton used to ride horses down here and spend the night. Everybody'd come. All the preachers. Everybody. There was always a crowd there.

Now in that storage room [L], they had everything in there. They even had cotton in there that they wove, and all such junk as that. They raised that cotton and they gathered it in the bolls back then, and then they had to pick it out of the bolls. They took it to them fireplaces and picked the seeds out, you know. They had cotton pickings, and they also had candy pullings—make old syrup candy and pull it, you know, and make it white? Did all that downstairs at that big fireplace, but they kept that cotton upstairs in those sealed-in storage rooms under the roof.

In the other end room [K], they had the spinning wheel in it that made the thread, and a loom down the middle of the room. Somebody took that spinning wheel and that made me hot because it could still be used. I've got a quilt in here that was made up there. Liza Hunter made it. It's got her initials in it somewhere. She made that quilt and gave it to John Rothell when he married Lois Singleton, and when he died, she gave it back to me. It was made upstairs right up there. They didn't know what a machine *was* whenever that thing was made!

The Hall   Marion's Room   Keith's Room

Rooms A and C were added to the original house about 1920, according to Mitch. He said, "I can remember when those were built. Those two rooms were a porch to start out with. The porch roof was straight to begin with, but when they added the two rooms, they made dormers in the porch roof at the same time. I think Fain Robinson built those rooms, and he built a big barn in the back at the same time. Keith probably helped him."

According to Moot, "There was a big hall tree setting out there [in the hall, room B] beside where you went up the stairs, and there was about eight or ten big rockers that set in there along the walls. Everybody wore a hat then, and so they also had hat racks all around —deer horns and things on the walls.

"And they had some slaves, and [room A] was for a colored man they kept. I was named after him. His nickname was 'Moose,' and they called me 'Mootie.' He used to pull me in an old red wagon. Now there was one bed in there and a dresser with a mirror and a wash-

PLATE 384   This is one of a number of
rocking chairs that sat in the hall.

stand. Marion, one of the Rothell girls, married a Dr. Sumter, and
after he died, she moved back to the house and moved into that
room. 'Moose' was gone by then.

"Keith moved into [room C] after the other boys was gone. It was
furnished the same way [as A]."

Amanda's Room

Apparently in the original house, room E was the living room and
room D was the kitchen. In the late 1920s or early '30s, D became the
living room and E was converted into a bedroom for boarding teachers. At that point, D was furnished with an organ, a settee, and some
chairs.

Much later, D became Amanda's bedroom, furnished, as Moot
said, with "a big bed, a big cherry cupboard that had drawers for
clothes, and on top of it, it had a big mirror. And there was an organ
in there, and benches to sit on with stove legs for legs. Some had four

legs and some were longer and had six. And those benches were covered with some red felt stuff. And then there was three more of them kerosene floor lamps."

The Teachers' Room

Schoolteachers from both the Pulliam and High Point schools boarded in the house because, according to Moot, "That was the only house that had room sufficient for them at that time. Back then they wouldn't let schoolteachers stay where they wasn't protected.

"They put four *fancy* beds in there, and big old stand-up battery radios, and one of those old-time windup [record players] with the horn on it. And there was washing stands and all kinds of stuff in there. That was a big room. I'll show you a clock that came off the fireboard in there. It hasn't got an iron cog in it. It's all wooden cogs, and it's got weights in it as big as window weights. It runs good, but Lord have mercy what a racket it makes. It makes the weirdest sound. When it strikes, you can hear it all over the house! They kept two peach seeds in there to keep it greased—one in the bottom and one in the top. Those peach seeds put out an oil, and so they never had to oil the clock."

Mitch added, "There was an old high poster bed in there that was once a rope bed. My father was a blacksmith, and he fixed that bed to where you used the rails and slats [instead of ropes]. He made the iron catches or locks to hold the rails to the posts. I remember that, because I helped him. The slats went on those rails."

The chimney and the fireplace in the teachers' room were re-worked while the Rothell children were still at home. Mitch said, "They put long curved rocks around the base of that chimney to help support it after water washed out the dirt from around the base. Those rocks came from the old porch [that was converted into rooms A and C]. There was a landing when you came out of that front door and the porch, and they had curved rock steps that went down to the ground from either side of the landing. That's the way the house was built to start with."

At the same time the chimney was buttressed, a cement slab was poured over the hearth of the fireplace, and hand prints and foot-prints were put into the wet cement. Moot said, "They didn't know what concrete was, and they just played all in it. One is Mother's and one is Ida's and one's John's. They just capped that rock over to make a flat place up there for them kids to play on."

Mitch laughed, remembering John's footprint. "Old John had a

PLATE 385 One of four identical pieces
that were in the teachers' room.

size thirteen or fourteen shoe. I remember an old doctor from out of
Lavonia would come up there to gig frogs, and he asked John what
size shoes he wore. 'Hell,' said he didn't know, but said it took two
cowhides and a half bushel of tacks to make him a pair of shoes! John
was a card, I'm telling you."

The Dining Room

In the dining room [F], according to Moot, "There was a hand-
painted chandelier that worked off of kerosene. And there was a big
table that's round when the leaves are out of it, but it pulls apart and
just *keeps* going out to put the leaves in, and in that house, all the
leaves were in it. There was a master chair and about eighteen of the
ones without arms around them. Then there was two big corner
cupboards—one for glass and china and one for silverware—and they
was thousands of dollars' worth of silver in there. They had big old

PLATE 386   The hand prints and footprint
in the fireplace hearth. The footprint is
John's.

heavy solid silver ladle spoons that'd weigh five and six pound apiece.
Then there was a buffet that had felt on the inside and a marble top."

The Boys' Room

"When I was young," said Moot, "the boys stayed in what they
called the boys' room. That was Keith, Cliff, John, and Bruce. Lord
have mercy, I slept in there a thousand times. There was four washstands with holes cut out in their tops and washbasins set down in
them where they washed their faces every morning and shaved. Then
there was dressers with mirrors beside each washstand, and there was
four beds and four of those stand-up kerosene lamps. All those lamps
in the house was just alike. They must have got them from the same
man.

"Those beds were solid oak, and they each had a roller at the end
with a wooden handle that you rolled the bedcovers up on to make
them up. And they were decorated. They had birds and animals
burned in the headboards with an iron. Them beds were so high they
couldn't go in a regular house, but that house had high ceilings."

The Kitchen

"At the last," Moot remembered, "they had an electric stove, but
when I was a boy they had one of them big wood ranges, and that

PLATE 387 This buffet was in the dining room . . .

PLATE 388 . . . as was this kerosene chandelier which hung . . .

PLATE 389 . . . over this table.

thing was enormous. It had [warming closets] on top of it and all that. They'd put biscuits up there at breakfast and they'd still be warm at dinnertime. That's the reason I stayed over there the biggest part of the time! The oven never got cool. There was thirteen of them, you know, and something had to be cooking almost all the time, so that stove hardly ever went out. The bread and potatoes and stuff was always hot. Had a stool I climbed up on and pulled them doors open up top on that old stove. Pshaw, every kid in this country was over there eating!

"And that stove had a hundred-gallon tank on the back of it and they kept hot water in it all the time. When we wanted to wash our feet, we'd go and turn that faucet on that tank and get us a tub of warm water.

"There was a big round table setting in the middle, and there was a cupboard about eight feet high, and they had a washing basin and table with water buckets and all setting on that thing. They never did get no running water at all. There never *was* none put in. To wash dishes, they had a big old thing that sat right to the left of the washstand like a sink, and they had a hollow bamboo cane going out from that. Didn't have no plastic pipe. They'd fill that sink with water from the stove to wash dishes, and then when they was done, they'd just let the water run off down the hill out of that bamboo pipe."

The Cellar

There was a full cellar big enough to stand upright in beneath rooms D and E. Moot recalled, "There was a big cellar there where they cut the meat and washed clothes and made hominy and everything. They'd build a fire under there right on the ground as big as a bonfire. Had a thing made out of rocks around it so the fire wouldn't get out. And they had an iron thing that a sixty-gallon pot sat on. Toted the water down there from the well. That's what they washed the clothes in and made hominy in. There was a clay pipe that run out of the side of the house to get the smoke out. They cooked lard down and everything under there, too. I used to go down there and watch them make cracklin's. That was a big place down under there at one time.

"They had about twenty-three hollow sections of chestnut log in there, too, to store meat in. They cured the meat first on big boards in the smokehouse. Then they'd take the side meat and slice it up into bacon and pack it into them logs after it was sliced up. Those were hollow on the inside, see, and they had them things full of meat."

PLATE 390   This washstand and the pitcher
and basin were in the kitchen. The clock was
on the mantel in the teachers' room.

Mitch remembered that they also had holes dug in the ground
where they kept their sweet potatoes and Irish potatoes covered up
through the winter.

Canned goods that were not stored in the cellar were kept in a
pantry built under the stairway that went from the first to the second
floor of the house.

Inevitably, members of the family died or moved away, one by one.
Toward the end, only Keith and Amanda were left. Then, as Moot
related, "After Keith died, Mandy stayed there by herself. I went over
there and slept a lot of times at night. She closed part of the house off
and stayed in the rest. That was home, and she wasn't gonna leave it.
[After she died, the family decided] they'd let it fall in rather than let
anybody rent it. Renters would have started taking the stuff out, one
piece at a time. One'd get this and one'd get that till it would all be
gone."

Mitch added, "Even at the end, Amanda hauled her water from the

PLATE 391   This hollow section of a chestnut
log, now filled with dirt and used as a planter,
used to stand in the cellar and hold salt-cured
bacon.

well. She had an electric stove and refrigerator, but the house never
was plumbed. Tough life. She thought the world of that place. Yes,
sir. You'd say something about her moving somewhere? She'd say,
'Aw, my furniture wouldn't fit there!' I offered to buy her a place out
there on Prathers Bridge Road—nice little house out there for sale
for $5,000. I mentioned it to her. Made her as mad as the very
dickens!''

PLATE 392 The Rothell house as it looked when purchased by Foxfire. From the outside, which was covered by siding, it was difficult to tell that the building was actually a log structure. Trees and vines had grown up, nearly covering parts of the house. The furniture had been removed, and many of the windows were broken out. The chimney shown here served room D.

PLATE 393 Another view of the house, looking along room G to the kitchen, H.

PLATE 394 The porch beyond rooms A and C had collapsed, so we began by removing the rotten debris and then tearing the siding off rooms A and C, which had been added to the original house in the 1920s.

PLATE 395 Beneath the long walls of the additions and the original house were solid foundations of flat rocks mortared by red clay. The foundation work beneath the entire building was one of its most striking features, most log houses being built simply on rock pillars. All the foundation rocks were loaded onto trucks and taken to the reconstruction site.

PLATE 396 The curved hand-cut rocks that once were steps are visible, stacked around the base of the chimney to help support it when years of rain finally washed the dirt out from under its corners. At the far left side of the photo, the end of room G is visible, supported by a post to keep it from collapsing before we could dismantle it. According to both Moot and Mitch, the bank visible under the room was not cut out by hand but was formed as the clay was eroded away from the house by rain.

PLATE 397 The siding for the F-H addition, or the kitchen wing, was removed first.

PLATE 398 In the kitchen addition, H, the rafters were round poles, lap-jointed and pegged.

PLATE 399 When the kitchen was removed, an elaborate piece of mortised and pegged work was revealed, supporting the roof line for the dining room, F, at a point where F and H had joined around the kitchen chimney.

PLATE 400

PLATE 401 The corner post beneath this point was supported by a diagonal brace . . .

PLATE 402 . . . the inside of which had been chiseled out by hand so that what was left matched the thickness of the walls. The diagonal support was mortised into the corner post and floor joist and pegged into place —a remarkable piece of work.

PLATE 403 The outside corners of the kitchen featured a similar construction, as did the outside corner of G.

PLATE 404 Upstairs in the original house we found hewed, pegged rafters and perfectly preserved interior log walls.

PLATE 405 The handmade window frames, which were pegged into the wall logs, were carefully removed, intact, to be used in the reconstruction.

PLATE 406

PLATE 407 Like the window frames, the door frames were also pegged into the wall logs—a technique that not only anchored the frames tightly into place, but also kept the wall logs separated and in line.

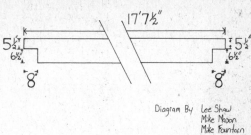

Diagram By Lee Shaw
Mike Mason
Mike Fountain

PLATE 408 Students from a Foxfire class helped former students Clay Smith and Darryl Garland set the foundation logs (sills) and floor joists for the two-story section into place first.

PLATE 409 The measurements for the floor joists for the first floor of the two-story section.

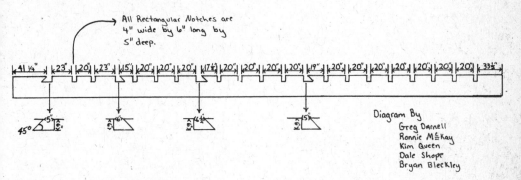

All Rectangular Notches are 4" wide by 6" long by 5" deep.

Diagram By
Greg Darnell
Ronnie McKay
Kim Queen
Dale Shope
Bryan Bleckley

PLATE 410 One of the sill logs for the F-G addition.

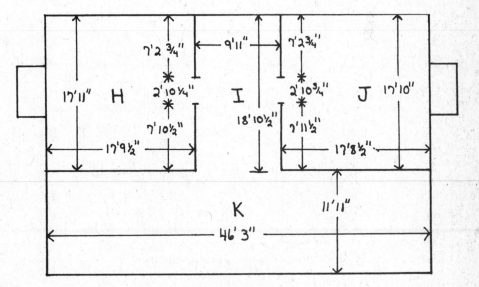

Diagram by
Greg Darnell

PLATE 411 The internal dimensions of the upstairs and downstairs portions of the house we actually moved to Mountain City.

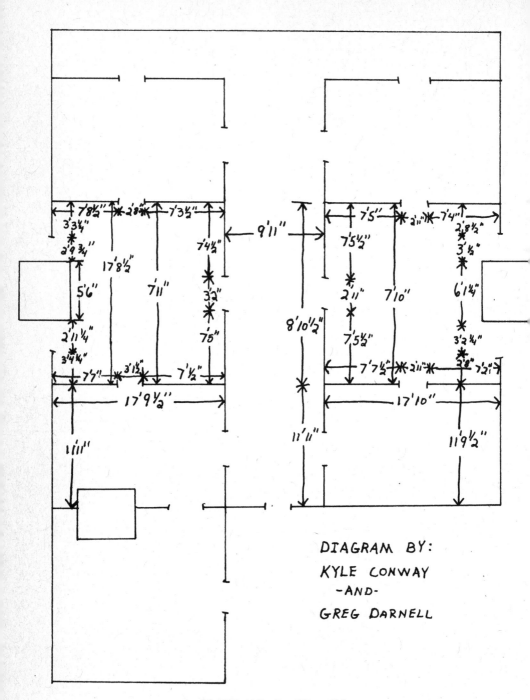

DIAGRAM BY:
KYLE CONWAY
-AND-
GREG DARNELL

PLATE 412   See Plate 411.

PLATE 413 The sill log diagrammed in Plate 436 is visible in this photo, set into place against the sill log for the two-story section. As the wall logs were set back into place on their new foundation, there was ample opportunity to plumb the walls again and straighten any portions that had sagged with age.

PLATE 414 From the lower side, the full basement foundation wall is as impressive as it was originally.

PLATE 415 Door jambs and window frames were repegged as in the original house.

PLATE 416 The two logs that support the floor joists for the second floor are each 48 feet long—the longest hewn logs we have ever worked with.

PLATE 417 Next, the wall logs for the second floor were added.

PLATE 418 With the final 48-foot-long wall logs anchored into place, the original rafters were replaced and pegged at their bases into the wall logs.

PLATE 419

PLATE 420 Their lap-jointed peaks were also repegged together.

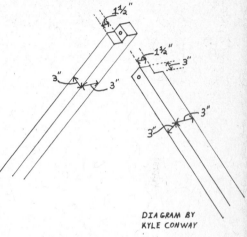

DIAGRAM BY
KYLE CONWAY

PLATE 421

PLATE 422 The lighter-colored logs in the end of the building are new logs that had to be cut and fitted to replace rotten ones.

PLATE 423

PLATE 424   A pegged mortise and tenon joint held the sills together at their corners. A mortise was also cut into the top of the corner to hold the base of the vertical corner post.

PLATE 425

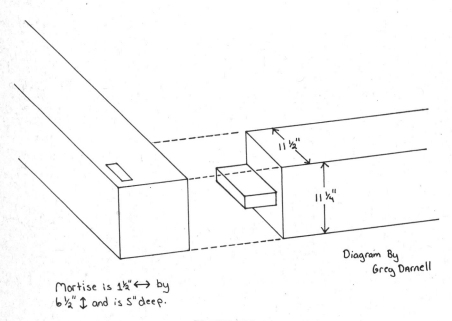

11 ½"

11 ¼"

Diagram By
Greg Darnell

Mortise is 1½" ↔ by
6½" ↕ and is 5" deep.

PLATE 426

All Notches are 3" ↔
by 1½" ↕ and 3"
deep. The Notches
are all 1½" away from closest edge.

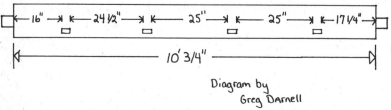

|← 16" →| |← 24½" →| |← 25" →| |← 25" →| |← 17¼" →|

|← 10' 3/4" →|

Diagram by
Greg Darnell

PLATE 427   The top of the long sill was also mortised at regular intervals to hold the vertical wall studs.

PLATE 428 The vertical corner post was fitted back into its mortise, and its diagonal brace was replaced and pegged.

PLATE 429

PLATE 430 The top of the diagonal brace was shaped to fit a mortise cut in the side of the vertical post.

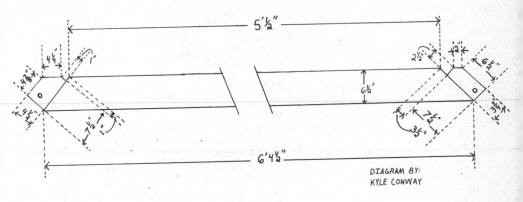

DIAGRAM BY:
KYLE CONWAY

PLATE 431

PLATE 432 The wall studs, diagonal braces, and sills were coded with Roman numerals by the original builders to show where each piece fitted.

PLATE 433 The top of each vertical corner post was shaped into tenons to hold the porch stringers.

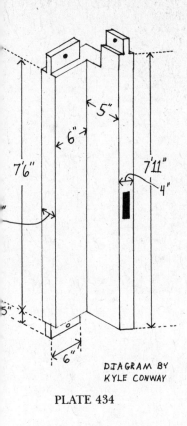

5"

6"

7'6"

5"

5"

7'11"

4"

6"

DIAGRAM BY
KYLE CONWAY

PLATE 434

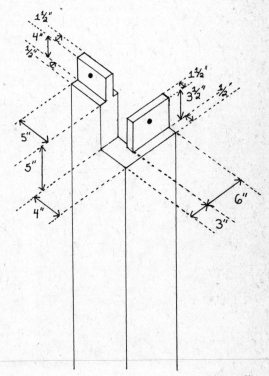

1½"

4"

½"

5"

5"

4"

1½"

3½"

½"

6"

3"

DIAGRAM BY
KYLE CONWAY

PLATE 435

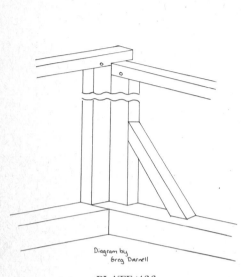

PLATE 436

PLATE 437   The reassembled corner.

PLATE 438

PLATE 439   This plate, the one that follows, and the accompanying diagram show how the two sections of the stringer that runs the length of the addition were shaped and joined and pegged in the middle.

PLATE 440

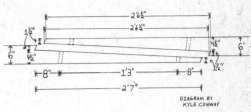

DIAGRAM BY
KYLE CONWAY

PLATE 441

PLATE 442 The porch stringers at each end of the addition not only fitted down over the mortises cut into the vertical corner support posts, but their opposite ends were also notched and pegged into the wall of the main part of the house itself.

PLATE 443

PLATE 444

PLATE 445 At the opposite end of the addition, the same construction was evident except for the section shown here (and mentioned earlier), built to support the roof line when the kitchen was added.

Since the chimney that stood between the kitchen and dining room addition (F and H) is not going to be replaced, new studs were cut and fitted into the hole in the wall left where the chimney used to stand.

PLATE 446

PLATE 447

PLATE 448 Each of the ceiling joists in the original addition was mortised into a wall log of the main house and notched on the underside of the opposite end to fit over the stringer that ran the length of the addition. One-by-eight-foot boards were nailed to the underside of these joists to form a ceiling, and the stud walls and log walls were paneled with the same material. This paneling was all salvaged and will be replaced.

PLATE 449 Standing on the addition's ceiling joists are Frank Hickox (left) and Pat Shields, who supervised the moving and reconstruction. They are preparing to add the rafters for the addition. On the ground is Scott Shope, maneuvering for a camera angle.

PLATE 451

PLATE 450 The house as it looks today. The location selected for the house is a wooded area with a view of the surrounding mountains from nearly all sides. The house overlooks a stream and what will eventually be a park.

As soon as the necessary funds are secured, the chimneys and shingle roof will be added, as well as the interior paneling, doors, windows, chinking, etc. On the side opposite the addition, a full porch will be added that will approximate the original as closely as possible and will afford a view of the park, the stream, and the mountains beyond.

PUNCHEON FLOORS

Some of the earliest Appalachian houses had dirt floors. Later on, people wanted wooden floors and if there wasn't a sawmill available, they had to figure out a way to make their wooden floors by hand.

One type of floor they came up with was called a puncheon floor. These were made of hand-split boards about six feet long, up to two feet wide, and two to three inches thick laid on top of hewn log joists. They were usually made of poplar wood, but some people told us that chestnut and oak were also used.

There is a diagram of a puncheon floor in the *Foxfire Book,* page 77, but we have looked for about fourteen years for one we could photograph and hadn't found one till now.

Wig was stripping the floor out of an old log house he bought and under it was an original puncheon floor. This was an exciting discovery for all of us, so we went to his house and photographed and measured several of the boards.

We also asked our grandparents what they knew about them. Dan's grandmother, Flory Rogers, and Charles's grandfather (who is Dan's uncle), Will Patterson, told us about the tools they used for making the puncheon boards. A wedge, sometimes called a glut, was used with a wooden maul to split the big logs. Usually a tree, at least twelve inches in diameter and often two feet or more, was cut into logs six to eight feet in length. Then these logs were split into widths of two to three inches by hammering the wedge in with the maul. A hand plane was used to smooth the top of the boards off.

Betty Jo Woods, a seventh-grade student, asked her grandfather Mark Snyder and her uncle Sam Snyder what they could tell her about puncheons. They added that the trees should be cut in early spring or late fall when the sap was down, and after the boards were split out, they should be stacked in ricks to air-dry for at least three months before being put down as the floor. Also they said that some people smoothed the boards with a foot adze and fitted them together with a tool called a floor dog, a tool that looks like a set of log grabs with a hook.

DAN CRANE AND CHARLES PHILLIPS

PLATE 452

PLATE 453 The puncheon in place on the joist, which is resting on the main log sleeper.

PLATE 455 Dan Crane showing top side of same board.

PLATE 454 Charles Phillips in front of Wig's log house, showing the underside of a puncheon board, this one made of poplar.

PLATE 456 This shows the whole floor.

CARLTON NICHOLS MAKES A MAUL

Carlton Nichols is my grandfather. He lives on Persimmon. Sometimes I go over to his house on weekends and stay with him, helping him work around the house and on his farm, and sometimes we take his dogs and go 'coon hunting together.

One weekend when I was over there, I noticed a wooden tool in the garage. I'd never seen one before, so I asked him what it was. He said that it was a maul for driving fence posts or splitting logs and that he made it himself.

When I started taking Foxfire courses I remembered the maul, and I asked him if he would let us interview him on how to make one. He was more than happy to help us out, and we started by looking for the right tree in the woods behind his house. After we located a good white oak sapling with a knot in the trunk, we chopped it down and carried out the piece we needed. He then gave us step-by-step directions for how to make this particular tool. The pictures that follow show how it was done.

My grandfather also gave us some tips on maul making and use that are not included in the directions and pictures. He cuts it out while the wood is green. Then he takes it indoors to the fireplace and allows it to bake for about two hours by a good hot fire. The big end should go toward the fire, and it should bake all the way around. This helps it cure out faster so that it won't split. Then he lets it air-dry in his shed before using it so that it will be good and hard.

My grandfather also said that you should keep the maul always in the dry and out of the weather. He also told us that a wooden maul should only be used with wooden wedges and not those made of steel.

CHRIS JARRARD

Article and photographs by Chris Jarrard and Dan Crane.

HOW TO MAKE A BROADAX HANDLE

This is an article about Frank Vinson making a handle for a broadax. A broadax handle is different from a regular ax handle in that it is shorter (only twenty-eight inches long), and is curved. A broadax is used for hewing the sides of logs off for a log house, and so

PLATE 457 Carlton, Dan, and Sandy, Carlton's dog, go to the woods to look for a white oak tree to make a maul.

PLATE 458 Carlton finds a good one while Dan watches.

PLATE 459 Chris carries the tree out to a flat place so he can cut the piece off that Carlton wants to make the maul out of.

PLATE 460   They carry it to the house to work on it.

PLATE 461   Carlton shapes the handle by hewing off the excess wood. There was a slight curve in the trunk, so Carlton hewed more off one side than the other so he'd have a straight handle.

PLATE 462   Chris helps, once Carlton gets the shape he wants.

PLATE 463

PLATE 464   "If you cut the timber on the new moon, you can set it up by the wall over there and it will bend, just like this is. I cut this one on the new moon so it would curve. If you cut it on the dark moon—that there's the first quarter—it'll stay straight. You saw the handles I already made? They're just as straight as they can be.

"Now I'm gonna make the handle. When I chop [score] all the way down one side like I'm a-goin' down here now, I turn it right around and it don't eat in. Now I'll take all of this side down, and then the other side, and I'll take it down thin enough for the ax handle."

PLATE 465   "What I'm using here is hickory. People would be after me for handles way back whenever my first kids were born, and my oldest girl's sixty-three year old. I once sold two fellows six handles apiece, and they said I'd die one of these days and they wouldn't be nobody else to make handles! Ain't hardly nobody left now can make 'em right."

PLATE 467 He takes the sides down a little more as Wig, William Brown, and Tony Whitmire watch and record.

PLATE 466 Once Frank has the piece of hickory chopped down into a rough rectangular slab, he rounds off the corners with his hatchet, and then he holds the axhead against one end to gauge his progress.

PLATE 468 As the handle approaches the right dimensions, Frank leaves the end that fits into the axhead larger, as well as the opposite end. He continues shaping, taking small, careful cuts. "I make that knot in the end so you can hold it there."

PLATE 469 When the handle is rounded off and shaped to roughly the correct dimensions, Frank clamps it at either end to a block of wood. Then he slips a wedge under the curve, hammers it in tightly, and clamps it there, too, so the handle will air-dry with the curve intact.

PLATE 470   After the handle has dried for several weeks inside his house, Frank brings it out and, using his rasps, does some final shaping.

PLATE 471   He works the end that the axhead fits onto down so that it is just slightly larger than the hole in the axhead. This ensures that the two will fit very tightly together.

PLATE 472

PLATE 473   When he is confident the handle will fit into the head, he takes his chisel and splits the head end open to a depth of four inches.

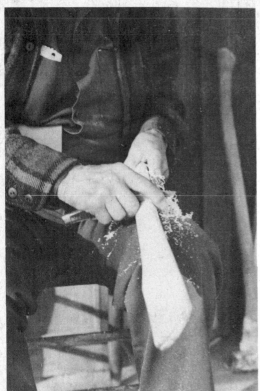

PLATE 474 Then, with the blade of his pocketknife held at right angles to the surface of the wood, he smooths off any ridges left from the rasp. Before he started using his knife for this job, he used the edges of pieces of broken glass.

PLATE 475 Finally he sands the whole handle so that it is completely smooth. Then he greases it thoroughly with linseed oil to help waterproof it and preserve it and keep it from cracking.

PLATE 476 Now he puts the handle into the axhead. He does this by getting the handle started into the hole and then striking the opposite end sharply six or eight times with a go-devil.

PLATE 477 When the handle is completely in place in the axhead, he takes a sharpened wooden wedge and drives it into the split he made earlier in the end of the handle. When the wedge is driven in as far as it will go, binding the axhead tightly into place, Frank cuts off the excess wood with a hammer and chisel.

PLATE 478   Now the job is complete. Frank charges five dollars apiece for his handles, no matter whether they are the twenty-eight-inch-long broadax handles like this one or the longer, double-bitted straight ax handles. He also can make handles for shovels, hoes, hatchets, mowing blades, and hammers, and he swears they'll last longer than the store-bought varieties.

PLATE 479   Frank Vinson with Cary Brown, Cecil Wilburn, and Tony Whitmire (left to right).

the handle is curved so that as the person hews, his hands will be out away from the side of the log and he won't skin his knuckles.

Cary Brown lives with his grandparents, Frank and Eva Vinson, and Cary and Cecil Wilburn are good friends and live close to each other on Scaley Mountain. Cecil found out about Frank's handle-making business and told us about it in the Foxfire class. Frank agreed to talk with us and show us how to make one. He already had a piece of hickory that was slightly curved and would do for the handles we wanted, and so he used that. He told us, though, that if we wanted a piece of hickory to have a really good curve in it, all we had to do was to cut the tree on the new of the moon, and cut off the piece for the handle, and as it began to dry it would curve in just the right way. If cut while the moon was in its dark phase (or waning), the timber would cure out straight.

The first day we went, Frank roughed out the handle and then put it in a press in such a way that it would finish curing with the curve intact. It took him about two hours to finish this phase. Several weeks later we returned, and he took the handle out of the press and did the necessary finishing work and then put it in a broadax head we had.

Article by Tony Whitmire, Cecil Wilburn, William Brown, and Cary Brown. Photographs by William Brown.

CAROLYN STRADLEY
"The worst feeling was being alone, never really feeling like I belonged."

The *Atlanta* Journal-Constitution's *Sunday magazine section of February 26, 1984, included an article about Mrs. Carolyn Stradley and her paving company. The article was posted on our classroom bulletin board and called to our attention. When I read the story my interest in Mrs. Stradley was sparked. I found it hard to comprehend that a young, orphaned girl (her mother died when Carolyn was eleven and soon after, she was abandoned by her father) could live alone in the often cruel mountains of northeast Georgia and survive to become a civil engineer and the owner of a successful paving company in Atlanta.*

Mrs. Stradley, born Carolyn Jones, has one brother, Eldon, who is four years older than she. He was at home in the mountains only occasionally, however, traveling back and forth from Atlanta to various jobs, so Carolyn was primarily on her own for her early teenage years. At the age of thirteen, she too packed up her few belongings and caught a ride to Atlanta. There she rented a small garage apartment with her brother, enrolled herself in a nearby high school, and got a job at the local Howard Johnson's. Two years after her move to Atlanta, Carolyn met and married Arthur Stradley. When she became pregnant during her junior year of high school, she left school. After her daughter Tina was born, she returned to night school to complete her education. She got a job as a secretary with a paving company, and over a period of several years worked her way up to a management position. As she progressed, the company offered to pay her tuition toward a certificate in civil engineering from Georgia Tech.

When Carolyn had advanced in the paving company to a point where she felt that she could go no higher, she left it. She, Eldon, and Eldon's wife, Shirley, collaborated and got a loan and started their own paving business. Thus began C&S (standing for Carolyn and Shirley) Paving, which she now runs.

We approached the small white one-story house with some hesitation one spring afternoon. Although we had followed very closely the directions that she

PLATE 480   Carolyn Stradley (right) at her secretary-receptionist's desk.

had given us, Carolyn's office was not quite what we were expecting. It was in an industrial area—small business offices on either side of the house proved this. Nevertheless, the friendly white cat that rubbed against our legs when we got out of the car, the well-trimmed lawn in front of the house, and the sound of barking dogs somewhere in the back were not, in our minds, characteristic of an average business office. However, as we knocked on the screen door at the top of the front steps, we could see a desk and file cabinets in the room. The secretary sitting at the desk confirmed for us that this was where we wanted to be.

The office is more of a home than a place of business. It is equipped with a small kitchen, an eating area, bathrooms, and offices where there were once three bedrooms and a den. We set our equipment in the eating area which was sparsely furnished with a drink machine, file cabinet, picnic table, and benches. On one end of the table a Crock Pot full of collard greens for someone's dinner slow-cooked as we set up our tape recorder at the other end.

When Mrs. Stradley strode into the room with a big grin and greeted us with a hearty "Hi, y'all!" our apprehensions of breaking the ice with her diminished immediately. She shook hands with the three of us with a firm, strong grip. The warm smile introduced us to a sparkling personality, and her bright blue eyes edged with laugh lines mirrored a shrewd, ever-clicking mind. That mind, plus a keen lust for learning, was the reason this woman had been able to survive, on her own, in the southern Appalachian mountains during the 1950s.

Mrs. Stradley is about five feet, eight inches tall and thirty-eight years old. She was attractively attired that day in maroon slacks and a pale pink blouse that complemented her thick, wavy shoulder-length red hair and fair, freckled skin. We found it difficult to picture her as a child leading the toilsome life she told us about because everything about Carolyn Stradley is notably refined and articulate.

Although the atmosphere was homelike, the office still had its business aspects. There was a constant **tap-tap** *of typewriters in the background accompanied by the occasional friendly greeting of the secretary answering the telephone. Our interview was interrupted several times by the jangling phone in another room and someone calling Mrs. Stradley to attend to business that just couldn't wait. In spite of those interruptions, Mrs. Stradley made us feel relaxed as if she had all afternoon to spend with us. It was obvious that she handles her business efficiently and yet with a warm, caring feeling for people and does her best to benefit everyone.*

Mrs. Stradley is not a typical Foxfire contact. She is young and she lives in an area that is south of the mountains. We were interested more in her way of life as a youth than anything else, but as we were putting together the article we realized that many of the other aspects of her life were too important to leave out. What resulted is an article full of joy and suffering, life and death, and happiness and triumph.

ALLISON ADAMS

Article and photographs by Allison Adams, Al Edwards, Eddie Kelly, Patsy Singleton, and Kelly Shropshire.

I was born in 1946 in the small community of Youngcane, which is in Union County near Blairsville in the mountains of northeastern Georgia. [Except for times when we moved to Atlanta for short periods] that's where I was raised until I was thirteen.

[My life before my mother's death] was probably just typical of the area. There was a garden, and we canned what we grew. We dried leather britches beans. I loved 'em.

Mother never worked outside the home [like in a store or factory]. Daddy worked in a sawmill and did a little moonshining and he hauled produce into the city. [There were times] when I felt like I lived out of a cardboard box! We'd move back and forth from Atlanta a lot of times. Daddy would get a job down here [in Atlanta] and we'd come down and stay in a tenement house. [My dad, mother, brother, and I] would live in two rooms while he worked. There would be like eight or ten families in one big house. Then we'd be moving back to the mountains because he'd get laid off or something.

I started grammar school out at the old Blairsville School [about

PLATE 481

1952]. Our school bus was a pickup truck with a wooden cover on the back and little wooden benches. And if it rained real bad, then we didn't go to school because the roads were so bad that the little truck couldn't get across the creeks. This was in the fifties, but very few people [in our area] had automobiles [and the roads were terrible]!

In the sixth and seventh grades, I was going to school over there at Youngcane. I can remember we did not even have electricity at that particular time. We were still using a kerosene lamp. When I first got into geometry in the seventh grade, it was very difficult at nights sitting by a kerosene lamp trying to get my geometry homework.

All [through] my life, I can't remember [ever] *not* being responsible for someone or something. As a small child, it was my responsibility to make sure there was water in the house. I went up to the spring and brought in water, carried in wood [for cooking and heat], and made sure that the chickens had been fed. These were all things that were necessary. Mama was often extremely sick. [When I was] a child, I can remember her being in the hospital a lot. She had had rheumatic fever [as a child] and she developed heart disease. [When my brother and I were small] she would get out and work like a man. She would do sawmilling with my father and pull a crosscut saw. Then she'd get really sick! [She died when] I was eleven. I believe I was in the sixth grade. There was so much anger inside because I couldn't understand what I had done wrong to make my mother die and leave me. You know, I really had this feeling: "What horrible thing have I done?" I really couldn't understand why this had happened to me.

She had been a very strong, independent person. She had grown to be that way with Daddy's habits of coming in one week and gone the next. There was never anything she could depend on.

First of all, please understand that I loved my father more than anything else in the world, but Daddy was an alcoholic. My mother died on a Sunday, she was buried on Tuesday, and the following weekend my father was remarried. He chose to live in the Atlanta area with his new wife. [He left my brother and me in our little house in Youngcane to look after ourselves.] He just did not get to the mountains to visit us that much [after Mother died].

My brother, Eldon, is four years older than I. [When we were children] his responsibilities were similar to mine. A lot of times he would do what they called "off-bearing" in a sawmill. Off-bearing is where someone catches the slabs that come off the side of the tree trunk whenever a tree is run through the saw. They'd catch those slabs and lay them somewhere else [away from the mill]. Even though he was a young boy, he was very strong and he would do that a lot of times for his money. [After Mother died] Eldon worked at the sawmill or cleaned out chicken houses—things like that. Whatever he could pick up! He would come in and live with me part of the time, between jobs.

Mother had managed to get the house paid off before she died. There wasn't much to it, but it was shelter. The winters get sort of severe over there and I can remember waking up sometimes and I'd have ice frozen across my face from the condensation of my breath. I think being cold was one of the things I remember most. It would be dark by the time the school bus got me home [and when Eldon worked away from home, I was there alone]. Some mornings I didn't properly cover the coals in the fireplace before I left for school and I would come in by myself in the evening and [the fire would be completely out and I'd] not have kerosene to start a new fire. I'd have to get a new fire going in the dark.

Bobby socks were the popular thing at that time and I only had one pair. I'd wash them [every night] and if they weren't dry by the next morning, I'd put them on wet. I think being laughed at and made fun of in school and never feeling like I was as good as anyone else were probably the worst things [I experienced]. When I was in the seventh grade, one of the things that I really remember most of all was this girl giving me a bar of soap for Christmas. Of course she was trying to be obnoxious, because she knew I had never had anything like that. [We made lye soap instead.] She didn't realize that was the best Christmas present I had. It was probably the only Christmas present I had that year. She thought she was being super mean to me, but I thought it was super good!

[Surviving] was a day-in, day-out process. I had learned to can vegetables and dry beans and dry apples and fix kraut so most of the time I had enough canned [food to last me].

I wore a lot of my brother's clothes, hand-me-downs. I worked hard through the summertime and usually would get enough money to buy enough clothes to just about last through the winter. [Farmers in that area grew vegetables for the big food companies like Campbell's Soup and Stokeley's. They sent big open trucks along the country roads to pick up people who wanted to work by picking the beans, peppers, or whatever in the summertime.] In the mornings, sometimes just at daybreak, big trucks came along near where I lived and picked us up and carried us to the fields and we would be in the fields all day. It might be where they'd be cutting cabbage and loading them into a sled or something, or they might be picking peppers. But mainly the thing that I did was pick beans because I was not fast enough to make any money the other ways. But beans—I learned to pick those quite well. I could make a quarter a bushel picking beans! One time, though, when I had worked picking beans all day, I got sun [burned] bad on my face and back because when I was bending over, my shirt had pulled up from my waistline. I had to take [all the money] I had made and go to the doctor. It cost me everything I made all that time for medication to repair the burns.

Also, I would keep people's children for them. I'd also take in laundry. Of course, up there [at that time], you had to either go to the creek or the spring to get water or draw up water if you were fortunate enough to have a well. And you either had a rub board, or again, if you were fortunate, you had the old-fashioned wringer washing machine. [I only had a spring and a rub board.]

Whenever school was in, I really had it made because I got one good hot meal a day. At school there was a long noontime recess and I would sweep the floors in the school at that time, and then wash dishes. That way I could have all I wanted to eat. That was how I got through the week.

I never begged. I never begged and I never had the first welfare check. And I never stole anything to eat. I'd wash the dishes or I'd watch the kids, or I'd mop floors or wash windows or whatever was necessary. I've never been ashamed of doing anything to make money that was honest and that I felt good about. And I've tried to do [every job] to the best of my ability.

To some degree I enjoyed my life in the mountains. The fact that I felt independent, the fact that I could card wool and could make a medicine out of herbs, could heat resin out of a pine knot to close a wound, made it almost enjoyable. These were things that I lived with day in and day out. I never felt that that was bad. I just felt a lot of emotional conflicts inside with the loneliness. That was the worst feeling. Being alone; never really feeling like I belonged. If I went to someone's house and they had children of their own, I felt like I was invading them. I never felt that I belonged anywhere. No matter where I went, I was like the fifth wheel. That's what I felt most of the time and so I spent a lot of time alone.

I've tried to look back at [that part of my childhood] as an adult and justify the things that people around me did, but I guess I have different feelings than they did at that particular time.

No one really cared. Everybody knew [about my living alone] and no one really cared. At that time, Daddy was making decent money in Atlanta and he dressed nice, you know. And I had an aunt tell me one time, "There's no way I'm going to take care of somebody else's child while he's off and making this kind of money and blowing it on some whore." Pardon me, but that's the way it was, and that was the attitude of the community. He was making good money and I was his responsibility. They probably never saw my side of it, yet I can see theirs.

One particular Christmas—I guess I was about eleven or twelve—I had been by myself. Daddy was down here in the city with his friends and Eldon was away. I had got a Christmas tree, and at school we'd colored little strips of paper and glued them into chains [for Christmas decorations]. It was Christmas Day, but I felt very much alone. So I thought, "Well, it's Christmas Day, and there's gonna be good spirit and good cheer at the preacher's house." I walked across the field, crossed the creek on a foot log, and then back up through another field to his house. When I went in, I didn't feel any kind of uncomfortableness. Their house was so nice and warm, and I was cold. I didn't have a fire [at my house] that day, and I was wet. [On my way over], I'd slipped off the foot log and fallen down into the creek, just like a kid will. The smells of turkey and dressing and all that food had my mouth watering. You've got to look at an eleven-year-old kid to understand what I'm saying. Anyway, I went in and the only thing I could think was, "Oh, boy! I'm gonna get something to eat because they wouldn't dare ask me to leave on Christmas Day. There's just no way."

And then all the family went in [to eat]. [I stood back because] I would never go into anyone's kitchen without being asked. Then the pastor came out and pulled me aside and he told me, "Carolyn, I don't get to spend much time with my family alone, and I would prefer to have this time alone. I would appreciate it if you could come back later." He didn't say, "Would you leave?" He said, "Come back later," but I knew what he meant. I'll tell you what. That was probably the only man I've ever hated in my life. That man was an A-number-one hypocrite. I disliked him then and I dislike him today, and he's dead. I still dislike anyone who even looks like him. I've had drunk guys in Atlanta come and try to rape me and I've fought them off with a butcher knife. I don't hate *them* the way I hate [that preacher] because they never professed to be loving and gentle and kind and then turn around and turn someone away.

And from that day on, I vowed that I would *never* ask for anything from anyone for as long as I live. I'm still pretty strict about that. I have found that to survive in this world, you have to ask for some things, but you don't beg for anything. I haven't, and with God's help, I won't. I'll beg God for help and forgiveness, but not another human being.

I think that if it had not been for my faith in Jesus Christ as being my friend, I probably would have died. I felt like He was the only friend I had and He would be there when no one else was. [When Mother was living] we didn't go to church that much. It was just something that I have felt strongly about all my life. Christ was the one friend that would never let me down. Even now I don't go to church regularly; I don't belong to a particular church or anything, but I feel very close to my Creator.

There were times I could almost literally leave my body, and it was like [the cold, the hunger, the troubles] were happening to someone else. I could just step aside and I wasn't cold anymore. I wasn't hungry. The Japanese have this theory that one can drink tea from an empty cup. That's the way I think I got.

Eldon and I couldn't really communicate about our feelings. We just went on day by day and we didn't say, "I hurt," or "I want to cry," or "I'm lonely," or "I'm hungry," or anything. We just did what we had to do one day at a time, and hoped that we lived until the next day or the next week.

I was about thirteen [when I moved to Atlanta]. I came by myself on the Greyhound bus. Three cardboard boxes held everything I had. That's really all there was to moving. Really, it was nothing for me to catch the bus and go.

Eldon was already working in Atlanta by then. He had been sleeping in the back of a station wagon [but when I came], we made enough money to rent a two-room garage apartment. He looked older [than seventeen] and so he worked for Blue Plate Foods, making mayonnaise and that sort of thing. I went to work for Howard Johnson's [Restaurant]. I would work in the evenings and go to school in the daytime. A lot of times Eldon would go to work at night and sleep in the day. [As we got a little money ahead, we moved from the garage apartment to a better place.] We would move every four or five months to a different place.

It took me a long time whenever I came to Atlanta [to make friends]. I was very much a loner. I was quite different [from other teenagers] in the fact that I could relate to people twenty years older than I. People my age in the city had never experienced anything like I had. But for some reason I was still determined to go to school, even though there was no one in my life making me go. Daddy couldn't read. He was a very intelligent man, but he was not educated at all. Mother could read, and she had a very strong appreciation for books and knowledge, but she was not well educated either. But to me, education was what I *lusted* after. In the seventh grade, I usually maintained all A's. And then in high school when I came to Atlanta, I was in the Beta Club. I wanted to learn and to understand, to be aware of what was happening around me.

[That was probably because I enjoyed reading so much.] In the mountains, one of the few ways I could find an escape [from the loneliness and fears I had after Mother's death] was through books from the library. It didn't make any difference to me what they were. I loved to read. I think that was what kept me strong as an individual, that ability to escape into a fantasy of books.

I have done skydiving, I'm a licensed pilot, and I'm a certified scuba diver, but I can imagine no excitement like that I have felt when I was reading. I felt that I was away in my own little world. I've traveled in the Mideast to Aswan, Luxor, the Valley of the Kings, but whenever I read, it is so much more exciting than actually going there. In the Bible I've read all about the walled city and going up to the Sea of Galilee. [I've traveled] to Jerusalem, and again, it's nothing in comparison to having traveled there in my mind through books.

[Going to school in Atlanta was certainly different for me. As in Youngcane] there was no one to supervise me [but here the authorities weren't aware of that]. Whenever I was absent, I wrote my own notes. No big deal. I signed my own report cards and all that kind of stuff. I didn't have any problems at all in school as far as the teachers or the school counselors went. Again, there was this attitude of, "Well, as long as the fees are paid, it doesn't make any difference." [I only ran into a problem once that I remember.] If we had any unexcused absences, we could not qualify for the Beta Club even though our grades were high enough. I forgot to write a note one day for an English class I missed, and of course the teacher was not familiar with my situation [and turned in an unexcused absence for me]. For that particular quarter, I was not allowed into the Beta Club.

[In the Atlanta high schools, there was a program at that time called] Distributive Education. I could get out of school earlier, so I left Howard Johnson's and got a job at a drugstore which was real close to the house [where we lived. This was much better because I had no car.] I was walking. It wasn't long hours and I was getting a guaranteed salary plus tips whereas at Howard Johnson's [my pay] was just tips.

[I met Arthur while working at that drugstore.] He was ten years older than I was, but I seemed a lot older, so we started dating. It was quite a different world for me because he was from a family of eight; we'd go on picnics and cookouts and to the lake with his family. His mother just took me under her wing and so we dated about a year and a half, and then got married. My brother was off dating a lady in the mountains and he was never [at our apartment] anymore. He had his own place. Therefore Arthur moved into the apartment with me after we married. It was something how Arthur moved in with *me* even though he was ten years older than I.

No one [at school] knew I was married, but when I got pregnant I had to quit. That was strictly taboo. I was in the eleventh grade. I only completed the tenth grade in regular high school.

After I married, we were the typical middle-class family. We had a daughter, Tina. She is our only child. We had bought a house and two new cars. Both of us worked but our payments were such that if one of us missed a payday, boy we were behind! Then Arthur took strep throat in January and it settled in his kidneys. It completely deteriorated the filtering system in his kidneys and he was completely disabled by June of that year.

Tina was nine when her daddy died and she still remembers what it was like to try to dialyze him. She knew what it was like for me to come in after working all day and trying to get the machine ready to put him on, trying to find the vein and an artery to stick him in. Then the machine might mess up at two o'clock in the morning or the power might go off and I would try to get the neighbors to help get him off the machine, because if we didn't, he could actually bleed to death. She's aware of these things for the four years that he was ill because she was in the middle of it. Again, I took it one day at a time. As a child, if I had thought about having to dialyze someone, then go to work, and to school, and come home and take care of Tina, Mighty God! Four years of this! I'll never make it. But I did—one day at a time, and we never took one penny of welfare.

It was necessary that I go back to school because I was not making enough money as a bookkeeper and a secretary to cover medical expenses and they were not totally covered by the insurance. I couldn't get prescriptions filled because I just didn't have the money. That's when I went back to school at night seriously. I chose civil engineering because I was working in that field as a bookkeeper-secretary for an asphalt paving company, and there was a demand there, with people that knew my circumstances and situation, and were ready and willing to pay for me to go to school. I earned a certificate in highway materials engineering and transportation from the civil engineering department at Georgia Tech.

There were no other women in the classes I had. There were only about eight percent women in the entire student body. [I was subject to ridicule] but for as many people that were bad to me because I was a woman, there were equally that many good to me.

I continued to be promoted throughout the time that I was with the paving company. I became division manager and had a new company car and expense account. I made very good money for a woman at that particular time. I think I made close to $25,000 per year. That was pretty good in the early 1970s. I realized that I could not really advance [much farther]. I had been there twelve years and I saw people who had been there twenty years who weren't any farther along than I was, except maybe their salary was a bit higher.

So then I started C & S Paving, Inc. We've still got most of the people that we started with. I borrowed money that first year to pay them in the wintertime [when there was very little work to do]. I care a lot about the people that work with me. I spent Christmas Eve one year at the Fulton County Jail trying to pay the bond so I could get a guy [that works for me] out of Grady [Hospital]. He had a DUI [drinking under the influence] and he tore himself up really bad in a car wreck on Christmas Eve. I went to the hospital to see him and they had him handcuffed to the bed.

Whenever the men work late, I buy their supper and bring it to them on the job site. [I feel it's very important] to do things like that.

We're still young as a company. We're still struggling. Most of it has been trial and error. We don't have it made by any means, but I think there's opportunity now because we have obtained a lot of tools that we need to really work. They weren't there in the past—we had to do with what we had. When I started the company, all we had was a pickup truck and the kitchen table, but with God's help we will continue to work and to grow and hopefully help people along, too.

If there is [a point at which big is too big], our company has not yet reached it. A lot of times, I think clients force you to grow. And as long as it's controlled growth rather than just in all directions, then I feel more comfortable with it. If you sort of guide it, then you're much better off. I won't take work if I know we can't do it.

PLATE 482

I'm not gonna lie about my past because I think too many people lie to themselves and to others. I think all human beings do that to some degree. I worshipped my father and yet I was torn with these feelings of knowing inside what he was doing was wrong, so how could I love him? Well, whenever Daddy was sober, he was a very kind man and he had personality plus, and I appreciate that.

[When we were still kids in Youngcane] we would come to Atlanta and live with Daddy for a while. He'd get drunk and come in and say, "Oh, Sis, I love you and I'm going to take care of you and everything's going to be all right from now on," but that'd last two or three weeks until [his new wife] would pitch a fit and say, "I'm not taking care of someone else's kids." So it would be back in the cardboard box to the mountains. We'd come down here [to Atlanta with my father] long enough to see the fights and go back!

The thing is, I don't think I'm by myself with this thing of people that are alcoholics and their coming home to their families and busting the television and breaking up the furniture and kicking down the door.

I had a relationship with Daddy as an adult that was just as stormy as the childhood thing. He'd say, "Well, I need a chain saw to cut firewood." I'd buy him a new chain saw and he'd take it and go pawn it and get the money and go get drunk for two or three weeks. Then he'd come back in [and say], "I'm sorry, Sis, I'm not going to do it anymore."

Of course, he'd go back to the same old things. "Well, I'll try one more time." That was the type of thing that it was. I feel that he was not dependable, but there was that magnetism in his personality.

I paid totally for his funeral. Of all those people who criticize me for being honest about what he was, not the first one has ever offered to pay any portion of his funeral or to have his house roofed or to get him out of jail—anything—whenever he needed it. I've repeatedly had some of them say, "Loan me the money and I'll pay you back." And I've done that before. I just think that there's a lot of hypocrisy in the world, and we have to look inside ourselves and really live for what we think is right. And if you do that on a day-in, day-out basis, then at the end of your life you can lie down and be peaceful with yourself. If you don't have peace inside of you, then you might as well hang it up, because you're not going anywhere.

I still furnish a place for my stepmother to live and try to help take care of her. She's a fine lady and I have a lot of compassion for her. It hurts her a lot of times whenever I talk about Daddy. That charisma that some people have was there and it just didn't have as great an impact on her as an adult as it did on me as a child.

I think a lot of times right now, I'm even more a child than I've ever been. I love to do things. I love going to the movies and I'm a sweet freak. I love to eat candy and popcorn—all the things you can imagine.

I try to tell the truth day-in and day-out. I try to live every day, everything I do, as if it's taped and recorded. If I'm going to face the world, then I'm not going to be ashamed of it. My standards and other people's standards may not be the same, but I don't feel ashamed of what I'm doing. God sees what I do behind closed doors. To me, that's the only one I've got to answer to. People say, "Oh, Carolyn, I can't believe you've got four houses, you've got this and you've got that." But to me, I don't have anything. This is something God's allowing me to use. A lot of people criticize me, saying, "Carolyn, people will take advantage of you." As long as I know what they're doing, it's not their taking. I feel comfortable in giving. And I just wish sometimes I had more to give. I really do.

EDITORIAL CONTRIBUTORS

STUDENTS

Allison Adams
Chris Beasley
David Brewin
Cary Brown
William Brown
Melanie Burrell
Pam Carnes
Tammy Carter
Rosanne Chastain
Vicki Chastain
Kyle Conway
Teresa Cook
Dan Crane
Chris Crawford
Leah Crumley
Greg Darnell
Hedy Davalos
Charles Dennis
Wesley Dockins
Dawn Dotson
Randy Dye
Al Edwards
Richard Edwards
Kim English
Kevin Fountain
Roger Fountain
Joseph Fowler
Lori Gillespie
Rance Gillespie
Aimee Graves
Curt Haban

Kim Hamilton
Dana Holcomb
Shane Holcomb
Carla Houck
Melinda Hunter
Chris Jarrard
Richard Jones
Tammy Jones
Eddie Kelly
Denise Layfield
Gwen Leavens
Karen Lovell
Bridget McCurry
Alan Mashburn
Teresa Mason
Stanley Masters
David Payne
Charles Phillips
Boyd Queen
Carol Ramey
Johnny Ramey
Lori Ramey
Vaughn W. Rogers, Jr.
Fred Sanders
Johnny Scruggs
Scott Shope
Kelly Shropshire
Oh Soon Shropshire
John Singleton
Patsy Singleton
Chris Smith

Clay Smith
Natasha Smith
Tracy Speed
Anthony Stalcup
Cheryl Stocky
Teresa Thurmond
Mark Turpin
Cheryl Wall

Sarah Wallace
Curtis Weaver
Chet Welch
Ronnie Welch
Kenny Whitmire
Tony Whitmire
Adam Wilburn
Cecil Wilburn

CONTACTS

Mitch Anderson
Jennie Arrowood
Wilma Beasley
Dorothy Beck
Agnes Bradley
Mrs. E. H. Brown
John Bulgin
Margaret Bulgin
Elvin Cabe
Nelson Cabe
Nola Campbell
Willie Campbell
Edith Cannon
Lola Cannon
Eula Cannon
Aunt Arie Carpenter
Florence Carpenter
Mrs. Eula Carroll
Mrs. Buck Carver
Ethel Corn
Ada Crone
D. B. Dayton
Barnard Dillard
Melba Dotson
Harriet Echols
Mrs. Albert Eckstein
Elizabeth Endler
Mrs. Clyde English
Diane Forbes
Beulah Forester

Moot Friar
Earl Gillespie
Mrs. Ollie Queen
 Glore
Louise Gravely
Blanche Harkins
Dan Hawkes
Annie Mae Henry
Bill Henry
Maelane Holcomb
Ruth Holcomb
Clyde Hollifield
Maude Houk
Oakley Justice
Leona Justus
Hazel Luzier
Numerous Marcus
Bob Mashburn
Henry Harrison Mayes
Lillie Mayes
Connie Mitchell
Frank Moore
Effie Mull
Jud Nelson
Carlton Nichols
Gladys Nichols
Mrs. Ed Norton
Margaret Norton
Cleland Owens
Ethel Owens

John Lee Patterson
Will Patterson
Laura Patton
Mrs. C. E. Pinson
Gladys Queen
Harv Reid
Ed Roane
Martha Roane
Roy Roberts
Flory Rogers
Kenny Runion
Lottie Shillingburg
Genelia Singleton
Mark Snyder
Sam Snyder
Samantha Speed
Billy Joe Stiles
Carolyn Stradley
Prudence Swanson

Amy Trammell
Amanda Turpin
Nellie Turpin
Bessie Underwood
Willie Underwood
Janice Van Buren
Frank Vinson
Jake Waldroop
Helen Wall
Lester J. Wall
Stella Wall
Von Watts
Catherine Weaver
Joe Weaver
Mrs. Verlan Whitley
Christine Wigington
Deborah Wilburn
Flora Youngblood

INDEX

Boldface numerals 8 and 9 refer to *Foxfire 8* and *Foxfire 9*, respectively.
Page numbers in italics indicate illustrations or their captions

ledger of, **9:**135
roughriders and, **9:**117
on William Patton Moore, **9:**116–28
Moore, Gialia Belle, **9:***123*
Moore, Harriet Naomi Gash ("Hattie"),
     9:88, **9:**116, **9:***123*
Moore, Henry, **9:***123*
Moore, Hubbie Ruth, **9:***123*
Moore, Ira William, **9:***123*
Moore, J. C., **9:**126
Moore, Jerry, **9:**133, **9:**135
Moore, Jim, **9:***123*
Moore, Joab Lawrence, **9:**88, **9:**89, **9:**92,
     9:93
Moore, John, **9:**88, **9:**89, **9:***123*
Moore, John Allen ("Jay"), **9:***123*
Moore, John Covington, **9:**87–93
Moore, J.V.A., **9:**133
Moore, Lawrence Richardson, **9:**88,
     9:*123,* **9:**128–29, **9:**136
   map drawn by, **9:**129, **9:***130–31*
Moore, Margaret Roxanna, **9:***123*
Moore, Martha Covington, **9:**88
Moore, Martha Patton, **9:**88
Moore, Mary Bryson, **9:**91–93
Moore, Mattie Ellen, **9:***123*
Moore, May Rosebud Moss, **9:***123*
Moore, Minnie, **9:***123*
Moore, Miriam, **9:**93
Moore, Mrs., **8:**69
Moore, Nannie Lou Chambers, **9:**87, **9:**88
Moore, Paul Henry, **9:***123*
Moore, Sarah Lou, **9:**88
Moore, T. C., **9:**93
Moore, Walter, **9:**128
Moore, Capt. William, **9:**127–28
Moore, William Patton (Irish Bill), **9:**88,
     9:116–28, **9:***123*
   in Civil War, **9:**116–17, **9:***118–19*
   horseback riding, **9:**122–23
   house of, **9:**117–20, **9:***121*
   prominence of, **9:**120–22
   Tusquittee letter of, **9:**125–27
Moore family, **9:**86–93
"Moose" (Rothell slave), **9:**400–1
Mops, cornshuck, **9:**150
Morgan, William L., **8:**393
Morgan Whitehackle chickens, **8:**393
Mormons, **9:**241
Mortising bit, **9:***284*
Moseley, Edwin Lincoln, **9:**77*n*
Mosley, Bruce, **8:**23, **8:**38–46, **8:***39,* **8:***40,*
     8:*43*
Mosley, Pank, **8:**40–41

Mosley, Polly, **8:**38, **8:**40–42
Mosley, Selma, **8:**23, **8:**38
Motorized pottery wheels, **8:**331
Moultrie, Ga., **9:**195
Mountain City, Ga., **8:**8–21, **8:**48–49
   experimental class, **8:**11, **8:***12*
   Foxfire Fund projects, **8:**11–21
   log house, **8:**18, **8:***19*
   from 1900s to 1930s, **8:**8–10
   solar home, **8:**15, **8:**18, **8:***18*
   tourists and, **8:**13–14
Mountain City Project, **8:**14, **8:***16–17,*
     8:21
Mountain Rug Company, **9:**322
Mount Grove Church school, **9:**152–53
Mourners' bench, **8:**60
Mucus, as burn remedy, **9:**48
Mud mills. *See* Pug mills
Muffs, **8:**417
Mugs, **8:**366
Muldawer, Paul, **8:**15
Mule business
   auctions and, **8:**501
   biggest trading time, **8:**508
   Depression and, **8:**492
   factories and, **8:**491
   government and, **8:**492, **8:**503
   stockyards and, **8:**501–2
Mules, **9:**31, **9:**124
   age of, **8:**495, **8:**504
   bad, **8:**505–8
   bellesed, **8:**496
   bleeding, **8:**498–99
   blind staggers of, **8:**498–99
   blood pressure of, **8:**499
   botulism in, **8:**499
   breathing of, **8:**495
   breeding, **8:**493–95
   bull, **8:**496
   color of, **8:**495
   current uses for, **8:**504
   dependency of farmers on, **8:**492
   determining age of, **8:**495
   diet of, **8:**496–97
   diseases of, **8:**496–99
   dog food made from, **8:**491–92
   ears of, **8:**495
   eyes of, **8:**495
   filing teeth of, **8:**499
   gums of, **8:**497
   horses compared to, **8:**510
   how to work, **8:**500
   infertility of, **8:**493–94
   intelligence of, **8:**508–9

With the publication of *Foxfire 9* in the fall of 1986, the series of numbered volumes documenting Appalachian crafts and traditions is now complete. The entire series is as follows:

The Foxfire Book: Hog dressing, log cabin building, mountain crafts and foods, planting by the signs, snake lore, hunting tales, faith healing, moonshining, and other affairs of plain living.

Foxfire 2: Ghost stories, spring wild plant foods, spinning and weaving, midwifing, burial customs, corn shuckin's, wagon making and more affairs of plain living.

Foxfire 3: Animal care, banjos and dulcimers, hide tanning, summer and fall wild plant foods, butter churns, ginseng, and still more affairs of plain living.

Foxfire 4: Fiddle making, springhouses, horse trading, sassafras tea, berry buckets, gardening, and further affairs of plain living.

Foxfire 5: Ironmaking, blacksmithing, flintlock rifles, bear hunting, and other affairs of plain living.

Foxfire 6: Shoemaking, 100 toys and games, gourd banjos and song bows, wooden locks, a water-powered sawmill, and other affairs of just plain living.

Foxfire 7: Ministers, church members, revivals, baptisms, shaped-note and gospel singing, faith healing, camp meetings, foot-washing, snake handling, and other traditions of mountain religious heritage.

Foxfire 8: Southern folk pottery from pug mills, ash glazes, and groundhog kilns to face jugs, churns, and roosters; mule swapping and chicken fighting.

Foxfire 9: General stores, the Jud Nelson wagon, a praying rock, a Catawba Indian potter—and haint tales, quilting, home cures, and log cabins revisited.

Research is now under way for a new group of future titles, also by our students, that will document other aspects of the Appalachian experience. *Sometimes a Shining Moment,* Eliot Wigginton's landmark work on education, will be available in paperback in the fall of 1986.